PUBLIC POLICY STUDIES IN AMERICAN GOVERNMENT

Edgar Litt, General Editor

THE NEW POLITICS OF AMERICAN POLICY

A Reader

THE NEW POLITICS OF AMERICAN POLICY

A Reader

EDGAR LITT

University of Connecticut

HOLT, RINEHART AND WINSTON, INC.

*New York Chicago San Francisco Atlanta
Dallas Montreal Toronto London Sydney*

To Matthew Bruce Litt, who will reap our public harvest or famine.

JK
274
.L576
1969

Foreword to the Series

A series devoted to the consequences of American public policy ought, at the outset, to indicate why it came into being. What has been lacking in the scholarly literature is overt analysis of the political consequences of policy on human institutions and the life style of human beings themselves. A review of the literature convinced the editor, and his colleagues who are to contribute to the series, that the vast analytical skills of political scientists have for too long been directed at the "input" side of politics, the ways in which policy is fashioned or administered out of the mélange of groups competing for public favor. Scholars have studied the behavior of organized interest groups, the calculations of administrative and policy experts, and the meaning of concrete policies for the totality of the political system itself. Yet, in an era where federal policies themselves are major sources of impact and innovations on society, it is crucial not to restrict the scope of our inquiries.

The scholar's responsibility extends to an evaluation both of policy forming agencies in terms of clear and realistic values, and of the impact of policy "outputs" on the social system. That responsibility has been asserted by one critical voice in the present epoch in this way:

> Of basic importance is the modern redefinition of "politics." No longer does the term refer to the promotion of justice or the search for the best organization of social life. The term now refers to "who gets what, when, how" or to some similar concept, which focuses not on justice but on power. This focus makes political science more quantifiable and political scientists more pliable and useful for the powers that be. At the same time it severs the study of politics from any direct bearing on the task of developing institutions and organizations in the service of human needs.[1]

The volumes in this series will raise this issue for the distribution of power in the American society, the civil liberties of the individual in times of immense governmental control, the quality of personal and political education received by black and white Americans, and the distribution of housing and other social goods in our urban centers. In our view, this perspective best accounts for the processes and quality of our political life. Moreover, these studies build on the intellectual tradition of public policy exploration that has importantly contributed to the maturation of the field of political science itself.

Storrs, Connecticut   E. L.

---

[1]Christian Bay, "The Cheerful Science of Dismal Politics," in Theodore Roszak (ed.), *The Dissenting Academy* (New York: Pantheon, 1967), p.3.

Preface

It is often useful for a preface to indicate the intellectual currents influencing an editor in compiling a book of this nature. *The New Politics of American Policy* includes original and reprinted contributions I thought relevant to the state of political science in the college classroom. Thus, I have been aware of the old concerns of teaching research studies, of the impact of behavioralism on the discipline, and of the mass influx of students into institutions of higher learning.

Moreover, this book is shaped on the anvil of new concerns that impose themselves on the study of politics — and, indeed, on all learning. It is time that political scientists took heed of the social and political relevances of their lectures and writings. It is also time that old assumptions be discarded, however painful that process may be. This book is an attempt to blend matters of social and political relevance with political science research of high quality. In particular, the emphasis on the problems of political knowledge and the universities sharpens the general theme for the inquiring student.

Whatever value a book of this nature has is due in large measure to the thoughts of colleagues who have turned to the issues of public policy and political knowledge. I appreciate in particular the original contributions of Christian Bay, Henry Pratt, and Tom Rose, three friends whose efforts have enriched the contents of this book.

Storrs, Connecticut
May 1969

E. L.

Contents

Introduction
Public Policy
and Politics

POLITICS AND INTELLECT

The focus of this anthology is on the policy consequences of American politics at midcentury. This orientation is dictated by the consideration of three related factors: the intellectual roots of public policy, the relation between policy and empirical study, and the prescriptive or value concerns of policy-oriented investigation. Although it is risky to speak of *the* guiding intellectual concern of political analysis, it is nevertheless realistic and important to sketch the main drift of such concerns for future generations. There has always been a close relationship between dominant political theories, the uses of political intellect, and the structure of public policy. This guiding concern has been with the processes of obtaining and retaining power, the varieties of decision-making techniques that sustain public institutions, and the piecemeal adjustments that resulted in accommodations to the

American policy. Behind these investigations lies the intellectual core of a pluralistic power system in which competing groups and social interests bargain for greater access to the formal and informal political processes.

Currently, the American polity—the total political organization—is well beyond the liberal hour during which the federal government served as the focal point for social welfare claims by articulate and organically distinct interest groups. It is increasingly clear that the American polity is the touchstone not only for the initiation of major social policies but for the fruition of those public values to be allocated authoritatively by government. Beyond the "nightwatchman" state that balances private forces, beyond the welfare service state that responds more or less to demands for better health, wages, and economic markets, lies the concept of politics as the search for the articulation and development of basic human needs. The task of the American polity in a nation at the height of its power and international commitments is the development of policies and institutions that expand the life chances of individuals, the self-respect of marginal social groups, and the cultural quality of the urban habitat in which most men and women will be born, live, and die.

This orientation rests on the claim that the *Pax Americana* has been originated and is maintained by an immense governmental apparatus whose systemic relations with every part of our social order (in religion, education, and commerce) are interlocking and critical to human well-being. In this unfolding process, the development and the execution of public policy are ongoing requirements that do not require specific interest group pressure or a sense of national crisis to sustain them. Just as the "temporary" pump priming of the New Deal was structurally incorporated into our political economy, so too have concerns about social welfare developed into an organic intellectual and policy concern of our political system. In fact, the social and political outcomes of these policy choices (often called "outputs" in the jargon of behavioral science) have become the most important political elements of our time. In almost every area of policy concern, the impact of policies and the rewards and sanctions allocated to effect them raise basic questions: What has been the impact of the American political presence in Southeast Asia upon the legitimacy of our governmental institutions? How have the stresses in our urban centers been related to the political matrix of power in these areas? How has the relationship between knowledge and power influenced the perception of policy questions and the efforts used to solve them? What do the political demands of disadvantaged groups tell us about the relation of popular participation to effective distributions of human and social valuables?

These social and political indicators become for the contemporary policy state what the contributions of Newton and Kepler were in the maturation of the natural sciences. Having committed ourselves to the consequences of global power abroad and prescriptions for social amelioration at home, we are required to reassess the human and political consequences of our policy processes. For here the structural and personal imperatives of national social policies have deeply influenced political managers, ordinary citizens, and those who articulate claims for greater amelioration of their social and economic distress.

POLITICS AND EMPIRICISM

In the not-too-distant past, scholars and commentators turned their attention to the formal properties of political systems—that is, to the constitutional and administrative arrangements most visible to inquiry. By the end of World War II a scholarly generation experienced in national politics and practical public service insisted that such institutional formalism obscured the intricate workings of the complex American polity. Henceforth, increasingly rigorous and sophisticated empirical theories and methodologies would be coined and applied to vigorous analysis of politics in field laboratories ranging from congressional committees to party conventions. In the process, research about political behavior has moved from a marginal academic interest to the core of a society engaged in the development and execution of major public policies.

The claims of total empiricism and the controlled social order have not withstood the test of contemporary stresses in the American polity. Empirical inquiry is now seen as part of a broad-based and painful effort to reconstruct social and political institutions through the analytical powers of a politically creative society. Seldom in human history has a nation expended so much of its organized and intellectual energies on research. Moreover, research and development have moved from the professional and trade language of scientific coteries to the neighborhood council, the public school system, and the welfare agency. Empirical research is now public knowledge relevant to political policy issues and is no longer clad in antiseptic academic garb.

Empirical inquiry about politics is now related to the major issues of war and peace, racism and poverty, and upon their solution depends the future of the Republic. Within one decade, the study of American politics has produced vibrant advances in knowledge and, in Veblen's appropriate phraseology, a trained incapacity to reexamine basic relationships between knowledge and politics. At a time when the unrest of the black, poverty-ridden communities shook the fabric of the American commonwealth, some scholars were elaborating "political socialization" research designed to prove that civic loyalty was guaranteed by subscription to abstract norms of the regime. At a time when the war in Vietnam had polarized the American electorate, the pervasiveness of apolitical divisions abounded in research reports. At a time when the substance of democracy is being tested, one often encounters a narrow empiricism in which general assent to propositions about the rule of the people, the importance of elections, and the ability to have some say with public officials are taken as evidence of democratic support. The selections in this book seek to link empirical studies with policy consequences rather than with a technical or procedural account of the political game.

POLITICS AND PRESCRIPTION

A third factor guiding this inquiry—one intimately related to the points previously mentioned—is the prescriptive meaning of the politics reviewed herein. It is a matter of irony and concern that at a time when political measures are so pervasive in our society, we have so little systematic knowledge of their personal impact on human beings. Some of the questions to be discussed are really ancient ones, such as the impact of political participation on individual and group esteem. Other questions are more current, such as the impact of urban desegregation on the political efficacy of blacks from the city's core. Throughout the book, the structural integrity of selections arises from the importance of social advantages and disadvantages as basic political values. Thus, each section contains articles that relate the social and political institutions involved in the distribution of human values to the more intimate personal relationships in which men spend their lives. For example, knowing the structure of racial segregation in housing is vital to understanding the mechanisms of the welfare industry with its professional-client relationships. Likewise, the political structure of urban education described by Robert H. Salisbury in Part IV highlights the more personal struggle in urban education portrayed in the editor's essay which follows it. And the politics of poverty viewed from several vantage points in Part V leads to considerations of new interest groups and policy strategies designed to cope with human deprivation.

I have sought to emphasize the impact of public politics upon groups and individuals in order to clarify an ancient truth: politics has an impact upon human beings—it is not a denatured academic enterprise. I have articulated value premises in the range of selections and the introductions to them. Moreover, thematic continuity is found in the proposition that the structure of power, knowledge, and institutions shapes the quality and quantity of human valuables among the citizenry. Some roots of political structure are debated in Part I, while some types of political demands are explored in the second section. The remainder of the book (Parts III, IV, and V) considers the distributive processes of key human values, namely welfare, enlightenment, and respect. In each case, I have begun with an article that establishes the context of the problem: for instance, the role of the black in urban America, the historic development of political education, and the importance of social advantage and deprivation as core political values.

The political analysis of policy is designed to increase our choices in dealing with the human condition. The stress upon the link among political intellect, values, and empiricism ought to inform the student that the political process and its methodological assumptions are not the property of any particular group of men. No political administration, no professional elite, and no sectarian cadre has a monopoly in these matters. The unthinkable is now commonplace in American politics, and we retreat to rigid and close-minded positions at our peril. It would be tragic if students of ameliorative public policies were blind to this reality.

PART I
THE ROOTS OF POLICY FORMATION IN AMERICA

Introduction

Policies that distribute power, enlightenment, esteem, and other values that enhance or diminish the human condition stem from the basic politics of a society. Thus, in a classic liberal society each interest group seeks access to government in order to register its political claims effectively. Once translated into political terms the dominant interests of labor, agriculture, and commerce influence the regulation of their sector so as to maximize their rewards and to minimize the sanctions they would receive from the official polity. Through these processes the governmental apparatus serves as a balancing and limiting mechanism for dispensing political rewards and punishments to competing groups.

However, as Theodore Lowi states in Selection 1, the limited relations among interest groups and governmental agencies no longer provides an adequate description of empirical realities. "Interest group liberalism," as Lowi defines contemporary arrangements, involves an extensive interaction of dominant groups with public governmental institutions. According to Lowi, the public philosophy debated in the period between 1932 and the end of World War II has become archaic. That debate centered on the role of federal government in supporting demands within the private economy. It produced liberal and conservative views about the dimensions of federal welfare policies. But the current debate is about the uses of governmental resources by all segments of a political economy in which "private" and "public" distinctions are not very significant.

Terence McCarthy (Selection 2) explores one powerful political sector, namely the military-industrial-defense research complex, which greatly influences all public policies. His purpose is to illustrate that a perpetual state of military crisis necessitates the draining of funds and other resources into the military sector. Although the breadth of control exerted by powerful military-defense groups is debatable, it is clear that the allocation of all public resources now exerts a significant and independent influence on the entire society.

The quality and distribution of knowledge has always been involved in the distributive impact of the American polity. Robert Lane (Selection 3) contends that a modern, authoritative form of public knowledge now guides policy makers and American social policies. Policy experts, influenced by empirical evidence and popular demands professionalize claims for human welfare. Science is at the service of democracy and the scientific elite who seek to improve policies rather than engage in ideological polemics. Christian Bay (Selection 4), on the other hand, is less certain about the policy elite's ameliorative effects and examines the relationship among expertise, the university, and the public interest. He sees the university as a critical site for genuine political freedom and representative democracy. Moreover, politics dedicated to meeting genuine human needs are distinct from "psuedo-politics," which stir mass emotions in the interest of powerful, self-serving groups. Despite these widely differing views of the current fit between knowledge and power, the Lane and Bay contributions in this section clarify the public impact of knowledge and research technology in the modern polity.

It was Ortega y Gasset, a conservative Spanish philosopher, who predicted that twentieth-century politics would be marked by systematic and unprecedented violence. We can no longer ignore the connections among actual and potential violence and the

American policy processes. Lewis Coser, in Selection 5, seeks to counter the prevailing adjustment-politics view held by most Americans by noting that social conflict and perhaps violence are productive in a modern polity, with its unequal distribution of human valuables. Tom Rose, in an important intellectual contribution written especially for this volume (Selection 6), ranges widely in exploring the theories and practices of violence in contemporary American politics. Rose demonstrates that violence is rooted in American life and that it evolves in a cycle of control and revolt toward which many current policy controversies seem directed. The use of police and riot squads, rebellion, and welfare policies form a complex network of public behavior. Rose's clarification of these relations provides a useful framework within which public policy can be studied and created in a manner appropriate to the conflicts of our epoch.

The decline of the self-balancing pluralistic system and the new forces of policy formation examined in these pages occurs amid salient political realities. The unequal distribution of advantages in human values is getting worse and calls for different political strategies within the Republic. In particular, non-bureaucratic group and personal demands have increased in the public sector, enhancing the import of dignity and respect as policy goals. In addition, the new importance of intellectual and policy skills requires sensitivity to the context and prescriptive premises of policies. These elements of human aspiration and intellectual skill are important at a time when older ways of resolving group demands fail us. The present fluid contextual situation involves important structural problems in understanding the nature of the new politics being acted out on the public stage.

1 The Public Philosophy: Interest-Group Liberalism*

THEODORE LOWI

Until astonishingly recent times American national government played a marginal role in the life of the nation.[1] Even as late as the eve of World War I, the State Department could support itself on consular fees. In most years revenues from tariffs supplied adequate financing, plus a surplus, from all other responsibilities. In 1800, there was less than one-half a federal bureaucrat per 1000 citizens. On the eve of the Civil War there were only 1.5 federal bureaucrats per 1000 citizens, and by 1900 that ratio had climbed to 2.7. This compares with 7 per 1000 in 1940 and 13 per 1000 in 1962—exclusive of military personnel.

[1] This article was made possible by a Social Science Research Council Fellowship. Thanks are also due Professors Richard Flathman, L. A. Froman, Jr., George LaNoue, and Grant McConnell for their many helpful criticisms and suggestions. For his considerable encouragement I am grateful to Max Ascoli of *The Reporter;* and to him, to Henry Kariel (in *The Decline of American Pluralism*) and to Grant McConnell I am doubly grateful for their early recognition of problems with pluralism.

*Reprinted by permission of the author and publisher from *The American Political Science Review,* 61: 1 (March 1967).

The relatively small size of the public sphere was maintained in great part by the constitutional wall of separation between government and private life. The wall was occasionally scaled in both directions, but concern for the proper relation of private life and public order was always a serious and effective issue. Americans always talked pragmatism, in government as in all other things; but doctrine always deeply penetrated public dialogue. Power, even in the United States, needed justification.

Throughout the decades between the end of the Civil War and the Great Depression, almost every debate over a public policy became involved in the larger debate over the nature and consequences of larger and smaller spheres of government. This period was just as much a "constitutional period" as that of 1789–1820. Each period is distinguished by its effort to define (or redefine) and employ a "public philosophy." . . .

INTEREST-GROUP LIBERALISM

The weaknesses of the old liberalism-conservatism were not altogether clear before the 1960s. This tardiness is due simply to the intervention of two wars and then an eight-year period of relative quiescence in policy making and in the saliency of politics and government to the masses. Truman's Fair Deal agenda, already left over from the end of the New Deal, held fire for over a decade until it became a major part of the Democratic agenda of the 1960s and comprised a very large proportion of the successful record of the 89th Congress, the most actively legislating Congress since 1933. Even the historic *Brown* v. *Board of Education* decision failed to bring about noticeable expansion and intensification of political activity until the Little Rock debacle of 1957. With increasing pace thereafter, new pressures began to be placed upon political institutions, and another round of governmental activity was in the making. In many ways the period that began in 1957 with Little Rock and Sputnik was as much a constitutional revolution as that of the 1930s. In this decade—as measured by Federal budgets, personnel, the sheer proliferation of service and other agencies, or the expansion of public regulatory authority—there have clearly been a civil rights revolution, an educational revolution, and a scientific and technological revolution.

All of this activity proves that there is no end to government responsibility. It is not possible to automate all the stabilizers. The new activity in the 1960s also proves that the political apparatus of democracy can respond promptly once the constitutional barriers to democratic choice have been lowered. However, that is only the beginning of the story, because the almost total democratization of the Constitution and the contemporary expansion of the public sector has been accompanied by expansion, not by contraction, of a sense of illegitimacy about public objects. Here is a spectacular paradox. We witness governmental effort of gigantic proportion to solve problems forthwith and directly. Yet we witness expressions of personal alienation and disorientation increasing, certainly not subsiding, in frequency and intensity; and we witness further weakening of informal controls in the family, neighborhood and groups. We witness a vast expansion of effort to bring the ordinary citizen into closer rapport with the democratic process, including unprecedented efforts to confer upon the poor and ineducable the power to make official decisions involving their own fate. Yet at the very same time we witness crisis after crisis in the very institutions in which the new methods of decision-making seemed most appropriate.

It is as though each new program or program expansion were admission of prior governmental inadequacy or failure without necessarily being a contribution to order and well-being. The War on Poverty programs have become as often as not instruments of social protest. The Watts riots, the movements for police review boards in many cities, the sit-ins and marches even where no specifically evil laws are being enforced against a special race or group, the strikes and protests by civil servants, nurses, doctors, teachers, transport and defense workers, and others in vital occupations—all these and many others are evidence of increasing impatience with established ways of resolving social conflict and dividing up society's values. Verbal and organizational attacks on that vague being, the "power structure," even in cities with histories of strong reform movements and imaginative social programs, reflect increasing rejection of pluralistic patterns in favor of more direct prosecution of claims against society. Far from insignificant as a sign of the times is emergence of a third and a fourth national party movement, one on either extreme but alike in their opposition to centrist parties, electoral politics, and pre-election compromise. Many of these new patterns and problems may have been generated by racial issues, but it is clear that that was only a precipitant. The ironic fact is that the post-1937 political economy, either because of or in spite of government policies and two wars, had produced unprecedented prosperity, and as the national output increased arithmetically the rate of rising expectation must have gone up geometrically—in a modern expression of the Malthusian Law. Public authority was left to grapple with this alienating gap between expectation and reality.[2]

Prosperity might merely have produced a gigantic race among all to share in its benefits. The expansion of the public sector might have

[2]The preceding two paragraphs were taken, with revision, from the Introductory Essay of my *Private Life and Public Order* (New York: W. W. Norton, 1967).

increased the legitimacy of government and other public objects through redistribution of opportunities to join the prosperity. Instead, the expansion of government that helped produce sustained prosperity also produced a crisis of public authority. Why? Because the old justification for that expansion had so little to say beyond the need for the expansion itself. The class of objects to which the new and appropriate public philosophy would have to apply should, it seems obvious, be the forms, structures and procedures of government control. There are vast technical, political and ethical questions involved in what are and what ought to be the consequences of the various ways in which power can be administered and employed. What constitutes "due process" in an age of positive government? What impact does one or another administrative process have upon society, upon the specific clientele whose compliance is sought, upon the sense of legitimacy among citizens, and upon the capacity of the next generation to respond, governmentally and otherwise, to the problems of its own time?

Out of the developing crisis in public authority has developed an ersatz political formula that does, for all its problems, offer the public man some guidance and some justification in his efforts to shape, form and provide for the administration of positive laws in the positive state. There are several possible names for this contemporary replacement of liberalism-conservatism. A strong possibility would be *corporatism,* but its history as a concept gives it several unwanted connotations, such as conservative Catholicism or Italian fascism, that keep it from being quite suitable. Another is *syndicalism,* but among many objections is the connotation of anarchy too far removed from American experience or intentions. However, the new American public philosophy is a variant of those two alien philosophies.

The most clinically accurate term to describe the American variant is *interest-group liberalism.* It may be called liberalism because it expects to use government in a positive and expansive role, it is motivated by the highest sentiments, and it possesses strong faith that what is good for government is good for the society. It is "interest-group liberalism" because it sees as both necessary and good that the policy agenda and the public interest be defined in terms of the organized interests in society. In brief sketch, the working model of the interest group liberal is a vulgarized version of the pluralist model of modern political science. It assumes: (1) Organized interests are homogeneous and easy to define, sometimes monolithic. Any "duly elected" spokesman for any interest is taken as speaking in close approximation for each and every member.[3] (2) Organized interests

[3]For an excellent inquiry into this assumption and into the realities of the internal life of the interests, see: Grant McConnell, "The Spirit of Private Government," *The American Political Science Review,* 52 (1963), 754–770;

pretty much fill up and adequately represent most of the sectors of our lives, so that one organized group can be found effectively answering and checking some other organized group as it seeks to prosecute its claims against society.[4] And (3) the role of government is one of ensuring access particularly to the most effectively organized, and of ratifying the agreements and adjustments worked out among the competing leaders and their claims. This last assumption is supposed to be a statement of how our democracy works and how it ought to work. Taken together, these assumptions constitute the Adam Smith "hidden hand" model applied to groups. Ironically, it is embraced most strongly by the very people most likely to reject the Smith model applied in its original form to firms in the market.

These assumptions are the basis of the new public philosophy. The policy behaviors of old-school liberals and conservatives, of Republicans and Democrats, so inconsistent with liberalism-conservation criteria, are fully consistent with the criteria drawn from interest-group liberalism: *The most important difference between liberals and conservatives, Republicans and Democrats*—however they define themselves—*is to be found in the interest groups they identify with. Congressmen are guided in their votes, Presidents in their programs, and administrators in their discretion, by whatever organized interests they have taken for themselves as the most legitimate; and that is the measure of the legitimacy of demands.*

The assumptions of the model and the concluding behavioral proposition constitute, for better or worse, an important part of the working methodology of modern, empirical political science. However, quite another story with quite different consequences is how all of this became elevated from an hypothesis about political behavior to an ideology about how the democratic system ought to work and then became ultimately elevated to that ideology most widely shared among contemporary public men.

Interest-Group Liberalism: An Intellectual History

The opening of the national government to positive action on a large scale was inevitably to have an impact upon political justification just as on political technique. However, the inventors of technique were less than inventive for justification of particular policies at

---

see also Clark Kerr, *Unions and Union Leaders of Their Own Choosing* (Santa Barbara: Fund for the Republic, 1957); and S. M. Lipset *et al., Union Democracy* (New York: Anchor, 1962). See also Arthur S. Miller, *Private Governments and the Constitution* (Santa Barbara: Fund for the Republic, 1959)

[4]It is assumed that "countervailing power" usually crops up somehow. Where it does not, government ought to help create it. See John K. Galbraith, *American Capitalism* (Boston: Houghton-Mifflin, 1952).

particular times. Hansen, for instance, has observed that Keynes was no social reformer, nor had he any particular commitments to particular social ends.[5] Keynes helped discover the modern economic system and how to help it maintain itself, but his ideas and techniques could be used, and indeed have been used, to support many points of view. "Collective bargaining, trade unionism, minimum-wage laws, hours legislation, social security, a progressive tax system, slum clearance and housing, urban redevelopment and planning, education reform," Hansen observed of Keynes, "all these he accepted, but they were not among his preoccupations. In no sense could he be called the father of the welfare state."[6]

Nor was the doctrine of popular government and majority rule, which was so important in the victory of liberalism over conservatism, adequate guidance after the demise of liberalism-conservatism. If one reviews the New Deal period and thereafter he will see how little propensity Americans have had to use the majority rule justification. The reasons why are fairly apparent. Justification of positive government programs on the basis of popular rule required above all a proclamation of the supremacy of Congress. The abdication of Congress in the 1930s in the passage of the fundamental New Deal legislation could never have been justified in the name of popular government. With all due respect to Congressmen, little discernible effort was made to do so. Statutory and investigatory infringements on civil liberties during World War II and during the Cold War, plus the popular support of McCarthyism, produced further reluctance to fall back on Congress and majority rule as the fount of public policy wisdom. Many who wished to use this basis anyway sought support in the plebiscitary character of the Presidency. However, "presidential liberals" have had to blind themselves to many complications in the true basis of presidential authority and to the true—the bureaucratic—expression of presidential will.[7]

The very practices that made convincing use of popular rule doctrine impossible—delegation of power to administrators, interest representation, outright delegation of power to trade associations, and so on—were what made interest-group liberalism so attractive an

[5]Alvin H. Hansen, *The American Economy* (New York: McGraw-Hill, 1957) pp. 152ff.

[6]Hansen, pp. 158–59. Keynes said ". . . the Class War will find me on the side of the educated bourgeoisie": quoted in Hansen, p. 158.

[7]No citations are necessary to emphasize the fact that presidential delegation and subdelegation to administrators is just as extensive as congressional. As to the popular basis of presidential authority, see Robert A. Dahl, *Preface to Democratic Theory* (Chicago: University of Chicago Press, 1956); and Willmoore Kendall, "The Two Majorities," *Midwest Journal of Political Science*, 4 (1960), pp. 317–345.

alternative. And because the larger interest groups did claim large memberships, they could be taken virtually as popular rule in modern dress. Interest-group liberalism simply corresponded impressively well with the realities of power. Thus, it possessed a little of science and some of the trappings of popular rule. Political scientists, after all, were pioneers in insisting upon recognition of the group, as well as in helping to elevate the pressure-group system from power to virtue. Political scientists had for a long time argued that the group is the necessary variable in political analysis for breaking through the formalisms of government.[8] However, there was inevitably an element of approval in their methodological argument, if only to counteract the kind of recognition of the group that Steffens and other progressives and Muckrakers were more than willing to accord. In 1929, Pendleton Herring concluded his inquiry with the argument that:

> [The national associations] represent a healthy democratic development. They rose in answer to certain needs. . . . They are part of our representative system. . . . These groups must be welcomed for what they are, and certain precautionary regulations worked out. The groups must be understood and their proper place in government allotted, if not by actual legislation, then by general public realization of their significance.[9]

Following World War II, one easily notes among political scientists the widespread acceptance of the methodology and, more importantly here, the normative position. Among political scientists the best expression of interest-group liberalism was probably that of Wilfred Binkley and Malcolm Moos. The fact that it was so prominent in their American government basic textbook suggests that it tended to reflect conventional wisdom among political scientists even in 1948. Binkley and Moos argued that the "basic concept for understanding the dynamics of government is the multi-group nature of modern society or the modern state."[10] Political reality could be grasped scientifically as a "parallelogram of forces" among groups, and the public interest is "determined and established" through the free competition of interest

[8]For pioneer expressions, see Arthur F. Bentley, *The Process of Government* (Chicago: University of Chicago Press. 1908); and E. Pendleton Herring. *Group Representation Before Congress* (Baltimore: Johns Hopkins Press, 1929). More recent arguments of the same methodological sort are found in David Truman, *The Governmental Process* (New York: Knopf, 1951); and Earl Latham, *The Group Basis of Politics* (Ithaca: Cornell University Press, 1952).

[9]Herring, p. 268.

[10]Wilfred Binkley and Malcolm Moos, *A Grammar of American Politics* (New York: Knopf, 1950), p. 7.

groups: "The necessary composing and compromising of their differences is the practical test of what constitutes the public interest."[11]

The fact that a doctrine has some support in the realities of power
certainly helps to explain its appeal as a doctrine.[12] But there were also
several strongly positive reasons for the emergence of this particular
doctrine. The first, and once perhaps the only, is that it has helped
flank the constitutional problems of federalism. Manifestations of the
corporate state were once limited primarily to the Extension Service of
the Department of Agriculture, with self-administration by the land
grant colleges and the local farmers and commerce associations.
Self-administration by organized groups was an attractive technique
precisely because it could be justified as so decentralized and permissive as to be hardly federal at all.[13] Here began the ethical and
conceptual mingling of the notion of organized private groups with the
notions of "local government" and "self-government." Ultimately direct interest group participation in government became synonymous
with self-government, first for reasons of strategy, then by belief that
the two were indeed synonymous. As a propaganda strategy it eased
acceptance in the courts, then among the locals who still believed the
farmer was and should be independent. Success as strategy increased
usage; usage helped elevate strategy to doctrine. The users began to
believe in their own symbols.

A second positive appeal of interest-group liberalism is strongly
related to the first. Interest-group liberalism helps solve a problem for
the democratic politician in the modern state where the stakes are so
high. This is the problem of enhanced conflict and how to avoid it. The
politician's contribution to society is his skill in resolving conflict.
However, direct confrontations are sought only by the zealous ideologues and "outsiders." The typical American politician displaces and
defers and delegates conflict where possible; he squarely faces conflict
only when he must. Interest-group liberalism offers a justification for
keeping major combatants apart. It provides a theoretical basis for
giving to each according to his claim, the price for which is a reduction

[11]Binkley and Moos, pp. 8–9. In order to preserve value-free science, many
pluralists ("group theorists") denied public interest altogether, arguing
instead that there is a "totally inclusive interest" and that it is served by
letting groups interact without knowing what it is. Cf. Truman, pp. 50–51.

[12]For discussions of the extent to which group theory is a satisfactory
statement of reality, see my "American Business, Public Policy, Case-Studies
and Political Theory," *World Politics,* 16 (1964), pp. 677–715, and the
excellent essays cited therein.

[13]For more on the expansion and justification of these practices in
agriculture see my "How the Farmers Get What They Want," *Reporter,*
May 21, 1964, pp. 35ff.

of concern for what others are claiming. In other words, it transforms logrolling from necessary evil to greater good. This is the basis for the "consensus" so often claimed these days. It is also the basis for President Kennedy's faith that in our day ideology has given over to administration. It is inconceivable that so sophisticated a person as he could believe, for example, that his setting of guidelines for wage and price increases was a purely administrative act. Here, in fact, is a policy that will never be "administered" in the ordinary sense of the word. The guidelines provide a basis for direct and regular policy-making between the President (or his agent) and the spokesmen for industry and the spokesmen for labor. This is a new phase of government relations with management and labor, and it is another step consistent with the interest-group liberal criterion of direct access.

The third positive appeal of interest-group liberalism is that it is a direct, even if pathological, response to the crisis of public authority. The practice of dealing only with organized claims in formulating policy, and of dealing exclusively through organized claims in implementing programs helps create the sense that power need not be power at all, nor control control. If sovereignty is parceled out among the groups, then who's out anything? As Max Ways of *Fortune* put it, government power, group power and individual power may go up simultaneously. *If* the groups to be controlled control the controls, *then* "to administer does not always mean to rule."[14] The inequality of power, ultimately the involvement of coercion in government decisions, is always a gnawing problem in a democratic culture. Rousseau's General Will stopped at the boundary of a Swiss canton. The myth of the group and the group will is becoming the answer to Rousseau in the big democracy.

President Eisenhower talked regularly about the desirability of business-government "partnerships," despite the misgivings in his farewell address about the "military-industrial complex." However, explicit and systematic expression of interest-group liberalism is much more the contribution of the Democrats. There is little reason to believe that one party believes more ardently than the other; but the best evidence can be found among the more articulate Democrats, especially in the words of two of the leading Democratic intellectuals, Professors John Kenneth Galbraith and Arthur Schlesinger, Jr.[15] To Professor Gal-

[14]Max Ways, " 'Creative Federalism' and the Great Society," *Fortune,* January 1966, p. 122.

[15]A third major intellectual of the Kennedy Administration was Professor Richard E. Neustadt. That he is a political scientist makes all the more interesting his stress upon the necessary independence of the Presidency rather than the desirability of presidential partnerships and countervailing power. See his *Presidential Power* (New York: Wiley, 1960).

braith: "Private economic power is held in check by the countervailing power of those who are subject to it. The first begets the second."[16] Concentrated economic power stimulates other business interests (in contrast to the Smithian consumer), which organize against it. This results in a natural tendency toward equilibrium. But Galbraith is not really writing a theoretical alternative to Adam Smith; he is writing a program of government action. For he admits to the limited existence of effective countervailing power and proposes that where it is absent or too weak, government policy should seek out and support or, where necessary, create the organizations capable of countervailing. Government thereby pursues the public interest and makes itself superfluous at the same time. This is a sure-fire, nearly scientific, guide to interest-group liberalism. Professor Schlesinger's views are summarized for us in the campaign tract he wrote in 1960. To Schlesinger, the essential difference between the Democratic and Republican parties is that the Democratic party is a truly multi-interest party in the grand tradition extending back to Federalist No. 10. In power, it offers multi-interest administration and therefore ought to be preferred over the Republican Party and:

> What is the essence of a multi-interest administration? It is surely that the leading interests in society are all represented in the interior processes of policy formation—which can be done only if members or advocates of these interests are included in key positions of government. . . .[17]

This theme Schlesinger repeated in his more serious and more recent work, *A Thousand Days*. Following his account of the 1962 confrontation of President Kennedy with the steel industry and the later decision to cut taxes and cast off for expansionary rather than stabilizing fiscal policy, Schlesinger concludes:

> The ideological debates of the past began to give way to a new agreement on the practicalities of managing a modern economy. There thus developed in the Kennedy years a national accord on economic policy—a new consensus which gave hope of harnessing government, business and labor in rational partnership for a steadily expanding American economy."[18]

[16]Galbraith, p. 118.

[17]Arthur Schlesinger, Jr., *Kennedy or Nixon—Does It Make Any Difference?* (New York: Crowell-Collier-Macmillan, 1960), p. 43.

[18]Arthur M. Schlesinger, Jr., *A Thousand Days,* as reprinted in *Chicago Sun-Times,* January 23, 1966, Section 2, p. 3.

Interest-Group Liberalism and Public Policies in the 1960s

A significant point in the entire argument is that the Republicans would disagree with Schlesinger on the *facts* but not on the *basis* of his distinction. The Republican rejoinder would be, in effect, "Democratic Administrations are *not* more multi-interest than Republican." And, in my opinion, this would be almost the whole truth. This principle has been explicitly applied in the formulation of a large number of policies, especially since the return of the Democrats to power in 1961. That is, policy makers have in numerous new programs added elements of official group representation and have officially applied "participatory democracy" to the implementation as well as the formulation of law as part of the justification of their action. There are additional policies where evidence of the application of interest-group liberalism is clear even though not as consciously intended or as much a part of the record of self-praise.

President Kennedy provides an especially good starting point because his positions were clear and because justification was especially important to him. No attention need be paid to the elements of liberalism-conservatism in his program[19] but only to the consistency of his requests with interest-group liberalism. John Kennedy was bred to a politics of well-organized and autonomous units of power. Locally they were more likely ethnic, religious and neighborhood organizations, but they had to be reckoned with as powerful interest groups. The national party he set out to win in 1956 was also a congeries of autonomous factions and blocs; and it has been said that he succeeded by recreating the "New Deal coalition." But there is a vast difference between pluralism inside political parties and legitimized pluralism built into government programs. The one does not necessarily follow from the other, unless leaders believe it is desirable. President Kennedy's proposals and rhetoric mark his belief in that desirability. Many of his most important proposals mark his very real contribution to the corporatizing of the government-group nexus in the United States.

The agriculture problem, high and early on the New Frontier

[19]By proper application of the old-school criteria, Kennedy was on balance conservative. . . . Examples include his "actuarially sound" medicare, his investment tax credit and tax cut proposals, his preference for expansion of housing through investment incentives, his reluctance to ask for new civil rights legislation, his appreciation for governmental contracting and other executive powers to deal with civil rights, his opposition to "Powell Amendments" and parochial school aid in federal education legislation his concerted effort to make agriculture controls work, his support for very permissive depressed areas legislation that would bail out needy businesses and industries while reducing needs or pressures of entrepreneurs to move to some other section of the country.

agenda, was to be solved somewhat differently from all earlier attempts, and that difference is much to the point. At local levels, federal agriculture programs had always been corporative, with committees of local farm dignitaries applying the state and national standards to local conditions.[20] President Kennedy proposed simply to bring this pattern to the center and to have the farmers, represented by group leaders, *set* the standards as well as apply them. Essentially, this was NRA applied to agriculture.

There was no attempt to reinstitute an industrial NRA pattern, but there were, just the same, moves toward recognition of the organized side of industry in the "interior processes" of government. First, as earlier observed, by direct presidential act guidelines for profits and wages were set up. Notice was thereby served that henceforth "industrial policy" would be made by direct bargaining between President and each and every leader of an industrial sector. Quite separately, but along parallel industrial lines, this meant the same sort of bargaining between President and union leaders. It is beside the point to argue whether Kennedy or Johnson has been more lenient in applying the guidelines to the unions. It is even beside the point to argue whether this new technique of control means more government involvement and direction than alternative techniques. The point is that the pattern of control and the manner of its impact is basically corporativistic. "Partnership" is the measure of success.

Many other relations of government to industry have tended toward the same pattern in the 1960s, whether they come this way full-blown from President or emerge from Congress this way only at the end. COMSAT is a combination out of 1930s Italy and 1950s France. Like the Italian practice of "permanent receivership," COMSAT is a combine of kept private companies, sharing in stock and risk with the government. Like the many French public and mixed corporations, there is direct "interest representation" on the Board. The "public" stamp is placed on it by adding to the interest-laden Board three presidentially appointed members; but one of these is a representative of Big Labor and one a representative of Big Industry. By the end of 1966, there was already talk among the carriers (the communications industries) of forming a combine within the combine to regularize and stabilize losses suffered by any of them as a result of obsolescence and competition.

The Trade Expansion Act of 1962, for another example, was the first American tariff based upon broad categories of goods rather than single items. From the beginning, categorization of goods paralleled the lines of jurisdiction of the leading trade associations and organized

[20]See for example, Lowi, "How the Farmers Get What They Want."

farm commodities groups.[21] The semi-official role of trade associations was expected to increase and expand through those parts of the new law providing relief through subsidy for injuries proven to have been sustained by tariff cuts.

There were, of course, many Kennedy proposals that are economy-wide in intention, but even some of these have one peculiarity or another that distinguishes them less from the interest-group policies than first appearances suggest. The investment tax credit, for example, was industry-wide, but it involved a reduction rather than an enlargement of the governmental sphere. Appalachia involved a bold regional concept overwhelmingly broader than any organized groups; however, the strong veto power given the state governors allows for, and was expected to allow for, maximum return of group representation through the back door. Appalachia is more clearly a case of interest-group liberalism if we include, as we should, state and local government agencies as groups to be directly represented in implementation of policies. This becomes an important characteristic of "creative federalism." In Appalachia the governors in the region commit Federal funds to development plans formulated by state agencies, local agencies, and private groups.

During the Johnson Administration the doctrines and policies of interest-group liberalism have been elevated to new highs of usage and rationalization. It is coming of age by being provided with new and appropriate halo words. The most important is "creative federalism," about which President Johnson and his Great Society team have spoken frequently and enthusiastically. This and related terms—such as partnership, maximum feasible participation, and, above all consensus—seem to be very sincerely felt by present government leaders. The sentiments are coming to be shared widely among non-government leaders and are at the bottom of the extraordinary business support Johnson received during his most active period of legislative creativity. Probably the most accurate and sympathetic analysis of creative federalism and the role it is playing in the Great Society has been provided by *Fortune Magazine*. As *Fortune* and many other observers would agree, creative federalism is not federalism. Federalism divides sovereignty between duly constituted levels of government. "Creative federalism" is a parceling of powers between the central government and *all* structures of power, governments and non-governments. In fact, little distinction is made between what is government and what is not. It is, according to the enthusiastic definition of *Fortune* writer Max Ways, "a relation, cooperative and competitive, between a limited

[21]See Raymond Bauer *et al., American Business and Public Policy* (New York: Atherton, 1963), pp. 73ff.

central power and other powers that are essentially independent of it."
The difference between federalism and "creative federalism" is no
mere academic distinction. Creative federalism involves a "new way of
organizing federal programs . . . [in which simultaneously] the power
of states and local governments will increase; the power of private
organizations, including businesses, will increase; the power of individuals will increase."[22]

In line with the new rationale, President Johnson and his Administration have expanded the degree to which private organizations and
local authorities become endowed with national sovereignty. Corporativistic programs inherited from the New Deal have been strengthened
in the degree to which they can share in the new, explicit rationale.
This has been particularly noticable in the power and natural resources
field, where policies are now quite explicitly left to the determination of those participants who know the "local situation" best. It is
quite at the center of Great Society expansions of existing programs.
When still Assistant Secretary for Education, Francis Keppel described
federal education policy this way: "To speak of 'federal aid' [to
education] simply confuses the issue. It is more appropriate to speak of
federal support to special purposes . . . an investment made by a
partner who has clearly in mind the investments of other partners—
local, state and private."[23]

The most significant contribution of the Great Society to the
growing ratio such corporativistic programs bear to the sum total of
federal activity is the War on Poverty, particularly the community
action program. To the old progressive the elimination of poverty was
a passionate dream, to the socialist a philosophic and historic necessity.
To the interest-group liberal, poverty is becoming just another status
around which power centers ought to organize. If one hasn't organized, then organize it. In so organizing it, poverty is not eliminated,
but inconsistency in the manner of government's relation to society is
reduced. Organizing the poor, something that once was done only in
the Threepenny Opera, helps legitimize the interest-group liberal's
preference for dealing only with organized claims. The "Peachum
factor" in public affairs is best personified in Sargent Shriver. In getting
the War on Poverty under way Shriver was misunderstood in many
matters, particularly on any insistence that the poor be represented in
some mathematically exact way. But one aspect of the doctrine was
clear all the time. This was (and is) that certain types of groups should
always be involved some way. As he listed them they are: "govern-

[22]Ways. p. 122.

[23]Quoted in *Congressional Quarterly Weekly Report,* April 22, 1966, p.
833.

mental groups," philanthropic, religious, business, and labor groups, and "the poor."[24] The significance lies primarily in the equality of the listing. "Governmental groups" are simply one more type of participant.

Interest-group liberalism thus seems closer to being the established, operative ideology of the American elite than any other body of doctrine. The United States is far from 100 percent a corporate state; but each administration, beginning with the New Deal revolution, has helped reduce the gap. And it is equally significant that few if any programs organized on the basis of direct interest representation or group self-administration have ever been eliminated. To the undoubted power of organized interests has now been added the belief in their virtue. There would always be delegation of sovereignty to interest groups in some proportion of the total body of governmental activities. The new context of justification simply means far more direct delegation than the realities of power, unsupported by legitimacy, would call for.

In sum, modern liberals are ambivalent about government. Government is obviously the most efficacious way of achieving good purposes in our age. But it is efficacious because it is involuntary; as one of the founders of modern social science put it, modern government possesses a monopoly of legal coercion in a society. To live with their ambivalence, modern policy makers have fallen into believing that public policy involves merely the identification of the problems toward which government ought to be aimed. It pretends, through "pluralism," "countervailing power," "creative federalism," "partnership," and "participatory democracy," that the unsentimental business of coercion is not involved and that the unsentimental decisions of how to employ coercion need not really be made at all. Stated in the extreme, the policies of interest-group liberalism are end-oriented. Few standards of implementation, if any, accompany delegations of power. The requirement of standards has been replaced by the requirement of participation. The requirement of law has been replaced by the requirement of contingency.

THE COSTS OF INTEREST-GROUP LIBERALISM

For all the political advantages interest-group liberals have in their ideology, there are high costs involved. Unfortunately, these costs are not strongly apparent at the time of the creation of a group-based program. As Wallace Sayre once observed, the gains of a change tend

[24]Jules Witcover and Erwin Knoll, "Politics and the Poor: Shriver's Second Thoughts," *Reporter*, December 30, 1965, p. 24.

to be immediate, the costs tend to be cumulative. However, it takes no long-run patience or the spinning of fine webs to capture and assess the consequences of group-based policy solutions. Three major consequences are suggested and assessed here: (1) the atrophy of institutions of popular control; (2) the maintenance of old and creation of new structures of privilege; and (3) conservatism, in several senses of the word.

1. In his *The Public Philosophy,* Lippmann was rightfully concerned over the "derangement of power" whereby modern democracies tend first toward unchecked elective leadership and then toward drainage of public authority from elective leaders down into their constituencies. However, Lippmann erred if he thought of constituencies only as voting constituencies. Drainage has tended toward "support group constituencies," and with special consequence. Parceling out policy-making power to the most interested parties destroys political responsibility. A program split off with a special imperium to govern itself is not merely an administrative unit. It is a structure of power with impressive capacities to resist central political control.

Besides making conflict-of-interest a principle of government rather than a criminal act, participatory programs shut out the public. To be more precise, programs of this sort tend to cut out all that part of the mass that is not specifically organized around values strongly salient to the goals of the program. They shut out the public, first, at the most creative phase of policy making—the phase where the problem is first defined. Once problems are defined, alliances form accordingly and the outcome is both a policy and a reflection of superior power. If the definition is laid out by groups along lines of established group organization, there is always great difficulty for an amorphous public to be organized in any other terms. The public is shut out, secondly, at the phase of accountability. In programs in which group self-administration is legitimate, the administrators are accountable primarily to the groups, only secondarily to President or Congress as institutions. In brief, to the extent that organized interests legitimately control a program there is functional rather than substantive accountability. This means questions of equity, balance and equilibrium to the exclusion of questions of overall social policy and questions of whether or not the program should be maintained or discontinued. It also means accountability to experts first and amateurs last; and an expert is a man trained and skilled in the mysteries and technologies of the program. These propositions are best illustrated by at least ten separate, self-governing systems (representing over 10 billion dollars per year in spending and loaning) in agriculture alone.[25] There are many other, although perhaps less dramatic, illustrations.

[25]Lowi, "How The Farmers Get What They Want."

Finally, the public is shut out by tendencies toward conspiracy to shut the public out. One of the assumptions underlying direct group representation is that on the boards and in the staff and among the recognized outside consultants there will be regular countervailing and checks and balances. In Schattschneider's terms, this would be expected to expand the "scope of conflict." But there is nothing inevitable about that, and the safer assumption might well be the converse. One meaningful illustration, precisely because it is an absurd extreme, is found in the French system of interest representation. Maurice Bye reports that as the communist-controlled union, the CGT, intensified its participation in post-war government it was able to influence representatives of interests other than the employees. In a desperate effort to insure the separation and countervailing of interests on the boards, the government issued the decree that "each member of the board must be *independent of the interests he is not representing.*"[26] After a 1964 review of the politics of agriculture and of five major efforts of their post-war administrations to bring the ten separate self-governing agriculture systems under a minimum of central control, I was led to the following conclusion:

> These systems . . . have become practically insulated from the three central sources of democratic political responsibility. Thus, within the Executive branch, they are autonomous. Secretaries of Agriculture have tried and failed to consolidate or even to coordinate related programs. Within Congress, they are sufficiently powerful to be able to exercise an effective veto or create a stalemate. And they are almost totally removed from the view, not to mention the control, of the general public. (Throughout the 1950s, Victor Anfuso of Brooklyn was the only member of the House Agriculture Committee from a non-farm constituency.)[27]

This, I suggest, is a tendency in all similarly organized programs.

2. Programs following the principles of interest-group liberalism create privilege, and it is a type of privilege particularly hard to bear or combat because it is touched with the symbolism of the state. The large national interest groups that walk the terrains of national politics are already fairly tight structures of power. We need no more research to support Michels' iron tendency toward oligarchy in "private governments." Pluralists ease our problem of abiding the existence of organized interests by characterizing oligarchy as simply a negative name for organization: In combat people want and need to be organized and

[26]Mario Einaudi *et al., Nationalization in France and Italy* (Ithaca: Cornell University Press, 1955), pp. 100–101, emphasis added.

[27]Lowi, "How The Farmers Get What They Want."

led. Another, somewhat less assuaging, assertion of pluralism is that the member approves the goals of the group or is free to leave it for another, or can turn his attention to one of his "overlapping memberships" in other groups. But however true these may be in pluralistic *politics,* everything changes when some of the groups are co-opted by the state in pluralistic *government.* The American Farm Bureau Federation is no "voluntary association" insofar as it is a legitimate functionary in Extension work. NAHB, NAREB, NAACP or NAM are no ordinary lobbies after they become part of the "interior processes of policy formation."

The more clear and legitimized the representation of a group or its leaders in policy formation, the less voluntary is membership in that group and the more necessary is loyalty to its leadership for people who share the interests in question. And, the more clear the official practice of recognizing only organized interests, the more hierarchy is introduced into the society. It is a well-recognized and widely appreciated function of formal groups in modern societies to provide much of the necessary every-day social control. However, when the very thought processes behind public policy are geared toward those groups they are bound to take on much of the involuntary character of *public* control. The classic example outside agriculture is probably the Rivers and Harbors Congress, a private agency whose decisions in the screening of public works projects have almost the effect of law. And, as David Truman observes, arrangements where "one homogeneous group is directly or indirectly charged with the administration of a function . . . [in a] kind of situation that characterizes the occupational licensing boards and similar 'independent' agencies . . . have become increasingly familiar in regulatory situations in all levels of government."[28]

Even when the purpose of the program is the uplifting of the underprivileged, the administrative arrangement favored by interest-group liberalism tends toward creation of new privilege instead. Urban redevelopment programs based upon federal support of private plans do not necessarily, but do all too easily, become means by which the building industry regularizes itself. An FHA run essentially by the standards of the NAREB became a major escape route for the middle class to leave the city for suburbia rather than a means of providing housing for all. Urban redevelopment, operating for nearly two decades on a principle of local government and local developer specifica-

---

[28]Truman, p. 462. For a profound appreciation of the public power of private authorities in occupational licensing, see York Willbern, "Professionalization in State and Local Government: Too Little or Too Much?" *Public Administration Review,* (Winter 1954). See also Arthur S. Miller, *Private Governments and the Constitution.*

tion of federal policy, has been used in the South (and elsewhere) as an effective instrument for Negro removal. Organizing councils for the poverty program have become first and foremost means of elevating individual spokesmen for the poor and of determining which churches and neighborhood organizations shall be the duly recognized channels of legitimate demand. Encouragement of organization among Negroes and the White and non-White poor is important. Early recognition of a few among many emerging leaders and organizations as legitimate administrators or policy-makers takes a serious risk of destroying the process itself (more on this directly below).

3. Government by and through interest groups is in impact conservative in almost every sense of that term. Part of its conservatism can be seen in another look at the two foregoing objections: Weakening of popular government and support of privilege are, in other words, two aspects of conservatism. It is beside the point to argue that these consequences are not intended. A third dimension of conservatism, stressed here separately, is the simple conservatism of resistance to change. David Truman, who has not been a strong critic of self-government by interest groups, has, all the same, identified a general tendency of established agency-group relationships to be "highly resistant to disturbance." He continues:

> New and expanded functions are easily accommodated, provided they develop and operate through existing channels of influence and do not tend to alter the relative importance of those influences. Disturbing changes are those that modify either the content or the relative strength of the component forces operating through an administrative agency. In the face of such changes, or the threat of them, the "old line" agency is highly inflexible.[29]

If this is already a tendency in a pluralistic system, then agency-group relationships must be all the more inflexible to the extent that the relationship is official and legitimate.

The war-on-poverty pattern, even in its early stages, provides a rich testing ground. I observed above that early official cooption of poverty leaders creates privilege before, and perhaps instead of, alleviating poverty. Another side of this war is the war the established welfare groups are waging against the emergence of the newly organizing social forces. Many reports are already remarking upon the opposition established welfare and church groups are putting up against the new groups. Such opposition led to abandonment of Syracuse's organize-the-poor project and the retreat of Sargent Shriver's Office of Economic Opportunity to "umbrella groups" sponsored

[29]Truman, pp. 467–468.

by City Hall.[30] Old and established groups doing good works might naturally look fearfully upon the emergence of competing, perhaps hostile, groups. That is well and good—until their difference is one of "who shall be the government?" Conservatism then becomes necessary as a matter of survival.

The tendency toward the extreme conservatism of sharing legitimate power with private organizations is possibly stronger in programs more strictly economic. Adams and Gray reviewed figures on assignment of FM radio broadcasting licenses and found that as of 1955, 90 percent of the FM stations were merely "little auxiliaries" of large AM networks. They also note that the same pattern was beginning to repeat itself in FCC licensing of UHF television channels.[31] The mythology may explain this as a case of "interest group power," but that begs the question. Whatever power was held by the networks was based largely on the commitment the FCC implied in the original grants of licenses. Having granted exclusive privileges to private groups in the public domain (in this case the original assignment of frequencies) without laying down practical conditions for perpetual public retention of the domain itself, the FCC had actually given over sovereignty. The companies acquired property rights and legally vested interests in the grant that interfere enormously with later efforts to affect the grant. Thus, any FCC attempt to expand the communications business through FM would deeply affect the positions and "property" of the established AM companies and networks. Issuing FM licenses to new organizations would have required an open assault on property as well as the established market relations. Leaving aside all other judgements of the practice, it is clearly conservative.[32] Granting of licenses and other privileges unconditionally, and limiting sovereignty by allowing the marketing of properties to be influenced by the possession of the privilege, are practices also to be found in oil, in water power, in the newer sources of power, in transportation, in the "parity" programs of agriculture.

Wherever such practices are found there will also be found strong resistance to change. Already the pattern is repeating itself in form and consequences in the policies regarding our newest resource, outer

---

[30]Witcover and Knoll.

[31]Walter S. Adams and Horace Gray, *Monopoly in America* (New York: Crowell-Collier-Macmillan, 1955), pp. 48–50.

[32]Cf. Adams and Gray, pp. 44–46, and their discussion, from a different point of view, of the "abridgement of sovereignty by grants of privilege." See also Merle Fainsod *et al., Government and the American Economy* (New York: Norton, 1959), pp. 400–404. They observe the same thing happening in television and for the same reasons.

space. As earlier observed, the private members of COMSAT very early in the life of the new corporation made arrangements to protect themselves against the impact of new developments on old facilities. In addition to that, and more significantly here, the constitutents of COMSAT have moved to exclude all other possible entrants and alternative ways of organizing the economics of space communication. In response to Ford Foundation's proposal for a separate satellite system for educational television, COMSAT officially moved to cut off any chance of a rival by (1) opposing Ford vigorously, (2) interpreting the statute and charter to be a grant of trust for the entire public interest in the field, (3) seeking a ruling to that effect from the FCC, (4) showing that stockholders in COMSAT and in the carrier members of COMSAT, such as A.T.&T., would be dealt an unfair blow, and (5) producing an alternative plan whereby the Ford system would be created within COMSAT, being underwritten by all the major carriers and "users" (i.e., the telephone and telegraph companies and the commercial networks).[33]

There are social and psychological mechanisms as well as economic and vested interests working against change. As programs are split off and allowed to establish self-governing relations with clientele groups, professional norms usually spring up, governing the proper ways of doing things. These rules-of-the-game heavily weight access and power in favor of the established interests, just as American parliamentary rules-of-the-game have always tended to make Congress a haven for classes in retreat. For example, as public health moved from a regulatory to a welfare concept, local health agencies put up impressive resistance against efforts to reorganize city and county health departments accordingly. Herbert Kaufman chronicles the vain forty-year reorganization effort in New York City.[34] An important

---

[33]See accounts in *New York Times,* August 2 and August 29, 1966, and *Time Magazine,* August 12, 1966, p. 38.

[34]Herbert Kaufman, "The New York City Health Centers," Interuniversity Case Program. Wallace Sayre and Herbert Kaufman in *Governing New York City* (New York: Russell Sage, 1960), chapter XIX, generalize on this pattern. They refer to "islands of functional power" as the formal power structure of the city. Each island enjoys considerable autonomy, each is a system of administrators and their "satellite groups," each resists interactions with other islands. The big city is possibly in an advanced stage of what in this paper is observed as an important tendency at the national level. Because of the tragic stalemate in the cities, these pronounced city patterns might serve as a better warning than my illustrations drawn from national practices. See also Herbert Kaufman, *Politics and Policies in State and Local Governments* (Englewood Cliffs, N.J.: Prentice-Hall, 1963), chapter V.

psychological mechanism working against change is one that can be found in criticisms of the electoral devices of proportional and occupational representation. PR tends to rigidify whatever social cleavages first provide the basis for PR, because PR encourages social interests to organize, then perpetuates them by allowing them to become "constituencies." This is all the more true as interests actually become not merely groups but parties represented by name and bloc in parliament.[35] Even in less formalized situations, legitimizing a group gives it the advantages of exposure and usage as well as direct power, access and privilege.

INTEREST-GROUP LIBERALISM AND HOW TO SURVIVE IT

Quite possibly all of these developments are part of some irresistible historical process. In that case policy-makers would never really have had any alternative when they created group-based programs. And in that case the ideology of interest-group liberalism simply reflects and rationalizes the realities of power. However, the best test of a deterministic hypothesis is whether real-world efforts to deny it fail. Thus, a consideration of remedies is worthwhile.

We might begin where Truman ended his extremely influential work on pluralistic America. After reviewing several possible "palliatives" Truman concludes essentially that the pluralistic political system is not doomed at all but, to the contrary, is self-corrective:

> To the extent that the kind of dynamic stability that permits gradual adaptation is a function of elements within the system itself, the key factors will not be new. The group process will proceed in the usual fashion. Whether it eventuates in disaster will depend in the future as in the past basically upon the effects of overlapping membership, particularly the vitality of membership in those potential groups based upon interests held widely throughout the society. The memberships are the means both of stability and of peaceful change. In the future as in the past, they will provide the answer to the ancient question: *quis custodiet ipsos custodes?* Guardianship will emerge out of the affiliations of the guardians.[36]

[35]Cf. Carl Friedrich, *Constitutional Government and Democracy* (Boston: Ginn and Co., 1950), pp. 291–294. See also a classic critique of occupational representation by Paul H. Douglas, "Occupational versus Proportional Representation," *American Journal of Sociology* (September 1923); and David Truman, pp. 525–526.

[36]Truman. p. 535.

But it is self-corrective only if there is overlapping and confrontation among groups, and too many examples above suggest that (1) there is a strong tendency, supported by a great deal of conscious effort, to keep confrontation to a minimum and that (2) "membership in potential groups" is confined to values about the "rules-of-the-game" about which there is strong consensus in general but, due to their generality, extreme permissiveness in particular, short-run situations. Thus, it cannot be assumed that the conditions necessary for the self-corrective system necessarily exist. It is wrong to assume that social pluralism (which is an undeniable fact about America) produced *political* pluralism.

However, the important question is not whether Truman and others are wrong but whether the conditions necessary for their self-corrective system can be deliberately contrived. The effort here is to propose some such contrivances. Two introductory observations should be made about them. First, it is assumed that positive government is here to stay and expand. Thus, proposals for return to a principle of lesser government and for policies in the lower left-hand corner of the Diagram, while logical and perhaps desirable, are not acceptable. Second, it is assumed that *real* political pluralism is a desirable form of democracy and that it is a desirable democratic antidote to the "incorporated pluralism" which has been the object of criticism throughout this essay.

1. The first part of the remedy is attractive precisely because it is so obvious. This is to discredit interest-group liberalism as official ideology. Essentially, this is the effort of this paper. Unless we are locked in a predetermined secular trend, a change of ideology can affect the pattern of power just as the pattern of power can affect ideology. Certainly the egalitarian ideology has affected the distribution of power in every country where it has had any currency at all. A change of ideology could keep to a minimum the number of programs that merely incorporate the forces responsible for passage. Some other ideology would provide a basis for resisting many of the most outrageous claims for patronage and privilege made by organized interests.

2. The second part of the remedy is institutional and also suggests the direction a new ideology ought to take. This is to push direct group access back one giant step in the political process, somehow to insulate administrative agencies from full group participation. This means restoration of the Federalist No. 10 ideology in which "factions" are necessary evils that require regulation, not accommodation. Madison defined faction as "a number of citizens, whether amounting to a majority or minority of the whole, who are united and actuated by some common impulse of passion, or of interest, *adverse to the right of other citizens, or to the permanent and aggregate interests of the*

community." As a manifestation of the ideology prevalent today, it is worth noting that Truman quotes Madison's definition but ends his quote just before the parts I. emphasized above.[37] That part of Madison's definition should be returned to full faith and credit, and the only way to do that and to be sure that it and the true self-regulatory character of pluralism can be institutionalized is *to keep group interests in constant confrontation with one another in Congress.* Once an agency is "depoliticized" or "made independent" by handing it over to its organized clientele, the number of "factions" is reduced from a competitive to an oligopolistic situation; competition lasts only until the remaining few groups learn each other's goals and each adjusts to the others. Lippmann is concerned for a "derangement of power" in which *governing* has been drained away from the executive to the assembly and to the electorate, and neither is qualified to govern. The American pattern would suggest another kind of derangement altogether, a derangement brought about by Congress's direct extension of its own principles of representation over into the executive.

Pushing group representation and "participatory democracy" back into Congress and away from the executive requires several relatively traditional steps. The first would be revival of a constitutional doctrine that is still valid but widely disregarded. This is the rule that the delegation of legislative power to administrative agencies must be accompanied by clear standards of implementation.[38] This involves revival of the rule of law to replace the rule of bargaining as a principle of administration. It does not involve reduction of the public sphere. It *is* likely to make more difficult the framing and passage of some programs; but one wonders why any program should be acceptable if its partisans cannot clearly state purpose and means. Revival of the rule of law would also tend to dispel much of the cynicism with which the most active citizen views public authority.

Another way to restore competition to groups and ultimately push them back to Congress is to foster a truly independent executive. Development of a real Senior Civil Service is vital to this in the way it would tend to develop a profession of public administration, as distinct from a profession of a particular technology and a career within a specific agency. The makings of a Senior Civil Service lie already within the grasp of the Civil Service Commission if it has the wit to

---

[37]Truman, p. 4.

[38]This rule is made more interesting for the argument here because it was given new currency in the *Schechter Poultry* and *Panama Refining* cases, both of which involved the most extreme instance of delegation of sovereignty to groups, the NRA. For a recent expression, see Judge Henry J. Friendly's *The Federal Administrative Agencies* (Cambridge: Harvard University Press, 1962), pp. 5ff.

perceive its opportunity in its Career Executive Roster and its Office of Career Development and its Executive Seminar Center. The independent Senior Civil Servant, who could be designed for weakness in agency loyalty, combined with the imposition of clearer standards and rules governing administrative discretion, together would almost necessarily centralize and formalize, without denying, group access to agencies. In turn this would almost necessarily throw more groups together, increase their competition, expand the scope of that competition, and ultimately require open, public settlement of their differences. This would throw groups back more frequently into Congress and would also increase presidential opportunity to control the bureaucracies. The legitimacy of these institutions would be further confirmed.

3. A third part of the remedy has to do with programs themselves, although the recommendation overlaps No. 2 in that it has much to do with institutional roles. This is to set a Jeffersonian absolute limit of from five to ten years on every enabling act. As the end approaches, established relations between agency and clientele are likely to be shaken by exposure and opposition. This is as important as the need for regular evaluation of the existence of the program itself and of whether it should be abolished, expanded or merged with some other program. There is a myth that programs are evaluated at least once a year through the normal appropriations process and that specialized appropriations and authorizations subcommittees review agency requests with a fine tooth comb. However, yearly evaluation, especially the appropriations process, gets at only the incremental and marginal aspects of most programs, rarely at the substance. Here is an example of the earlier distinction between functional and substantive accountability. The very cost-consciousness and detail that makes yearly review functionally rational is the basis of its weakness as a substantively rational process.

This proposal, like the proposal for a return to a rule of law, injects an element of inefficiency into the system. But our affluence is hardly worth the trouble if we cannot spend some of it on maintaining due process, pluralism and other system values. It also injects instability, but it is the very sort of instability that is supposed to make the pluralistic system work. It is amazing and distressing how many 1930s left-wing liberals have become 1960s interest-group liberals out of a concern for instability.

4. The fourth and final part of a reform program bears some resemblance to an old-line constitutional argument. Restoration of the *Schechter* and *Panama* requirement would tend to do more than strengthen the rule of law, enhance real political competition, and dispel political cynicism. It might also provide a basis for establishing some practical and functional limitations on the scope of federal

power. That is to say, if an applicable and understandable set of general rules must accompany every federal program, then, except in some clear emergency, federal power could not extend to those objects for which no general rules are either practicable or desirable. Where regional or local variation is to be encouraged, State Government is really the proper unit. Argument for restoration of State Government is not based on mere antiquarian admiration of federalism or fear of national domination. It is an immensely practical argument. State Governments have been systematically weakened by Home Rule, by federal absorption of tax base and by federal-local relations. Yet the cities, even with federal help, have proven unable to cope because the problems have outgrown their boundaries. The State possesses all the powers of its cities plus the territorial containment of most of the new metropolitan realities. The State may be the only governmental unit capable of coping with contemporary problems. Unconditional rebates of federal revenues to the States and obedience to a rule of law may leave the way open for expansion of federal activities in which there is reasonable chance of success without loss of federal control and without loss of legitimacy.

No individual interest group can be expected to take fullest account of the consequences of its own claims. This is what Presidents and Congresses are for, and this is what will continue to be delegated away as long as the ideology of interest-group liberalism allows. In effect this means that restoring pluralism as an effective principle of democratic politics requires destroying it as a principle of government. If this is to be accomplished, reform must begin with the replacement of interest-group liberalism with some contemporary version of the rule of law. The program of reform must include at least: debate that centers upon the actual consequences of public policies and of their forms of implementation; a legislative process that regularly treats enabling legislation rather than revision; political brokers that have to deal in substantive as well as functional issues; and adaptation of public controls to local needs through choice of appropriate level of government rather than through delegation of the choice to the most interested parties.

2 The Garrison Economy*

TERENCE McCARTHY

I

In September 1965 the Federal Reserve Bank of Philadelphia, in its *Business Review,* reassured the nation that "So far the Vietnam buildup ordered by the President apparently will funnel an extra $3 or $4 billion into the war effort between now and the second quarter of 1966. . . . The nation's manufacturing plants are presently working at about 90 percent of capacity and the additional expenditures anticipated would amount to less than one percent of the current rate of national output and would scarcely dent the existing rate of utilization. . . . The added defense spending must also be viewed against a record rate of capital spending which will make even more industrial capacity available."

That was in the tranquilizer stage of statistical pronouncements

*Reprinted by permission of the author from *The Columbia University Forum,* 9:4 (Fall 1966). Copyright 1966 by The Trustees of Columbia University in the City of New York.

about Vietnam. It was as though somebody somewhere had sat down to estimate just how much war the United States could afford within guidelines: no increases in prices or interest rates, no rise in imports, no effects upon balance of payments, and—above all—no inflation. The war in Vietnam was looked upon as a no-cost operation, involving only a narrow increase in the utilization of resources employed below their optimum; that is, an exercise in the maximization of output. Events have proved the contrary. Instead of the *Fröhlichkrieg* described by the Philadelphia Federal Reserve Bank, the war in Vietnam is proving bloody, costly in resources, and inflationary in its economic results. The $3–4 billion cost estimate was an illusion. It has been shown that, econometrics or no, one cannot have war without price. In June 1966 the Federal Reserve Bank of San Francisco, in its *Monthly Review,* reported: "Last year's commitment of substantial ground forces to the conflict in Vietnam suddenly increased the pressures on defense-related sectors and accelerated the pace of activity throughout the entire U.S. economy. And the impact will continue, as resources are strained by the cost of perhaps $20 billion or more associated with a buildup to 400,000 troops in Vietnam." The buildup to 400,000 men will be completed at about the end of 1966; to be followed, according to general expectations, by a further buildup to 625,000 men by summer 1967.

These numbers are extraordinarily important to the economy. The Philadelphia Reserve Bank predicted: "The increase in the armed forces will probably have a minimum impact on labor markets. Most of those who will be drafted are in the age brackets which possess few developed skills and where unemployment is high." But increase of committed troops beyond 400,000 will require some withdrawal of men from manufacturing industries; a call up of reservists, for example, would have precisely this effect. At the same time, the proportion of manufacturing output going to noncivilian uses will increase as procurement steps up and as depleted military stocks are replaced. A question therefore arises as to whether abundance of civilian goods can be assured as the proportionate output of military items increases and skilled industrial labor grows even scarcer.

The scarcity of skilled labor is already acute. This summer, unemployment among skilled workers, excluding temporary layoffs, was a bare 1.2 percent—close to an irreducible minimum. So far—and it is a genuine accomplishment—there has been no measurable decline in the productivity of industrial labor since the buildup began. Nor has productivity increased; it has simply stood still. The scarcity of skilled labor combined with static productivity not only limits output but, unhappily, is likely to *increase* unemployment among the unskilled. It is now beginning to be recognized, by Mr. Gardner Ackley I am pleased to note, that as unemployment among skilled laborers approaches zero the amount of injected purchasing power needed to eliminate unemployment among the unskilled approaches infinity. That is, the inflation attendant upon total employment of the skilled drives into the labor market more unskilled young and superannuated persons than obtain employment.

The net effect of the Vietnam escalation, from July 1965 to July 1966, has been a 9.9 percent increase in monthly wage and salary disbursements—compared to a 9.2 percent increase in industrial output during the same period. But a large part of the increased output is not available to consumers because it consists of defense-related products or of capital goods. Production of consumer goods has risen only one third as fast as production of equipment, which has risen 19.2 percent.

America's inflation has its roots in this most fertile soil. Additions to purchasing power are exceeding additions to civilian products available for purchase, and the great increase in purchasing power is occurring in industries other than those producing commodities. In July 1966, the annual rate of wage and salary disbursements exceeded that of the previous year by $35.4 billion, about $10 billion higher than had there been no war in Vietnam. Consumer credit, excluding home mortgages, rose by $8.4 billion, about $1 billion more than if there had been no war. Of the $35.4 billion increase in wage and salary disbursements, only $14.2 billion has been paid to workers in commodity-producing industries; $6.7 billion has gone to people in distributive industries; $5.3 billion in service industries; $9.2 billion in federal and state government.

What the war in Vietnam has brought about, it is clear, is a malformation in economic growth. Consider, then, the condition we can expect in the economy with an additional buildup in Vietnam between now and next summer. Assuming the whole of the $20 billion expenditure on the buildup to 400,000 men to be complete by the end of 1966, it is reasonable to estimate that maintenance of this force, a buildup to 625,000 troops thereafter, and replacement of depleted military stocks will cost $22–24 billion in the period between July 1966 and July 1967. In short, from May 1965 to July 1967 the direct costs of the war in Vietnam can be estimated at about $33–35 billion—an average annual rate of $15–16 billion over the period and an annual rate of $26–30 billion from fall 1966 until summer 1967.

If these amounts startle one—they should not, for modern war is no pauper's game—let us refer again to the June 1966 *Monthly Review* of the San Francisco Federal Reserve Bank. It tells us: "Although troop commitment does not yet match Korea-war levels, troop costs per man are much more expensive than in that earlier period. Average military pay is 40 percent higher than during Korea; today's F-4C fighter costs six times as much as the earlier F-86 model; and ammunition usage is higher, especially since today's M-16 rifle shoots five times as many rounds per minute as the earlier M-14.

Moreover, each B-52 sortie from Guam to Vietnam costs $13,000 in operational costs plus $30,000 for each planeload of sixty 75-pound bombs."

Vietnamese rice exports used to range between 300,000 and 400,000 tons per year; the country now must import that amount—all paid for, directly or indirectly, by the United States. Internal shipments have suffered too. Rice movements to Saigon from the Mekong Delta dropped by about 300,000 tons, or 40 percent, in 1965. The United States, from domestic resources and purchases abroad, has had to take responsibility for filling Saigon's rice bowl. And aircraft losses suffered by the United States totaled some $700 million through August 1966 and may approximate $1 billion by 1966 year-end.

Ask not, then, American citizen, for whom the price of Vietnam rises. It rises for thee. And so it should, for no people has the moral right to embark upon war without paying its cost—as no people ever, whatever the circumstances, should enjoy the privilege of waging war by sending into combat only those "in the age brackets which possess few developed skills and where unemployment is high."

By July 1967, in short, wages and salaries may exceed those of July 1965 by an annual amount of $87 billion, an insupportable inflation of purchasing power. By as early as December 1966, in fact, the annual rate of salaries and wages paid may exceed that of December 1964 by about $67 billion, itself inflationary enough.

The inflation would have been worse had merchandise imports not increased $2.1 billion in the first half of 1966, easing the pressure of purchasing power on available consumption items. Merchandise exports rose $1.4 billion in the first quarter, but only $337 million in the second, with a sharp decline in nonagricultural shipments. First quarter expectations as to support for the balance of payments have therefore been belied. Deterioration in the balance of payments was mitigated by the inflow of nearly $400 million of foreign funds attracted by the extraordinary increase in interest rates in this country in the second quarter. Therefore, if government action were to force interest rates down, the recent inflow of capital would be reversed, bringing about a serious balance of payments predicament by year-end. However, unless consumer goods imports rise more sharply than exports in the months to come and are encouraged to do so, the foreseeable enormous generation of purchasing power will not be offset by a sufficient supply of consumption goods. Moreover, the war is generating an extraordinary demand for capital goods that cannot be met readily unless machinery and equipment exports are depressed and imports increased.

Thus, because of Vietnam, the United States is faced with a most uncomfortable choice: between aggravating the balance of payments deficit or aggravating the domestic inflation. Whichever is chosen, the price will be high. The position of the dollar in the world will be jeopardized in either case, but the injury from domestic inflation is likely, in my judgment, to be much the greater.

Continued inflation will accelerate the gold drain—$600 million in the twelve months to September 9, 1966—and jeopardize the gold cover of the Federal Reserve notes issue. The law requires that for each $1 of Federal Reserve notes in circulation the Federal Reserve maintain 25 cents of gold backing in the form of a claim on the U.S. Treasury stock of gold. At September 8, 1965, this gold cover was 37.4 percent; at September 9, 1966, 32.8 percent. A comparable decline, easily foreseeable, would reduce the gold cover of U.S. currency to about 28 percent by September 1967. Before that point, experience dictates, the gold cover would have to be reduced or removed. There is already sentiment in the Congress for its removal. The currency of the United States may be without gold cover by fall 1967.

This is not the place to argue the merits or demerits of gold. It is the place to argue that, whatever these merits, gold and the dollar will be severed if the war in Vietnam continues. In fact, removal of the gold cover will be essential if the recent rate of borrowings from large commercial banks continues. Suspension of the 7 percent investment tax credit may reduce the rate of increase in demand for loans; it will hardly deter borrowers faced with demand for products beyond their capacity to supply. The borrowing pressure on bank resources is extreme. The prime rate in September 1966, ostensibly 6 percent, was actually closer to 8 percent because of requirements by banks that borrowers maintain compensating balances. Removal of the gold cover might make increased assets available for lending. But the inflation would gather pace. Vietnam is proving to be no petty cash venture.

What the economic effect might be of moving land forces into North Vietnam is sheer conjecture. Indeed, we have no sound reason to believe that invasion of North Vietnam is part of the unfolding strategy. But we do know that there has been cessation of the clamor to mine the harbor of Haiphong and to bomb the harbor installations, and that simultaneously the oil depots and transportation infrastructure of North Vietnam have become targets of continuous attack from the air. These are classic preconditions for invasion from the coast. It is possible that strategists are contemplating amphibious landing of troops at Haiphong as part of a drive on Hanoi. This is not something I predict. But it is precisely the sort of possibility that could bring about a formal declaration of war involving wartime controls on the economy. The point is that we are already at war without wartime controls. And that is why we have an inflation.

II

In the real world of today, the central purpose of a civilian economy is the maintenance and growth of social standards; the art of civil government is to facilitate what the citizen can accomplish for himself and his society. A war economy denies this purpose; it subordinates civilian aims to the single objective of gaining victory in battle over a specific enemy in a specific situation. The civilian sector is required to facilitate what it is the purpose of government to accomplish—a total, though temporary, inversion of the relation between state and citizen.

The garrison economy differs crucially from both. It is that permanent economic ordering of the nation-state responsive to the view that what is foreign is threat; that this threat is not ultimate but immediate, not specific but universal; and that the magnitude of this threat increases as technical, industrial and social advance occurs abroad, whatever the technical, industrial and social advance occurring at home.

In the garrison economy, the size and character of military spending in part determine the qualities of the economy as a whole. Born out of the allocation of existing resources, the garrison economy evolves toward greater though not total control over future resource allocation. Interpenetration of the military and the civilian sectors of the economy proceeds so far that significant demarcation between them becomes impossible. At that point—which has been reached in the United States, as in the Soviet Union—military appropriations, with their effects upon income and capital creation, become the most important stabilizing factors in the economy.

Even more important, the size and character of military spending at home becomes a function of economic evolution taking place abroad, for the garrison economy hypothesizes that all economic evolution is ultimately military in its capability. Hence, amelioration of economic backwardness abroad, especially change in the social framework of which backwardness may be the concomitant, is seen as intensifying the threat to the nation-state even when such change occurs among powers considered friendly. Growth in foreign civilian economies consequently tends to excite the preparedness psychology at home. Ability to meet all present and potential threats to the security of the nation-state—the normal objective of every military establishment—takes on quite new qualities. Analysis is undertaken of the eventual military potential of all significant economic developments occurring in all foreign nations. And the concept of preparedness becomes transmuted into the concept of ability to meet all these eventual threats simultaneously and in the present.

And so the garrison economy ends up by practising the theory which was its starting point, namely, that all the world is enemy and all foreign progress a threat.

Paradoxes result. The garrison economy will gladly aid a strategic backward country on the condition that it refrain from economic activity which might develop a capacity to produce the means of war. But since the garrison economy regards all economic development as of this character, it is led to pursue a policy of selective deterrence of change abroad, intended to limit total evolution of foreign economies. It disarms its allies economically by supplying them the means of war. Or the reverse may happen. In the case of Egypt, violation of the agreement to finance construction of the High Dam at Aswan— dictated by premonitions of the jeopardy inherent in economic evolution abroad—led to an extraordinary diversion of Egyptian resources into military preparedness, bringing into being the very military capability foreseen as a long-run likelihood.

The garrison economy, then, is no isolationist phenomenon. On the contrary, it represents, and implements, a specific world view: that some change abroad is inescapable but that it is the function of diplomacy to limit change. The garrison economy and its associated diplomacy, consequently oppose, politically and militarily, fundamental changes in social relations, especially in systems of landholding, in areas of large and growing population. No critical change can be permitted in social relations abroad except in areas that are, in effect, military outposts of the garrison state. The garrison economy's ability to prevent such change requires demonstration from time to time. And so, on occasion, military excursions must be mounted in order that the military power of the garrison economy may be a credible deterrent to foreign peoples tempted to proceed in directions the garrison economy interprets as containing elements of danger to itself.

Hence Vietnam, commanding the attention of all the world, can be seen in reality as an incident, a demonstration in credibility, of the evolving garrison economy. Vice President Humphrey, interviewed by *The Christian Science Monitor* (August 16, 1966), put the matter aptly: "I believe the United States can't be a world power—which we are—with half-world interests. We are an Asian power, a Pacific power. It takes a growing up on the part of liberal intellectuals—the liberal and articulate spokesmen—to see our relationship to the Asian area and the fact that we are and have to be involved."

It does indeed take a growing up on the part of liberal and articulate spokesmen. For the full meaning of the garrison economy has gone unnoticed. The world view that it represents has gone unchallenged. Its implications for future political actions have not yet been examined. The garrison economy does not echo the naive domino theory of Mr. Dulles. In its view, every foreign power, friend or foe today, is equally menace tomorrow. Does not this mean, in the end, that all the world outside the garrison economy must cease its independent change? Or that, where economic advance is permitted abroad, it must integrate into the garrison economy, preferably by occupation by the military and civil arms of the garrison state?

Upon the civilian sector of the garrison economy is thus imposed, beyond a certain point, the obligation to support a growing number of military outposts and ventures overseas. The proportion of social output going to military purposes increases; the strain upon resources creates the need for *de facto* controls at home. New and enduring changes occur in social relations, all adverse to civilian interests. And as these changes come about, the nation approaches in effect a permanent state of war, permanent even though military actions are intermittent and local in character. The garrison economy is then fully developed.

The search for any reasonable alternative must begin with rejecting the interpretation of economic development abroad that motivates the garrison state. For all today's trouble spots—from Algeria to Cuba, from the Dominican Republic to Vietnam, India and Pakistan, and all the nations bordering on Mainland China—are countries of appalling backwardness. It is not their attempts to escape backwardness but their insistence that progress be based on transformation of social institutions which brings the U.S. garrison economy, in country after country, into open conflict with the local populace. For the United States, it seems, has determined that while aid shall be extended, no attempts at basic change in social relations shall be tolerated.

These social relations cluster around the single factor of land ownership. The late Morris Forgash, in a NATO paper titled "Plan For An International Bank For Economic Acceleration Of Backward Countries," eloquently described examples of landholding systems in areas within the American sphere of influence.

In all the trouble spots of Latin America, the basic and unanswered question is what we plan to do about the landless peasant and the hungry farmer. . . .

In Panama, for example, no less than 67 percent of all landholdings, representing about 40 percent of the land under cultivation, are cultivated by persons who have no title whatever to these lands, who are subject to eviction without recourse, have no security of tenure, no reason to improve their farm practices, and no guarantee that tomorrow they will be tilling the land which they are tilling today. Of the land area under cultivation in Panama, 22 percent of the holdings are less than two hectares in size, and of these 22 percent, less than one-tenth is farmed by farmers who own their land. . . . The landless farmer having no legal rights to the soil he works is the principal system of farming in Panama.

In Paraguay very much the same conditions exist. It has been estimated that 60 percent of the inhabitants of the country are concentrated in an area representing only 2 percent of the land surface, and that the system of tenure, based on the agricultural census of 1942-1943, is such that 63 percent of all farm holdings are cultivated by squatters with no legal right to the land they work, while landowners farm only 16 percent of the land. . . .

But in the [Costa Rica] Sierra farms of less than 10 hectares average only 2.1 hectares in size, insufficient to sustain a farm family, and these minute holdings form 90 percent of all the farm properties in the Sierra. This 90 percent controls only 16.4 percent of the total farmlands in the region while the large estates of 1,000 hectares or more control 41 percent of the farm area but represent only fifteen one hundredths of 1 percent of the number of farms.

As a result, the landless farmer of the Sierra is seldom paid a money wage. Unlike his brother in the Costa, what he is paid for working the great estates is the use of a small plot of land or grazing and watering rights for his small herd of sheep. This is serfdom in no way different from that of Europe 800 years ago, except that the standard of life of the virtual peon of the Sierra is lower than that of Europe's serfs of the twelfth century.

Yet even in the Sierra, the large estates, the haciendas, have brought only 10 percent of the land into cultivation and for Ecuador as a whole only 4.5 percent of the country was in cultivation in 1951. And the dreadful fact is that unused land withheld by its owners from use and the hunger of the landless farmer conspire to cause the poor to work for less than subsistence because they have no other means of providing sustenance for their wives and children.

India's basic program of land reform calls for the ultimate redistribution of almost 161 million acres of land, or more than 250,000 square miles. The total cost for compensation has been estimated at no less than $400 million at recent rates of exchange for the rupee. This is actually less than $2.50 per acre, a negligible price to pay for land reform in Western values, but beyond the financial ability of India's peasantry and beyond the present purse of India's Government. . . .

Exactly the same is true of Pakistan. By 1953, land reform had already transferred close to 275,000 acres to the farmers and 279,000 persons were made landowners. But this program covers only 5.5 percent of the cultivated area of the Punjab, and the Government of Pakistan itself has declared that land reform is impeded by "lack of sufficient funds. Vested interests are, of course, opposed to any attempt for adjusting the maldistribution of the land. Most of the farms are too small to pay their way. Credit facilities are inadequate, cultivators are, generally speaking, illiterate and their number runs into millions. No satisfactory organization exists to carry technical information to the bulk of our rural population."

Is more evidence needed as to the garrison state's intent to maintain existing social relations in Latin America and Asia?

From May 1965 to the end of 1966 some $20 billion will have been spent on the war in Vietnam. One quarter of this amount—$5 billion, a bagatelle by garrison economy standards—would suffice to finance redistribution of uneconomically farmed land, *without* confiscation and under the guidance of international agencies, throughout India, Pakistan, the coastal areas of Asia, and the whole of Latin America. Reformation of landholding systems, and substitution of incentive farming for subsistence farming, would dampen the peasant unrest general in these areas by removing the primary cause of widespread discontent. Why should not the United States abandon its militarist stance and take the leadership in the peasant rebellion, a constructive attitude leading toward rapid peaceful conversion of the landholding systems of half the globe? Related to such a program is the manifest need for technical education and guidance in agriculture throughout the underdeveloped world. The United States will shortly have sent more than 600,000 men to fight in Vietnam. If they were withdrawn from combat they could be educated and trained in technical assistance work to accompany the transformation in landholding to be financed by reduction in military spending overseas. These two steps alone would go far along the road to an alternative to the garrison economy.

To further ease international tensions, and to make the search for economic alternatives multilateral in effect, I propose the undertaking of a perpetual inventory of the producer goods and capital needs of all developing nations, and a specific income tax to be levied by the UN upon the gross national products of all developed nations. This would permit international supply and coordination of capital advances and grants by developed nations to underdeveloped nations as a matter of comity and of concern for the natural rights of our fellow man.

We would find, I think, that a number of domestic satisfactions would follow naturally in the path of such steps abroad as the civilian economy enlarged at home. By progressive stages of $5 billion per year, the arms budget of the United States could be reduced to a level calculated to defend this nation's shores. The sums so saved could be transferred from the spending and taxing power of the federal government to the states and municipalities, on the condition that these organs of civilian government pledged to cooperate in a coordinated plan for community development on a national basis. Such community plans would include the redesign and rebuilding of this country's decaying central cities, development of an adequate network of mass transportation media, necessary medical and educational facilities, and the establishment of modern industrial parks.

To stimulate the civilian economy, I would further propose the institution of a graduated system of corporate income taxes such that each one percent gain in productivity attained by individual corporations would be rewarded with a corresponding reduction in corporate profits tax. To this end, federal credits ought to be made available to commercial banks to enable them to make designated productivity loans at low and regulated rates of interest.

The cost of these programs would be but a fraction of annual expenditures of individual nations on fruitless wars. Even if large, it would be a small price to pay for some insurance against the suicide toward which the human race is so quickly moving.

3 The Decline of Politics and Ideology in a Knowledgeable Society*

ROBERT E. LANE

From reports on the growth and changing character of contemporary knowledge, it is argued that we live in a "knowledgeable society" with certain epistemological characteristics, among which are the development of more fruitful categories of thought, increased differentiation of ego from inner and outer worlds, as imagination of situations contrary to fact, reflective abstraction, changing truth criteria, and a changed philosophy of knowledge. This increase in knowledge and change in thoughtways lead to changes in policy-making procedures. There is increased application of scientific criteria for policy determination at the expense of the usual short-term political criteria and ideological thinking as well. In this situation, social knowledge is creating its own attitudinal disequilibrium.

It has been a common thing to speak of a "democratic society," and recently of an "affluent society." Could one, in some analogous sense,

*Reprinted by permission of the author and publisher from *The American Sociological Review*, 31 (October 1966).

speak of a "knowledgeable society," or perhaps historically of an "age of knowledge"? Good scholars are likely to be so aware of what they do not know to regard the term as pretentious, yet they are familiar with, and perhaps accept the implications of conventional statements on the "scientific age." The purpose of this piece is to explore the concept of a knowledgeable society, and to examine some of its political implications.

The strands of thinking which may be woven into such a conceptual fabric are many and varied and curiously isolated from one another. There are, in the first place, certain early sociological and anthropological thinkers, each with a somewhat different interpretation of the stages of development of knowledge.[1] The Marxian dialectic offers a further developmental analysis, in the tradition of the sociology of knowledge.[2] Students of social change,[3] historians of science,[4] and philosophers of science[5] add to the picture. Knowledge is cognition—psychologists dealing with cognitive processes and concept formation and thinking illuminate the microprocesses given greater

[1]See Auguste Comte, *A General View of Positivism*, trans. by J. H. Bridges, Stanford: Academic Reprints, 1958; and comments in Howard Becker and Harry Elmer Barnes, *Social Thought from Lore to Science*, New York: Dover, 1961, 3d ed., Vol. 2, pp. 573–74; Emile Durkheim and Marcel Mauss, *Primitive Classification*, trans. by Rodney Needham, Chicago: University of Chicago Press, 1963; Bronislaw Malinowski, *Magic, Science and Religion*, Garden City, N.Y.: Doubleday Anchor, 1955; A. L. Kroeber, *Configurations of Culture Growth*, Berkeley: University of California Press, 1944.

[2]See Marx's discussion of consciousness and of ideas as superstructures in his "Economic and Philosophical Manuscripts" and "German Ideology," in *Marx's Concept of Man*, edited by Erich Fromm, New York: Ungar, 1961; Karl Mannheim, *Ideology and Utopia*, trans. by Louis Wirth and Edward Shils, London: Routledge & Kegan Paul, 1949; Robert K. Merton, *Social Theory and Social Structure*, New York: Free Press, 1957, rev. ed., Parts 3 and 4.

[3]See, especially, "Social Evolution Reconsidered" (1950), in *William F. Ogburn On Culture and Social Change*, edited by Otis D. Duncan, Chicago: University of Chicago Press, 1964.

[4]Derek J. de Sola Price, *Science since Babylon*, New Haven: Yale University Press, 1961; Herbert Butterfield, *The Origins of Modern Science*, New York: Crowell-Collier-Macmillan, 1961, rev. ed.

[5]Alfred N. Whitehead, *Science and the Modern World*, Cambridge: Cambridge University Press, 1933; Carl G. Hempel, *Fundamentals of Concept Formation*, Chicago: University of Chicago Press, 1952, Vol. 2, No. 7 of the *International Encyclopedia of Unified Science*; Hans Reichenbach, *The Rise of Scientific Philosophy*, Berkeley: University of California Press, 1953.

emphasis in an age of knowledge.[6] Even economists have recently dealt with knowledge.[7] The organization and professionalization of knowledge is analyzed in the works of contemporary sociologists.[8] The relationship of science to government has many contemporary students, some of them gathered together in a recent collection.[9] Finally, the current controversies dealing with the "end of ideology" on the one hand, and the place of the intellectual in modern society on the other, bear on the matter.[10] Obviously the scope of the problem is large, the complexity great, and the various treatments disparate. Nevertheless in discussing the concept of a knowledgeable society, we have the help of many others.

"Knowledge," of course is a broad term and I mean to use it broadly. It includes both "the known" and "the state of knowing."[11] Thus a knowledgeable society would be one where there is much knowledge, and where many people go about the business of knowing in a proper fashion. As a first approximation to a definition, the knowledgeable society is one in which, more than in other societies, its members: (a) inquire into the basis of their beliefs about man, nature, and society; (b) are guided (perhaps unconsciously) by objective standards of veridical truth, and, at the upper levels of education,

[6]For a general overview, see D. E. Berlyne, *Structure and Direction in Thinking,* New York: Wiley, 1965; a developmental (individual and social) view is presented in O. J. Harvey, D. E. Hunt, and H. M. Schroder, *Conceptual Systems and Personality Organization,* New York: Wiley, 1961; I have found Milton Rokeach's work especially helpful (*The Open and Closed Mind,* New York: Basic Books, 1960.)

[7]Fritz Machlup, *The Production and Distribution of Knowledge in the United States,* Princeton: Princeton University Press, 1962.

[8]Bernard Barber, *Science and the Social Order,* New York: Free Press, 1952; Florian Znaniecki, *The Social Role of the Man of Knowledge,* New York: Columbia University Press, 1940; Everett C. Hughes, *Men and their Work,* New York: Free Press, 1958; T. H. Marshall, *Class Citizenship and Social Development,* especially chap. VI, Garden City, N.Y.: Doubleday, 1964; H. L. Wilensky, "The Professionalization of Everyone?" *American Journal of Sociology,* 70 (1964), pp. 137–58.

[9]Robert Gilpin and Christopher Wright, (eds.) *Scientists and National Policy Making,* New York: Columbia University Press, 1964; Don K. Price, *Government and Science,* New York: New York University Press, 1954.

[10]Daniel Bell, "The End of Ideology in the West" in *The End of Ideology,* New York: Free Press, 1960; Edward Shils, "The End of Ideology?," *Encounter,* 5 (November 1955), pp. 52–58; S. M. Lipset, "The End of Ideology?," in *Political Man,* Garden City, N.Y.: Doubleday, 1960.

[11]Machlup, *The Production and Distribution of Knowledge,* p. 13.

follow scientific rules of evidence and inference in inquiry; (c) devote considerable resources to this inquiry and thus have a large store of knowledge; (d) collect, organize, and interpret their knowledge in a constant effort to extract further meaning from it for the purposes at hand; (e) employ this knowledge to illuminate (and perhaps modify) their values and goals as well as to advance them. Just as the "democratic society" has a foundation in governmental and interpersonal relations, and "the affluent society" a foundation in economics, so the knowledgeable society has its roots in epistemology and the logic of inquiry.

In order to support such an epistemological effort, a society must be open, i.e., free discussion must be allowed on every topic, with the outer limit posed not by threats of social change, but by concern for survival as a society. It must be stable enough to maintain the order necessary for the process of inquiry, trusting enough to encourage cooperative effort and acceptance of each other's "findings,"[12] rich enough to educate its population in the modes of inquiry, dissatisfied or curious enough to want to know more.

Obviously this definition and these conditions raise more questions than can be answered easily: Who are these paragons? What power have they? What standards of knowledge qualify a man or a group or a society? How shall we deal with mystical and religious knowledge? With poetical and artistic knowledge? What about the basis for the epistemology itself—is not this the crudest act of faith? This is only an approximate definition of a model of a "knowledgeable society." The elements are present in some degree in every society; in the knowledgeable society they are present to the greatest degree. . . .

THE THOUGHTWAYS OF A KNOWLEDGEABLE SOCIETY

The knowledgeable society is characterized by a relative emphasis upon certain ways of thinking, a certain epistemology, or, at the very least, a certain knowledge about knowledge. Is this epistemological skill more characteristic of modern, particularly American, society, than of societies in previous periods? It is possible to speak of the development of epistemology somewhat as one speaks of economic and political development, and to construct a sketch of the "thoughtways" of a knowledgeable society. The view that these qualities are more widely distributed today than ever before (one of the themes of Whitehead's *Science and the Modern World*), and are more thoroughly understood by a governing elite of professional and managers, is

---

[12]Daniel Lerner, *The Passing of Traditional Society,* Cambridge, Mass.: MIT Press, 1965, pp. 112–158.

reinforced by research showing the impact of modern education upon thinking processes.[13]

Anthropomorphic and Analogical Thinking

The first stage of thought is labelling, i.e., assigning things to classes—a more complicated process than at first appears.[14] Durkheim and Mauss argue that primitive classification was first developed according to social categories: "the first classes of things were classes of men, into which things were integrated. It was because men were grouped, and thought of themselves in the form of groups, that in their ideas they grouped other things, and in the beginning the two modes of grouping were merged to the point of being indistinct." So, also, "the unity of knowledge is nothing else than the very unity of the collectivity. . . . Logical relations are thus, in a sense, domestic relations."[15] This view has been criticized in detail,[16] but the general point, seen in animistic thought everywhere, is valid: Men classified the unfamiliar in terms of the homely, familiar concepts developed in daily living. Even in the history of science the use of familiar analogies dominated thought. For example, it is said that Aristotle thought of causal effects in terms of a horse drawing a cart and that Galileo thought of heavenly bodies as something like ships moving in an ocean without friction.[17] The knowledgeable society is one where, by successive approximation, categories and classes of things move from the immediate, personal and familiar, to more abstract concepts with a better fit (more adequate to account for the properties of the phenomena observed).

Differentiation of Ego from Inner World and from Environment

The more a person responds "unselfconsciously" to his inner moods and fantasy life, without conscious thought, or to the stimuli of

[13]See Harold Webster, Mervin B. Friedman, and Paul Heist, "Personality Changes in College Students," in Nevitt Sanford, ed., *The American College*, New York: Wiley, 1962, pp. 811–846.

[14]See the discussion of "concept attainment" in Jerome S. Bruner, Jacqueline J. Goodnow, and George A. Austin, *A Study of Thinking*, New York: Wiley, 1956.

[15]*Primitive Classification*, pp. 82–84.

[16]See Rodney Needham's excellent introduction to Durkheim and Mauss, *Primitive Classification*, pp. vii–xlviii.

[17]Stephen Toulmin, *Foresight and Understanding*, New York: Harper Torchbook, 1961, pp. 52, 54.

his environment, reactively, the less able he is either to schedule his drives and maximize his purposes or to master and control the environment. Somehow he must be "separate" from his inner world and his outer world; he must have ego strength to think through his problems, synthesize his desires and control his behavior. These qualities are said to be lacking in primitive man, as they are demonstrably lacking in a child. Indeed as one ascends the phylogenetic scale, the separation of ego from inner and outer worlds becomes more and more marked.[18] This is sometimes mistaken for alienation; in reality it is a necessary element in thought and a necessary ingredient of the knowledgeable society.

Imagining Situations Contrary to Fact or beyond Experience

In *The Passing of Traditional Society,* Daniel Lerner reports on surveys where Middle Eastern subjects are asked to imagine themselves as editors of a newspaper, Governor or President of their society, or residents in a foreign country. Those with the most limited experience and the most parochial orientations cannot do this; they boggle at the very thought. Lerner refers to this imagination of the self in the place of another as "empathy."[19] A more general notion is the "assumption of a mental set willfully and consciously," as distinguished from a capacity to respond only in terms of a given and familiar state of affairs and an inability to manipulate concepts in the mind so as to reconstruct them in an ungiven manner.[20] Any society which relies upon widely distributed initiative, ambition, and innovation must encourage these qualities of imagination: men must think of themselves and of elements of their situation as other than they are.

Holding Simultaneously in Mind Various Aspects of a Situation

Primitive and uneducated people can learn a task, a creed, a message, a set of conventions, but it takes special qualities to grasp the "essential" parts, to see how they are put together, to compare them, in short, to analyze them. Comparison and contrast implies holding and

---

[18]This point and several following are derived from Harvey. Hunt. and Schroder's explication and development of Goldstein and Scheerer's concept of a concrete-abstractness dimension of thought. originating from studies of children and brain-damaged patients. See Harvey *et al., Conceptual Systems.* pp. 24–49.

[19]*The Passing of Traditional Society,* New York: Free Press, 1958, pp. 47–52.

[20]Harvey *et al.. Conceptual Systems.* p. 29.

bringing together at least two things at once.[21] Rote learning, as in many traditional schools, does not develop these special analytical qualities; it only teaches parts, or, perhaps, sequences. To analyze is to question, and questioning is regarded as dangerous.

The Reflective Abstraction of Common Properties and the Formation of Hierarchic Concepts

The capacity to compare and analyze, to disintegrate a whole, is usually paired with the more difficult task of integrating and organizing parts into a new pattern: analysis and synthesis. In the most primitive societies, the concept of abstract numbers, in contrast to concrete instances, is sometimes missing.[22] Once possessed of the idea of, say, "fiveness" it is not difficult to assign groups with five discrete elements to this class; but to invent, from a multiplicity of objects, the concept of "five" or any other abstract number is the act of genius. The knowledgeable society is not only endowed with a great variety of useful concepts, it actively encourages concept formation to create classes and relationships which give a better account of observable phenomena. The pre-knowledgeable society employs the concepts given by tradition.

The qualities discussed above fall along a dimension of concreteness-abstraction. The concrete style of thinking is stimulus-bound, unreflective, unanalytic, unsynthetic, and unimaginative. Present in all societies, it is most evident in primitive societies. Harvey, Hunt and Schroder believe it has social consequences, which can be summarized in these ways:[23] Greater concreteness tends to be accompanied by absolutism, categorical thinking, and stereotyping; it is likely to be expressed in attribution of external causality and "oughtness" to rules; it disposes toward catechisms and word magic; it tends to be accompanied by negativism and resistance to suggestion; and it encourages ritualism. In these ways, as readers of *The Authoritarian Personality* and of *The Open and Closed Mind* will recognize, the dimension of concreteness-abstraction has political and social implications: concreteness is related to authoritarianism and to dogmatic, rigid, and

[21]See the discussion of "conceptualizing in political discourse," in my *Political Ideology*, New York: Free Press, 1962, pp. 346–363.

[22]H. Werner, *Comparative Psychology of Mental Development*, New York: International Universities Press, 1957 rev. ed. quoted in Harvey *et al.*, *Conceptual Systems*. p. 33.

[23]Harvey *et al.*, *Conceptual Systems*, pp. 36–46.

opinionated thinking;[24] The democratic society in contrast is marked by abstract thinking.

Employment of Objective Truth Criteria

A knowledgeable society is not only one where more people value knowledge, but one where knowledge is more likely to be valued if it can be shown to be true by certain objective criteria. In the words of Ithiel Pool:

> To evaluate assertions primarily by a criterion of objective truth is not a natural human way of doing things; it is one of the peculiar features of the Graeco-Roman-Western tradition. . . . The Western criterion of truthvalue . . . assumes that a statement has a validity or lack of it inherent in itself and quite independent of who says it and why. . . . In most societies facts must be validated by an in-group authority before they can be considered credible.[25]

In most societies, statements are true according to whether the spokesman is powerful and likely to dominate others, whether he is "one of us," whether it is expressed with appropriate politeness, and so forth. Moreover, in Eastern philosophies a thing can both be true and not true at the same time; there is no rule of the undistributed middle.[26] In a sense, this is a facet of a much larger problem analyzed by Rokeach: the processing of information according to its "intrinsic merits." In his discussion of the open and closed mind, he says that the "basic characteristic that defines the extent to which a person's system is open or closed," is "the extent to which the person can receive, evaluate, and act on relevant information received from the outside on its own intrinsic merits, unencumbered by irrelevant factors in the situation arising from within the person or from the outside." By irrelevant internal pressures Rokeach means unconscious intruding habits and poses, irrational power needs or needs for self-aggrandizement, the need to allay anxiety, to create an impression, and so forth. The irrelevant outside factors are attitudes of dislike towards

[24]T. W. Adorno, Else Frenkel-Brunswik, Daniel J. Levinson, and R. Nevitt Sanford, *The Authoritarian Personality*, New York: Harper and Row, 1950; Rokeach, *The Open and Closed Mind*, see footnote 6.

[25]In Wilbuhr Schramm, "The Mass Media and Politics," *Public Opinion Quarterly*, 31 (1963), p. 242.

[26]Schramm, "The Mass Media and Politics," pp. 242–244.

the source, conformity pressures, the rewards and punishments implied by acceptance and rejection.[27] The knowledgeable society screens out more of the irrelevant internal and external factors for more people.

Tolerance of Dissonance and Ambiguity

The authoritarian personality, according to Else Frenkel-Brunswik, is intolerant of ambiguous stimuli; he needs quick, sharp resolution of his doubts. Thus he likes sharply defined art, quick (and usually easy) answers, people who are decisive.[28] The person with a closed mind, according to Rokeach, does not bring together conflicting elements of his belief system; rather he compartmentalizes them, linking them only through the authority of the dogma or the party line or the dominant spokesmen's view.[29] Similarly the capacity and inclination to hold simultaneously in view opinions or attitudes each of which "implies" the reverse of the other (a favored message from a hated source) varies greatly in the population, and generally forces various kinds of reconceptualization to reestablish a consonant emotional posture.[30] More than others, the members of a knowledgeable society are endowed with the capacity to tolerate ambiguity, conflict and dissonance.

Changed Views of Metaphysics and Religion

Comte, writing in the early nineteenth century, held that social progress was produced by a changing epistemology and metaphysics. Societies pass (necessarily, he thought) through certain stages marked by the dominance in modes of thought and emphasis first, of theology, then of metaphysics, and finally of science associated with industrial development, centrally planned and controlled with the help of extensive sociological studies which give the controllers knowledge of the laws of society.[31] The agency of change is, however, unclear; there is no epistemological dialectic. Yet one can at least accept the idea that

[27]Rokeach, *The Open and Closed Mind*, p. 57.

[28]"Intolerance of Ambiguity as an Emotional and Perceptual Variable." *Journal of Personality*, 18 (1949), pp. 108–143.

[29]Rokeach, *The Open and Closed Mind*, pp. 67–97.

[30]I think the most useful short account of the general phenomenon of cognitive dissonance and cognitive balancing is in Milton Rosenberg *et al.*, *Attitude Organization and Change*, New Haven: Yale University Press, 1960, pp. 112-163.

[31]*A General View of Positivism*, passim.

in the knowledgeable society theological and metaphysical modes of thought shrink in contrast to scientific modes.

Within this framework, however, certain kinds of religious thought seem to have encouraged the growth of science. Merton expressed his position as follows: "It is the thesis of this study that the Puritan ethic, as an ideal-typical expression of the value-attitudes basic to ascetic Protestantism generally, so canalized the interests of seventeenth-century Englishmen as to constitute one important *element* in the enhanced cultivation of science. The religious *interests* of the day demanded in their forceful implications the systematic, rational, and empirical study of Nature for the glorification of God in His works and for the control of the corrupt world."[32] A knowledgeable society, then, emerges from and is reinforced by religious beliefs which, however framed, focus attention upon this world, and allow for or encourage a scientific epistemology. Today, scientists and professional people are much less likely to be religious or believe in God than businessmen, bankers, and lawyers.[33]

Changed Philosophy of Knowledge

The mind vs. matter problem appears in many guises: as the contrast between "words and things", as rationalism vs. empiricism, as idealism vs. nominalism, and so forth. Whitehead considered that the great difference between the modern scientific age and all other periods was the wedding together of speculative and theoretical modes of thought with empirical and systematic modes of investigation.[34] Similarly Reichenbach has argued that the rise of scientific philosophy is grounded in a shift from "*transcendental* conception of knowledge, according to which knowledge transcends the observable things and depends upon the use of other sources then sense perception," to a "*functional* conception of knowledge, which regards knowledge as an instrument of prediction and for which sense observation is the only admissible criterion of nonempty truth."[35] There are not two worlds, an ideal and a real one, but one integrated world of thought and experience. The knowledgeable society is marked by an increased acceptance of this view. "The opium of the intellectuals" is not so much, as Raymond Aron thinks, Marxism,[36] as it is philosophical idealism.

[32]*Social Theory and Social Structure*, pp. 574–575. (Merton's emphasis).

[33]S. M. Lipset, *Political Man*, p. 314.

[34]*Science and the Modern World*, p. 3.

[35]*The Rise of Scientific Philosophy*, p. 252.

[36]*The Opium of the Intellectuals*, trans. by T. Kilmartin. New York: Norton, 1957.

One facet of this changed concept of knowledge has been an emphasis upon operationalism, i.e., the position that concepts are related, however indirectly, to the operations which measure them, and by intersubjective testability. Knowledge in the knowledgeable society must be public, its sources indicated and its conceptual boundaries marked by something other than incommunicable experience.

From Symptomatology to Taxonomy to Explanation

The history of the biological and behavioral sciences, reveals a tendency first to report observations on phenomena (the naturalist and the journalist), then, with greater care, to group these observations into classes and syndromes, and then, with experimental or controlled observational techniques, to attempt to understand causal relationships, to explain why the phenomena change as they do. When this latter phase is successful, control is more feasible and social policy is likely to be more adequate to the situation. In the knowledgeable society, the intellectual emphasis is more likely to be upon laws of behavior, change, and control. Attaching metrics to phenomena often improves our understanding and our control. The knowledgeable society increasingly employs mathematical modes of expression and thought.

The Contribution of the Philosophy of Science

We have been discussing the complex of attitudes and skills which equip men to deal realistically with the events which impinge upon their lives—policy-formation at the micro-level. This is related to but separate from the ways of thinking of scientists and philosophers who are interested in social policy. This history of social thought reveals the importance of analogical thinking: If geometry yields results from axiomatic methods, so should sociology; in an age of mechanics the model may be clockworks or hydraulics to some (cf. Freud); organismic theories dominate certain periods: a primitive set of anatomical analogies seems to have been prevalent in the Middle Ages.[37]

It seems to me that the emergence of a coherent philosophy of science or logic of inquiry represents a crucial change in this groping toward a method of studying society, particularly as it has matured and increased the scope given to imagination. If one goes back no

[37]Karl Deutsch has an interesting discussion of these analogies in his *The Nerves of Government,* New York: Free Press, 1963, pp. 24–38; The anatomical metaphor in medieval political thought is most explicit in Otto Gierke, *Political Theories of the Middle Ages,* trans. by F. W. Maitland, Boston: Beacon, 1958.

further than the beginning of this century, with the rise of analytic philosophy in Austria (the Vienna Circle) and in England, the development of the "unified science" group at Chicago, perhaps the general systems theorists, and the widespread teaching of the philosophy of science today, a change in intellectual posture toward man and society so great as to represent a watershed is evident. Other knowledgeable societies, marked by Kroeher's "bursts" of culture growth, have not sustained their performance. I believe the development and widespread acceptance of the philosophy of science as a basis for social inquiry represents a "take-off" phenomenon in social science, promising sustained growth in social interpretation.

PROFESSIONALISM AND THE "PRE-FORMULATION" OF POLICY

The discussion so far has sought to illuminate the development of the knowledgeable society, and to show its characteristic thoughtways. Now we turn to the application of this knowledge to public policy. The people who make this application are, in the first instance the professionals, organized in their own associations, governing and staffing institutions devised to develop and teach the new knowledge and apply it to current problems. Within the professions there are tendencies to allocate responsibility for knowledge domains and hence responsibilities for working out "solutions" of social problems relevant to these domains. One aspect of professionalization is the establishment of standards of performance well above actual performance. The gap between the actual and the idea creates within the profession a kind of strain towards remedial action. The consciousness of meeting or failing to meet standards enlists professional ambition, reputation, credit and blame. Staff conferences, annual meetings, and new research studies set up strains for better performance, better instruments, better laws, and new agencies to meet the new standards. In the knowledgeable society, much policy is made first through professional intercourse, concerning what solutions to press upon the government and what men to advance to positions of influence as well as what standards to impose. In some ways this is only a change of venue for political maneuvering, but in an important sense it implies a change in criteria for decision-makers from immediate political advantage to something within the professionalized domain of knowledge.

KNOWLEDGE IS ENCROACHING ON POLITICS

If one thinks of a domain of "pure politics" where decisions are determined by calculations of influence, power, or electoral advantage, and a domain of "pure knowledge" where decisions are determined by calculations of how to implement agreed-upon values with rationality and efficiency, it appears to me that the political domain is shrinking and the knowledge domain is growing, in terms of criteria for decisions, kinds of counsel sought, evidence adduced, and nature of the "rationality" employed. Some of the evidence for this direction of change may be suggested in the following sampling of recent events:

a. With due allowance for political slippage, there has been a gradual expansion of the civil service based on competitive examinations from 23 percent of personnel employed in the executive branch of the Federal government in 1891, to 87 percent in 1962.

b. The General Accounting Office, established in 1921, and the General Service Administration, established in 1949, supervise government business operations so as to encourage economic rather than political criteria.

c. The Council of Economic Advisers was set up in 1946, symbolizing the introduction of economic criteria into the monetary and fiscal operations of government.

d. The professionalization of the attack on poverty is illustrated by the contrast between the methods and programs of the Works Progress Administration (1933) and the Office of Economic Opportunity (1965).

e. The growing use of extra-governmental organizations, like Rand and the university research centers, to study social and technical problems and formulate policy proposals, introduces a variety of less political (if not value-free) criteria for policy-making.

f. Similarly the growing employment of Presidential Commissions and Committees and White House Conferences changes the nature of the criteria employed in policymaking.

g. An enlarged governmental apparatus has been created to enlist scientific advice on a variety of topics (not just what is coming to be called the management of "science affairs"), as seen in the President's Scientific Advisory Committee and the Office of Science and Technology, and even the Office of Science Adviser to the Secretary of State.[38]

Moreover, the dominant scholarly interpretation of policy-making processes has changed in the direction of emphasizing the greater autonomy of political leaders and legislators: with respect to the role

---

[38]Much of this is reported and commented upon in Gilpin and Wright, *Scientists and National Policy Making.* Here (on page 109) one will find Wallace Sayre making the point that "politics is inescapable." Nothing in this section should be read as implying anything contrary to this maxim.

of pressure groups,[39] the power elite,[40] and the electorate.[41] If leaders and other legislators are less bound by the domain of pure politics than we had thought. Then they are freer to be guided by the promptings of scientists and findings from the domain of knowledge. Studies of the legislative process reinforce this view. A massive literature documents four relevant points: (a) the rising influence of the bureaucracy is based in large part on bureaucratic command over the sources of knowledge; (b) state and national legislators respond to the growing importance of technical knowledge both with increased standards for their own mastery of subject-matter fields and with demands for greater staff resources to help them meet the challenge; (c) there is an increased reliance on the kind of professional help enlisted by the executive; and (d) the power of the lobby is less likely to be based on electoral sanctions than upon specialized information helpful (however self-interested) in formulating policy change.[42]

THE CHANGED APPROACH TO PROBLEMS

Of course there will always be politics; there will always be rational-ized self-interest, mobilized by interest groups and articulated in political parties. But, if political criteria decline in importance relative to more universalistic scientific criteria, and if the professional problem oriented scientists rather than laymen come to have more to say about social policy, the shift in perspective is likely to occasion some differences in policy itself. What would these be?

[39]E. E. Schattschneider, *Politics, Pressures and the Tariff*, Englewood Cliffs, N.J.: Prentice-Hall, 1935; Peter H. Odegard, *Pressure Politics*, New York, Columbia University Press, 1928; Raymond A. Bauer, Ithiel de S. Pool, and L. A. Dexter, *American Business and Public Policy*, New York: Atherton, 1963.

[40]Floyd Hunter, *Community Power Structure*, Chapel Hill: University of North Carolina Press, 1953; Robert A. Dahl, *Who Governs?*, New Haven: Yale University Press, 1961.

[41]"Toward a More Responsible Two-Party System," Supplement to *American Political Science Review*, XLIV (1950) No. 3; and, see, for example, Warren E. Miller and Donald E. Stokes, "Constituency Influence in Congress," *American Political Science Review*, LVII (1963), pp. 45–56.

[42]See, for example, John Wahlke, Heinz Eulau *et al.*, *The Legislative System*, New York: Wiley, 1962; James D. Barber, *The Lawmaker*, New Haven: Yale University Press, 1965; Bauer, Pool, and Dexter, *American Business and Public Policy*; Robert L. Peabody and Nelson W. Polsby, eds., *New Perspectives on the House of Representatives*, Chicago: Rand McNal-ly, 1963; Donald R. Matthews, *U. S. Senators and Their World*, New York: Random House Vintage, 1960.

In the first place there is the question of the very *consciousness* of a problem. The man in the middle of the problem (sickness, poverty, waste and especially ignorance) often does not know there is anything problematic about his state. He may accept his condition as embodying the costs of living: if one accepts his lot in life, one accepts lesions, hunger, overwork and unemployment. For this reason such people are often hard to reach. As Harrington says, "First and foremost, any attempt to abolish poverty in the United States must seek to destroy the pessimism and fatalism that flourish in the other America," the America of the poor.[43] Often it takes years of dedicated agitation to make people aware that they live in the midst of a problem. The curious thing about modern times is the degree to which government itself undertakes to do what, in the past, has so often been the task of the agitator. The New Deal helped to organize labor, and the New Frontier and the Great Society help Negroes to demand more of society, and help organize the poor to pursue their own interests. Admittedly there are political benefits in these acts, and they can be attributed only in minor part to the growing insights into the nature of poverty and apathy. Yet consciousness of a problem may come *first* to the authorities, scientific and governmental. People may have to be told, not that they are miserable, but that the conditions of their lives are, in some sense, remediable.

Beyond consciousness is something else, the analysis of the nature of the trouble: its causes, and what should be done about it. Here the main point is the environmentalism of the authoritative scientific or governmental view, in contrast to the personalism of the man involved. The problem as it presents itself to these two attentive persons is in each case different. For the unemployed worker, his problem is to find a job; for the economist, the problem is to analyze the causes of unemployment and sometimes to suggest remedial action. To the worker the "cause" of his plight is that he was let go; to the economist, the cause of the worker's plight may be insufficiency of demand due to higher interest rates and a budgetary surplus. What is cause to the worker is to the economist only a symptom, so different are their perspectives.

The view of a problem by scientific or governmental authorities is very often an analysis of the environment in which it occurs; the causes for the scientist are the factors which make the "problem" for the individual. In consequence, the political demands of the affected group and the demands of the professionals interested in the group's condition, may lead in different directions.

For people within a system (hospital, market, watershed, commu-

[43]Michael Harrington, *The Other America*, New York: Crowell-Collier-Macmillan, 1963, p. 163.

nication network), the boundaries and budgets seem fixed; they bargain for limited resources and more for them seems necessarily to imply less for someone else. An authoritative overview can change that perspective by introducing the possibility not of reallocating limited values but of generating an increase in values. Thus an economist today considers the problems of equity and efficiency in distribution in conjunction with the problem of growth. For the medical sociologist, the problem of the distribution of hospital facilities is paired with the problem of more and better facilities and better health; he is unsatisfied simply with a redistribution of untreated illness in a more equitable fashion. Political scientists have failed to understand this point, because their attention to "the authoritative allocation of values" has tended to obscure another facet of government: the generation of values.

KNOWLEDGE IS ENCROACHING ON IDEOLOGY

If we employ the term "ideology" to mean a comprehensive, passionately believed, self-activating view of society, usually organized as a social movement, rather than a latent half-conscious belief system,[44] it makes sense to think of a domain of knowledge distinguishable from a domain of ideology, despite the extent to which they may overlap. Since knowledge and ideology serve somewhat as functional equivalents in orienting a person toward the problems he must face and the policies he must select, the growth of the domain of knowledge causes it to impinge on the domain of ideology.

Silvan Tomkins has developed a theory of a basic ideological left-right dimension in virtually all domains of life, turning on the questions, "Is man the measure, an end in himself, an active, creative, thinking, desiring, loving, force in nature? Or must man realize himself, attain his full stature only through struggle toward, participation in, conformity to, a norm, a measure, an ideal essence basically independent of man."[45] He believes that arguments along these lines develop in passionate forms (in philosophy, mathematics, jurisprudence, etc., as well as in politics) wherever men are least certain of their ground. These arguments thrive on uncertainty and ignorance. "When the same ideas [that men have been arguing over in these ideological terms] are firmly established and incorporated into the

[44]See my *Political Ideology*, pp. 13–16; also footnote 10 above. Of course there are many definitions of ideology referring to a wider range of "mental products."

[45]"Left and Right: A Basic Dimension of Ideology and Personality," in Robert W. White, ed., *The Study of Lives*, New York: Atherton, 1963, pp. 391–392.

fabric of a science or tested and found wanting, they cease to constitute an ideology in the sense in which we are using the term. At the growing edge of the frontier of all sciences there necessarily is a maximum of uncertainty, and what is lacking in evidence is filled by passion and faith and by hatred and scorn for the disbelievers. Science will never be free of ideology, though yesterday's ideology is today's fact or fiction."[46] The theory, then, is of an "ideo-affective" orientation toward the world directed towards subjects about which there is doubt. If the doubt is clarified by knowledge, this ideological orientation moves on to some other marginal and uncertain area. Increasing knowledge about man, nature, and society can be said to reduce the target area for ideological thinking.

A second way in which the characteristics of a knowledgeable society may be thought to reduce ideological thinking, is through the reduction of dogmatic thinking. Following Rokeach, we may conceive of dogmatic thinking as a selection and interpretation of information so as to reinforce a previously established creed, dogma, or political ideology. Information is used, not so much to understand the world as it really is, but as a means of defending against conflict and uncertainty.[47] The knowledgeable society is marked by a relatively greater stress on the use of information veridically, relying on its truth value and not on any adventitious defense, popularity, or reinforcement value. This should be associated with a decline in dogmatic thinking. The decline of dogmatism implies the decline of ideology, in the narrower sense of the term used here.

In the third place, consider the way in which knowledge may limit Mannheim's thesis that political thinking is inevitably biased. He says "all knowledge which is either political or which involves a world view is inevitably partisan"; and later "at the point where what is properly political begins, the evaluative element cannot easily be separated out," and still later, "the peculiar nature of political knowledge, as contrasted to the 'exact' sciences, arises out of the inseparability, in this realm, of knowledge from interest and motivation."[48] Mannheim has in view only the thinking of those who are themselves engaged in political strife; he does not envisage the possibility of such studies as *The Legislative System* and *The American Voter*,[49] which, although evaluative in many ways, nevertheless narrow the range of partisan,

[46]"Left and Right" p. 389.

[47]See footnote 29.

[48]"The Prospects of Scientific Politics," in *Ideology and Utopia*, pp. 132, 168, 170.

[49]Angus Campbell, Philip E. Converse, Warren E. Miller, and Donald E. Stokes, *The American Voter*, New York: Wiley, 1960.

irrational and evaluative thought. Granting that interested parties form their ideas about politics into ideological constructs it seems likely that knowledge may constrict the scope of their ideology.

This narrowing effect was, in fact, experienced by the participants at the conference of the Congress for Cultural Freedom in Milan in 1955 out of which the theme of "the end of ideology" developed. These scholars and scientists came expecting, indeed inviting, a great confrontation of world views. Under the pressure of economic and social knowledge, a growing body of research, and the codified experience of society, ideological argument tended to give way to technical argument, apparently to the disappointment of some.[50] The debate remained evaluative and partisan, but the domain of ideology was shrunken by the dominance of knowledge.

KNOWLEDGE AS DISEQUILIBRIUM

What happens when the scientific apparatus of the knowledgeable society produces some important findings: existential, causal, remedial, or whatever? Here are some examples from the social sciences:

> Among the nations of the world, the United States ranked 16th in rate of infant mortality in 1961.[51]

> "To raise every individual and family in the nation now below a subsistence income to the subsistence level would cost about $10 billion a year. This is less than 2 per cent of the gross national product. It is less than 10 percent of tax revenues. It is about one-fifth of the cost of national defense."[52]

> "The reinforcing experience for convicted criminals while in jail results in high rates of recidivism: about three-fourths of those entering jail have been there before. And the younger the person at the time of first offense, the higher the rate of recidivism and the sooner it occurs."[53]

> "Today, more American school children die of cancer than from any other disease. So serious has this situation become that Boston

[50]See footnote 10.

[51]*United Nations Statistical Yearbook,* 1962, New York: United Nations, 1963, p. 50.

[52]James N. Morgan *et al., Income and Welfare in the United States,* New York: McGraw-Hill, 1962, pp. 3–4.

[53]Bernard Berelson and Gary Steiner, *Human Behavior,* New York: Harcourt, 1964, p. 630.

has established the first hospital in the United States devoted exclusively to the treatment of children with cancer. . . . One of the earliest pesticides associated with cancer is arsenic. . . . In the United States the arsenic-drenched soils of tobacco plantations, of many orchards in the Northwest, and of blueberry lands in the East easily lead to pollution of water supplies."[54]

"The more an individual engages in personal interaction with persons of different race, religious, or national background, the lower is his general level of prejudice. This result holds not only for majority group prejudices but also for minority prejudices against the majority group and other minorities. It is true of youths as well as their elders. It has been confirmed in 14 different samples, involving about 6000 persons."[55]

Such knowledge—discovered, organized, and communicated by professional men—creates a pressure for policy change with a force all its own. Knowledge (and what is regarded as knowledge) is pressure even without pressure groups, and without reference to an articulated forensic ideology. If the reader of these statements experiences some kind of policy-oriented speculation, so, I believe, do policy-making officials. The source of the tension is not difficult to discover. In skeleton form, the sequence may be as follows:

a. A state of affairs is presented, conveying new or more precise information than that previously known (infants and children are dying at a "high" rate; poverty could be eliminated).

b. A value is engaged (early death is bad; poverty is worse than prosperity).

c. In some cases the information applies to particular groups whose needs and values are especially significant to an observer (Northwest apple growers, Southern Negroes and Whites, delinquent youth).

d. Remedial action may be suggested (subsidies to the poor, policing of pesticides, enforced integration).

e. Social, economic, and political costs are implied (taxation for subsidies to the poor, expensive re-education for prisoners, the opposition of tobacco growers).

f. Certain "pre-political ideological" positions on man and society are enlisted (Can man control his own fate? Is poverty "necessary"? Is human nature a constant?).

---

[54]Rachel Carson, *Silent Spring,* Boston: Houghton Mifflin, 1962, pp. 221–223.

[55]Robin M. Williams, quoted in Berelson and Steiner, *Human Behavior,* p. 519.

g. Certain ideological postures toward the business of government are enlisted (Is every increment of government a bad policy in itself? Is government too corrupt an instrument to employ in changing conditions? Are tax dollars better spent by private organizations and individuals?).

Let us suppose, as seems likely, that knowledge like that presented above sets up a kind of "disequilibrium" in a person's mind. The restoration of equilibrium, then, is the problem-solving process, perhaps by questioning the data or the source, perhaps by changing one's own priorities of action, perhaps by selective inattention, perhaps by delegation (real or symbolic), perhaps by purely expressive as opposed to instrumental behavior, perhaps by rationalization, perhaps by scapegoating, perhaps by advocating simplistic solutions, and so forth.[56] But the point is that knowledge, with little more, often sets up a disequilibrium or pressure which requires compensating thought or action.

SUMMARY

In this article I have tried, first, to develop the idea of a knowledgeable society, with special attention to questions of growth and epistemology. Then, assuming that the concept applies to modern American society, I have suggested that the professionals and their associations have a role in the preformulation of policy, not all good, but generally responsive to the needs of society. Further, in comparing two "pure" domains, that of politics and that of knowledge, I have suggested that the criteria and scope of politics are shrinking while those of knowledge are growing. This has created a difference in perspectives of policy-makers: a different kind of consciousness, an environmentalist approach, and a concept of the generation of values. Like politics, ideology is declining as a *necessary* ingredient in change, partly because, given present values, knowledge sets up a powerful kind of attitudinal disequilibrium all its own.

[56]Dan Berlyne's *Structure and Direction in Thinking* illuminates the processes of "problematicity" and problem-solving, especially pp. 236–293.

4 Academic Government and Academic Citizenship in a Time of Revolt*

CHRISTIAN BAY

This is a time of accentuated conflict between the generations, with less respect for inherited wisdom and greater insistence on the part of many young people that they want a major part in shaping their own future society. . . .

I

"The highest function of education, I would maintain," writes Edgar Z. Friedenberg, "is to help people understand the meaning of their lives, and become more sensitive to the meaning of other people's lives and relate to them more fully. Education increases the range and complexity of relationships that make sense to us, to which we can contribute, and on which we can bring to bear competent ethical and practical

*A lecture in the series *Contemporary Trends,* presented at the University of Wisconsin-Milwaukee on March 5, 1968. Printed by permission of the author.

judgment."[1] Friedenberg is merely plagiarizing Plato, of course. "Know thyself" was the highest commandment among the wise men of ancient Athens, twenty-five centuries before Freud invented a fresh approach toward the same goal. An unexamined life is not worth living, Socrates taught; he might have said or have been translated as saying an "uneducated life"; self-education, or philosophy, he saw as the highest intrinsic value or aim of human life. . . .

By "education" I mean liberation of the intellect and its latent powers—or, more broadly, the liberation of the self, the achievement of freedom of expression, emotional as well as rational. Liberation, first of all, from crippling anxieties—though it is perhaps better to speak of this part of the process as therapy, and to say that therapy may be a prerequisite to education for those who are severely afflicted with neurotic problems. It is conceivable that some psychotics and probable that some brain-damaged individuals can never become educated, but in other cases when some person or people are termed "uneducable" the chances are that no adequate educator, or no tolerable circumstances, have been available.

For the psychologically able, at least, "education" refers to their liberation from social and cultural and ideological obstacles to the independent quest of each developing mind, for bearings and attitudes to suit its temperament, and for answers and beliefs to satisfy its curiosity and powers of reason. The educated man is an intellectual, an eternal student of life, a philosopher not in the Oxford sense perhaps but in the Socratic sense; by temperament he may be more of an artist, more of a scientist, or more of a freewheeling explorer of life; he may be primarily an estheticist or an ethicist; but he is not a conformist for conformism's sake, not an automation, not a flagwaver who responds to cues from authorities, not a good member of a mob.[2]

The fully educated man does not exist, of course, but as an ideal type he would be the person whose behavior is in full harmony with his own full range of basic human needs, needs that are no longer antagonistic to those of others because he has resolved or faced up to his anxieties, and relationships to most others are seen as rewarding or indifferent but not menacing; he has become conscious of a shared stake in humanity and in lasting community with others.

The obstacles to education are of course formidable in every gerontocratic society—the older generation, or more strictly speaking

[1]Edgar Z. Friedenberg, *Coming of Age in America* (New York: Vintage Books, 1967), p. 221.

[2]Bertrand Russell writes, somewhere, that the failure of education is well illustrated by the extent to which the public, almost any public, will pay attention to the glib orator with cocksure opinions, rather than to the scholarly and less flamboyant speaker who admits to doubts about the general validity of some of the points he makes.

a very small part of it, is in nearly complete control, here as in almost every other country. It is true that once in a rare while charismatic leaders of successful revolutions have been young men, but these have seldom stayed in power for very long, or stayed young in spirit. Fidel Castro is possibly an exception. But the normal state of affairs is certainly the gerontocratic oligarchy, whether you have outright dictatorship or alleged democracy.[3] Now, every administrator prefers subjects to citizens, individuals who will live in peace or go to war on cues from the leadership. And every sensible gerontocrat, every sensible person over fifty . . . prefers young people who cut their hair the way we do and, above all, who believe what we tell them, especially when we are taking the trouble to explain what's good for them. Nobody really wants young people to become intellectuals; nobody wants effective education as here defined—well, almost nobody, except a few odd educators and intellectuals.

What is wanted by the people who count, and who pay the bulk of the taxes, is well-trained, well-molded young persons, with the skills and trained intelligence to do the jobs specified for them by our gerontocratic industries and government agencies, and with the manners and attitudes and motivations to make them work diligently on the tasks set out for them. Take the biggest employer of them all, President L. B. Johnson: independent intellectuals like J. W. Fulbright or Wayne Morse or Eugene McCarthy are the last people he would want to employ; his preference is for highly trained minds with no independent convictions to interfere with their complete loyalty to his strategies and purposes, whatever they may be. But virtually every other employer has the same preferences: he seeks useful, pliable employees without stubborn principles or independent integrity. "Ask what you can do for America," exhorted our late President; he didn't suggest that you first ask what America under his leadership is up to. Uncritical patriots are wanted, not intellectuals, whose sense of patriotism would compel them to be loyal to the nation's best interests as they see them, and perhaps disobedient to laws and policies that appear to be disastrous for the nation's best interests, or grievously unjust.

Who wants educated men and women? No government does; hardly any employer does; very few parents do (the average family, too, is a gerontocracy); only a very few educators and intellectuals do, and an occasional educational administrator.

Everybody, of course, favors education in the conventional sense as a means to success, and as a way of keeping youngsters off the streets and off the job market for a few years, while furnishing them

---

[3]Although JFK was "only" in his forties and very handsome, he picked older men for most of his advisors and continued most of the policies, foreign and domestic, of the Eisenhower regime.

with skills and good manners and attitudes and eventually a diploma. I am not questioning anyone's integrity; there is nothing inherently dishonest in acquiring, say, engineering skills or in learning to root for the home team, on the football field or in Vietnam. But for present purposes I wish to separate the acquisition of such skills and attitudes sharply from the acquisition of an independent mind, and I shall reserve the term "education" for the latter processes. Training is to achieve skills to hold jobs; molding is for getting along and being accepted by your elders and thus facilitating conventional careers. Education is for coming alive as human beings and for becoming self-governing citizens rather than passive subjects. Merely trained and molded people compete for existing jobs and careers and invest their lives for the purposes of their superiors, their corporations, or their government. Educated men are able to choose what to do with their lives; working together, they can shape the jobs to fit their own needs, and perhaps eventually shape society to fit their own ideals and aspirations as human beings, instead of passively adjusting and accepting and competing for the carrots held out for them by the existing establishment.

But this leads me to the subject of politics.

II

"Politics" is a term now in low repute. I shall argue in all seriousness that we need a new approach to the very term if we are going to improve the processes of politics, or even those of university government. Or perhaps I should say that we need to return to the oldest usage of "politics" in our Western literature, namely that of Plato and Aristotle. Politics, Plato taught, is the art and science of promoting justice and virtue (meaning by "virtue" not chastity but honesty, charity, and sense of civic duty); he distinguished "politics" sharply from "rhetoric", or the art of persuading for fun or profit, regardless of purpose. Aristotle taught that all sciences exist for the good of man, and that the science of politics is the most valuable of them all, for it bears most directly on the good of man-in-community or man-in-society, and draws on all the other sciences.

Plagiarizing Plato and Aristotle, I shall define "politics" as the art and science of studying and promoting human welfare and freedom; or more succinctly, of promoting freedom for all men equally (since freedom presupposes welfare, and "freedom for all men equally" implies that those who are suffering the most severe deprivations, whether by design, tradition, or accident, must have the prior claim on political redress). I shall call "pseudopolitics" all other activities that take place on the public arena, which are concerned with the promotion of private or private interest group objectives—be they neurotically or rationally conceived.[4] Rhetoric is an art that is of course still very much alive and kicking. In fact, it has become institutionalized to the tune of the billions that we spend each year on advertizing, public relations, propaganda, and research on how to improve our already so smooth manipulation techniques. Some of the persuasion agencies work for political ends (in my sense) some of the time, but the vast majority of our modern rhetorics industries work for pseudopolitical or entirely commercial private objectives.

Now, I hold to the view that social science is valuable to the extent that it enables us to understand and cope with human and social problems; "problem" here refers to any important discrepancy between what exists and what should be (and here I imply *could be* as well). If it is accepted that the proper purpose of politics, and therefore of government, is to promote the freedom of all men equally, then political science is of value first of all to the extent that it helps us understand the nature and determinants of human freedom and to cope with the obstacles to its fuller realization. The value of political science to be sure depends also, at least secondarily, on its relevance and use in relation to other categories of social problems as well, but I think social problems are important and should command political attention mainly to the extent that important freedoms or rights of men are at stake.

Mind you, the life and health of the person is the most basic aspect of his freedom; death destroys all rights and ill health cripples them all. To put the issue more sharply, within the definition of politics as the struggle to promote the freedom of all men equally, we must stress the primacy of life itself. I shall insist that the first priority objective of politics is identical with that of medicine, namely the protection and prolongation of life, along with the reduction of needless suffering. The good doctor will give first attention to the patients whose health is worst, or who are in greatest danger of death. Similarly, the *good* politician will give redress first of all to those groups in the population who are most severely afflicted with ill health—in the form of poverty or other disabling conditions.

In every stable order that we know, certainly including this one, the actual practice in politics is of course the opposite: the wellest patients are given the most favorable attention by the politicians. The people whose demands are most likely to be heeded are those who have the money to give to campaign kitties or to buy mass media influence, or who have family or friendly connections, or the organiza-

---

[4]Logically, one could think of a third type of activity, which opposes the public interest *without* serving any private interest, not even a neurotically misanthropic interest. Surely we can for practical purposes leave such hypothetical behavior to one side.

tion to control the votes. And the worst part of it is that this has come to be accepted. Politics has not only in fact become a great game in which all privileged groups are out to enhance their advantages, but our pluralist liberal philosophy has endorsed this state of affairs as the essence of democracy.

Orthodox theory in political science nowadays holds that our low political participation[5] indicates a widespread satisfaction with this state of affairs. It is far more accurate, in my view, to diagnose the low participation as the outcome of the sense of political impotence of those who might otherwise have believed in politics, in the Greek sense (that is, as the art of promoting justice and the public interest, or the freedom of all).[6] But our political arena has been taken over by the entrenched forces of pseudopolitics, who are practicing their buying and selling like any other category of businessmen, for profit rather than public service, and with the inevitable result, as in all big business, that the man of small means is either crowded out or allowed to stay in at the price of giving up his independence and integrity.

This is democracy, our political science establishment tells us; this is the nature of politics in a developed country; and our comparative politics people in effect keep asserting that all countries, however underdeveloped and benighted, should develop this kind of democracy, too, and emulate our achievements. Their priorities of freedoms should become the same as ours; with freedom of speech, private enterprise and competing political parties at the top of the list; with the right to a dignified and secure existence for the disabled, the below-average intelligent, the poor and the unemployed way down on the list. Michael Harrington has called our economic system "socialism for the rich, free enterprise for the poor" and this is not far off the mark. Our privileged minorities are not only able to enjoy and expand their privileges without much risk-taking; they have been able also to make the rest of society, including the bulk of the academy, internalize *their* political ideology down to the very definitions of our key political terms: "freedom" is by almost everyone automatically associated, not with elementary dignity and choice for the average person but with free speech for the articulate and free enterprise for the man of means; "patriotism" not with love of people and concern for human welfare but with pledges of allegiance to the government and whatever it is up to; "national security" not with political efforts toward a

[5]Perhaps one or two percent are politically active, beyond voting and occasionally having a bumper sticker on the car. For a survey of the literature on political participation see Lester W. Milbrath. *Political Participation* (Chicago: Rand McNally, 1965).

[6]This position is taken by Richard Lichtman in his critique of Robert Dahl's *Who Governs* (New Haven: Yale University Press 1966). See Lichtman.

peaceful, just and secure world but with military deterrence, even military intervention against popular movements in other countries.

And last but not least, "politics" has come to be understood, not in the classical sense, not in the sense of efforts to promote freedom and justice, but as the pursuit of private and group interest within the permanent, never to be challenged rules of the pluralist game, rules made out to favor the status quo, rules based on conventioneering, electioneering, engineering of support, and all the rest.

No wonder people turn away from this kind of politics, and especially the young who by now constitute a very large minority of the American population (a majority of Americans are now under 25, but that, of course, includes infants and children). Adult politics is becoming almost as irrelevant to most people's problems as traditional student government has been to the real problems of students in the past: enterprising individuals can get themselves elected to office allright but have no power and also very little incentive to try to change things. Until recently, students interested in politics as distinct from pseudopolitics would have nothing to do with student governments but were active mostly off campus in work for peace, civil rights, and so forth. In the adult community as well, increasing numbers of those who feel deeply about political as distinct from pseudopolitical issues have tended to despair of our major political parties and our electioneering games, in which the economic and even psychological cards are so heavily stacked against them, and to resort to direct action and threats of direct action of many kinds.

It testifies to the viability of our pluralist system, supported as it has been by generations of liberal ideologues and academicians who have adorned it with all the pride and symbols of triumphant democracy achieved, that it has been able to withstand for so long the dire consequences of Washington's know-nothingism about what goes on in the rest of the world, or even in this country. The well-to-do and the articulate (or even half-articulate, if well-to-do) still establish the frame of reference of what little we have of political dialogues; the down-and-outers are treated as objects of stingy welfare policies at best, and many of them are driven into mental illness, drug addiction, crime or apathetic desperation. At this time, at least, increasing numbers among the dispossessed are driven to revolt. . . .

It is from this perspective on education and on politics that I want to address myself to the subject of academic government and citizenship in a time of revolt. What a university *can* and *should* accomplish at its best can be made clear only when education is understood as something quite different from the training in skills and the molding of accepting apolitical attitudes; and when "politics" is understood as something quite different from pseudopolitics. For the most urgent task of the university is to restore politics to our western civilization; our most crucial task is to develop self-governing *citizens* in greater numbers, instead of the submissive, privatist or pseudopolitical *subjects* we have been and are turning out. . . .

The universities will probably have to play a crucial part, if American politics is to be restored from its present moral degradation and pseudopolitical impotence. Today, when our political order is cracking, the university cannot and must not claim to be apolitical while in fact continuing to support the established order on its path to self-destruction. In W.H. Auden's phrase, this would amount to an insistence on the continuation of a lecture on navigation while the ship is going down.[7] Political action is needed, but action based on radical inquiry and the use of political reason. Alas, political reason is a scarce resource, and becomes more scarce the more badly it is needed.[8] But it is a resource that our universities are in a better position to supply than any other agencies; nowhere else is an enlightened political dialogue and free, sustained inquiry as *possible* today as in our universities. To be sure, the professors in many of our North American universities—and the students in virtually all—are still treated as subjects, not citizens, of their own academic communities. Paradoxically, however, it is precisely in these communities that real citizenship and democratic government are most feasible in our time, as I shall try to show.

III

This is indeed a time of revolt and a time of revulsion. This is all to the good, when we consider on the one hand the monstrous scale of man's inhumanity to man, and on the other hand the gigantic technical opportunities today for abolishing extreme poverty and other indignities of human life all over the world. It would be sad indeed if men, especially young men and women, no longer had the inclination to feel revulsion and to advocate revolutionary changes, by nonviolence if possible, by violence if necessary, to reduce the institutionalized violence committed against our children each day, in the ghettoes and elsewhere, to say nothing of the children in Vietnam or Latin America.

Perhaps the worst part of the molding that takes place in American universities and schools today, under the guise of education, is the

---

[7]Quoted by Richard Lichtman in his "The University: Mask for Privilege?" *The Center Magazine* (Box 4068, Santa Barbara, Calif.), Vol. I (January 1968), p. 6.

[8]This last statement is in part, but only in part, a tautology. Scarcity of reason automatically increases the need for reason, but other factors, too, like technological and social change, increase the need for reason while also placing higher demands on its powers.

training toward indifference—indifference toward anything not bearing directly on one's own academic grades, one's paycheck or one's future career prospects. Intellectual indifference is only part of the problem— I mean the ingrained habit of studying, listening, discussing topics according to schedules suitable to a university bureaucracy rather than according to one's own interest in the various topics (perhaps an inevitable problem in very large universities). The worst part is the emotional indifference we try to breed into our youngsters, if we have become sufficiently indifferent to human suffering ourselves—as easily happens, especially when one gets over thirty. "Don't get involved," we counsel; "don't stick your neck out—some day you might lose a job opportunity." A respected senior political scientist stood up at the business meeting of our last convention and counselled us never to change the American Political Science Association's constitutional ban on political stands—even against having APSA officers work with the CIA!— (a *political science* association which must not speak to the great political issues!) on the ground that we might lose our tax exemption. . . .

I think politics may be on its way back, chiefly thanks to our student militants, if also due to the peace movement more generally and to the black power movement. And, of course, due to the monstrosity of the events brought about by our obsolete political system.

With particular reference to the emerging politics inside our university communities, as distinct from the emerging concern among academics, young and old, for politics in the world outside, most university administrators have resisted and will continue to resist this development even more stubbornly than they resist student and faculty concern with what goes on in the outside world. "Extreme" student or (worse, but less frequent) faculty critiques of powerful men and policies carry limited weight outside; while nervous university Presidents may worry about repercussions, there are likely to be few that will matter; the worst static will come from those alumni of the alma mater who learned the least while they were there. But if students and faculty take it in their heads to demand changes in the structure of the university itself, this is a far more serious matter, for this could well become an irreversible process that would end the university's role as a servant of the established powers; it might end up becoming an agency for liberating the minds of the young to the extent of enabling them to build not only a new university but a new social order!

Fortunately for the young, and for the prospects for political change, most university administrators behave as mere managers of the status quo, and not as institution-building leaders, in Philip Selznick's sense; their apparent concern has tended to be with resisting symptoms of change, not with anticipating new circumstances and utilizing opportunities to promote enduring values.[9] Alexander Meiklejohn is said to have defined "administration" as "placing ideas in charge of circumstances;" more often, when cries of "student power" are heard, the circumstances that can be controlled appear to be placed in charge. Most university governments when faced with student unrest have seen the unrest as the problem, not the conditions that had given 'rise to the unrest. In a society dominated by large concentrations of economic power and by status-quo oriented pseudopolitics, most university governments even in a time of revolt are mainly worried about their budgets and the university image and public relations on which the rise or decline in operating budgets may hinge; to placate their student militants, obviously a minority anyway, usually is of far lesser concern. Of least concern, it often appears, are ideas about the aims and nature of the university as a servant of man, not of particular men. How can such priorities be reversed? How should academic governments ideally be organized? I shall now discuss (IV) what steps toward better education and better politics are possible in the major North American universities today, and then (V) what we should aim for as the best kind of academic government and citizenship.

IV

I assume, at least for the sake of my argument, an agreement that more of our students should become educated, in the sense of developing independent minds and an individual sense of justice—the quality that according to Aristotle separates men from animals. I furthermore assume that it would be good if our universities to a greater extent would develop a sense of responsibility for defining and looking out for the public interest. It may be hard to agree on what is and what is not in the public interest when you come to specifics, but surely there are some objectives that we can all agree on, and not only for the sake of discussion: conservation of natural resources for our children's and their children's and grandchildren's generations is an obvious example; the reduction of lawless violence and needless suffering in our own world, at least in the abstract, is another.

No other type of agency, I have said, is as potentially able to look out for the public interest as the university; no other community is as potentially able even to define the public interest disinterestedly as is the academic community. But I hasten to add that by "academic

[9]See Selznick, *Leadership in Administration* (New York: Harper & Row, 1957).

community" I mean professors and students together, not administrators, and not the professors alone.[10]

The first thing to realize is that our hallowed taxpayers nowadays are at least as dependent on the university as the university is on them (or us, if you like). For all his reputed eminence on the screen, this is one thing that Governor Ronald Reagan has never understood: California's prosperity is in no small measure the result of and continually dependent on the eminence of the University of California. If eminent professors are driven away, new industries depending upon university brainpower will also tend to locate elsewhere, at about the same rate. And such processes can snowball; both academics and industries migrate very easily nowadays. "The meta-message of (Clark Kerr's) writings is that the federal government cannot survive without the university's help", writes one of the young student militants, and he is right.[11] Unfortunately, it was the other side of the dependency relationship that President Kerr tended to stress, to say nothing of university administrators more timid and less resourceful than he.

My first recommendation for the here and now, then, is that it be more generally realized that university administrators, or whoever is authorized to speak for the universities, do have power in the world outside, if they care to exercise it. I know there are many university presidents who always stand ready to rush over to the state capital, hat in hand, at the first sign of government or senatorial displeasure with goings on at the university; this attitude strikes me as not only undignified but harmful for the university; for it supports expectations in the government to the effect that the President of the university is their man on the campus. If he is to be anybody else's man than his own he should most emphatically be the academic community's own man, not its political overseer.

My second recommendation is that the more political-minded students and professors must get together and organize. It is our supreme obligation not only to the university but to the country and to

[10]Here I take issue with Dean Robert A. Nisbet, who in a recent paper champions the oldfashioned disregard of student criticism of established ways of scholarship and learning; he is particularly enamored of Italian academic establishments, in which all power rests with the senior professors, who apparently have been unconcerned with or even oblivious of student unrest. In fairness, his paper was written before this winter's massive Italian student rebellions. See his "Is There a Crisis of the University?" *The Public Interest*. No. 10 (Winter 1968), pp. 55–64.

[11]Stephen Saltonstall. "Toward a Strategy of Disruption". W. H. Ferry (ed.) *Students and Society; Report on a Conference* (Santa Barbara: Center for the Study of Democratic Institutions, Occasional Papers, Vol. I, No. 1 1967), p. 29.

humanity, as I see it, to do what we can to become citizens in the Socratic sense and to politicize the university—not of course to support politics in the usual sense of pseudopolitics but to accentuate public purpose and moral commitment; to do what we can to bring about not only democratic university government some day but, more important over the short run, to extricate the university from its present stance of indifference and passive or active support to ugly government policies like the war in Vietnam. This can be attempted by minorities of professors and students, for example by way of picketing or even non-violently obstructing the campus hiring activities of organizations like Dow Chemical Co. or the Central Intelligence Agency.

A couple of years ago some of us tried to launch, perhaps prematurely, a Stanford Association of University Scholars. It was shortlived but something like it may well rise again, at Stanford and elsewhere. Minimally, this was an association to improve communication and dialogue between professors and students. Maximally, this could eventually have become the embryo of a new kind of counter-government of the University, if such an association had built up enough support to feel entitled to speak for the academic community, whose rightful constituents are, of course, the scholars and aspiring scholars, not absentee trustees or administrators deriving their powers from them.

My third recommendation is that we realize to a fuller extent the scope of the revolutionary developments in our time not only in engineering-type technology but in the techniques of social organization and social action as well. The potential power of the moral individual with guts has not diminished—it has greatly increased with our increasingly complex society. . . .

My fourth immediate recommendation on this occasion is that we all, as professors and students, insist on our rights and responsibilities as self-governing citizens—of our country and first of all of our university communities. This means, most basically, that we in principle insist on being the final judges of our own acts, and assume moral responsibility for the foreseeable consequences and implications of what we are doing. More concretely, this means (a) that we are not to lend ourselves to the support of monstrously unjust causes even if required to do so by law; and (b) that we insist on the right to participate effectively in the shaping of the rules that we are asked to live by, in the larger society and especially in the university community. I am certainly not advocating indiscriminate civil disobedience, or disobedience for the sake of disobeying; and still less am I advocating civil disobedience when it suits our convenience to break the law, as J. Edgar Hoover appears to believe about people of my persuasion. Civil disobedience and lawlessness are not the same.

What I advocate is responsible citizenship in the Socratic sense of caring more to please the gods, or justice, than to please the powers that be, whether the popular court of the city of Athens or the legislation that suits the powers that be in these United States. It is inconvenient and can be costly to break the law. It should be done sparingly, not as self-administered therapy for a feeling of revulsion but only after dispassionate study of chances of good effects and of relevance to a crucial moral cause or objective.

Fifthly and finally, we should immediately try to push harder for the principle that education, including political education, is for everybody, rich and poor, young and old, sick and healthy (though the sick may need treatment prior to education). This I see as perhaps the chief failing of the multiversity: it has come to take instruction from vested interests, and especially the United States government and its military establishment, about what this country needs. It has abandoned its own responsibility for determining and then supporting the public interest. It has given up being a university in the sense of serving the universality of mankind; it has tended to serve itself instead, its own corporate interest, by providing whatever services can be paid for most handsomely. It tends toward becoming, in Theodore Roszak's phrase, an "all-purpose brothel."[12] Very few universities have refused military money for research on new weapons of destruction; and I know of only one university once deeply implicated in such work which was finally extricated from it after stubborn and tenacious student and faculty protests. The past events at the University of Pennsylvania now serve as a shining example of academic political citizenship in successful action.[13]

In Berkeley the students have most often had to do it alone, except in the days of the great FSM victory of November 1965, which was ensured in part by faculty support at the crucial moment. The Berkeley administrations, past and present, have placated student protestors when it was deemed necessary but have not felt responsible for trying to educate even its own alumni, let alone the general public or the politicians, to what is the nature of education and of the university. I see this omission as Dr. Kerr's greatest failure, and as the failure of most university administrators. Few of them (names like Robert M. Hutchins and Harold Taylor stand out as exceptions[14]) have been educators in my sense, and leaders of men rather than caretakers

[12]See his "On Academic Delinquency" in his (ed.) *The Dissenting Academy* (New York: Pantheon, 1968), p. 12.

[13]See Gabriel Kolko, "Uneasy Alliance: Universities and the Pentagon," *The Nation*, Vol. 205, No. 11 (October 9, 1967), pp. 328–332.

[14]See Hutchins, *The Higher Learning in America* (New Haven: Yale University Press, 1936); *Education for Freedom* (Baton Rouge: Louisiana State University Press, 1943); *The Conflict in Education* (New York:

and PR-conscious mediators among powerful pseudopolitical interest groups.

V

Now I come, finally, to the question of academic government and citizenship as things ought to eventually become. But the following is not intended as a description of a utopia. I shall argue that this is a practical scheme, and rest my case on that empirical proposition. You will force me to retreat if you can show that I am less than realistic. Crackpot idealism has no greater appeal to me than crackpot realism. Furthermore, I shall argue that the recommended next steps, just discussed, if implemented would bring this desired state of academic government much nearer, with or without Berkeley-type confrontations on the way from here to there.

Being way past thirty, I may be forgiven for being a gradualist. I believe in Freedom Now and Power Now for the blacks but not in Power Now for the Students, handed to them with the trustee's best wishes. I think the students' fight to win their freedom and power from their intransigant elders is a vital requirement for developing a moral and political consciousness among many more students. I don't want to see boards of trustees abolished in the next ten years but to see them include and then gradually increase the proportion of professors and students as voting members. In the final analysis, though, I would like to see boards of trustees given purely ceremonial functions, with or without academic representation.

Ultimately, I would like to see universities governed democratically much as other communities ought to be, but with the great difference that in the academic community democracy just might work—that is, democracy as envisaged by the classic theorists. For in academic communities people are relatively well educated, relatively nondesperate or nonmiserable, and there are optimal opportunities for a constructive dialogue on normative issues and for recourse to research as a way of resolving the more empirical controversial issues, on any questions of fact subject to dispute.

Ideally, the total voting power of faculty and students should be approximately equal, which raises ticklish questions of differential weighting of votes, because of the far greater number of students,

Harper & Row, 1952); *The University of Utopia* (Chicago: University of Chicago Press, 1953 and 1964); and *Freedom, Education and the Fund* (New York: Meridian Press, 1956). Also see Harold Taylor, "Individualism and the Liberal Tradition" in Willis D. Weatherford (ed.), *The Goals of Higher Education* (Cambridge: Harvard University Press, 1960); and Taylor (ed.), *Essays in Teaching* (New York: Harper & Row, 1950); and Taylor, *On Education and Freedom* (New York: Abelard-Schuman, 1954).

especially undergraduates. John Stuart Mill in his day argued eloquently for differential voting in Great Britain, on the theory that some categories of citizens are likely to be wiser or more conscientious than others.[15] I don't buy this argument as applied to Great Britain, then or now; nor would I buy it for university governments. Granted, professors may average more experience but this is offset by the fact that students, when given political responsibility, may well average not only a fresher vision but quite possibly a much broader and deeper vision of the public interest, being less specialized, that is, having fewer trained incapacities. There are some issues so simple, it has been said, that it takes experts *not* to understand them.

My argument for some kind of differential voting so as to achieve rough parity hinges instead on the view that the welfare of the university and the contributions it can make to society depends on the kind of cooperation that can be achieved, only on a basis of equality I believe, between the two main components of the academic community, professors and students. If one side always were in a position to vote the other side down, the dialogue would suffer and the representative institutions would soon cease representing the minority in any real sense, or so the minority would come to feel.

I would not anticipate any oppression comparable to the experience of the blacks in the United States, who have almost always faced the certainty of being voted down. I would rather compare with the French in Canada; intelligent citizens of that country nowadays realize that Canada can never become united until the achievement of a constitution that grants equal powers, in many areas, to the French minority. Some English-Canadians are as lacking in understanding any basis for the French gripes as some professors and deans are failing to see any merit in the demands for student power; but that does not dispose of the problem of self-government and citizenship for students, or for Quebec in Canada.

It might not be a bad idea to begin by giving students, and especially undergraduates, rather less of a voting representation than would seem fair as a permanent arrangement; first, it may take a little time to get used to exercising new powers and responsibilities and, secondly, it would not be a bad idea to hold back on their rights until a real political demand has been developed. Democratic forms without substance are of little use; witness the decline of democratic participation of Sarah Lawrence as described by Harold Taylor; although these

[15]See chapter VIII, "Of the Extension of the Suffrage" in his *Representative Government* (1861), reprinted in Mill, *Utilitarianism, Liberty and Representative Government* (New York: Everyman's Library, E. P. Dutton, 1951) pp. 371–393.

hazards of insufficiently challenging issues are, alas, less likely to be encountered in the years to come.[16]

I shall not go into detail about academic constitution-making. The names and routine functions of administrative offices might not change a great deal; the key point is that the governing boards, with powers corresponding to those of present day boards of trustees, would be elected by professors and students and would be composed of professors and students only (and possibly research scholars and librarians). The administration would be responsible to an executive committee of the Academic Senate, perhaps on a year-to-year basis; I should prefer a university president who would not submit to detailed board supervision but who would report regularly and at maybe yearly intervals see if he still had the Board's confidence.

Within this democratic framework there would still be alienated minorities of students to berate "the system." It would be disquieting if this were not to be the case. The point is not that democratic government with student-faculty power would please everyone; but that a rational, politically responsible dialogue would be brought about which would help educate to citizenship many students who are now robbed of an education and merely acquire skills and attitudes; and the university community as a whole would be far better able than now to contribute to political enlightenment and to political action in the local public interest, in the larger society, and in the international world.

There would presumably be political party slates; hopefully they would be joint student-faculty parties rather than tribal student parties separate from faculty parties; hopefully there would even be an occasional engineer among the humanists and social scientists who might dominate the slates on the left. Presumably there would be proportional representation, with members at large to give minority voices a hearing in the assembly. And surely there would be a bill of individual rights so as to place limits of the majority's powers to infringe on essential human rights such as freedom of speech, of association and so on.

Among the benefits of democratic government on the campus two categories stand out, in my judgment: the likely demonstration that democracy can work, and the likelihood that the university can become true to its own essential mission of universality in the pursuit and transmission of knowledge, and in the fostering of education as a liberating force from oppression, individual and collective.

If democratic government can work on the campus, surrounding

[16]See Taylor, "Freedom and Authority on the Campus," chapter 23 in Nevitt Sanford (ed.), *The American College* (New York: John Wiley), pp. 774–804.

communities will take note; if students can become self-governing citizens, so can perhaps at a later stage alumni; if full freedom of expression is achieved on the campus, then the normal stifling of radical dialogue in Washington and in most mass media and in many communities will not be tolerated much longer. Real democracy on a national scale may still be a quite utopian ideal, but at least we will all learn the difference between pretended democracy and the real thing, and we will cease paying respectful attention to those who now control our destinies when they keep on talking as if democracy has already been achieved in this country. The universities, perhaps starting with campuses like Berkeley, Wisconsin, Harvard, Yale, Stanford, Michigan and Chicago can become the first demonstration projects in urban America that will show what democracy is and how it can work. If this development can be brought about gradually, I rather think these universities will remain in the front rank among our most distinguished centers of higher learning; and the various political and financial establishments will for their own good (short range, at least) have to put up with us.

How can a democratically governed university hope to become more of a universal city of learning than a trustee-governed one, or a professor-governed one on the continental European models [which in practice tend to function as real gerontocracies, with the influence of youngsters under fifty even more limited than here]? I think the last decade has amply demonstrated that a universalistic moral vision, a disinterested concern for justice is encountered far more often among students than among the faculty, to say nothing of the bulk of university administrators, who so often have been trained to become practical, hard-headed servants of their corporations. What the typical North American and the typical European university have in common today is precisely the absence of effective student influence (official student governments have traditionally been little more than a parody on adult pseudopolitical governments; by hook or by crook, most administrators have had "friendly" immature apoliticals to work with, although the days of this convenient kind of arrangement now appear to be numbered). . . .

The forces that work against full intellectual integrity and against achieving the universal city of learning are in part a matter of PR-conscious university governments, sometimes supported by large sections of the senior faculties as well, who prefer to stifle or forestall dissent by hiring or giving tenure or promotions only to meek or conformist professors. In larger part the problem is that the major foundations and the government and the other main sources of funds and of status and creature comforts outside the universities are exhibiting just the same kinds of preferences: political radicalism is not to be encouraged; it makes people excited, especially the brighter but still immature and malleable students; it rocks the boat, and it is bad business for the university.

But radical intellectual and political inquiry, and perhaps radical politics as well (though about the latter I don't wish to be equally emphatic) is more essential than ever in a world that changes so fast. The really impractical utopians among us are those who believe that our social order can continue to exist without basic changes. Only sheltered societies can sometimes persist unchanged, relying on the conventional wisdom of their unchallenged gerontocrats; in our fast-changing world the premium is on maximal rationality, and political inquiry can be fully rational only to the extent that it is radical, taking no empirical assumptions for granted, however comfortable or crucial they may seem from the perspective of the established powers. Para-doxically, the more turmoil brought about by confrontations between old and young, ins and outs, experts and laymen, and so forth, the greater the prospect that significant parts of our heritage can be adapted to new situations and preserved.

5 Some Social Functions of Violence*

LEWIS A. COSER

American social science has traditionally been somewhat remiss in examining social conflict and social violence because of its excessive commitment to models of social harmony; this has resulted in a tame view of social structures. This paper proposes to redress the balance somewhat by discussing three social functions of violence: violence as a form of achievement, violence as a danger signal, and violence as a catalyst. A plea is made that the study of social violence be given greater emphasis in further research.

The folklore of psychology has it that animals in experimental studies display systematically different behavioral characteristics depending on the investigator. Rats described by American observers are seen as frenetically active, given to a great deal of motor activity, forever dashing in and out of mazes, always trying to get somewhere—though

*Reprinted by permission of the author and publisher from *Annals of the American Academy of Political and Social Science*, 364 (March 1966).

not always certain of exactly where. In contrast, experimental animals seen through the lens of German investigators, apes, for example, seem given to long and intense periods of pensive deliberation and musing cogitation. This jest highlights an important truth. There *are* systematic differences in the ways a particular scholarly community at a given moment in time chooses to approach the manifold data with which it is confronted. In sociology, for example, even if most American social theorists would readily agree in the abstract that conflict as well as order, tension as well as harmony, violence as well as peaceful adjustment characterize all social systems in varying degrees, social theory actually has settled mainly for a remarkably tame and domesticated view of the social world. This is so despite the fact that European social thinkers such as Marx, Weber, and Simmel, upon whose works so much of American theorizing depends for its inspiration, had an entirely different orientation.

It seems as if American social science, developing in a society which, its birth through revolution notwithstanding, has only known one major internal upheaval throughout its history, has failed to be sensitized to the pervasive effects of violence, conflict, and disorder which to the European thinker were facts that they could not but be acquainted with intimately. While to the European thinker the fragility of the social fabric and the brittleness of social bonds seemed self-evident experiences, American social science proceeded from a world view in which social violence was at best seen as a pathological phenomenon. As Arnold Feldman has recently argued:

> Violence is conceived as being *incidental* to the basic character of social structures and processes. Indeed the very conception of social structure ordinarily excludes the source of structural destruction.[1]

As long as American sociology confined its attention mainly to a limited view of the contemporary American scene, its neglect of conflict and violence was, perhaps, none too disabling, at least until recently. But at present, when sociology has happily awakened to the need of doing comparative studies of social structures in both geographical space and historical time, this domesticated vision of the social

[1] Arnold S. Feldman, "Violence and Volatility: The Likelihood of Revolution," *Internal War*, ed. Harry Eckstein (New York: Free Press, 1964), p. 111. See also, Ralf Dahrendorf, *Class and Class Conflict in Industrial Society* (Stanford, Calif.: Stanford University Press, 1959) and a series of later papers collected in the author's *Gesellschaft und Freiheit* (Munich: R. Piper, 1961).

world can be severely hampering. In addition, it seems that even the proper study of American society can no longer profit from exclusive emphasis on models and constructs in which conflict and violence are deliberately or unwittingly minimized. Just as analyses of, say, contemporary South Africa, Latin America, or Southeast Asia, or of seventeenth-century England or nineteenth-century France, would be patently unrealistic if they ignored the functions of political violence, so it has become increasingly evident that such ignoring would be just as unrealistic in the study of the current racial scene in the United States.

For a number of years I have urged a correcting of the traditional balance in theoretical and empirical emphasis in studies of social conflict and social order and have suggested that it is high time to tilt the scale in the direction of greater attention to social conflict.[2] Though much of my work was more generally concerned with the wider topic of social conflict rather than with the somewhat narrower area of social violence, a number of propositions previously advanced apply to violence as well. There is no need, therefore, to reiterate them in this paper. Instead, I shall focus selectively on but a few functions of social violence: violence as a form of achievement, violence as a danger signal, and violence as a catalyst. It is to be understood that this is by no means an exhaustive list of the functions of violence, nor will its dysfunctions be dealt with in this paper.

VIOLENCE AS ACHIEVEMENT

Certain categories of individuals are so located in the social structure that they are barred from legitimate access to the ladder of achievement, as Merton has argued in convincing detail.[3] Moreover, as Cloward and Ohlin[4] have shown more recently, certain categories of persons may find themselves in structural positions which effectively prevent them from utilizing not only legitimate channels of opportunity

[2]Lewis A. Coser, *The Functions of Social Conflict* (New York: Free Press, 1956); Lewis A. Coser, "Social Conflict and the Theory of Social Change," *British Journal of Sociology*, VIII, 3 (September 1957), pp. 197–207; Lewis A. Coser, "Some Functions of Deviant Behavior and Normative Flexibility," *American Journal of Sociology*, LXVIII, 2 (September 1962), pp. 172–181; Lewis A. Coser, "Violence and the Social Structure," *Violence and War*, Vol. VI of *Science and Psycholanalysis*, ed. Jules Masserman (New York: Grune and Stratton, 1963).

[3]Robert K. Merton, *Social Theory and Social Structure* (rev. ed.; New York: Free Press, 1957), chaps. 4 and 5.

[4]Richard A. Cloward and Lloyd E. Ohlin, *Delinquency and Opportunity* (New York: Free Press, 1960).

but criminal and illegitimate channels as well. I shall argue that when all such channels are barred, violence may offer alternate roads to achievement.

Cloward and Ohlin take as a case in point adolescents in disorganized urban areas who are oriented toward achieving higher positions and yet lack access to either conventional or criminal opportunity structures. "These adolescents," they argue,

> seize upon the manipulation of violence as a route to status not only because it provides a way of expressing pent-up angers and frustrations but also because they are not cut off from access to violent means by vicissitudes of birth. In the world of violence, such attributes as race, socioeconomic position, age, and the like are irrelevant; personal worth is judged on the basis of qualities that are available to all who would cultivate them. The acquisition of status is not simply a consequence of skill in the use of violence or of physical strength but depends, rather, on one's willingness to risk injury or death in the search for "rep."[5]

In the area of violence, then, ascriptive status considerations become irrelevant. Here, the vaunted equal opportunity which had been experienced as a sham and a lure everywhere else, turns out to be effective. In the wilderness of cities, just as in the wilderness of the frontier, the gun becomes an effective equalizer. Within the status structure of the gang, through a true transvaluation of middle-class values, success in defense of the "turf" brings deference and "rep" which are unavailable anywhere else. Here the successful exercise of violence is a road to achievement.

Nor need we rest consideration with the case of juvenile delinquency. One can make the more general assertion that in all those situations in which both legitimate and illegitimate socioeconomic achievement seems blocked, recourse to aggressive and violent behavior may be perceived as a significant area of "achievement." This may help to explain the ideal of *machismo* in the lower classes of Latin America. Here, as in the otherwise very different violence in disorganized urban areas of American cities, men tend to feel that only prowess in interpersonal violence and in aggressive sexual encounters allows the achievement of personal identity and permits gaining otherwise unavailable deference. Where no social status can be achieved through socioeconomic channels it may yet be achieved in the show of violence among equally deprived peers.

Somewhat similar mechanisms may be at work in the intrafamilial aggression and violence of American lower-class fathers. These men

---

[5]Cloward and Ohlin, p. 175.

tend to compensate for inadequate rewards in the occupational world at large by an aggressive assertion of male superiority within the little world of the family—as Donald McKinley has recently argued with much cogency.[6] The disproportionately high rate of interpersonal violence among Negro males may yield to a similar explanation. Since Negroes are assigned lowest position in all three major dimensions of the American status system—ethnicity, class, and education—and since their mobility chances are nil in the first and minimal in the second and third, it stands to reason that achievement in the area of interpersonal violence might be seen as a channel leading to self-regard and self-enhancement—at least as long as conflict with the dominant white majority seems socially unavailable as a means of collective action. This does not preclude that violent acting out may not also at the same time call forth a feeling of self-hatred for acting in the stereotypical manner in which the Negro is accused of acting by the dominant white.

Revolutionary violence, both in the classical revolutions of the past and in the anticolonialist liberation movements of the present, can also be understood in this manner. Participation in such violence offers opportunity to the oppressed and downtrodden for affirming identity and for claiming full manhood hitherto denied to them by the powers that be. Participation in revolutionary violence offers the chance for the first act of participation in the polity, for entry into the world of active citizenship. In addition, participation in acts of violence symbolizes commitment to the revolutionary cause. It marks to the actor, but also to his circle, the irrevocable decision to reject the *ancien régime* and to claim allegiance to the revolutionary movement. This has been well described by the late Frantz Fanon, an active participant in the Algerian movement of liberation and one of its most powerful ideological spokesmen. "For colonial man," he writes,

> violence incarnates absolute *praxis*. . . . The questions asked of militants by the organization are marked by this vision of things. "Where did you work? With whom? What have you done?" The group demands that the individual commits an irreversible deed. In Algeria, for example, where almost all of the men who called for the struggle of national liberation were condemned to death or pursued by the French police, confidence in a man was proportional to the degree of severity of his [police] case. A new militant was considered reliable when he could no longer return to the colonial system. It seems that this mechanism was at play among the Mau Mau in Kenya where it was required that each

---

[6]Donald G. McKinley, *Social Class and Family Life* (New York: Free Press, 1964).

member of the group strike the victim. Hence everyone was personally responsible for the victim's death. . . . Violence once assumed permits those who have left the group to return to their place and to be reintegrated. Colonial man liberates himself in and through violence.[7]

The act of violence, in other words, commits a man symbolically to the revolutionary movement and breaks his ties with his previous life and its commitments. He is reborn, so to speak, through the act of violence and is now in a position to assume his rightful place in the revolutionary world of new men.

Similar considerations may also account for the otherwise puzzling fact that women, normally much less given to violence than men, have played leading roles in classical revolutionary movements and in such modern liberation movements as that of Algeria. Here one may suggest that situations where the old norms have broken down differ significantly from normatively stable situations. In the latter, women, having internalized the acceptance of their lower status relative to men, tend to have low rates of active violence. Their suicide as well as their homicide rates are much lower than those of men. Being more sheltered in their lower status positions, women tend to have less motivation for aggression whether directed toward self or toward others. The situation is different, however, when the old norms are challenged, as in revolutions. Here many observers have noted high female participation rates in violent crowds and in street riots. In certain key revolutionary events, such as the March to Versailles of October 1790, and in later food riots, women were predominant. Writes the foremost student of revolutionary crowds, George Rudé, "On the morning of October 5 the revolt started simultaneously in the central markets and the Faubourg Saint-Antoine; in both cases women were the leading spirits."[8]

Revolutionary situations topple the status order and allow underdogs to aspire to equal participation. They provide the occasion for women to act like men. It is as if women were to say to themselves:

If all these extraordinary actions have become possible, then it is perhaps permissible to entertain the extraordinary idea that women need no longer accept their inferior status and can aspire to achieve a hitherto unattainable equality.

[7]Frantz Fanon, *Les Damnés de la Terre* (Paris: Francis Maspero, 1961), pp. 63–64.

[8]George Rudé, *The Crowd in the French Revolution* (Oxford: Clarendon Press, 1959), p. 73.

Here, as in all the other cases considered, violence equalizes and opens to the participants access to hitherto denied areas of achievement.[9]

VIOLENCE AS A DANGER SIGNAL

The late Norbert Wiener once remarked that cancer is so peculiarly dangerous a disease because it typically develops through its early stages without causing pain. Most other diseases, by eliciting painful sensations in the body, bring forth bodily signals which allow early detection of the illness and its subsequent treatment. Pain serves as an important mechanism of defense, permitting the medical readjustment of bodily balance which has been attacked by disease. It seems hardly far-fetched to apply this reasoning to the body social as well.

A social dysfunction can, of course, be attended to only if it becomes visible, if not to the total community, at least to certain more sensitive and more powerful sectors of it. But the sensitive usually lack power, and the powerful often lack sensitivity. As Merton has phrased the issue, there are latent social problems, "conditions which are . . . at odds with values of the group but are not recognized as being so,"[10] which can become manifest, and hence subject to treatment, only when particular groups or individuals choose to take cognizance of them. Merton urges that it is the task of the sociologist to make latent social problems manifest; at the same time he stresses that

> those occupying strategic positions of authority and power of course carry more weight than others in deciding social policy and so . . . in identifying for the rest what are to be taken as significant departures from social standards.[11]

Granted that the social perceptions of those in power and authority may be influenced by social scientists calling attention to previously neglected problems, it would be an indulgence in unwarranted Comtean optimism to assume that such enlightenment will at all times be sufficient to alert them. It is at this point that the signaling functions of social violence assume importance.

Although there are individual, subcultural, and class variations in the internalized management and control of anger in response to

[9]I have dealt with this in a somewhat different framework in "Violence and the Social Structure."

[10]Robert K. Merton, "Social Problems and Social Theory," *Contemporary Social Problems,* ed. Robert K. Merton and Robert A. Nisbet (New York: Harcourt, 1962), p. 709.

[11]Merton, p. 706.

frustration, I take it to be axiomatic that human beings—other than those systematically trained to use legitimate or illegitimate violence— will resort to violent action only under extremely frustrating, ego-damaging and anxiety-producing conditions. It follows that if the incidence of violence increases rapidly, be it in the society at large or within specific sectors of it, this can be taken as a signal of severe maladjustment. I would further suggest that this signal is so drastic, so extremely loud, that it cannot fail to be perceived by men in power and authority otherwise not noted for peculiar sensitivity to social ills. This is not to say, of course, that they will necessarily respond with types of social therapy that will effectively remove the sources of infection. But I suggest that outbreaks of social violence are more apt than other less visible or sensitive indicators at least to lead them to perceive the problem.

To be sure, outbreaks of violence can be seen as mere manifestations of underlying conditions. Yet, perhaps because of this, they may lead power-holders to effect a change in these conditions. Two illustrations will have to suffice. Conventional historical and sociological wisdom has it that the British Chartist movement of the first half of the last century and the often violent and destructive popular movements which preceded it were but manifestations of temporary imbalances brought by the Industrial Revolution upon the British social and political scene. These imbalances, it is argued, were progressively eliminated through a variety of social-structural changes, more particularly through an increase in structural differentiation which gradually provided the homeostatic forces that led to the restabilization of British society in the second part of the nineteenth century.[12] In this view, Chartism was a symptom of a temporary pathological condition, and its defeat highlighted the return to equilibrium and stability.

This view seems to be seriously deficient, if for no other reason than that it ignores the impact of Chartism and related movements on the political decision-makers. It ignores, in other words, the determining contribution of this movement. Far from being but an epiphenomenal manifestation of temporary maladjustment, Chartism had a direct impact by leading to a series of reform measures alleviating the conditions against which it had reacted. Violence and riots were not

---

[12]Cf. Neil J. Smelser, *Social Change in the Industrial Revolution* (Chicago: University of Chicago Press, 1959) and the same author's *Theory of Collective Behavior* (New York: Free Press, 1963). In the latter work, social movements are seen as always involving the "action of the impatient" who "short-circuit" the process of social readjustment by "exaggerating reality," see pp. 72–73. In this perspective one might be justified in concluding that had impatient Christians not short-circuited the adjustment process in ancient Israel, the Jews would have readjusted in time—and spared the world the spectacle of much later impatient religious action.

merely protests: they were claims to be considered. Those involved in them assumed that the authorities would be sensitive to demands and would make concessions. And it turned out that they were right.[13]

Historians will hardly deny that the condition of the laboring poor, and more particularly the industrial working class, between the beginning of the Industrial Revolution and the middle of the nineteenth century was appalling. Nor is it subject to debate that for a long time these conditions were barely perceived by those in power. Finally, it is not to be doubted that legislative remedies, from factory legislation to the successive widening of the franchise and the attendant granting of other citizenship rights to members of the lower classes,[14] came, at least in part, in response to the widespread disorders and violent outbreaks that marked the British social scene for over half a century. Let me quote from Mark Hovell, one of the earliest, and still one of the best, of the historians of the Chartist movement.

"The Chartists," he writes:

> first compelled attention to the hardness of the workmen's lot, and forced thoughtful minds to appreciate the deep gulf between the two nations which lived side by side without knowledge of or care for each other. Though remedy came slowly and imperfectly, and was seldom directly from Chartist hands, there was always the Chartist impulse behind the first timid steps toward social and economic betterment. The cry of the Chartists did much to force public opinion to adopt the policy of factory legislation in the teeth of the opposition of the manufacturing interests. It compelled the administrative mitigation of the harshness of the New Poor Law. It swelled both the demand and necessity for popular education. It prevented the unqualified victory of the economic gospel of the Utilitarians. . . . The whole trend of modern social legislation must well have gladdened the hearts of the ancient survivors of Chartism.[15]

The often violent forms of rebellion of the laboring poor, the destructiveness of the city mobs, and other forms of popular disturbances which mark English social history from the 1760s to the middle of the nineteenth century, helped to educate the governing elite of

[13]Eric J. Hobsbawm, *The Age of Revolution* (London: Weidenfels and Nicholson, 1962), p. 111.

[14]Cf. T. H. Marshall, *Class, Citizenship and Social Development* (New York: Doubleday Anchor Books, 1965).

[15]Mark Hovell, *The Chartist Movement* (London: Longmans, Green, 1918), pp. 210–211. See also Edouard Dolléans, *Le Chartisma* (Paris: Marcel Riviére, 1949).

England, Whig and Tory alike, to the recognition that they could ignore the plight of the poor only at their own peril. These social movements constituted among other things an effective signaling device which sensitized the upper classes to the need for social reconstruction in defense of a social edifice over which they wished to continue to have over-all command.[16]

My second example concerning violence as a danger signal will be brief since it deals with recent experiences still vivid in social memory: the civil rights movement and the war against poverty. The plight of the American Negro and of the urban poor until recently had a very low degree of visibility for the bulk of the white population and the decision-makers on the American scene. Much of it was physically not visible in the sense that it took place in segregated areas not customarily visited by "good people." Much of it, on the other hand, though physically visible, was yet not socially perceived. The sociology of social perception, a sociology elucidating why people sometimes look and why they sometimes look away, it may be remarked in passing, still is to be written. Be that as it may, the shock of recognition, the jolt to conscience, occurred only when the Negroes, through by-and-large nonviolent action in the South and through increasingly violent demonstrations and even riots in the North, brought the problem forcibly to the attention of white public opinion and the white power structure. To be sure, a whole library of books has been written on the dehumanizing consequences of the racial caste system. Yet all this became a public issue only after a number of large-scale social conflicts, beginning in Montgomery, Alabama, helped to highlight the issue. No doubt, the slow process of structural differentiation might have taken care of the problem some time in the indeterminate future. In fact, something was done about it here and now mainly because Negroes, no longer satisfied with promises and having gained some advances, now raised their level of expectations, indicating in quite drastic a manner that they were no longer prepared to wait, that they wanted *Freedom Now*. (I shall return to the topic in the last part of this paper.) Much as one might deplore the often senseless violence displayed in such racial riots as those in Los Angeles, one cannot help feeling that they, too, constituted quite effective signaling devices, perhaps desperate cries for help after other appeals had been unavailing. They indicated a sickness in the body social which demands immediate remedy if it is not to undermine social order altogether.

[16]On the politics of rioting and crowd action see, among others, George Rudé, *The Crowd in History* (New York: John Wiley & Sons, 1964); *The Crowd in the French Revolution* by the same author, also his *Wilkes and Liberty* (Oxford: Clarendon Press, 1962); Eric J. Hobsbawm, *Labouring Men* (London: Weidenfels and Nicholson, 1964) and his earlier *Social Bandits and Primitive Rebels* (New York: Free Press, 1959).

VIOLENCE AS A CATALYST

Marx once remarked: "The criminal produces an impression now moral, now tragic, and hence renders a 'service' by arousing the moral and aesthetic sentiments of the public." Marx here anticipated by many years similar formulations by Durkheim and Mead stressing the unanticipated functions of crime in creating a sense of solidarity within the community.[17] Here I shall argue a related idea, namely, that not only criminals, but law-enforcing agents also, may call forth a sense of solidarity against their behavior. More particularly, the use of extralegal violence by these officers may, under certain circumstances, lead to the arousal of the community and to a revulsion from societal arrangements that rest upon such enforcement methods.

It is common knowledge that the violence used by sheriffs and other Southern officers of the law against Southern Negroes engaged in protest activities and voting-registration drives has had a major impact upon public opinion and federal legislation. The fact is that such methods had been relied upon by Southern police for a very long time without any marked reaction against them. Why, then, did they suddenly become counterproductive? Two major factors seem to account for this reversal. First, modes of control involving the extralegal uses of violence worked well as long as the acts in question could be committed with a minimum of publicity and visibility. They became suicidal when they were performed under the glare of television cameras and under the observation of reporters for national newspapers and magazine.

Everett Hughes, in discussing the Nazi case, has argued that all societies depend for their maintenance on a certain amount of "dirty work" by shady agents of the powers that be, and he added that such dirty work is usually performed far from the sight of "good people."[18] Indeed, the usefulness of those doing the "dirty work" may well come to an end when it must be performed in full view of "good people." If, as Hughes argues, those who do the dirty work "show a sort of concentrate of those impulses of which we are or wish to be less aware," then it stands to reason that they cease to be useful if they have to operate in full view. The solid middle-class citizen of Nazi Germany seems, by and large, to have been unconcerned with what was being done to the Jews; even the early public degradation of Jews in city streets seems to have left them unaffected. But the Hitler regime showed very good judgment indeed in carefully hiding and camouflaging its later murderous methods. One may doubt that the death camps

[17]For the relevant quotations from Marx, Durkheim, and Mead, see Coser, "Some Functions of Deviant Behavior."

[18]Everett C. Hughes, "Good People and Dirty Work," *Social Problems,* X, 1 (Summer 1962), pp. 3–11.

could have been operated except in secret. Similarly, solid middle-class citizens in both North and South may have been aware of the extralegal uses of violence habitually resorted to by Southern sheriffs and police. Yet as long as such knowledge did not intrude too much in their visual field, they remained unconcerned. Matters changed drastically when these inhuman methods were fully exposed to the public at large. Now visibility could no longer be denied. Had these officials become conscious of the changed circumstances under which they were now forced to operate, they might well have abandoned these methods in favor of more subtle means of intimidation. As it turned out, they were subject to the "trained incapacity" upon which Veblen and Kenneth Burke have commented. They adopted measures in keeping with their past training—and the very soundness of this training led them to adopt the wrong measures. Their past training caused them to misjudge their present situation.[19] The very exercise of violence which had been productive of "order" in the past now produced a wave of public indignation which undermined the very practice.

The matter of publicity, powerfully aided by the recent "communication revolution," though crucially important, is not the only one to be considered here. It is equally relevant to observe that violent tactics of suppression tend to be much less successful when used against people who are publicly committed to the principle of nonviolence. Violence by the police, even extralegal violence, may be approved, or at least condoned, when it can be justified by reference to the supposed actual or potential violence of the offending criminal. That is, such behavior seems to be justified or condoned when there exists, or seems to exist, a rough equivalence between the means used by both sides. A tooth for a tooth tends to be a maxim popularly applicable in these cases. But the matter is very different when the presumed offender is committed in principle to a politics of nonviolence. The nonviolent resisters in the South, as distinct from other cases where nonviolence was not based on principle, had consciously assumed the burden of nonviolence. That is, they had made a commitment to the public not to have recourse to violence. When violence was used against them, this hence came to be seen as a breach of a tacit reciprocal commitment on the part of those they opposed. What is ordinarily perceived as a multilateral relationship in which both sides actually or potentially use violence, came now to be perceived as unilateral violence. This impression was still accentuated when acts of official or semiofficial violence were being directed against ministers, that is, against men who enjoy specific mandates and immunities as men of peace.

For these reasons, extralegal violence habitually used in the South

[19]Kenneth Burke, *Permanence and Change* (New York: New Republic, 1936), p. 18.

to maintain the caste system turned out to be a most effective triggering device for measures to abolish it. One need, perhaps, not go so far as to argue, as Jan Howard has recently done,[20] that the very effectiveness of the nonviolent methods used depended on the assumption or expectation that it would encounter violent reactions that would arouse the public conscience. The violent reactions did not have to be anticipated. But it was nevertheless one of the latent functions of Southern violent response to the nonviolent tactics used to lead to the arousal of a previously lethargic community to a sense of indignation and revulsion.

Nor is the Southern case unique. Even in earlier periods extralegal violence on the part of law-enforcement agencies has often been suicidal. The Peterloo Massacre of 1819 in Manchester, when a crowd of listeners to speeches on parliamentary reform and the repeal of the Corn Laws was charged by soldiers who killed ten and injured hundreds, became a rallying cry for the reformers and radicals. The wholesale massacre of participants in the French Commune of 1871 created a sense of intimate solidarity, but also a alienation from society at large, among large sectors of the French working class. In these latter cases the impact was not on the total society but only on particular sectors of it, but in all of them the show of violence on the part of officialdom was suicidal in so far as it transformed victims into martyrs who became symbols of the inquity and callousness of the rulers.

Lest it be understood that I argue that unanticipated and suicidal uses of violence are limited to cases involving law-enforcement agents alone, let me remark, even if only in passing, that there are clearly other groups within society whose resort to violence may under specifiable circumstances bring forth similar suicidal consequences. In particular, when minority groups appeal to the public conscience and attempt to dramatize the fact that they are treated with less than justice and equity, their resort to violence may effectively hamper their cause. They must depend in their appeal on winning to their side previously indifferent and unconcerned sectors of the public. Resort to violence, however, even though it may serve as a danger signal, is also likely to alienate precisely those who are potential recruits for their cause. Hence groups such as the Black Muslims and other extremist Negro organizations may, if they resort to violence, bring about suicidal results by turning previously indifferent or potentially sympathetic bystanders into hostile antagonists.

CONCLUSION

The preceding discussion has identified and examined a series of cases in which violence may perform latent or manifest functions. The

[20] In *Dissent* (January–February 1966).

approach was meant to be exploratory and tentative rather than exhaustive and systematic. It is hoped, however, that enough has been said to show that the curiously tender-minded view of the social structure which has generally predominated in American social theory is seriously deficient and needs to be complemented by a more tough-minded approach.

6 Violence as Political Control and Revolt*

THOMAS ROSE

PROPENSITIES TO VIOLENCE

Violence is central to politics and society because people and institutions are committed to it as a logical and useful style of life. American culture tolerates, approves, propagates, and rewards violence.[1] The glamour of violent acts and the glorifications of violent men create an idealization of violence in America.[2] It is generic and fundamental to the substance of American life, a major theme, ingrained in our life

[1]Frederick Wertham, M.D., *A Sign for Cain: An Exploration of Human Violence* (New York: Crowell-Collier-Macmillan, 1966).

[2]See Robert Coles, "The Gunman Needs A Climate of Hate," *New York Times Magazine,* April 21, 1968, and "America Amok," *The New Republic,* August 27, 1966.

*This selection was prepared especially for this book by Thomas Rose, Instructor in Sociology at The Federal City College, Washington, D. C.

I would like to thank Warner Bloomberg, Jr., Edgar Litt, and H. L. Nieburg for their helpful comments and suggestions on earlier drafts.

style, and is part of the individual character as well as the sociopolitical structure. We have so interiorized our own violence that it has engulfed many of us.

Writers and the mass media "invent almost any conceivable device and method not to *conceal*, but to *introduce* violence and provide occasions for showing it in detail."[3] Violence is a reflection of our social reality, and it is tolerated as a solution to personal and social problems. An excessive display of violence exists against the background of a whole system of defense arguments, alibis, and rationalizations.

The sound of violence reverberates throughout American history. From the earliest beginnings of this nation until the present there has been no period without considerable violence. William Appleman Williams points out that the major feature of American history is that Americans force others to be the way they want them to be. A governing minority has always imposed its will on the majority by force and said that what is good for it is good for others.[4] In the political policies of social control, organized violent control is the might, the cannon, that sanctions and upholds authority and tradition.

The policy of violent control has a long history, especially in race relations, the cities, the Southern and Appalachian region, among farmers in the plains states, and in union-management relations (conflicts). There has been a steady stream of violent control in order to dissipate the strength of violent revolt and dissent.[5] Violent revolt has only been tolerated when those in control felt it would strengthen the consensus of American politics.

A few examples should set a historical mood and sense of perspective. It is easy to forget how we violently dispossessed a native population. Slavery was maintained by violence, and after slavery officially ended there were 3700 lynchings between 1889 and 1930, a period of forty years. DuBois credits troops attacking John Brown at Harper's Ferry as the first violent battle of the Civil War; and the war itself, like other civil and world wars we have fought in, was conducted by a policy of violent attempts to control the South.[6] Janowitz points out that before the Civil War the state militia helped maintain slavery.[7]

[3]Wertham, p. 327.

[4]William Appleman Williams, *The Contours of American History*, (Chicago: Quandrangle, 1966).

[5]Irving Louis Horowitz, (ed.), *The Anarchists* (New York: Dell, 1964).

[6]W. E. B. DuBois, *John Brown* (New York: International Publishers, 1962).

[7]Morris Janowitz, *Social Control of Escalated Riots*, Chicago: University of Chicago Center for Policy Study (pamphlet), 1968.

The prerevolutionary and revolutionary periods of American history were filled with violence. There were riots over the Stamp Act: "a politics of the street—was replacing the old politics—the politics of the assembly hall."[8] Stamp Act rioters took to the streets because they had no other way to express their grievances and political goals. The Boston Massacre and the Battle of Golden Hill are other situations in which people were crushed by a policy of violent control.

Troops were required to subdue rioting farmers in 1790, rioting tax protesters in 1794, rioting laborers in the 1860s and 1880s, and rioting railroad workers in 1877.[9] "The railroad strikes of 1877 were suppressed by federal troops waging small-scale battles with rioting crowds."[10]

Violence in urban industrial history includes the Homestead strike in 1892, the Pullman strike in 1894, and riots in the steel mills of Ohio, Illinois, and Pennsylvania in the 1930s. In 1892, several hundred Pinkerton detectives fought armed battles against steel workers to enforce a reduction in wages in Homestead. Federal troops smashed Eugene V. Debs' strike against the Pullman company in 1894.[11] Urban history is filled with other violent events, including nationalist groups rioting against each other, such as the Germans and Poles in Milwaukee.

The Molly Maguires, a secret society of Irish miners, plundered and destroyed property in the anthracite regions of Pennsylvania in the 1860s and 1870s. It is easy to forget about our rural and urban anti-Catholic traditions, particularly before the 20th century. Violence was directed against other religious groups, including Jews and Mormons; and almost all immigrant groups went through periods of unpopularity during which resentment and hatred often took the form of mobs, riots, and violence. Most history books say little about the horrible Draft Riots that took place in New York City in the summer of 1863, when more than two thousand people were killed in a week of riots.[11]

These examples of violence and conflict in American history must

[8]Jessie Lemisch, "The American Revolution Seen from the Bottom Up," in Barton J. Bernstein (ed.), *Towards a New Past: Dissenting Essays in American History* (New York: Pantheon, 1968).

[9]Marvin E. Wolfgang (ed.), "Patterns of Violence," *Annals,* March 1966.

[10]Theodore Draper, *The Roots of American Communism* (New York: Viking, 1957), p. 21.

[11]See the excellent study by Joel Tyler Headley, *The Great Riots of New York, 1712-1873* (New York: E. B. Treat, 1873). This will be reissued in 1970 by Bobbs-Merrill with an introduction by Thomas Rose and James Rodgers. Also see John Higham, *Strangers in the Land* (New York: Atheneum, 1967).

be coupled with an understanding of present policies. It is obvious that a policy of violent control is being used to try and stop rebellion in our cities and an increasing resistance to the draft and to the war in Vietnam. Policy makers are having difficulty, to say the least, in finding the causes, and then solutions, to growing revolt, which is sometimes violent. Although the daily press does not always report on the policy of violent control, the liberal weeklies continually tell of growing intimidation, repression, brutal clubbing, gassing, and other, more sadistic violence, especially against women who oppose the war and the draft. The following report by Harvey Mayes, an English Professor at Hunter College and a participant in a Washington antiwar demonstration, is the rule rather than the exception when the authorities are angered.

One soldier spilled the water from his canteen on the ground in order to add to the discomfort of the female demonstrator at his feet. She cursed at him, understandably, I think, and shifted her body. She lost her balance and her shoulder hit the rifle at the soldier's side. He raised the rifle, and with its butt, came down hard on the girl's leg. The girl tried to move back but was not fast enough to avoid the billyclub of a soldier in the second row of troops. At least four times that soldier hit her with all his force, then as she lay covering her head with her arms, thrust his club swordlike between her hands into her face. Two more troops came up and began dragging the girl toward the Pentagon. . . . She twisted her body so we could see her face. But there was no face: all we saw were some raw skin and blood. We couldn't even see if she was crying—her eyes had filled with blood pouring down her head. She vomited, and that too was blood. Then they rushed her away.[12]

VIOLENCE AS CONTROL AND REVOLT

Violence as control and revolt are generic to American sociopolitical life. Violence and conflict are a specific property of social and political associations central to a definition of the political process. Violence is critical for an understanding of social and political questions, and implies a conflict model.

Traditionally social scientists assumed that the model for understanding American life is one of consensus and accommodation, because they are so enamored and wedded to these kinds of politics. Because social scientists are hooked to the consensual model, to

[12]Committee of the Professions, *Pentagon: War and Protest,* Advertisement in the *New York Times,* December 3, 1967.

harmony, to adjustment, and to equilibrium, they tend to cover conflict and violence with a kind of "patriotic garb and cool neutrality." "A relentless commitment to his own country may cause an American to glide over the elements of brutality in American history."[13]

Because social scientists have insisted that we are a "peaceful" nation that is generally affluent, they have been unable to describe society as it is but, rather, give a distorted view based on how they want it to be and how they want others to see us. One indicator of this is the tragic lack of information about conflict and violence. When violence and conflict are discussed, they are perceived as being marginal rather than integral to an understanding of American politics and society.[14]

Consensus has avoided the basic issue of how conflicts arise. Conflict situations are not transitory, but have consequences of lasting duration.[15] A theory of political and social conflict is a better solution to the problems of a democracy. But more important, violence and other sociopolitical problems cannot be resolved within a consensual or systems model, where everything is adjusted and patched up, and where conflict is left smoldering, like social and political dynamite, just below the surface. Finally, conflict is important because America is in dire need of change. Positive conflict, rather than consensus, will help alter the course of this nation.

Violence can best be understood in human affairs as the idea of the violation of "personhood," violation of dignity. Violence, or violation, occurs in any combination of four different forms depending upon

[13]Howard Zinn, "History as Private Enterprise," in *The Critical Spirits Essays in Honor of Herbert Marcuse* edited by Stein, *et al.* (Boston: Beacon, 1967).

[14]The lack of articles in the social science journals tells us more about the socialization of social scientists than they do about violence. In the subject index of *Dissertation Abstracts* from 1961 to 1966 there are three titles with the word violence. In the cumulative index of the *American Journal of Sociology* from 1895 to 1965, in the subject index, there were four articles under violence. In the cumulative index of the *Midwest Journal of Political Science* from 1957 to 1966 there was nothing listed under violence, force, or terror. In the cumulative index of the *American Political Science Review* from 1906 to 1963 there was one reference to violence in the word index, although there have been a few articles on violence in developing nations since 1963, and one on "Power and Violence" by E. V. Walter in 1964. In the *Annals of the American Academy of Political Science* there was a special issue on violence in March 1966, but the editor "refrained" from discussing revolution, war, and revolt in our cities.

[15]Irving Louis Horowitz, *Three Worlds of Development* (New York: Oxford, 1966); see especially chapter 12, "Consensus and Dissensus."

whether ". . . the violence is personal or institutionalized, and whether the violence is overt or covert and quiet."[16] Institutional violence is most severe and most obvious when people are systematically deprived of choices. We often fail to see the similarities between individual violence, overt or covert, and large-scale violence of the state. Violence can be physical action or harm and/or symbolic expression, which includes power over others, the various techniques of inflicting, influencing, or overpowering the individual, and in its ultimate extension could include the annihilation of a people or state. Violence includes the various techniques—personal, institutionalized, overt, or covert—of inflicting harm by mental or emotional means, psychic and spiritual as well as physical.

Violent control restrains and regulates and is a method of sociopolitical control. Violent revolt is dissent and strives to create change. Both violent control and revolt seek to influence, but because they are constantly conflicting (consensus is nearly impossible), both impose various gradations along the continuum. For control this may mean large-scale military movements in big cities or various forms of manipulation. Violent revolt thrives on conflict, and when influence is unable to create conflict and change, the threat and use of greater violence is possible. *It is the precarious balance between control and revolt that makes violence central to a discussion of politics.* Both are basic to American life, but they are usually implemented differently through a constant interaction, which I explain as a cycle of violence as revolt and control.

Albert Camus indicated that we are able to ". . . find all direct violence inexcusable and then to sanction that diffuse form of violence which takes place on the scale of world history." We are horrified when a teen-ager tosses a brick, but not when a corporation steals millions of dollars. Many people have the attitude that state violence is defensive and even sacrosanct, but individual violence is murder. Often those who cry most about individual violence in the streets are themselves willing to resort to violence on an institutional level.[17] The lack of comprehension about the interrelationship and interconnections between individual and institutional (collective) violence runs throughout the literature. ". . . Large-scale violence exercised by the state sets a pattern for and dwarfs acts of individual violence. The symbol of

[16]See Newton Garver, "What Violence Is," in Thomas Rose (ed.), *The Violence Reader* (New York: Random House, 1969).

[17]See Eric Fromm, "Different Forms of Violence," *Fellowship,* March 1965. There are many forms of violence, including overt, covert, peaceful, symbolic, physical, unperceived, theft (individual and corporate), state, individual, murder, counterviolence, city rebellions, a garrison state, revolt, violence disguised as love, pathological, playful, revengeful, compensatory, as a substitute for creativity, control, revolt, and archaic bloodthirst.

violence nowadays is not the anarchist's (or ghetto dweller's) puny bomb, but the state's magnificent hydrogen horror."[18]

VIOLENCE AS CONTROL

Violence is one form of sociopolitical control. Its most basic function is to support and sustain the *status quo* and regulate change. There are a series of intricately related social controls. They include custom, or folkway, which rests on conformity by expectation; fashion and convention (mores), which are enforced by community opinion; law, which is regulated by punishment; rational uniformity; ethical rules, which have profound influence on human action even in the absence of external sanctions; and institutional controls, which are upheld by institutions.[19]

There is a dual continuum of violence as a sociopolitical control. Violence includes combinations of many of the above types of control. Sociopolitical control can be used to socialize deviant groups and check potential rebellions, but it can also be used as brute force, as large-scale military movements in ghettos, and in civil and world wars.

The continuum can include both direct and indirect sociopolitical control, obvious manipulation, or a more diffused and amorphous control. Indirect influence works from afar—control is distant—whereas direct influence is more complicated. Indirect control may be termed "potential" (threat) control or direct actual control. An example of direct control is a police officer pushing a young man, which often provokes a very different kind of response than the officer's indirect influence, which would mean asking him in a friendly way to move on.

There are important differences between the kind of violent control threatened and used by governmental institutions and by semiprivate groups and individuals. One is officially legal and has the power of the state behind it, and the other is supra- or extra-governmental. Semiprivate groups and individuals feel that the official ones, legitimate law-enforcement agencies, are unable to control or do not recognize violent revolt. Examples of these supragovernmental groups and individuals include the Minute Men, the American Nazi Party, the Ku Klux Klan, labor organizations, corporations, and the Black Muslims. They are able to exert various gradations of violent control. Often the state does not interfere with supragovernmental groups.

[18]Richard Drinnon, *Rebel in Paradise: A Biography of Emma Goldman* (Chicago: University of Chicago Press, 1961)

[19]See Hans Gerth, and C. Wright Mills, *Character and Social Structure: The Psychology of Social Institutions* (New York: Harcourt, 1963)

The problem of neutral control is an important one, and is made especially complex by the interrelations between local, state, and national law-enforcement agencies. When the local police are unable and/or unwilling to control (or protect), the state and national police are sometimes called in. Often these agencies are more neutral or legitimate; this is the very reason they *are* brought in.[20] The definition of violent control and the question of whether it is needed are both complex and devolve from local custom, community opinion, and other forms of control. The problem of coordination and unity of violent control is complex in a democratic society because there are different levels of control, including three branches of government. The possibilities for total control are, theoretically, fewer than in a totalitarian nation, but in America one unit or branch of government can overpower another; for instance, the federal government has the authority to take over the University of Mississippi and the city of Detroit.

Sociopolitical Control

Violence is social control and authority, and a technique, or a tool, of social control.[21] Violence means physical assault and other methods of inflicting harm or power by mental or emotional means. Lasswell explains that violence may become total—control over the entire populace and over each individual's life, ". . . in order to control, atomize, terrorize them, [and] . . . capture them ideologically."[22]

Absolute violence may be defined as terror: concentration camps, totalitarian regimes, and some forms of overpowering. Terror depends on the techniques of social control, or in the case of a terroristic regime, social organization.[23] Walter clarifies terror by talking about the *process of terror*, which involves a combination of "the act or threat of violence, the emotional reaction, and the social effects."[24] He

[20]Arthur Waskow, *From Race Riot to Sit-in* (New York: Doubleday, 1966)

[21]See E. V. Walter "Power and Violence," *American Political Science Review,* June 1967; Hans Gerth, and C. W. Mills, *From Max Weber*: *Essays in Sociology* (New York: Oxford, 1958); C. Wright Mills, *The Power Elite* (New York: Oxford, 1959); and Harold Lasswell, "The Garrison State," *American Journal of Sociology,* Vol. 46. (1941), p. 455.

[22]Lasswell, "The Garrison State," p. 456.

[23]E. V. Walter, "The Rise and Fall of the Zulu Power," *World Politics* (April 1966), p. 456–463.

[24]E. V. Walter, "Violence and the Process of Terror," *American Sociological Review* (April 1964), p. 248. See also Walter's *Terror and Resistance*: *A Study of Political Violence* (New York: Oxford, 1969).

restricts his discussion to terror as an emotional state "caused by specific violent acts or threats," and distinguishes this from a system of terror, a zone of terror, a siege of terror, and a regime of terror.

The process of terror should be separated from force, coercion, and power. That is, power is all forms of influence and compulsion; force is an agency that compels a person to do something he does not want to do; and coercion is social compulsion or institutionalized force. Finally, he calls violence destructive harm. "Violence may occur without terror, but never terror without violence."[25] Various forms of violence easily shift over during the process of terror-controlling disobedience and resistance, sapping their potential in advance, breaking the power to resist. E. V. Walter comments,

> Every state has the necessary conditions for terrorism, namely, a staff of men obedient to the directors of the system and equipped with instruments of violence, as well as a population capable of experiencing fear. The sufficient conditions invite our exploration, and we must search for them. To identify controlling factors, we must construct a ladder going from actual to potential terrorism, with three levels: (1) situations in which terrorism is practiced; (2) situations in which the agents of violence are not practicing terrorism at the time, but nevertheless are disposed to initiate violence if people were to behave in a certain way; (3) situations in which terror is absent, but in which there is a threshold of stress beyond which an armed staff will be converted into a terroristic apparatus and a regime of terror established.[26]

Totalitarian systems or states—Russia under Stalin, Nazi Germany, Haiti, South Africa—and concentration camps, including totalitarian prison camps, come closest to a process of terror in which the final stages of absolute violence coincide with the destruction of humanity. Hannah Arendt points out that a totalitarian government operates only by the law of nature or history, which is really translated as lawlessness: totalitarian domination. Total terror leaves nothing arbitrary. It creates a "band of iron" that holds people so tightly together that their plurality disappears into one gigantic mass.[27]

Violence as a Failure of Power

It is a common argument of social scientists and social philosophers that the conditions of mass society have injured or destroyed the foundations of political community. They say that the politicized mass

[25]Walter, p. 251.

[26]Walter, p. 257.

[27]Hanna Arendt, *The Origins of Totalitarianism* (New York: Meridian, 1966) p. 464–465.

has replaced the political community. If people do not control their social and political lives and communities, if the power of the people fails, then violence may become *the* significant force in the community. A pattern of violent control would be established as political participation wanes and is coupled with absolute deprivation among various groups. A high degree of participation and political obligation lessens the emergence of institutionalized violence used as control.

Another frequently held position is that the ultimate kind of power is violence.[28] The holders of power, the "power elite," determine the degree of violent controls. (This tends to determine the *amount* of revolt according to the cycle presented later.) The state has exclusive claim to the resources of violent control, which means that ". . . those who control the state inevitably enjoy great power."[29] Tillich worries that the state is able to use violent control to its ultimate limits: overpowering by punishment or liquidation.[30] Whereas Dahl defines power as influence, Tillich realizes it has a much greater use: liquidation by overpowering.

As participation of the public wanes, the power of the state will increase. It is possible for violence to become the primary element in sociopolitical life. We may call this the "politics of impotence."

Force

John Dewey argues that we are "moralizing" force, and that no ends are accomplished without the use of force.[31] He believes, in addition, that force is most often used unwisely and ineffectively, and defines the organization of force as efficiency, making the distinction between power or energy, coercive force (such as the prison), and violence. Power "denotes effective means of operation; ability or capacity to execute, to realize ends. Granted, an end which is worthwhile, and power or energy becomes a eulogistic term. . . . Not to depend upon and utilize force is simply to be without a foothold in the real world."[32] Coercive force, according to Dewey, is the middle ground between power as energy and power as violence. He argues that at the end of any discussion of these terms,

There remains a difference between narrow and partial ends and full and far-reaching ends; between the success of the few for the

[28]See Walter, "Power and Violence," p. 355.

[29]Dahl, Robert A., *Modern Political Analysis* (Englewood Cliffs, N.J.: Prentice Hall, 1963).

[30]Tillich, Paul, *Love, Power, and Justice* (New York: Oxford, 1960).

[31]Dewey, John, "Force, Violence, and Law," in *John Dewey's Philosophy* (New York: Random House, 1939).

[32]Dewey, "Force, Violence, and Law."

moment and the happiness of the many for an enduring time; a difference between identifying happiness with the elements of a meagre and hard life and those of a varied and free life.[33]

Hanna Arendt comments that,

Just as the rule of law, although devised to eliminate violence and war of all against all, always stands in need of the instruments of violence in order to assure its own existence, so a government may find itself compelled to commit actions that are generally regarded as crimes in order to assure its own survival and the survival of lawfulness.[34]

Niebuhr argues that the risk of violence is often necessary in "preserving national societies." "The law tends always to become to some extent the instrument of the *status quo* and an instrument for resisting change."[35] This should have different meanings for people who live in democratic, representative nations and those where the people have no access to the *status quo*.

For Sorel, writing at the turn of the century, Marxism becomes a theory of revolutionary syndicalism or a philosophy of history in which the essential factor is violence. Sorel's most significant contribution is the distinction between force and violence—acts of authority and acts of revolt. Too often, he warned, we believe violence and force are one. Because of this ambiguity, he argues, "*the term violence should be employed for acts of revolt; we should say, therefore, that the object of force is to impose a certain social order in which the minority governs, while violence tends to the destruction of that order.*"[36]

Sorel's argument is all the more important because he feels that the orthodox Marxists did not make this distinction. He believes that the Marxists made a grave error in thinking the proletariat must acquire force like the middle class. "The mass of the producers would merely change masters." Sorel comments further,

Whether force manifests itself under the aspect of historical acts of coersion, of fiscal oppression, or of conquest, or labor legisla-

[33]Dewey, "Force, Violence, and Law."

[34]Arendt, Hanna, *Eichmann in Jerusalem: A Report on the Banality of Evil,* (New York: Viking Compass, 1965), p. 291.

[35]Nieburg, H. L. "Uses of Violence," *Journal of Conflict Resolution,* March 1963.

[36]Sorel, George, *Reflections on Violence,* (New York: Crowell-Collier-Macmillan, 1961).

tion, or whether it is wholly bound up with the economic system, it is always middle-class force laboring with more or less skill to bring about the capitalist order of society. [37]

Proletarian violence for Sorel is the general strike, which he compares to Napoleonic battles—both crush the adversary. Revolutionary syndicalism and the general strike are the crucial elements in a Marxist revolution. They keep the minds of the workers alive and ready to strike, but only when accompanied by violence. Sorel's argument is all the more important because he feels, in counterdistinction to Marx and Engles, that force does not play a revolutionary role, but that violence does. Engles commented that it is force that "shatters the dead, fossilized forms."[38] Walter points out that the translation of Engles, and whether he meant force or violence, is a debatable question. Sorel felt he was talking about force, but Frantz Fanon, the Algerian Marxist, translates Engles "Force Theories" as violence.[39]

Control by Fear

Control is maintained by encouraging the public to be fearful and anxious about violence. The institutionalized symbols of violence are "those" people and groups who are violent. "We" fear the ghetto, the hippie, the Indian, and the Mexican because "we" are socialized to believe "they" are violent. The rationale for control is "them." Of course communists are very violent, and most Americans have an almost psychotic fear of "them." As long as "we" believe this, then "we" will use all our power, influence, and resources to control "them." Control is maintained by fear. Ronald Laing, a British psychoanalyst, points out that,

The invention of Them creates Us, and We may require to invent Them to reinvent Ourselves.

Violence attempts to constrain the other's freedom, to force him to act in the way we desire, but with the ultimate lack of concern, with indifference to the other's own existence or destiny.[40]

---

[37]Sorel. *Reflections on Violence.*

[38]Engles. Frederick, *Anti-Duhring*, (Moscow: Foreign Languages Publishing House, 1962). See especially part two, "The Force Theory."

[39]Fanon, Frantz, *The Wretched of the Earth,* (New York: Grove, 1966).

[40]Laing, R. D., and D. G. Cooper, *Reason and Violence*, (London: Tavistock, 1964).

This is a classical psychological pattern: projection of ourselves as good and of others as evil. We are warped, fearful, hateful, frustrated, but more specifically, we suffer status anxiety. Perhaps the dialectic has come full circle. "We" feel that only "they" are violent. "We" insist, often with anger, that "they" be kept in "their" place, and that "they" are the cause of all the trouble: violence in the streets and antiwar protesters and others who do not know "their" place. We are unable to look ourselves in the mirror and see ourselves as we really are. Sartre points out that as the dialectic unfolds, "they" will look in the mirror at "our" violent reflection and meet "us" with all the violence "they" can muster.[41]

VIOLENCE AS REVOLT

Violent revolt is characteristic of the American political process and should not be considered as outside sociopolitical life. Violent revolt can be explained as gradations on a continuum, and as in the discussion of control, there are two sets of actors: institutional and groups individuals. We do not include governmental revolt, because in America the state does not revolt, however, various institutions in it do, for instance, a political party. Most often violent revolt is directed against the state, the *status quo*, or a combination of the two. The basis of most violent revolt is a desire for sociopolitical and socioeconomic change. Violent revolt, such as rebellions in big cities, often has deeper roots, which may lead to revolution. One episode often leaves a cumulative tradition—it helps build a tradition of successful revolt. This pattern is currently present in the 1960s and ranges from marches in Selma to big city rebellions and to accelerated antiwar revolt and resistance.

At the other end of the continuum is the kind of violent revolt that seeks to overturn the government by the use of wholesale revolution. The American Revolution and the Civil War are the most obvious examples, but Door's Rebellion in the mid-19th century is another less-known example of an attempt to overturn the American government. Such attempts have obviously been rare, but the threat often exists. In theory, the threat is advocated in the literature of some groups who want to revolt, such as Students for a Democratic Society, but it is not the same as an overt advocacy of violent revolt.

For some individuals and groups there can be a very special meaning to violent revolt on the continuum: at one end it can mean a reaffirmation of life and at the other it can mean suicide. This is one of the main concerns of existentialism: freedom or death. Albert Camus argues that rebellion is a reaffirmation of existence. "I rebel therefore

[41]Fanon, see introduction by Jean-Paul Sartre.

we exist."[42] At the other end of the continuum, Kenneth Clark's comment that "revolt is akin to suicide, an attempt to destroy what is intolerable," is a good example. Millenarian movements are another example of how, in effect, a group of people turn against themselves as they predict the violent end of the world.

Justification of Violent Revolt

Hook argues that the real issue concerning violent revolt is its justification by subordinate groups who want to capture power, influence, and the ability to bargain. He points to the moral issues:

> . . . devotion to the values of peace and serenity is higher than devotion to life itself. . . . the use of violence against violence cannot be sanctioned; but where other values are considered as intrinsically desirable as serenity or blessedness, the use of violence may be extenuated as the necessary, even if painful, means of achieving them.[43]

Hook indicates further that humanity, love, and reason have always provided justification for violence.

Reinhold Niebuhr explains the ethical consequences of violence. He considers the influence of violence as a *moral* instrument of social change and argues that nothing is intrinsically immoral or moral, nor natural and inevitable. Violent revolt must be situationally understood. Each instance must be examined, and it is this that Americans have been unable to do. They have wanted to say all violence is bad. Niebuhr takes the realistic position that it is possible to establish justice through violence. He concludes,

> A distinction must be made, and is naturally made, between propaganda which a privileged group uses to maintain its privileges and the agitation for freedom and equality carried on by a disinherited group.

> Equal justice is the most rational ultimate objective for society. . . . Violence may tend to perpetuate unjustice, even when its aim is justice. . . . A social conflict which aims at the elimination of these injustices is in a different category from one which is carried on without reference to the problem of justice.[44]

[42]Albert Camus, *The Rebel* (New York: Vintage, 1958).

[43]Sidney Hook, "Violence," *Encyclopedia of Social Sciences,* 1934, p. 265.

[44]Reinhold Niebuhr, *Moral Man and Immoral Society* (New York: Scribner, 1932), p. 234–235, 245.

Individuals and groups have a "higher moral right" to challenge their oppressors than the oppressors have to maintain a system by violent control. Niebuhr points out that there is no impartial tribunal who can judge the claims of either group. There is, for example, no neutral community within America, although, he points out, oppressed nationalities in other nations ". . . have always elicited a special measure of sympathy and moral approbation from the neutral communities."[45] One might argue that the United States Supreme Court is a neutral community or body, but perhaps it is not really neutral since one must have money to reach that level of justice. At any rate, it is always easier to see and feel revolt that is distant!

Social Change

There is little agreement as to whether violence brings about social change or whether social change heightens the possibilities of violent revolt. It seems likely that there is most often some of each: change is not unidimensional. Under normal conditions of social change there is primarily "frictional" violence: grievances are adjusted through debate, legislation, public policy, and contact. There is little violent revolt. As social change increases, as conflict between white and black (or between the oppressed and the oppressors) increases and the normal methods (frictional) of control are unsuccessful, violence becomes "political."[46]

According to Nieburg, political violence ". . . addresses itself to changing the very system of social norms which the police power is designed to protect."[47] Spontaneous acts of violent revolt are encouraged, and it becomes obvious that the peaceful procedures of social and political processes are closed. Nieburg concludes that, "To understand the role of political violence, we must see it as part of the continuum of the total [formal and informal] polity."[48]

As social change increases at a faster rate there will be more violent revolt. There are three assumptions in this statement: under normal conditions violence is spasmodic; as abundance rises for the majority, violent revolt increases among the less affluent; and in Mertonian terms, violent revolt is caused by an imperfect coordination

---

[45]Niebuhr, p. 238.

[46]See H. L. Nieburg, "Violence, Law, and the Social Process," in a special issue of the *American Behavioral Scientist* on violence, March-April 1968. Also see Nieburg's *Political Violence* (London: St. Martin's, 1969).

[47]Nieburg, "Violence, Law, and the Social Process."

[48]Nieburg, "Violence, Law, and the Social Process."

of culturally prescribed aspirations and socially structured avenues for reaching these aspirations.

The preconditions of violent revolt as influence and revolution are similar. Briton lists three preconditions of revolution: uneven distribution of the fruits of progress; a government corrupt or ineffective in trying to institute reforms; and the development of a social consciousness by intellectuals.[49] Certainly all three existed (with some question about the third) before the American Revolution and the Civil War, and one has only to stretch the imagination a little to see that these prodromal symptoms have had an important effect on the civil rights movement and big city rebellions in the 1960s. Some of the more resistant types of revolt against the war in Vietnam originating from the universities has had all three preconditions. These symptoms also apply in some of the more violent union revolts and where violence has only been threatened.

Violent revolt can be an agent of social change. When some groups and individuals are oppressed—"the other America" for example,—they begin to understand and believe that social change will take place only if they revolt.

This was the position of Emma Goldman, an American anarchist, who felt the oppressed were caught in a tight net of forces that finally made them lash out violently.[50] She had Kroptkin's dream that anarchy would offer more than a mystique of violence: "it would be an inevitable concomitant of significant social change."[51] Even when she did not agree with violent acts, she understood the impelling motives behind them. Although she rejected the ethic of individual acts of violence, ". . . she still had not, at the end of her life, discarded the illusion that large-scale violence. . . could bring about her ultimate ends of peace, freedom, and justice."[52] Her realism was change achieved through the influence of revolt. Her dreams, utopia, was a violent revolution leading to a new life without oppression.

Social Movements and Violent Revolt

Nieburg points out that "any group whose interests are too flagrantly abused or ignored is a potential source of violent unrest." He argues in favor of the accommodation of these interests in order to

[49] Crane Briton, *Anatomy of Revolution* (New York: Vintage, 1956) p. 5.

[50] Drinnon, p. 83.

[51] Drinnon, p. 37.

[52] Drinnon, p. 314.

avoid violence and to retain stability.[53] We can assume that the number and influence of social movements grow in proportion to the resulting accommodation, or that lack of accommodation results in conflict.

Social movements are concerned with bringing about a fundamental change in the social order. They are a response and stem from a feeling of unrest or dissatisfaction with present conditions. In varying degrees all social movements involve various pronouncements and attempts at violent revolt. *Organization* is the crucial factor of success for a social movement.[54]

The successful use of violent revolt, recently discussed from a Marxist perspective, involves a need to organize people, to form alliances and coalitions, even if they are temporary and wavering. Power and influence do not come out of the barrel of a gun.[55]

Andrew Kopkind argues that recent big city rebellions produce a new kind of ghetto with more organization.[56] He argues that a primitive new politics has emerged out of the summer of 1967 in the ghettos. Tough black street leaders have become "new" political leaders. "They are half guerilla, half ward heeler. They work between organization and revolution, groping for a way in which a bitter and mobilized minority can change a system they know will never accept them as they are." Tom Hayden, writing about Newark,[57] wrote of the unifying effect of violence: seeing friends and kin being hurt, makes one become a part of their lives. "It touches people personally and springs a commitment to fight back."[58] Tom Parmenter wrote that some experts involved in community organization see the rebellions as an

> . . . opportunity to assert leadership in building a community. They see more value in organization than in looting. They view organization as a constructive solution. Riots may run out of gas in a week but if organization can begin, it can keep going.[59]

[53]Nieburg, "Uses of Violence," p. 50.

[54]See Saul D. Alinsky, *Reveille for Radicals* (Chicago: University of Chicago Press, 1946) and Lasswell, "The Garrison State."

[55]Ernest Kaiser, "Negro History: A Bibliographical Survey," *Freedomways* (Fall 1967), p. 370.

[56]Andrew Kopkind, in the *New York Review of Books*, August 24, 1967.

[57]Tom Hayden, *Revolt in Newark*, (New York: Dell, 1967), p. 211.

[58]Tom Hayden, *Revolt in Newark*.

[59]Parmenter, "Breakdown of Law and Order," *Transaction*, September 1967.

Sidney Hook points out that Christianity and the Jacobins were compelled to use violence. He shows that violence has been "an invariable concomitant of all mass movements of social reform."[60] Hook is aware that, from one end of the continuum to the other, the threat or shadow of violent action has played a powerful part in social movements aimed at both influence and overthrow.

American history is filled with movements of violent revolt. Jack O'Dell comments,

> . . . Nat Turner's *rebellion,* or of Denmark Vesey's *revolt* and of the more than 200 other slave *revolts.* These were violent efforts by men, individually or collectively, to throw off the chains of slavery exploitation. . . .
>
> More than a century before these freedom revolts by African slaves under the rule of the American Republic, a series of similar events had shaken British rule in the colony of Virginia. In 1676 the Governor's plantation was stripped of its crops and domestic animals, and a militia was organized among the planters, farmers, and white indentured servants to back up their demands for lower taxes, and an end to corruption and favoritism in the government. This was known as "Bacon's Rebellion."[61]

The threat and use of violent revolt has deep roots in American history. The growing number of groups arguing for violent revolt against America's position regarding civil rights and the war in Vietnam seems to be cutting across racial and class lines, whereas in the past most social or mass movements were more specifically based on these lines. The black power movement is an obvious exception.[62]

Violent Revolt and the Ethic of Crisis

Crisis and drama help create change, develop mass movements, and instill fear in those at whom the revolt is aimed. Sorel advocated an ethic of crisis: the accentuation of dramatic social change. For Sorel, crisis and drama were a technique of keeping the middle class in a state of fear and of illuminating the conflict of ethical values. Even a few violent acts would suffice. Small violent insurrectionary acts in defiance of all authority dramatize the spirit of violent revolt. For Sorel, however, they have historical value only if they are a "clear and

---

[60]Hook, "Violence."

[61]Jack O'Dell, "The July Rebellions and the Military State," *Freedomways,* Fall 1967, vol. 7, No. 4. p. 288.

[62]See Janowitz, *Social Control of Escalated Riots* on the difference between community and commodity riots.

brutal expression of the class war: middle classes must not be allowed to imagine that, aided by cleverness, social science, or high-flown sentiments they might find a better welcome at the hands of the proletariat."[63]

This basic ideology has threads throughout American history. The Student Nonviolent Coordinating Committee and other groups in recent years have used all sorts of violent, dramatic threats and actions which have made the middle class fearful but which, more important, have united the black community. Crisis and drama are organizing devices around which a movement for violent revolt can be built. Citizens can read material on violence with the same thrill that adolescents read "marriage manuals" as pornography and that others nightly view violent westerns on television. Certainly films and novels about urban crime, violence in the streets, and war are also ways of "hooking" and organizing people in and around the crisis and drama of violence. Violence turns America on!

The use of dramatic production to show the violence of organized society and control and/or the need for violent revolt is frequent in the works of Bertolt Brecht, especially in *Mother Courage,* which shows the horrors, suffering, and violence of war. Many films place fantastic emphasis on violence. *Bonnie and Clyde,* produced in 1967, and nominated for an award as the best motion picture of that year, is a magnificent study of violence in America and shows the continual crisis ethic of violence as a way of life. Every decade in American history is filled with literature and films about gang life. An interesting example is Warren Miller's *The Cool World.* In 1968 the state of Massachusetts banned a brilliant documentary film about violence in a state mental institution. Documentaries about violence which strip bare "distasteful" facts have often been kept from the public.[64]

The use of Guerrilla Theater, using some of Artaud's ideas,[65] is making Americans understand their own violence, especially to see the relationships of domestic and international violence. Various groups of black teen-agers are using drama to show their anger and revolt to the white 'world, for instance, Youth For Service in San Francisco and the Blackstone Rangers in Chicago. Guerrilla Theater groups have sprung up on a number of university campuses in the past few years.

Violent Revolt as Bargaining Influence

The threat of violent revolt should create a willingness to bargain politically in a democratic state, but not all groups are invited to the

[63]George Sorel, *Reflections on Violence* (New York: Crowell-Collier-Macmillan, 1965).

[64]See Robert Coles' review, "Stripped Bare at the Follies," *New Republic,* January 20, 1968.

[65]Antonin Artaud, *The Theater and its Double* (New York: Grove, 1958).

bargaining table. Those groups that threaten and use violence as revolt are not given the same rights and means of bargaining power or influence as those that use violence as control. There is always a highly skewed power relation between the controllers and the revolters. This basic inequality of power in the bargaining process may itself produce violence as revolt. Potentially violent groups are often somewhat accommodated by authority to avoid violence and retain stability.[66] *But those who advocate violent revolt do not want accommodation but equal bargaining power.* This does not mean token change or resolution of disputes with tokenism.

Jessie Lemisch points out that poor colonial seamen resisted the Royal Navy before the American Revolution. "The seamen were fighting, literally, for their life, liberty, and property, and *their violence was all the politics they could have.*"[67] Violence may be considered a continuation of bargaining by other means. "Here all the attenuated politically-socialized forms of indirect power are brushed aside. The threat of force moves into action. . . ."[68] Violence is a political resource when the bargaining process provides no other alternatives, or at least when some groups perceive no other alternatives.[69]

Violence becomes bargaining power. Sometimes violence represents success. Traditionally social scientists and others have argued that violence was not a political resource, that it could never mean success, but rather, that it signified despair and defeat for those using it. This can also be turned around: violence as control has made minorities in America feel despair, defeat, powerlessness, and alienation..It is because violent revolt was forbidden and violent control was so successful that we have black power today. Black power—black political power—simply says that the traditional bargaining process does not work for those who are poor and black. The solution, a way to stop despair and defeat, powerlessness and alienation, is found in the use of the threat and demonstration of violent revolt.

In larger perspective, minorities and dissenting groups have always used violent revolt as threat and demonstration to gain power, influence, and status in the larger society. Minorities, it can be argued, have never been a part of the democratic bargaining process. They have often been (lived, worked, and so on), in effect, *outside* the system. That society has created institutions and values that keep the poor and other minority groups outside, by not allowing them to have affluence, status, a sense of community, and bargaining power.

Violent revolt has often been the only alternative other than despair or powerlessness. This statement is not the result of a flash of

[66]Nieburg, "Uses of Violence," p. 50.

[67]Lemish, "The American Revolution Seen from the Bottom Up."

[68]Nieburg, "Violence, Law, and the Social Process."

[69]Nieburg, "Violence, Law, and the Social Process."

anger—we are discussing bargaining power and not accommodation. Most social scientists have discussed the accommodation process and not the equal participation as bargaining agents of minorities. It was impossible for them to discuss violent revolt as a potential source of influence because they are so enamored of the "peaceful change" and accommodation theories.

Violent revolt and the threat of violent revolt can have lasting advantages if used successfully as a political-bargaining instrument, as a method of developing policies. Roosevelt created a Fair Employment Practices Commission and Truman desegregated the armed forces because in both instances A. Philip Randolph threatened mass demonstrations and marches if they did not. The March on Washington in 1963 forced Congress to pass a civil rights act. During the past few years rebellions in large cities have violently convinced the government into a reallocation of resources and a number of studies. Vast amounts of money are now being used for control. Continual stories in the *Milwaukee Journal* indicate that the threat of violence by the NAACP Youth Council and Father Groppi has sat as an invisible agent at the bargaining table, and has caused the city of Milwaukee to spend vast sums of money to create stability, or at least the feeling of stability (as opposed to threat and fear) for the larger white community. Stokely Carmichael has pointed out that those blacks jailed in big city uprisings will not be going to Vietnam.[70] This shows a form of bargaining power using violent revolt. The nation needs those men on the battlefront, but they remain in Newark and Detroit prisons. Violent revolt may be termed successful when by the creation of lasting disruptions and conflict in the system, they are also able to create policies and the demand for policies that get at the causes of revolt rather than suppress it.

Violent Revolt as Threat

Violence as revolt may range on the continuum we have discussed, which includes threat. Violence may have actual and potential use, demonstration and threat.[71] Lasswell discusses the expectation of violence.[72] Fanon writes of passing from an atmosphere of violence to violent acts.[73] The threat of potential violence is often effective before it is actually demonstrated. Neiburg points out that,

---

[70]Stokely Carmichael and Charles V. Hamilton, *Black Power: The Politics of Liberation in America* (New York: Vintage, 1967).

[71]Nieburg, "Uses of Violence."

[72]Harold Lasswell, *World Politics and Personal Insecurity* (New York: Free Press, 1965).

[73]Fanon, *The Wretched of the Earth* (New York: Grove, 1967).

The actual demonstration of violence must occur from time to time in order to give credibility to its threatened outbreak; thereby gaining efficacy for the threat as an instrument of social and political change. The two aspects, demonstration and threat, cannot be separated, *The two merge imperceptibly into each other.* If the capability of actual demonstration is not present, the threat will have little effect in inducting a willingness to bargain politically. In fact, such a threat may provoke "pre-emptive" counter violence.[74]

How can those groups who use violence as threat have some assurance this will not provoke "preemptive" counterviolence? This question has often been raised by those groups using nonviolence because the state (the controllers) has assumed that "nonviolent" demonstration would become violent. Seldom during the nonviolent civil rights movement of the 1960s have the nonviolent demonstrations become violent, but the police and the public often have. Can we assume that this is why nonviolence has become a technique of the past, and that now most civil rights demonstrations see the failure of nonviolence and use the threat of violence? When H. Rap Brown tells black people they had better get guns, he frightens the white public into the same action. The threat, therefore, often brings about "preemptive" violence on the part of those who control. The stages in the cycle we discuss next can become "preemptive." Repression may be termed a form of "preemptive" violence by control in order to prevent the threat and use of violence.[75]

Violent Revolt Is Functional

Frantz Fanon, the Algerian psychiatrist, argues that violent revolt makes it possible for the masses to understand social truths and insists that only a violent struggle will create significant revolutionary changes for black Americans (whom he considers to be a colonial people).[76] Lewis Coser commented in the previous article in this volume that violence is functional as an alternative road to achievement, as a danger signal, and as a catalyst. Whereas Coser stresses the integrative functions of violence, Dahrendorf indicates that violence has diverse functions, and that the disruptive functions of violence and conflict are more important than the integrative functions.[77] Let us conclude this

[74]Nieburg, "Uses of Violence."

[75]Also see T. M. Tomlinson, "The Development of a Riot Ideology among Urban Negroes," *American Behavioral Scientist,* March-April 1968.

[76]Fanon, *The Wretched of the Earth.*
[77]See Ralf Dahrendorf, *Class and Class Conflict in Industrial Society* (Stanford: Stanford University Press, 1960).

section with a letter that Frederic Douglass wrote on the functions of revolt in 1849.

> The whole history of the progress of human liberty shows that all concessions, yet made to her august claims, have been born of earnest struggle. The conflict has been exciting, agitating, all-absorbing, and for the time being putting all other tumults to silence. It must do this or it does nothing. If there is no struggle, there is no progress. Those who profess to favor freedom, and yet depreciate agitation, are men who want crops without plowing up the ground. . . They want the ocean without the awful roar of its many waters.

> . . . Power concedes nothing without a demand. It never did, and it never will. Find out just what people will submit to, and you have found out the exact amount of injustice and wrong which will be imposed upon them; and these will continue till they are resisted with either words or blows, or with both. The limits of tyrants are prescribed by the endurance of those whom they oppress. In light of these ideas, Negroes will be hunted at the North, and held and flogged at the South, so long as they submit to those devilish outrages, and make no resistance, either moral or physical. Men may not get all they pay for in this world; but they certainly pay for all they get. If we ever get free from all the oppressions and wrongs heaped upon us, we must pay for their removal. We must do this by labor, by suffering, by sacrifice, and, if needs be, by our lives, and the lives of others.[78]

THE CYCLE OF VIOLENCE

Many conflict theorists argue that conflict prevents the ossification of society by a constant pressure for innovation and creativity. Because conflict has *diverse, integrative,* and *disruptive* functions it can lead to fundamental positive social change. A conflict model, and conflict situations, are operative at various levels or zones in society. American society is often defined by the ". . . quality and types of conflict situations tolerated if not openly sanctioned."[79] Conflict functions and is a struggle within the structure or system over status, power,[80] laws, norms, values, and resources. It is *not outside* the system, but gives

[78]See Frederick Douglass in *The Black Power Revolt* edited by Floyd B. Barbour (Boston: Porter Sargent, 1968).

[79]Horowitz, *Three Worlds of Development,* p. 372.

[80]There are two models of power. One is violence as the failure of power or what may be called power responding to cooperation. This is minimizing violence and conflict. The other is political power or violence as the

direction to change, helps produce necessary change, and contributes to the settlement of issues and problems. It is a problem-solving vehicle.

Political, social, and economic conflict are often *cyclical* in the United States, a nonequilibrated nation. Conflict and violence, within a cycle of control and revolt are more likely when there is absolute deprivation in socioeconomic and political terms rather than relative deprivation. Conflict is a more intensive dynamic component and process because various groups and institutions in our society are in such severe disequilibrium. It is possible for conflict to be violent or nonviolent and to occur at any point in the cycle, or for it to be the basis of revolt or control. More equilibrium, recognition of the positive factors of conflict, greater democratic organization and participation, and more effective parliamentary institutions should decrease violence.

Continual violent revolt has had a formative influence on the policy response of violent control. Various policies evolve and respond within a cycle of control and revolt. Traditionally there has been a balance between revolt and control, but America is moving in a direction where violent control, repression, and suppression become policy and where revolt is quelled.

Both control and revolt are moving on a continuum toward greater escalation, and the increasing conflict is caused in part by a nation that insists that conflict and violence must be interpreted as dysfunctional. Too seldom are policy makers able to understand and cope with the causes of the conflict and violence. Violence of the oppressed is proportional to the violence exercised by the majority of the oppressors. Resistance or expectations of resistance increase the probability of violence. The probability that any group or movement using violent revolt will thrive in America is nil. Influence gets some results, but plans for revolution do not. Finally, repression can effectively crush movements of revolts, but at the same time, public renunciation of the use of violent revolt undercuts the very fabric of American democracy, where balance, conflict, and dissent are such critical ideologies.

Conflict theory is best illustrated by a cyclical theory of violence as control and revolt that has become a generically recurrent pattern in American politics. Tom Hayden, writing about the disorders in Newark during the summer of 1967, argues that (1) official violence (control) has been used for years to quell the aspirations, rights, and demands of the black community; (2) the response of the ghetto was rebellion or revolt with various degrees of violence, (3) the controllers

property of power where there is a maximizing of conflict. Power is central to violence and conflict. "Violence from this perspective may be seen as a decisive form of power responding to conflict." Violence and conflict take on a political character, a political identity.

(the government, the local and national guard) used violent control as a destructive technique (authority and repression); and (4) each side escalated with greater violence.[81]

Stage One

Violence has become an efficient means of control. According to Lasswell, we are moving into an era where violence will dominate the society. More specifically, specialists on violence are becoming the most powerful group in society. They dominate the instruments of violence.[82] Wolfgang argues that the greater the participation which members of society have in its maintenance, control, and direction, the less vulnerable that society will be to the emergence of collective violence.[83] Democratic bargaining processes break down because violent control becomes centralized. Fear of violent revolt often produces preemptive violence. There is an escalation, or buildup, of violent control in anticipation of future violent revolt.

The increase of violent control has been created by a society that is more and more unidimensional: domination of the individual, paralysis of criticism, lack of meaningful opposition, an overriding concern with preserving the *status quo*, the obliteration and integration of opposites, and the merging and swallowing-up of alternatives.[84] Many people feel trapped. Violent control is also being created by greater absolute deprivation among some groups and the lack of participatory politics. There is a need for organizations on a neighborhood and small community level run by the residents.

Stage Two

Violent revolt, as Janowitz points out[85], "seems to establish a vague political presence." People are asking for recognition by a kind of "defiance" politics. Retaliation against growing control is an affirmation that society is neither peaceful nor participatory. The factors in stage one increase the threat and demonstration of violent revolt. Those who wish to revolt have a philosophical base in many ideas and in the Declaration of Independence, which clearly opens the door for, and in fact encourages, revolt. Throughout American history, racial, ethnic, and political minorities have felt oppressed and *outside* the processes of participation and bargaining. They have felt that they had

---

[81]Hayden, *Revolt in Newark,* p. 148.

[82]Lasswell, "The Garrison State."

[83]Wolfgang, "Patterns of Violence."

[84]See Herbert Marcuse, *One-Dimensional Man* (Boston: Beacon, 1964).

[85]Janowitz, *Social Control of Escalated Riots.*

no influence on making adjustments or drastic changes. Violent revolt appeared to be the only alternative. Engles has argued that the masses are thus *forced* to use violence.[8].

As people become more aware of inconsistencies, tensions rise, and violent revolt becomes a fact. Calvert[87] indicates that at this stage occur direct forms of violent revolt, including strikes, demonstrations, and riots, which have an "overriding political purpose." When the propaganda effect is highly disproportionate to the objectives of these acts, they tend to perpetuate the cycle.[88] Less communication and less confrontation between revolters and controllers increases the probability of greater violence by both sides. Horowitz points out that

> . . . the use of violence to counter the force of the state wherever it occurred—in the Haymarket affair, in Coxey's Army, the American Federation of Labor Dynamiters, Centralia Steel unionization, by the Wobblies of the West—all came to a frustrating and dismal end. . . . the state unleashed a steady stream of counterviolence. . . .[89]

Stage Three

Control as counterviolence to knockout violent revolt and repression are increased. Revolt is put down or smashed. Dissent and other deviant behavior is prohibited. Violence becomes a decisive form of political power in response to conflict.[90] If resistance from those revolting increases, those in control use counterresistance. Ultimate repression and control are overpowering. Repressive legislation in reaction to revolt is appearing on the local, state, and national levels. The New York Civil Liberties Union said 1967 had not been a good year for individual rights and warned "that state reprisals against peaceful protest could lead to increased violence." They continued:

> Escalation of violence in protest demonstrations can thus become difficult to reverse as escalation of violence in international relations. . . . the mere fact of overregulation, quite apart from the merits of any particular regulations, is destructive of individual dignity and individual liberty.[91]

[86]Friedrich Engles, *Selected Writings* (New York: Penguin Books, p. 54, 1967) pp. 123–137.

[87]P. A. B. Calvert, "Revolution: The Politics of Violence," *Political Studies* (Oxford) February 1967.

[88]Lasswell, "The Garrison State."

[89]Horowitz, *The Anarchists*, p. 42.

[90]Walter, "Power and Violence."

[91]Reported by Douglass Robinson in the *New York Times,* "1967 Called Bad For Civil Rights," January 1, 1968.

Stage Four

Repression, suppression, and exceptional social control, which render those revolting as outlaws, bring counterviolence against the state which has firmly established control. Counterescalation occurs on both sides when adjustments are not made. As blood is spilled a pattern of violent control and revolt intensifies. Rebellions often spread from one city to another or from one strike to a series. The National Guard is called out (private police were used in earlier years) and the various agents of violent control are equipped with highly technical weapons. In 1968 both armored trucks and such chemical agents as Mace were being used. As a nation, perhaps we have not reached this last stage, the phase of spiraling control and revolt; but it is possible to speak of pockets of overpowering control and intervention: the National Guard took over Detroit and Newark; they moved into Little Rock and the University of Mississippi; and the government has created intense fear and hatred in many of our cities, which may explode in a cumulative series of events. At this junction, a kind of overpowering totalitarian policy of control may evolve. In sum, the policy of violent control and repression has never been an anomaly. Violent revolt has traditionally been political, and when control is threatened it retaliates with policies of violent control.

CONCLUSION

In order to develop creative constructive policies to deal with violence it must first be understood. "We cannot say that because violence *should* not exist, we might as well proceed as if it did not."[92] It should now be obvious that we cannot eliminate violence, but it can hopefully be regulated and reduced without escalation of a policy of violent control.

A theory of conflict resolution addresses itself to the causes rather than the expressions of social conflict. Its purpose is not the elimination of causes. Regulation will replace suppression and repression. Suppression will only force conflict under the surface, where it will eventually erupt. Horowitz points out that "to plan for social change very often means to anticipate social conflict and devise programs for meeting the problems which arise out of such conflict. . . . The rejection of conflict is an invitation to violence and coercion. Conflict may often turn out to be a 'safety valve' for minimizing violence. . . ."[93] Violent revolt will have to increase in order to educate the larger society.

[92]Bruno Bettleheim, "Violence: A Neglected Mode of Behavior," in *Annals,* March 1966.

[93]Horowitz, *Three Worlds of Development,* p. 379.

We are in a position not only to tolerate conflict, with a low yield of violence, but induce dissensus—for the purpose of avoiding all-out conflict which is unstructured. Political parties, voluntary social organization, and athletic events are examples of the safety-valve factor in such forms of conflict. By taking conflict as a social constant it may yet be possible to avoid the consequences of *maximum* conflict. There is abundant evidence that low-yield violence is at least as plausible within a world of programmed conflict as it is in the diplomatic world of compromise.[94]

The causes of conflict and violence and their relationship to the policy of violent control must be understood, and the will to solve problems inherent in those causes must be developed. It must be made clear that poor Americans, and especially blacks, find that life in this nation is now unacceptable. America now has a grotesque inversion of priorities; there are incompatible demands being made upon our values and resources. Too often fear has been the basis of a policy of violent control because Americans wanted to be protected from those who are excluded from any real participation in American life rather than to create a more equalitarian society. We can now make an effort to understand and alleviate the causes of violent conflict and revolt, or we can continue to be reactionary and suppress conflict and revolt—which may result in irrepressible conflict.

[94]Horowitz, *Three Worlds of Development*, p. 389.

PART II
POLITICAL DEMANDS ON THE PUBLIC POLICY STATE

Introduction

The present era is a time during which the masses have become politically visible. The instant impact of television, the changes in political structure, and the new techniques of mass protest have brought about new demands on the central polity. The contributions to this section investigate diverse political choices involved in making effective demands. First, the articles by Rustin, McWilliams, and Marvick (Selections 7, 8, 9) sharpen our focus on the problem of political potency for more disadvantaged groups in society. Bayard Rustin is writing in the face of "black power" militancy among ghetto blacks, and his writing preceded the assassination of Dr. Martin Luther King. Reviewing the antecedents of the cleavage between integrationist and separatist (or black power) strategies in Negro history, Rustin takes his cues from the assertion that it is "the growing conviction that the Negroes cannot win—a conviction with much grounding in experience—which accounts for the new popularity of 'black power.' "

Carey McWilliams offers a broader perspective. Noting that the concentration of political power in America has become more intense since the United States entered World War II, he finds this situation important in understanding the growth of antimovements, that is, protest and action without politics rooted in profound feelings of institutional powerlessness. Dwaine Marvick's balanced essay utilizes empirical data to discover the personal and group means by which American blacks accommodate themselves to the practical realities of their daily lives. He points to the practical significance of personal and party politics, and to the legacy of disadvantage in which public outlooks are formed. Two implications seem very important, namely that blacks have had to find functionally equivalent ways of accomplishing political ends, and that problems in organizing their own lives have been primary concerns. Thus, efforts to socialize blacks to predetermined rules of the political system or of the white middle-class society are not likely to be highly successful.

We are faced with several important questions when we combine these three contributions. First, to what extent are major shifts in institutional and group power required to reduce spiraling frustrations when public demands are not met? (The article by Piven and Cloward in Part III is also relevant). Second, how relevant are existing political institutions, such as our urban and party structures, in meeting political demands by disadvantaged and highly political groups? Third, how meaningful is much of our writing on political participation in stressing the political apathy of disadvantaged people? Consideration of these issues indicates the enormously complex and sensitive nature of effective public policy in a time of mass demands and political action. Here traditional ideological clichés are of little help. The classic conservative defenses of political repression and limited value distribution simply infuriate politicized masses and endanger the stability of the political order upon which responsible conservatism depends. The radical ideology calling for drastic redistribution of existing political power and social goods is undermined when disadvantaged groups have not been prepared to exercise power and to distribute social justice. The classic middle ground of welfare liberalism no longer guarantees either political order or the massive redress of grievances. The ambiguities of our political era must be understood before we are able to cope with them in articulating and implementing public demands upon the polity.

This understanding is necessary if we are to consider the conditions and consequences of our political options within institutional structures.

The last two selections in Part II explore the politically significant terrain of interest-group behavior among advantaged and skillful members. Lewis Froman (Selection 10) is concerned with the relationships among the strength of interest groups in American state politics, the characteristics of state constitutions, and the methods of selecting state officials. Employing techniques of modern political science, he establishes positive relationships between interest group strength and the malleability of state political structures. Strength of interest groups is a major factor in explaining why states vary in the ease with which constitutional amendments are made. Moreover, states with strong interest groups rely more heavily on election of state officials than do states with weaker interest groups. The stronger the interest groups, the greater the number of elected officials, the greater the number of state agencies with elected officials, the greater the likelihood that public utility commissions will be elected, and the greater the probability that judges on state courts of last resort will be elected. Froman's message is clear—interest-group strength can effectively shape the political institutions in order to effectuate its demands and enlarge its political access.

The impact of the university faculty upon the contractual relations between the university and the Department of Defense can be gleaned from Gabriel Kolko's report (Selection 11). An activist antiwar minority prevailed because the nature of the modern university is such that even if a small number within the university community wish to accept or reject military research, the faculty can define the rules, pushed by a skillful minority in the name of the entire university. Here the resources used are academic and political knowledge, so that the needs of an outside governmental agency can be resisted by the university community. While Froman looks at the "external impact" of potent interest groups upon political institutions, Kolko focuses upon the "internal impact" of a university faculty within the highly politicized multiversity. These two accounts of interest-group politics alert us to the critical pressure points within ongoing and seemingly impregnable major institutions. Awareness of major political institutions can significantly improve the quality and efficacy of demands made by disadvantaged groups.

Moreover, the significance of shared power within key institutions applies to the volatility and apathy of the masses. It is only when previously erratic or apathetic groups can anchor their behavior in collective enterprise that the quality participation required in modern society can be sustained. Therefore, structured political demands countervail against the tendencies to explosive and withdrawn behavior of the masses, who have no clear structural relationship to the larger polity.

7 "Black Power" and Coalition Politics*

BAYARD RUSTIN

There is no question, then, that great passions are involved in the debate over the idea of "black power"; nor, as we shall see, is there any question that these passions have their roots in the psychological and political frustrations of the Negro community. Nevertheless, I would contend that "black power" not only lacks any real value for the civil-rights movement, but that its propagation is positively harmful. It diverts the movement from a meaningful debate over strategy and tactics, it isolates the Negro community, and it encourages the growth of anti-Negro forces.

In its simplest and most innocent guise, "black power" merely means the effort to elect Negroes to office in proportion to Negro strength within the population. There is, of course, nothing wrong with such an objective in itself, and nothing inherently radical in the idea of pursuing it. But in Stokely Carmichael's extravagant rhetoric about "taking over" in districts of the South where Negroes are in the

*Reprinted by permission of the author and publisher from *Commentary*, copyright © 1966 by the American Jewish Committee.

majority, it is important to recognize that Southern Negroes are only in a position to win a maximum of two congressional seats and control of eighty local counties.[1] (Carmichael, incidentally, is in the paradoxical position of screaming at liberals—wanting only to "get whitey off my back"—and simultaneously needing their support: after all, he can talk about Negroes taking over Lowndes County only because there is a fairly liberal federal government to protect him should Governor Wallace decide to eliminate this pocket of black power.) Now there might be certain value in having two Negro congressmen from the South, but obviously they could do nothing by themselves to reconstruct the face of America. Eighty sheriffs, eighty tax assessors, and eighty school-board members might ease the tension for a while in their communities, but they alone could not create jobs and build low-cost housing; they alone could not supply quality integrated education.

The relevant question, moreover, is not whether a politician is black or white, but what forces he represents. Manhattan has had a succession of Negro borough presidents, and yet the schools are increasingly segregated. Adam Clayton Powell and William Dawson have both been in Congress for many years; the former is responsible for a rider on school integration that never gets passed, and the latter is responsible for keeping the Negroes of Chicago tied to a mayor who had to see riots and death before he would put eight-dollar sprinklers on water hydrants in the summer. I am not for one minute arguing that Powell, Dawson, and Mrs. Motley should be impeached. What I am saying is that if a politician is elected because he is black and is deemed to be entitled to a "slice of the pie," he will behave in one way; if he is elected by a constituency pressing for social reform, he will, whether he is white or black, behave in another way.

Southern Negroes, despite exhortations from SNCC to organize themselves into a Black Panther party, are going to stay in the Democratic party—to them it is the party of progress, the New Deal, the New Frontier, and the Great Society—and they are right to stay. For SNCC's Black Panther perspective is simultaneously utopian and reactionary—the former for the by now obvious reason that one-tenth of the population cannot accomplish much by itself, the latter because such a party would remove Negroes from the main area of political struggle in this country (particularly in the one-party South, where the decisive battles are fought out in Democratic primaries), and would give priority to the issue of race precisely at a time when the fundamental questions facing the Negro and American society alike

[1]See "The Negroes Enter Southern Politics" by Pat Watters, *Dissent,* July–August 1966.

are economic and social. It is no accident that the two main proponents of "black power," Carmichael and McKissick, should now be
co-sponsoring a conference with Adam Clayton Powell and Elijah
Muhammad, and that the leaders of New York CORE should recently
have supported the machine candidate for Surrogate—because he was
the choice of a Negro boss—rather than the candidate of the reform
movement. By contrast, Martin Luther King is working in Chicago
with the Industrial Union Department of the AFL-CIO and with
religious groups in a coalition which, if successful, will mean the end or
at least the weakening of the Daley-Dawson machine.

The winning of the right of Negroes to vote in the South insures
the eventual transformation of the Democratic party, now controlled
primarily by Northern machine politicians and Southern Dixiecrats.
The Negro vote will eliminate the Dixiecrats from the party and from
Congress, which means that the crucial question facing us today is who
will replace them in the South. Unless civil-rights leaders (in such
towns as Jackson, Mississippi; Birmingham, Alabama; and even to a
certain extent Atlanta) can organize grass-roots clubs whose members
will have a genuine political voice, the Dixiecrats might well be
succeeded by black moderates and black Southern-style machine politicians, who would do little to push for needed legislation in Congress
and little to improve local conditions in the South. While I myself
would prefer Negro machines to a situation in which Negroes have no
power at all, it seems to me that there is a better alternative today—a
liberal-labor-civil rights coalition which would work to make the
Democratic party truly responsive to the aspirations of the poor, and
which would develop support for programs (specifically those outlined
in A. Philip Randolph's $100 billion Freedom Budget) aimed at the
reconstruction of American society in the interests of greater social
justice. The advocates of "black power" have no such programs in
mind; what they are in fact arguing for (perhaps unconsciously) is the
creation of a *new black establishment.*

Nor, it might be added, are they leading the Negro people along
the same road which they imagine immigrant groups traveled so
successfully in the past. Proponents of "black power"—accepting a
historical myth perpetrated by moderates—like to say that the Irish
and the Jews and the Italians, by sticking together and demanding their
share, finally won enough power to overcome their initial disabilities.
But the truth is that it was through alliances with other groups (in
political machines or as part of the trade-union movement) that the
Irish and the Jews and the Italians acquired the power to win their
rightful place in American society. They did not "pull themselves up by
their own bootstraps"—no group in American society has ever done
so; and they most certainly did not make isolation their primary tactic.
In some quarters, "black power" connotes not an effort to increase the
number of Negroes in elective office but rather a repudiation of

non-violence in favor of Negro "self-defense." Actually this is a false issue, since no one has ever argued that Negroes should not defend themselves as individuals from attack.[2] Non-violence has been advocated as a *tactic* for organized demonstrations in a society where Negroes are a minority and where the majority controls the police. Proponents of non-violence do not, for example, deny that James Meredith has the right to carry a gun for protection when he visits his mother in Mississippi; what they question is the wisdom of his carrying a gun while participating in a demonstration.

There is, as well, a tactical side to the new emphasis on "self-defense" and the suggestion that non-violence be abandoned. The reasoning here is that turning the other cheek is not the way to win respect, and that only if the Negro succeeds in frightening the white man will the white man begin taking him seriously. The trouble with this reasoning is that it fails to recognize that fear is more likely to bring hostility to the surface than respect; and far from prodding the "white power structure" into action, the new militant leadership, by raising the slogan of black power and lowering the banner of non-violence, has obscured the moral issue facing this nation, and permitted the President and Vice President to lecture us about "racism in reverse" instead of proposing more meaningful programs for dealing with the problems of unemployment, housing, and education.

"Black power" is, of course, a somewhat nationalistic slogan and its sudden rise to popularity among Negroes signifies a concomitant rise in nationalist sentiment (Malcolm X's autobiography is quoted nowadays in Grenada, Mississippi as well as in Harlem). We have seen such nationalistic turns and withdrawals back into the ghetto before, and when we look at the conditions which brought them about, we find that they have much in common with the conditions of Negro life at the present moment: conditions which lead to despair over the goal of integration and to the belief that the ghetto will last forever.

It may, in the light of the many juridical and legislative victories which have been achieved in the past few years, seem strange that despair should be so widespread among Negroes today. But anyone to whom it seems strange should reflect on the fact that despite these victories *Negroes today are in worse economic shape, live in worse slums, and attend more highly segregated schools than in 1954* Thus—to recite the appalling, and appallingly familiar, statistical litany once again—more Negroes are unemployed today than in 1954; the gap between the wages of the Negro worker and the white worker is

---

[2]As far back as 1934, A. Philip Randolph, Walter White, then executive secretary of the NAACP, Lester Granger, then executive director of the Urban League, and I joined a committee to try to save the life of Odell Waller. Waller, a sharecropper, had murdered his white boss in self-defense.

wider; while the unemployment rate among white youths is decreasing, the rate among Negro youths has increased to *32 percent* (and among Negro girls the rise is even more startling). Even the one gain which has been registered, a decrease in the unemployment rate among Negro adults, is deceptive, for it represents men who have been called back to work after a period of being laid off. In any event, unemployment among Negro men is still twice that of whites, and no new jobs have been created.

So too with housing, which is deteriorating in the North (and yet the housing provisions of the 1966 civil-rights bill are weaker than the antidiscrimination laws in several states which contain the worst ghettos even with these laws on their books). And so too with schools: according to figures issued recently by the Department of Health, Education and Welfare, 65 percent of first-grade Negro students in this country attend schools that are from 90 to 100 percent black. (If in 1954, when the Supreme Court handed down the desegregation decision, you had been the Negro parent of a first-grade child, the chances are that this past June you would have attended that child's graduation from a segregated high school.)

To put all this in the simplest and most concrete terms: the day-to-day lot of the ghetto Negro has not been improved by the various judicial and legislative measures of the past decade.

Negroes are thus in a situation similar to that of the turn of the century, when Booker T. Washington advised them to "cast down their buckets" (that is to say, accommodate to segregation and disenfranchisement) and when even his leading opponent, W. E. B. Du Bois, was forced to advocate the development of a group economy in place of the direct-action boycotts, general strikes, and protest techniques which had been used in the 1880s, before the enactment of the Jim-Crow laws. For all their differences, both Washington and Du Bois then found it impossible to believe that Negroes could ever be integrated into American society, and each in his own way therefore counseled withdrawal into the ghetto, self-help, and economic self-determination.

World War I aroused new hope in Negroes that the rights removed at the turn of the century would be restored. More than 360,000 Negroes entered military service and went overseas; many left the South seeking the good life in the North and hoping to share in the temporary prosperity created by the war. But all these hopes were quickly smashed at the end of the fighting. In the first year following the war, more than seventy Negroes were lynched, and during the last six months of that year, there were some twenty-four riots throughout America. White mobs took over whole cities, flogging, burning, shooting, and torturing at will, and when Negroes tried to defend themselves, the violence only increased. Along with this, Negroes were excluded from unions and pushed out of jobs they had won during the war, including federal jobs.

In the course of this period of dashed hope and spreading segregation—the same period, incidentally, when a reorganized Ku Klux Klan was achieving a membership which was to reach into the millions—the largest mass movement ever to take root among working-class Negroes, Marcus Garvey's "Back to Africa" movement, was born. "Buy Black" became a slogan in the ghettos; faith in integration was virtually snuffed out in the Negro community until the 1930s when the CIO reawakened the old dream of a Negro-labor alliance by announcing a policy of non-discrimination and when the New Deal admitted Negroes into relief programs, WPA jobs, and public housing. No sooner did jobs begin to open up and Negroes begin to be welcomed into mainstream organizations than "Buy Black" campaigns gave way to "Don't Buy Where You Can't Work" movements. A. Philip Randolph was able to organize a massive March on Washington demanding a wartime FEPC; CORE was born and with it the non-violent sit-in technique; the NAACP succeeded in putting an end to the white primaries in 1944. Altogether, World War II was a period of hope for Negroes, and the economic progress they made through wartime industry continued steadily until about 1948 and remained stable for a time. Meanwhile, the non-violent movement of the 1950s and 60s achieved the desegregation of public accommodations and established the right to vote.

Yet at the end of this long fight, the Southern Negro is too poor to use those integrated facilities and too intimidated and disorganized to use the vote to maximum advantage, while the economic position of the Northern Negro deteriorates rapidly.

The promise of meaningful work and decent wages once held out by the anti-poverty programs has not been fulfilled. Because there has been a lack of the necessary funds, the program has in many cases been reduced to wrangling for positions on boards or for lucrative staff jobs. Negro professionals working for the program have earned handsome salaries—ranging from $14- to $25,000—while young boys have been asked to plant trees at $1.25 an hour. Nor have the Job Corps camps made a significant dent in unemployment among Negro youths; indeed, the main beneficiaries of this program seem to be the private companies who are contracted to set up the camps.

Then there is the war in Vietnam, which poses many ironies for the Negro community. On the one hand, Negroes are bitterly aware of the fact that more and more money is being spent on the war, while the anit-poverty program is being cut; on the other hand, Negro youths are enlisting in great numbers, as though to say that it is worth the risk of being killed to learn a trade, to leave a dead-end situation, and to join the only institution in this society which seems really to be integrated.

The youths who rioted in Watts, Cleveland, Omaha, Chicago, and Portland are the members of a truly hopeless and lost generation. They can see the alien world of affluence unfold before them on the TV screen. But they have already failed in their inferior segregated schools. Their grandfathers were sharecroppers, their grandmothers were domestics, and their mothers are domestics too. Many have never met their fathers. Mistreated by the local storekeeper, suspected by the policeman on the beat, disliked by their teachers, they cannot stand more failures and would rather retreat into the world of heroin than risk looking for a job downtown or having their friends see them push a rack in the garment district. Floyd McKissick and Stokely Carmichael may accuse Roy Wilkins of being out of touch with the Negro ghetto, but nothing more clearly demonstrates their own alienation from ghetto youth than their repeated exhortations to these young men to oppose the Vietnam war when so many of them tragically see it as their only way out. Yet there is no need to labor the significance of the fact that the rice fields of Vietnam and the Green Berets have more to offer a Negro boy than the streets of Mississippi or the towns of Alabama or 125th Street in New York.

The Vietnam war is also partly responsible for the growing disillusion with non-violence among Negroes. The ghetto Negro does not in general ask whether the United States is right or wrong to be in Southeast Asia. He does, however, wonder why he is exhorted to non-violence when the United States has been waging a fantastically brutal war, and it puzzles him to be told that he must turn the other cheek in our own South while we must fight for freedom in South Vietnam.

Thus, as in roughly similar circumstances in the past—circumstances, I repeat, which in the aggregate foster the belief that the ghetto is destined to last forever—Negroes are once again turning to nationalistic slogans, with "black power" affording the same emotional release as "Back to Africa" and "Buy Black" did in earlier periods of frustration and hopelessness. This is not only the case with the ordinary Negro in the ghetto; it is also the case with leaders like McKissick and Carmichael, neither of whom began as a nationalist or was at first cynical about the possibilities of integration.[3] It took countless beatings and 24 jailings—that, and the absence of strong and continual support from the liberal community—to persuade Carmichael that his earlier faith in coalition politics was mistaken, that nothing

---

[3] On Carmichael's background, see "Two for SNCC" by Robert Penn Warren in the *Commentary*, April 1965—Ed.

was to be gained from working with whites, and that an alliance with the black nationalists was desirable. In the areas of the South where SNCC has been working so nobly, implementation of the Civil Rights Act of 1964 and 1965 has been slow and ineffective. Negroes in many rural areas cannot walk into the courthouse and register to vote. Despite the voting-rights bill, they must file complaints and the Justice Department must be called to send federal registrars. Nor do children attend integrated schools as a matter of course. There, too, complaints must be filed and the Department of Health, Education and Welfare must be notified. Neither department has been doing an effective job of enforcing the bills. The feeling of isolation increases among SNCC workers as each legislative victory turns out to be only a token victory—significant on the national level, but not affecting the day-to-day lives of Negroes. Carmichael and his colleagues are wrong in refusing to support the 1966 bill, but one can understand why they feel as they do.

It is, in short, the growing conviction that the Negroes cannot win—a conviction with much grounding in experience—which accounts for the new popularity of "black power." So far as the ghetto Negro is concerned, this conviction expresses itself in hostility first toward the people closest to him who have held out the most promise and failed to deliver (Martin Luther King, Roy Wilkins, etc.), then toward those who have proclaimed themselves his friends (the liberals and the labor movement), and finally toward the only oppressors he can see (the local storekeeper and the policeman on the corner). On the leadership level, the conviction that the Negroes cannot win takes other forms, principally the adoption of what I have called a "no-win" policy. Why bother with programs when their enactment results only in "sham"? Why concern ourselves with the image of the movement when nothing significant has been gained for all the sacrifices made by SNCC and CORE? Why compromise with reluctant white allies when nothing of consequence can be achieved anyway? Why indeed have anything to do with whites at all?

On this last point, it is extremely important for white liberals to understand—as, one gathers from their references to "racism in reverse," the President and the Vice President of the United States do not—that there is all the difference in the world between saying, "If you don't want me, I don't want you" (which is what some proponents of "black power" have in effect been saying) and the statement, "Whatever you do, I don't want you" (which is what racism declares). It is, in other words, both absurd and immoral to equate the despairing response of the victim with the contemptuous assertion of the oppressor. It would, moreover, be tragic if white liberals allowed verbal hostility on the part of Negroes to drive them out of the movement or to curtail their support for civil rights. The issue was injustice before "black power" became popular, and the issue is still injustice.

In any event, even if "black power" had not emerged as a slogan, problems would have arisen in the relation between whites and Negroes in the civil-rights movement. In the North, it was inevitable that Negroes would eventually wish to run their own movement and would rebel against the presence of whites in positions of leadership as yet another sign of white supremacy. In the South, the well-intentioned white volunteer had the cards stacked against him from the beginning. Not only could he leave the struggle any time he chose to do so, but a higher value was set on his safety by the press and the government— apparent in the differing degrees of excitement generated by the imprisonment or murder of whites and Negroes. The white person's importance to the movement in the South was thus an ironic outgrowth of racism and was therefore bound to create resentment.

But again: however understandable all this may be as a response to objective conditions and to the seeming irrelevance of so many hard-won victories to the day-to-day life of the mass of Negroes, the fact remains that the quasi-nationalist sentiments and "no-win" policy lying behind the slogan of "black power" do no service to the Negro. Some nationalist emotion is, of course, inevitable, and "black power" must be seen as part of the psychological rejection of white supremacy, part of the rebellion against the stereotypes which have been ascribed to Negroes for three hundred years. Nevertheless, pride, confidence, and a new identity cannot be won by glorifying blackness or attacking whites; they can only come from meaningful action, from good jobs, and from real victories such as were achieved on the streets of Montgomery, Birmingham, and Selma. When SNCC and CORE went into the South, they awakened the country, but now they emerge isolated and demoralized, shouting a slogan that may afford a momentary satisfaction but that is calculated to destroy them and their movement. Already their frustrated call is being answered with counter-demands for law and order and with opposition to police-review boards. Already they have diverted the entire civil-rights movement from the hard task of developing strategies to realign the major parties of this country, and embroiled it in a debate that can only lead more and more to politics by frustration.

On the other side, however—the more important side, let it be said—it is the business of those who reject the negative aspects of "black power" not to preach but to act. Some weeks ago President Johnson, speaking at Fort Campbell, Kentucky, asserted that riots impeded reform, created fear, and antagonized the Negro's traditional friends. Mr. Johnson, according to the New York *Times,* expressed sympathy for the plight of the poor, the jobless, and the ill-housed. The government, he noted, has been working to relieve their circumstances, but "all this takes time."

One cannot argue with the President's position that riots are destructive or that they frighten away allies. Nor can one find fault with his sympathy for the plight of the poor; surely the poor need sympathy. But one can question whether the government has been working seriously enough to eliminate the conditions which lead to frustration-politics and riots. The President's very words, "all this takes time," will be understood by the poor for precisely what they are—an excuse instead of a real program, a cover-up for the failure to establish real priorities, and an indication that the administration has no real commitment to create new jobs, better housing, and integrated schools.

For the truth is that it need only take ten years to eliminate poverty —ten years and the $100 billion Freedom Budget recently proposed by A. Philip Randolph. In his introduction to the budget (which was drawn up in consultation with the nation's leading economists, and which will be published later this month), Mr. Randolph points out: "The programs urged in the Freedom Budget attack all of the major causes of poverty—unemployment and underemployment, substandard pay, inadequate social insurance and welfare payments to those who cannot or should not be employed; bad housing; deficiencies in health services, education, and training; and fiscal and monetary policies which tend to redistribute income regressively rather than progressively. The Freedom Budget leaves no room for discrimination in any form because its programs are addressed to all who need more opportunity and improved incomes and living standards, not to just some of them."

The legislative precedent Mr. Randolph has in mind is the 1945 Full Employment bill. This bill—conceived in its original form by Roosevelt to prevent a postwar depression—would have made it public policy for the government to step in if the private economy could not provide enough employment. As passed finally by Congress in 1946, with many of its teeth removed, the bill had the result of preventing the Negro worker, who had finally reached a pay level about 55 percent that of the white wage, from making any further progress in closing that discriminatory gap; and instead, he was pushed back by the chronically high unemployment rates of the 50s. Had the original bill been passed, the public sector of our economy would have been able to insure fair and full employment. Today, with the spiralling thrust of automation, it is even more imperative that we have a legally binding commitment to this goal.

Let me interject a word here to those who say that Negroes are asking for another handout and are refusing to help themselves. From the end of the 19th century up to the last generation, the United States absorbed and provided economic opportunity for tens of millions of immigrants. These people were usually uneducated and a good many could not speak English. They had nothing but their hard work to offer and they labored long hours, often in miserable sweatshops and unsafe mines. Yet in a burgeoning economy with a need for unskilled labor, they were able to find jobs, and as industrialization proceeded, they were gradually able to move up the ladder to greater skills. Negroes who have been driven off the farm into a city life for which they are not prepared and who have entered an economy in which there is less and less need for unskilled labor, cannot be compared with these immigrants of old. The tenements which were jammed by newcomers were way-stations of hope; the ghettos of today have become dead-ends of despair. Yet just as the older generation of immigrants—in its most decisive act of self-help—organized the trade-union movement and then in alliance with many middle-class elements went on to improve its own lot and the condition of American society generally, so the Negro of today is struggling to go beyond the gains of the past and, in alliance with liberals and labor, to guarantee full and fair employment to all Americans.

Mr. Randolph's Freedom Budget not only rests on the Employment Act of 1946, but on a precedent set by Harry Truman when he believed freedom was threatened in Europe. In 1947, the Marshall Plan was put into effect and 3 percent of the gross national product was spent in foreign aid. If we were to allocate a similar proportion of our GNP to destroy the economic and social consequences of racism and poverty at home today, it might mean spending more than 20 billion dollars a year, although I think it quite possible that we can fulfill these goals with a much smaller sum. It would be intolerable, however, if our plan for domestic social reform were less audacious and less far-reaching than our international programs of a generation ago.

We must see, therefore, in the current debate over "black power," a fantastic challenge to American society to live up to its proclaimed principles in the area of race by transforming itself so that all men may live equally and under justice. We must see to it that in rejecting "black power," we do not also reject the principle of Negro equality. Those people who would use the current debate and/or the riots to abandon the civil-rights movement leave us no choice but to question their original motivation.

If anything, the next period will be more serious and difficult than the preceding ones. It is much easier to establish the Negro's right to sit at a Woolworth's counter than to fight for an integrated community. It takes very little imagination to understand that the Negro should have the right to vote, but it demands much creativity, patience, and political stamina to plan, develop, and implement programs and priorities. It is one thing to organize sentiment behind laws that do not disturb consensus politics, and quite another to win battles for the redistribution of wealth. Many people who marched in Selma are not prepared to support a bill for a $2.00 minimum wage, to say nothing of supporting a redefinition of work or a guaranteed annual income.

It is here that we who advocate coalitions and integration and who object to the "black power" concept have a massive job to do. We must see to it that the liberal-labor-civil rights coalition is maintained and, indeed, strengthened so that it can fight effectively for a Freedom Budget. We are responsible for the growth of the "black power" concept because we have not used our own power to insure the full implementation of the bills whose passage we were strong enough to win, and we have not mounted the necessary campaign for winning a decent minimum wage and extended benefits. "Black power" is a slogan directed primarily against liberals by those who once counted liberals among their closest friends. It is up to the liberal movement to prove that coalition and integration are better alternatives.

8 Protest, Power, and the Future of Politics*

CAREY McWILLIAMS

A preoccupation with power—black power, student power, flower power, poor power, "the power structure"—is the most striking aspect of the American political scene at the moment. Oddly enough, obsession with power goes hand in hand with a fear of power. Some of the New Left groups that talk the toughest about power are extremely reluctant to see power operate in institutional form; within their own organizations, they shun "hierarchies" and formally structured relations of authority. What the preoccupation with power reflects, essentially, is a deep-seated, pervasive feeling of powerlessness. The feeling is not restricted to particular groups; most citizens, a majority perhaps, are bedeviled by it. "A feeling of having no choice," Mary McCarthy has noticed, "is becoming more and more widespread in American life."

So intense is the feeling of powerlessness that it has given rise to "anti-movements" and "anti-politics." Instead of building new, strong,

*Reprinted by permission of the author and publisher from *The Nation*, January 15, 1968.

viable organizations, through which to exercise political power, the tendency—at least on the Left—has been to move in the reverse direction, that is, to reject the instruments of politics. Discussion has been superseded by "uproar," debate by demonstrations, dialogue by confrontation, civil disobedience by overt resistance. Often in the past, young voters have bade "farewell to reform" and then turned to radical politics; this time they have swung toward no politics at all. The idea of government by and through elected representatives is seriously questioned by some and indignantly rejected by others. The very process of politics has come under direct attack from young and old alike.

Apart from increasing evidence of this active disaffection, there is among those who have by no means despaired of politics a widespread anxiety about what Walter Lippmann has called "the rot of the American political system." On November 10, NBC presented an analysis of voter attitudes on the 1968 election, and found that most voters had little faith that any major candidate for the Presidency could master either of the two major problems we face (war and race), and worse, seemed to feel that the electorate was being denied live options on most issues. The survey indicated "a stunning lack of confidence in the President and in his political opponents." A mountain of supporting evidence might be cited. Yet despite the active disaffection and the mounting general concern, little attention has been focused on what it is that accounts basically for the malfunctioning of the political system. The problem has two aspects. Power has been concentrated in our society in such a way, and to such a degree, that normal political processes are perhaps no longer able to cope with it. But one can't be sure of that because if certain specific weaknesses in the political system not directly related to the concentration of power, were remedied (at the moment they are not widely recognized, much less discussed) the reform might go far to remove the "rot" from the system. (In this paragraph I have drawn on a most interesting paper, "Social and Psychological Preparation for War," presented by Jules Henry at the Conference on Dialectics of Liberation, London, July 1967.)

On the first aspect, that of power, Thomas C. Cochran, the economic historian, has reminded us that "the modern centralized, militarized, and welfare-directed state" did not come into being overnight; it is the result of a complex internal evolution. Not consciously planned, it is a response to fears: first of internal economic collapse; second of external dangers and "enemies." The New Deal, a war against impending economic collapse, was fought as any war is fought. Emergency agencies, with extraordinary powers, came into being overnight; crash programs were rushed into motion; executive decisions took precedence over cumbersome legislative processes; and more and more power was vested in the Presidency. At the same time, and as part of the same process, economic power was increasingly concentrated. On the eve of World War II, a study made by a group including six members of President Roosevelt's Cabinet ("The Structure of the American Economy," 1939), expressed, even then, growing alarm at the political consequences of tightly held economic power.

The concentration of power became much tighter after we entered World War II. Under the stress of rapid mobilization, a remarkable fusion of economic and political power took place; more accurately, perhaps, a fusion of economic and administrative or Executive power. This had been true also in World War I, but unlike the procedure after 1918, the war-making machine of World War II was never fully dismantled. The swift onset of the cold war, then the fighting in Korea and Vietnam, set the pattern for a permanent war economy. The rapid pace of military technology, which began to diverge sharply from civilian advances, created a political rationale for continuous research and improvement in weapons systems and the like. Nuclear weapons and virtually instantaneous delivery systems authorized an ever-larger permanent military establishment; in any future war, it was said, there would be "no time to mobilize." In the past, industries had "converted" to war production and then "reconverted" to peacetime production. After 1945 new defense industries came into being specifically to manufacture military hardware. At the same time the magnitude of the military budget revolutionized government finance. Defense-related expenditures will this year probably exceed $100 billion. In a recent survey, the AP referred to the Pentagon as wielding "the mightiest concentration of economic power in the world today."

In his famous farewell address, General Eisenhower expressed misgivings about our ability to control "the military-industrial complex" by normal political processes. More recently, the same concern has been more specifically voiced by others. "The huge size of military budgets," said Dr. Arthur F. Burns, "and incomplete disclosure concerning their management, carry with them the dangers of political abuse"—as by building military stockpiles of certain raw materials to maintain price levels during periods of overproduction or of stepping up defense spending as an offset to declining employment. Dr. Charles J. Hitch, an expert on defense planning, now president of the University of California, has made a similar observation: "Certainly the defense budget is a large and powerful tool for the government, and one is tempted to seek its uses to solve an array of problems. . . . Defense spending has become a substantial and more or less normal factor in the economic reckoning of many American businesses."

Senator Fulbright spoke most soberly on this point in the Senate on December 13:

More and more our economy, our government and our universities are adapting themselves to the requirements of continuing war—total war, limited war and cold war. The struggle against militarism into which we were drawn twenty-six years ago has become permanent, and for the sake of conducting it, we are making ourselves into a militarized society . . . For all the inadvertency of its creation and the innocent intentions of its participants, it [the military-industrial-academic complex] has become a powerful new force for the perpetuation of foreign military commitments, for the introduction and expansion of expensive weapons systems and, as a result, for the militarization of large segments of our national life. Most interest groups are counterbalanced by other interest groups, but the defense complex is so much larger than any other that there is no effective counterweight to it except concern as to its impact on the part of some of our citizens and a few of our leaders, none of whom have material incentive to offer.

For this reason, the defense complex has not been challenged by either party; in fact both have been about equally responsible for it. But it is doubtful that the growth of the complex could have been arrested even if one of the major parties had been willing to incur the risk of such a stand. And it is doubtful today that the Republican Party can bring itself to challenge the disastrous course of present policies, not because it is blind to the dangers or fails to appreciate the political possibilities in capitalizing on the existing discontent, but because power is now so bipartisan in structure that the opposition party cannot, apparently, muster the resources or the will to make the effort. James Reston notes, moreover, that the powerful Eastern Establishment in the GOP is by no means unanimously displeased with Johnson and his policies.

As the militarization of the society has proceeded, the power of the Congress relative to the Presidency has steadily declined. The recent report of the Senate Foreign Relations Committee on "National Commitments" (November 20) points out that the last twenty years have seen a nearly complete reversal of the positions of the Executive and legislative branches in the area of foreign affairs. Dr. Ruhl Bartlett, of the Fletcher School of Law and Diplomacy, told the committee that "the greatest danger to democracy in the United States and to the freedom of its people and to their welfare—as far as foreign affairs are concerned—is the erosion of legislative authority and oversight and the growth of a vast pyramid of centralized power in the Executive branch of the government." Dr. Edgar Eugene Robinson of Stanford suggested in a recent speech that the acquisition by the President of immense power over foreign affairs during the last twenty years means that the Constitution is outdated. "There is no possibility," he says, "of real change in the President's foreign policy except by removal . . . by death, resignation, impeachment or defeat at the polls." What in his view makes this development particularly dangerous is the dexterity with which the President can fuse two constitutional functions: his role as commander in chief and his responsibility for the conduct of foreign affairs. Once war has become an instrument of national policy, it is hard to tell which role a President is playing. If his foreign policy is challenged, he can always assert his powers as commander in chief, and these powers are almost unlimited. (See, also, Sen. Frank Church's speech, October 29, on "President and Congress in Foreign Policy: The Threat to Constitutional Government.")

The process by which political and economic power have been concentrated through expansion of the war-making machine has been hastened by a series of postwar "revolutions": the organizational revolution, the scientific and technological revolution, the cybernetic revolution and, most notably, the communications revolution. As Dr. Robinson also pointed out, the communications revolution has made it possible for a new Presidential order, decision or proclamation to be carried instantaneously by radio and television. "Consequently, the effectiveness of that action is amplified millions of times by the miracle of swift communication."

Over the past twenty years the power of appropriation, which is supposed to be the bedrock of Congressional control, has been seriously eroded. A study of how the military budget has been handled in successive Congresses since the end of World War II would demonstrate that it is now firmly controlled by the Executive. And the military budget is today so immense, particularly if expenditures for NASA and the AEC are included, that the power to manipulate it conveys, as a side effect, power to shape the whole national budget.

The fallacy in the guns-and-butter proposition, as Dr. Burns has pointed out, is that "Financial transactions and the price system are merely mechanisms for putting a nation's resources to work and for distributing what is produced among people and their government. The resources that we devote to national defense are not available for making consumer goods or for adding to the stock of industrial equipment or for public uses in the sphere of education, health, or urban development. To the extent that we allocate labor, materials, and capital to national defense, we cannot satisfy our desires for other things. . . . Bombs or missiles add nothing to a nation's capacity to produce, while new equipment serves to augment production in the future. The real cost of the defense sector consists, therefore, not only of the civilian goods and services that are currently foregone on its account; it includes also an element of growth that could have been achieved through larger investment in human or business capital." In fact a former member of President Eisenhower's Council of Economic Advisers, Dr. Paul McCracken, has expressed the opinion that the Executive's seizure of decision-making has resulted in a federal budget whose expenditures, in the technical sense, are now out of control.

Any erosion of the power of Congress is an erosion of the power of the people. Given a society in which for a period of twenty years—almost the span of a generation—the real power of decision has been increasingly ceded to the President, it is not hard to account for the prevalent sense of "powerlessness." Just as the ghetto dweller feels that he lives in "occupied territory," so many people come to feel that they have been "displaced" from their role as electors. A force which they cannot control or directly influence has taken charge of their lives and destinies. "There are many signs," writes A. H. Halsey (*New Society,* October 26), "from love-ins in the Haight-Ashbury district of San Francisco to the 'privitization' of affluent workers . . . that a theory of the impotence of politics is being accepted." If the country has in fact been "occupied" by a power not sanctioned by the Constitution, then it must be "liberated." But given the degree to which power has been concentrated, can the direction of policy be reversed by conventional political means? In such a situation, public protests become increasingly directed against the symbols of power, and that has the effect of diverting energies from the political process and, at the same time, discrediting it.

In the nature of things, it is difficult for "anti-movements" to cooperate with movements—of any kind. The objectives, the sense of tactics, the style of action, are different or divergent. That some of the "anti-movements" share with the infinitely larger movement of "concerned" and "dissatisfied" citizens the short-term objective of stopping the war does not mean that they see the war in the same terms or that they agree on other objectives. The "anti-movement" of Negro nationalists does not even share the short-term objective of stopping the war (at least, it is not for them a priority objective). And, to complicate matters, the larger movement is itself not well organized and lacks sufficient program.

By and large, "anti-movements" are not elated when a dove defeats a hawk; they have lost confidence in the political process as it now exists—not without reason—and they want to discredit it, the better, no doubt, to fill the political vacuum with a new politics. If the "anti-movements" openly espoused revolutionary objectives, then a measure of "parallel" politics might be possible (it may still be, depending on developments). But as of now, the Black Nationalists and the New Activists, as William Appleman Williams has observed, "have no vision of a Socialist commonwealth, let alone even the beginnings of serious proposals to create and govern such a society." They seem less concerned with the concentration of power, and the growing political vacuum which could set the stage for an American fascism, than with the hateful discrepancy between liberal ideals and liberal practice. They give little thought to the possibility that something about the functioning of a capitalist economy may lead to the concentration of power. The heroes of the "anti-movements" are Debray and Che Guevara, not Gramsci who thought that the proper place to find those who aspired to lead revolutionary movements was in the reading rooms of public libraries. Because they are not really concerned with the *political* consequences of particular protests and demonstrations, they discount polls which show that certain recent demonstrations have stimulated a reaction and strengthened the President's hand. This, of course, is a logical attitude for those who have lost confidence in the political process. But it carries a distressing echo of the "social fascism" line that the Communist Party pursued in the early 1930s.

However, the "anti-movements" have had some highly desirable political consequences. The stress on personal commitment, on values, on life styles, the exposure of liberal pretense, have released new energies, focused attention on particular issues, and pointed up the relation between morality and politics. One of the only means whereby individuals can make what they think and feel relevant in a society in which power is highly concentrated is to stress the morality—or immorality—of public policies. But it is precisely in such a period that as Iris Murdoch has noted, "political moralizing comes to be thought of as an idle idealism, a sort of utopianizing which is just a relief from looking at unpleasant facts." This was the position into which many cold-war liberals were driven, or into which they retreated, when they decided that there was little point in attempting to bring moral judgments to bear in the field of foreign policy. Today many of these same individuals have recoiled in horror from the consequences of the "crackpot realism" of Dulles and Acheson and Rusk. For this shift in attitude, the "anti-movements" are entitled to some credit. But if we are to answer the cynic in ourselves, moral judgments, as Miss Murdoch stresses, must be *realistic enough* to be political judgments as well. For the ultimate cynicism is to conclude that politics is a futile game. Such a conclusion severs the relation between morality and politics. To stress the immorality of the war in Vietnam, while rejecting the possibility of stopping it *by political means,* is self-defeating. Before anyone declared politics obsolete, he should at least try to identify the rot which has brought such discredit upon the institution.

Perhaps the most important single cause of the rot has been adherence to a bipartisan foreign policy. Politics does *not* stop at the water's edge. In today's world, one might well say that it begins there. The American party system had its origins in a dispute over foreign policy. The bipartisan concept dates from Roosevelt's determination to secure ratification of the UN charter by obtaining Republican support in advance. But the cold war came along almost before the Charter had been ratified, and what had been projected as a temporary expedient crystallized as a national dogma. The policy that resulted has been one of preserving the *status quo,* of pushing American economic expansion throughout the world under cover of a rigid "anti-Communist" ideology. At the same time the fear of communism—in part real, in part concocted—made it relatively easy to wrest cold-war appropriations from Congress, particularly military appropriations. Since the major interest groups all benefited directly or indirectly—if not evenly—they became adherents to bipartisan cold-war policies and the country, enjoying the prolonged boom, acquiesced.

Given the generally conservative cast of successive postwar Congresses, the emphasis on military spending in support of mostly reactionary cold-war policies won majority bipartisan support. For one thing, it was a way of keeping domestic spending for welfare and other purposes under control. Then, as military spending increased, the influence of the military on foreign policy also increased, as did the power of the President. The public hearings which the Senate Foreign Relations Committee staged in 1966 are generally conceded to represent the first significant attempt by that committee in the postwar period to regain some of the power it once possessed. Not to debate foreign policy assumptions and alternatives was, in today's world, to forgo significant debate on domestic issues as well. It was as though both parties had agreed to a twenty-year moratorium on significant politics. Today the rot that this moratorium produced is all too evident.

But there are signs—and they are multiplying—that the bipartisan consensus is breaking up. Senator Morton's dramatic announcement last summer—"I was wrong. Our country has been painted into a corner out there. There's going to have to be a change"—was an event of major political importance. Since then, as Don Oberdorfer points out in *The New York Times Magazine* (December 17), the "wobble" on Capitol Hill has become increasingly evident. "The summer and fall of 1967 have been a time of switching . . . a scurrying in many directions, in search of a stance that took account of the growing distaste for the war." The splendid spadework on Vietnam undertaken by a 29-year-old freshman Republican, Rep. Donald W. Riegle, Jr., and some of his colleagues is a sign that the twenty-year infatuation with bipartisan cold-war policies is beginning to lose its appeal to

Republicans. Never before have so many dissenting voices begun to link foreign affairs with domestic politics (Dr. Martin Luther King is an example), which suggests that in the end the crisis in domestic affairs will force a reconsideration of foreign policy. But even as the ferment spreads, efforts are made to reimpose the "consensus," to choke off partisan debate before it gets started. General Eisenhower has said that any Republican who departs from the official line on Vietnam "will have me to contend with. . . . That's one of the few things that would start me off on a series of stump speeches across the nation"—a statement not calculated to encourage the Republicans to offer an alternative policy and program. However, increasing numbers of Republicans continue to "wobble."

Adherence to a bipartisan foreign policy was made all the easier when the Left collapsed after World War II. By Left, I mean all those elements that might have been disposed to challenge the assumptions on which the coldwar policy rested. Twenty years of systematic redbaiting, conducted not by private but by government agencies, and financed by public funds, gravely distorted the political spectrum; it shifted the center of gravity in both parties well to the right. The Left, in the European sense, was never strong here; during the McCarthy phase it ceased to exist. Nor was this merely a matter of disrupting certain organizations; currents of "undesirable" critical opinion were driven underground, individuals censored their own thoughts, organizations purged their own ranks.

The collapse of the old Left in the postwar period meant that the liberals of the Democratic Party were subject to no pressure or competition except from conservative or right-wing sources (much the same state of affairs prevailed in the trade union movement). The official liberalism of the Democratic Party, which was really "the new conservatism," lived off the store of ideas that had been developed in the 1930s. It responded to new issues and new problems by offering "more of the same," that is, extending the programs of the New Deal.

More important, the collapse of the Left has deprived us all of a comprehensive critique of American society, its values, its direction, its performance. The New Deal was not based on any carefully thought-out assumptions; its programs were mostly improvisations. The continued failure of the liberal Democrats to provide a serious alternative to the "reformism" of the early progressive movement had the effect of minimizing ideological differences of all kinds, including those between Democrats and Republicans. Both parties professed the same values, the same purposes, essentially the same policies. Both parties have accepted the ideology of "free enterprise," joined in the "American celebration," and endorsed the objectives of an expansionist foreign policy. Both have pushed the new American imperium. No partisan challenge has been offered to the Administration's assertion of a right of unilateral military intervention wherever it feels that vital "interests" have been threatened.

The collapse of the Left is an essential key to explaining the rot because the absence of ideological differences has been the historic weakness of American politics. Not only has the American Left contributed to this weakness; the lack of a consistent ideological drive explains the feebleness of the Left itself. "The American Left," as Michael Davie points out, "has always been more eccentric than effective. In Europe, men have had to battle for the establishment of their basic rights, and have needed a theory of drastic social change to go to war with." But not here. As Tom Hayden, one of the leaders of the New Left observes: "How *do* you act as a revolutionary against a nation-state that celebrates your values while betraying their substance?" Even in the fiercest American struggles, everyone of major political importance has believed in the same basic things. "The mainstream of the American political tradition," to quote Davie again, "thus flows between firm banks (though it is not yet clear whether they can contain the Negro revolution) and features a steady belief in the sanctity of private property, the importance of economic individualism, and the unifying influence of greed. . . . Outside Portugal, Marx has had less influence in the United States than on any country in the Western world. . . . The most wretched victims of the American system [are kept] safely in the mainstream of the American political tradition— convinced that only luck or geography, never the system itself, stand between them and all-American prosperity." Al Capone once said to Claud Cockburn that "This American system of ours . . . gives to each and every one of us a great opportunity if we only seize it with both hands and make the most of it." Capone's view is still shared by most Americans. That it was never really true Indians and Negroes and others can testify, but it seemed to be true until fairly recent times. In the past, a debilitated American Left tried to mount a critique of the prevailing ideology, but the collapse of the Left in the postwar period silenced this type of criticism precisely when it was most needed.

The abdication of the Left in the postwar period, and the failure of the New Left thus far to fill the vacuum, have meant that the idea of a radical politics and the function it can serve in our kind of political system has been forgotten. Radical political pressures played a role in bringing the Republican Party into being. Radical political pressures also helped to shape the New Deal. Radical politics revivified the labor movement in the 1930s. Recently J. H. Plumb reviewed a collection of papers by American planners on environmental problems. In not one of these papers, he noted, had thought been given to the kind of politics that would be needed if any of the plans were to win a fair hearing. What he said has direct relevance to the rot in the political system:

> Environment problems get too easily abstracted from social problems, and social problems from their historical roots.
>
> How can planning work in a society which has sharp social divisions due to disparity in wealth as well as differences in color? How can planning work in a society in which profit, personal or corporate, must be a more urgent motive than control or conservation?
>
> So long as society is structured as it is there will be slums. . . . No amount of thinking about environment, no amount of planning the optimum space and minimal communal facilities can be effective without political action, and that means political action of a radical nature.
>
> The history of the last hundred years shouts that fact aloud. Human beings are like carrion crows, not Christians. They will not give up what they have to the poor, they have to be scared before they will disgorge.

A radical politics, whether organized as a party or as a movement, is needed today—as it has always been needed—to goad the two major parties, to offer a general critique of the society, and to give *political* expression to the discontents that can gain a hearing in neither major party. The New Left may meet this need; it has not done so to date.

A secondary but relevant explanation of the rot is that the major parties are hopelessly old-fashioned. On essential matters they have changed little in the last century. At the *national* level they are loosely organized. They spend a pittance on research and planning, and even less on education. They rally briefly during national elections but for the rest of the time are "demobilized" and lethargic. This slackness of organization mirrors the attitude of most voters, who are content to limit their political enterprise to the ritual act of voting every two years—when they bother to vote. The professionals who run the parties do not encourage any greater activity. The parties engage the active support of perhaps not more than 3 to 5 percent of the membership. There was a time when various organizations and interest groups participated directly in political decision-making, but this pluralistic pattern has almost vanished, and today most of the interest groups are long since "integrated" into the power structure, i.e., they are more dependent on the party in power than it is on them. The New Left groups, therefore, quite properly attempt to build new bases of local administrations in meaningful bargaining. Even if this were to occur, however, national political decisions would still need to be local administrations in meaningful barganing. Even if this were to occur, however, national political decisions would still need to be made, national priorities established, and for that purpose well-organized national parties are indispensable.

At the national level, both major parties are still loosely organized coalitions formed for the purpose of conducting campaigns. The Republican coalition, established at the time of the Civil War, was ascendant until the successful New Deal coalition was put together in 1932. Since then, the Republicans have been unable or unwilling to form a new coalition and the New Deal coalition is now disintegrating. At the moment it would be difficult to say which party is the more sharply divided internally. Neither seems able to confront the new issues (too risky) or appeal to the new constituencies which have emerged since 1932 (to do so, just now, would endanger what is left of the old coalition). Yet recent polls show that a large—perhaps a third or more—and steadily increasing percentage of the electorate is dissatisfied with the candidates and programs and styles of both parties and therefore disinclined to participate actively in politics.

Instead of addressing themselves to the new issues and the new constituencies, both parties evade their responsibilities by resort to excessive "personality politics," TV-style (with the result that rising campaign costs threaten to make the Senate once more the "millionaire's club" that it was in the 1890s). The effect of all this is to encourage the feeling of "powerlessness" and enforce the conviction that political action is futile. It needs to be stressed that whereas at one time national coalition parties functioned reasonably well, today's problems are much more complex, the resistances to be overcome are much greater and the concentration of power is formidable. To make politics alive once more, national parties must be coherently and purposefully organized, and they must command enough energy, not merely to secure adoption of new programs but to make certain that they are properly administered. Neither party today is so qualified.

A related cause of the rot is the failure of the Republican Party to function as an opposition party. Since 1932 it has been obvious that the two-party system was endangered by the failure of the GOP to offer effective opposition by urging alternative programs and policies. It was generally assumed in 1952 that President Eisenhower would reorganize the party which had been, even then, much too long out of power. He had the prestige and the power, but he showed not the slightest interest in the problem, and a great opportunity was lost. The

Goldwater explosion of 1964 was the logical consequence of failure to renovate the party and, judging by recent events, the need is still there. The party system has been further weakened by a new situation. A combination of factors, with heavy emphasis on the mass media, has made a measure of "direct democracy" possible. Representative government is at best slow, cumbersome, exasperating. Nowadays many decisions must be made quickly if they are to be effective. Let's say that the mayor announces the immediate closing of a city hospital. There isn't time to distribute leaflets, interview officials, petition the parties, organize a campaign. So those opposing the closure chain themselves to the office furniture, after first giving the TV news rooms notice of time and place. A vast audience is immediately alerted, with little effort, at minimal expense.

In a sense, *the new media become a substitute for the party.* Often official reaction is swift and responsive; whereas when petitioners go through channels, elected officials can stall, appoint commissions, order investigations, etc. A pamphlet by John Morris on "Direct Democracy," published recently in London, explains the theory. The universal defect of representative democracy, so the argument goes, is the formation of controlling elites. Such government lets the people vote periodically for politicians or for parties, but seldom for policies. This, of course, merely echoes Michels' cynical comment: "The one right which the people reserve is the ridiculous privilege of choosing from time to time a new set of masters." Representative government was once a neccessity; people had to *send* representatives to the capital. But modern communications have made a degree of direct democracy possible and people are beginning to like it. Polls have somewhat replaced primaries as a means of registering voter preference. Experiments are being made to test the possibility of "instant" opinion polls by the use of computer techniques. Up to a point, there is much to be said for direct democracy and we shall see more of it; but it cannot substitute for partisan debate on significant issues, much less for representative government which extends and clarifies the partisan debate and, in the end, should resolve it. Direct democracy can stimulate and supplement representative government; it can never replace it.

Given the extent of the rot that currently besets the American political system—and given the degree to which power is concentrated— it is not surprising that many people feel powerless, or that they have lost confidence in politics or are voicing doubts about representative government and liberal political institutions. Nor is it surprising that many young people have turned to "anti-movements" of one kind or another and taken to the streets to air their grievances and express their frustrations. What *is* surprising, given these factors, is the way in which "concerned" and "dissatisfied" citizens have tried to find new but democratic ways of expressing their judgments and preferences, with no aid and little encouragement from either party. It was not until the President began to escalate the war in 1965 that serious misgivings about it arose. Until then it had seemed merely another "police action" in furtherance of cold-war policies which had been pursued by both parties for twenty years without serious question or opposition. But once Mr. Johnson suggested the need for an increase in taxes, once it became clear that the war had been "Americanized," once the manpower requirements and the casualties began to increase, public dismay mounted rapidly. It took a quantum leap early in the summer. Between July and September, the percentage of the public supporting the war dropped 14 points; between September and October it declined a further 11 percent.

Now, in part as a reaction to certain recent demonstrations, opinion seems to be shifting back a bit in support of the Administration. But during the last two years, there has been a sharp increase in concern and it has found expression through a variety of ingenious devices and forms *in spite of* the political rot. Most of these forms had to be improvised. Abhorrence of the war has found expression in advertisements, petitions, pamphlets, art exhibits, poetry readings, sit-ins, teach-ins, pray-ins, and all manner of protests and demonstrations. Criticism has been voiced in newspaper polls, and in informal referenda. Students have been polled; professional organizations have canvassed their members; faculties have done the same. In Cambridge, Mass., and San Francisco, the issue has been forced on the ballot with results that under the circumstances have been truly impressive. What this rising protest lacked, until recently, was any semblance of national political leadership; and what it still lacks, in general, is a sustained political emphasis. In a way, it represents a kind of "anti-politics" since neither political party has, to date, seen fit to respond to it.

All the same, the prospects for a reversal of policy, for a redirection of American power, are not nearly as bleak as they have been pictured. An enormous volatility, as yet unexpressed, just might ignite in 1968. In any case, it would be a sad mistake to write off the political prospects as unrealistic and improvise a kind of guerrilla "anti-politics" until an attempt was made to overcome the rot in the political system and to infuse it with an energy equivalent to what now finds expression in demonstrations and protests, many of which lack direct political relevance. It may be impossible, in the end, to cope with the concentration of power that exists today by normal political processes, but we shall never know until we give the system a chance to function. It is not a question of either/or but of both, a great deal more of both. Action protests can be combined with radical politics; action protests can also be combined with conventional politics. But action protests without politics will not stop the war, much less reverse the direction of American policy, much less open the structural changes needed by American society. The task of those who are concerned with these objectives, then, is to concentrate, for a change, on the political problems.

9 The Political Socialization of the American Negro*

DWAINE MARVICK

American Negroes perforce "came to terms" historically with a locality-circumscribed political world. A huge northward migration has occurred, and the younger Negro has gradually become aware of metropolitan as well as national American political processes as they affect him. Opinion-survey evidence reveals clear contrasts by region and generation in Negro attitudes toward public officials; it also suggests that Negro evaluations of political opportunity sometimes approach parity with matched counterpart groups of underprivileged whites. A shift has also occurred in Negro leadership, away from accommodationist civic dignitaries, tapped by whites as liaison spokesmen for the Negro subcommunity, to Negro professional politicians, negotiating from positions of pivotal electoral power both in Southern localities and Northern metropolitan districts. The middle-class leadership of the National Association for the Advancement of Colored People (NAACP) and Urban League, moreover, has been supplemented and jostled into new militancy by the direct-action protest organizers of the Southern Christian Leadership Conference (SCLC), the Congress of Racial Equality (CORE), and the Student Nonviolent Co-ordinating Committee (SNCC). Full and mundane possession by

*Reprinted by permission of the author and publisher from *The Annals of the American Academy of Political and Social Science*, 361 (1965).

Negroes of a reformulated place in the American polity depends, however, on the proliferation of community-level opportunities to learn new skills and roles in civic affairs.

In the middle of the twentieth century, the political socialization of the American Negro is rapidly and drastically changing. In part, the trends involve and reflect a massive migration from the rural South into Northern metropolitan slums. In part the trends are embodied in the perspectives of successive generations—those under forty today, whose awareness of American political life is therefore exclusively post-World War II, and their elders, who grew up in a prewar or wartime climate of opinion.

These key dimensions—migration and generation—will be repeatedly considered as we sift the findings available from recent research into how people are inducted into their political culture, which is what we mean by the phrase "political socialization." And because change is the outstanding feature in considering both dimensions, the findings raise questions about "resocialization" quite different from those involved in teaching civics to children or in other ways giving young people a "feel for politics." Protest, alienation, reconciliation, reintegration: these are all relevant terms when we examine how Negroes adjust to the rules and arrangements of American politics.

Political socialization refers to one's induction into a political culture, and perhaps one's capacity to change it. As a learning process, it needs to be seen as often painful, embarrassing, and even stultifying. It is a school of hard knocks for those on the receiving end as American Negroes are. It is not a pleasant academic routine of lessons learned and grades achieved in a civics class. It is the process by which adults come to learn what is expected of them as citizens and, perhaps, leaders.

Political socialization, then, is concerned with how a person "comes to terms" with the roles and norms of the concentric political worlds—local, regional, and national—into which he passes as he grows up. Necessarily it focuses on formative experiences—in the family, school, and primary group contexts of childhood—that shape ideals and give insight into political aspects of life. It requires consideration of a set of motivational factors—rooted in each individual's private problems of psychic management, including also the patterned goals and goads to which he responds with some regularity. Negro Americans in many ways are excluded from the dominant political culture of their community and nation, and are denied its rewards. Norms and roles for political performance are learned in a special Negro subculture, which is at present undergoing basic changes, creating for the next Negro generation new prototypes for political action, and creating also new tensions and new frustrations for the individual.

But the psychological transformation—the "internalized revolution"—in the way Negroes are being inducted into American political life still confronts the would-be "new Negro" with some practicalities that can make all the difference. The study of political socialization requires attention also to situational insights and beliefs—sets of ideological, group-oriented, or self-interested calculations made by a person which largely determine the level of his involvement and participation in any specific occasion or process. Attitudes of skepticism may be widely prevalent among Negro citizens, but they are surprisingly differentiated from person to person, and from situation to situation. And linked to these situational appraisals also is the question of what resources can be marshaled. A full analysis of the changes occurring in Negro political socialization would take into account a long list of capabilities—skills, knowledge, contacts, style, energy, strength, reputation, access, control of organizations—each of which is distributed unequally within the Negro population, and each of which implies control by an active intelligence to be effectively invoked.

Finally, political socialization is not simply the study of how people come to terms with the conventional practices and arrangements which are manifestly referred to as "political" or "governmental" in the institutional sense. It involves examination also of a set of functional equivalents, ways of doing indirectly what cannot be done directly. Because of the history of Negro exclusion—both nationally and in his residence localities—from active and accepted participation in the conventional processes of governance, it is especially relevant to look at his political education as it is functionally acquired, even though the ostensible processes are those of community-service groups, fraternal associations, or church affairs.

This, then, is a brief inventory of the range of problems embraced by the study of political socialization. Applied to an inquiry about the American Negro, it is, perhaps, a useful approach. But certain risks should be pointed out. First, learning what is expected and how to perform in either basic or specialized roles is an undertaking that seems to imply a rather homogeneous political culture, housed in monolithic institutions and with standardized induction norms. Second, it is likely to suggest that the things to be learned are, on the surface, straightforward, manifest political events and governmental patterns. Third, these, in turn, imply that learning depends upon the initiative of each student; some will get A's and others F's. Fourth, it conveys a rather static picture. Allowing for variations in milieu, the old textbook should continue to apply; if one is not politically inducted into the same culture, at least it is into a progressively unfolding political culture. These are all comfortable illusions.

In any extensive society there is a plurality of political milieus into which a person coming to adulthood passes. They are not equally challenging, nor easy, nor stable. In the South, a Negro "knew where he stood" and what to expect—or he used to. In the North, impersonal treatment is functional on the surface. It means access to public accommodations, a chance to vote, due process of law, and so forth. It also means isolation, exclusion, hypocrisy, and ambiguity about where the Negro stands socially.

Change does not necessarily mean revolutionary change. The actions of those in a political culture *are* largely what reaffirm or modify its norms and practices, and incidentally serve to integrate or disjoin it from other political cultures. The accretion of small changes in political practice, moreover, includes not only innovations made on purpose and by forceful leaders, but the modifications as well that result from improvisation, from fumbling, from shortsighted maneuvers, from unwillingness to continue in familiar roles, and so forth.

To learn the political game only once is not enough, whether one treats it as a spectator sport, a hobby, or a vocation. Change is too basic; resocialization is too necessary. Especially is this so in the rapidly changing arenas of America's racial politics. Recent collective efforts at direct action have multiplied Negro opportunities for political experience; the organizational scaffolding of leadership and cadre roles has vastly increased the list of political tasks to be done at the same time that it has made those roles more desirable and more differentiated. New organizing skills, analytical abilities, and communication talents are being found and encouraged in the distinctive circumstances of "protest politics." Yet, in looking at the changing patterns of Negro role-playing and Negro skill-acquisition, it is still difficult to gauge the changes in Negro attitudes and motivations. It is necessary to remember the backlog of frustration, self-doubt, and anger which the neophyte must somehow control if he is to learn anything effectively. That he often fails, and in the process learns other lessons about himself and the political system, are other aspects of the problem.

This inquiry, then, becomes a case study in the use of a new conceptual paraphernalia—that of "political socialization"—applied to the complexity and recalcitrance of actual politicizing situations, as reported by Negro informants. Analyzing some of the available data in these terms is at least a way of highlighting the flimsiness of our theoretical apparatus in this area. And because it is impossible to consider the acquisition of political capacities, skills, and beliefs by a sizable segment of the population without asking what difference it is likely to make to the political system in which they will be used and are being used, this inquiry also links interpretation of Negro potentialities to the developmental prospects for the American polity. Let us turn then to a consideration of the resources and difficulties of Negro Americans in coming to terms with the political worlds that surround them.

THE NONCOMPATIBILITY OF NEGRO AND WHITE CIRCUMSTANCES

In special ways as well as common ones, American Negroes occupy inferior statuses. Almost from birth they are discriminated against and made to feel inadequate, useless, and undesirable by the dominant white community. As a group also they tend to be poor, marginally educated, and maladapted economically.

In these latter respects, many whites living in the same localities are in similarly depressed circumstances. Some of the apathy and skepticism about American political life which we expect to find among Negroes is probably due to these socioeconomic disabilities. At the same time, the political viewpoints and roles of typical Negro citizens must substantially be seen as a response to the animosities and prejudices they experience because of their ethnic distinctiveness.

Within the Negro community as elsewhere, there is a spectrum of affluence and poverty, prominence, and ordinariness. It is increasingly hard to find a "typical" Negro. How old should he be? Does he live in a Northern city? Does he work at a menial job? Does he earn less than $5000 a year? For every such Negro, an equal number can be found in contrasting circumstances.

Only a composite picture begins to convey at once the "central tendencies" and the "scatter" in Negro characteristics. Sample surveys, by interviewing representative cross-sections of the citizenry, secure just this kind of composite picture for the nation as a whole. Complications arise, however, when a segregated and disadvantaged subgroup like the Negroes in such a sample are compared with the larger majority-status sample of whites.

In the spring of 1960, the National Opinion Research Center (NORC) undertook a national survey of the United States, as part of a five-nation study of contemporary patterns of political socialization. Reported elsewhere, that project has disclosed many fascinating parallels and contrasts between American, British, German, Italian, and Mexican publics.[1] Many subsidiary problems were scarcely touched upon in their transnational study, although their data are directly relevant. One such problem area concerns the American Negro's past and potential induction into politics.

To investigate carefully those aspects of Negro political socialization that seem distinctive for the ethnic group, and at the same time

---

[1]Gabriel Almond and Sidney Verba, *The Civic Culture* (Princeton, N.J.: Princeton University Press, 1963).

identify attitudes and beliefs about political matters that equally characterize a set of whites in comparable socioeconomic circumstances, a matching procedure was followed. One hundred interviews had been taken with Negro respondents, as part of the NORC survey. These were now classified by region (South or North), by urban or rural residence, by age (over and under forty), by income levels (over and under $5000 a year for family units), and by sex. Invoking all five points of distinction as either-or dichotomies produced thirty-two exclusive categories, each with two to five Negro respondents. The 870 white respondents in the national sample were then divided into the same thirty-two subsets. Random selection methods were used to choose as many white counterparts in each subset as there were Negro cases. Thus a composite group of one hundred whites was defined, deliberately matched with the Negro group on five dimensions.

In each component, hereafter called the Negro and the Counterpart groups, approximately half were male, under forty, big-city dwellers, Northerners, and earning over $5000 a year. The other half were not. So far as the national white cross-section was concerned, proportions quite different from fifty-fifty were found on most of these same counts.

A few other points of comparability deserve mention. In both Negro and Counterpart samples, approximately half grew up in rural, small-town, or farm environments. In both samples, two-thirds were married, and just under two-fifths had large families—three or more children. In both groups, also, at least three-fourths intended to stay in their current locality of residence.

On all of these points, moreover, the national white cross-section registered quite similar levels. Once having come to terms with a community, a young adult marries, raises a family, and intends to stay there. In all these respects, both the Negro and Counterpart groups are typically American.

Looked at from another vantage point, what sociologists call status-crystallization operates in ways that are dysfunctional to the Negro's most elementary solution—to move. This is illustrated by the impossibility—using the kinds of matching procedures noted—of securing a good match between Negroes and their Counterparts on either occupational or educational counts; there were simply not enough whites in menial job categories or with limited educational backgrounds, once age, sex, region, income, and residence area dimensions were stipulated.

Cumulative social constraints box in an American Negro. Unskilled or semiskilled (76 percent) and poorly educated (56 percent), his problem is further exacerbated by the region and locality in which he lives and *wants to remain living*. Of the Counterpart group, only 58 percent hold similarly low-status jobs, and only 44 percent had comparable educational handicaps. For the larger white cross-section, these percentages dropped to 40 percent and 32 percent, respectively. The Counterparts are considerably closer to the Negroes on these counts than are most white Americans. Their disadvantages, nevertheless, are not so cumulative; they are not so "locked in."

The "first solution"—migration—is, of course, widely used by Negroes. In our sample, only half now live in the South, but nine-tenths were born there. Nearly half the Counterparts but only 36 percent of the Negroes reported that they had always lived in their current locality.

The underlying point, however, relates to the generational aspect of the socialization phenomenon. For many Negroes, although not for all, "coming to terms" with a political world is almost irreversible. Basic life premises are involved. Some kinds of adult activity are so difficult, once foresworn, as to be impossible to undertake later in life. Some sets of events are so remote that they do not really touch one's daily life, however relevant, as news developments about public policy or group demonstrations, they may seem to the observer. Politics is the "art of the possible." And in school, on the job, in dealings with police or government officials, learning the art of the possible is not an abstract problem. Instead, it is a practical question of getting along with a specific teacher, a particular foreman, a well-known sheriff, a certain postal clerk or building inspector.

. . . Asked in 1960 whether government officials were likely to give them "equal treatment" in matters like housing regulations or taxes, 49 percent of the Negro sample and 90 percent of the white Counterpart group said yes. On a parallel question, asking about encounters with the police over traffic violations or similar minor offenses, a slightly reduced margin was found, with 60 percent of the Negroes and 85 percent of the Counterparts expecting "equal treatment."

Probing to learn what kind of treatment was expected, that is, how considerate and reasonable, the same patterns were found. Among both Negro and Counterpart groups, substantially fewer persons expected either bureaucrats or policemen to "give serious consideration" to their explanations. Counterparts are close to the scores registered on these counts by the larger white cross-section; the Negroes are about half again as likely to be pessimistic. This is a level of caution and distrust among Negro Americans toward representatives of the law with whom they have dealings which may well be substantially realistic.

It is when North-South contrasts and younger-older comparisons are made that the dynamics of Negro resocialization are suggested. While 60 percent of the Northern Negroes expected equal treatment from officials in government agencies, only 40 percent of the Southern Negroes were so optimistic. And, however equal the treatment might be, only 44 percent of the Northern group and 18 percent of the Southern expected agency officials to take their viewpoint seriously. Not only has the trek north to the metropolitan slums been accompanied by a measurable growth in confidence of equal official treatment, but also it represents a heightened feeling that the character of official treatment is not deaf or insensitive to their points of view.

Northern Counterpart whites, to be sure, are more confident (93 percent) than Northern Negroes (60 percent) of equal treatment. When the quality of that treatment is brought into question, however, they register only 49 percent confidence of being listened to. The 44 percent level on this point among Northern Negroes thus approaches parity.

If we look next at the parallel question of police treatment, the direction of change is just opposite. While only 47 percent of the Northern Negroes expected equal handling by the police, 76 percent of the Southern Negroes did. Moreover, this latter figure approaches parity with the level of confidence scored by the white Counterpart—and even the white cross-section.

Only 29 percent of the Northern Negroes expected the police to listen to their story. Here again the level of confidence registered by Southern Negroes (44 percent) matches that found among the Southern Counterpart. In sum, in the South of 1960 a random sample, economically and socially, of Negroes and their white counterparts reported roughly equal treatment by the police in their home communities. Equally, too, they reported that treatment to be reasonable and considerate.

A glance at the generational breakdown on these points is useful. It is younger Negroes, not those over forty, whose confidence in the police had risen to a near parity with that registered by their white Counterparts. It is younger Negroes, too, whose expectations of considerate attention from officials—although not equal treatment—had risen to a parity level.

THE NEGRO MIGRATION INTO AMERICAN URBAN LIFE

By 1960 half of America's Negro population lived outside the states of the old Confederacy, and nearly a third lived in the twelve largest metropolitan centers. More than half of the residents of Washington, more than a third of those in Detroit, Baltimore, and Cleveland, and easily a quarter in Chicago and Philadelphia were Negroes. In a ten-year period, a million and a half Negroes had left the South. No immigrant wave in American history was ever so large or came so quickly into the urban centers of the nation. In 1930, half of the Negro population lived in rural Southern areas and another quarter in the towns and cities of the South. By 1940, the ratio was one Northern to every two Southern Negroes. And while the proportion living in Northern localities went, decade by decade, from a quarter to a third to half, the size of the Negro population in absolute numbers had nearly doubled.

This massive influx of Negro citizens flooded the metropolitan slums with newcomers who, by reason of their opportunity-deprived upbringing, often lacked the incentives and goads to get ahead found among previous immigrant groups. Earlier ethnic minorities had come from culturally intact backgrounds in Europe which provided them with distinctive but, usually, well-defined standards of conduct for political life. The slave-period traditions for Negroes who had been field hands in the Delta, members of a domestic class in a plantation system, or personal servants for white masters in the urban South were quite disparate, but in all cases were heavily weighted in terms of imitating white patterns.

While this long spiral of migration continued, other trends were also at work. Technological advances in industry and commerce were displacing unskilled and semiskilled labor—Negro labor—at an accelerating pace. Metropolitan programs for meeting transportation, education, recreation, and housing demands were inevitably displacing families—both long-established and newly come—from blighted neighborhoods.

Now some glimpse of the magnitudes involved in the attitudinal reorientation of Negroes toward local government. In 1960, asked how important was its impact on their daily lives, nearly the same proportion—one-third—of Negroes and whites felt that the answer was "great impact." Among Northerners, whites (41 percent) were somewhat more inclined to this view than Negroes (29 percent).

Asked to evaluate the contribution of local government, only 50 percent of the Negroes, compared with 72 percent of their Counterparts, felt it had generally been helpful in their lives. In the North, however, the 60 percent scored by Negroes was rather close to the Counterpart figure of 69 percent. On the other hand, only 42 percent of the Southern Negroes made this evaluation, while 75 percent of their white Counterparts did so. When generations are compared, the margin by which whites make more favorable evaluations is similar for younger and older sets.

Those interviewed were asked to consider what could be done to prevent the village or city council from adopting a regulation which "you considered very unjust or harmful." For the national white cross-section, only 24 percent felt it was almost impossible for them to change a bad local ordinance. Somewhat more (31 percent) of the Counterpart whites and fully 38 percent of the Negroes felt this way. Asked whether they had, in fact, ever tried, 70 percent of the national cross-section of whites and 73 percent of the Counterpart whites admitted never having done so, but 86 percent of the Negroes had never tried.

When attention is given to the regional and age breakdowns, again the attitudinal transformation can begin to be seen. Not alienation, but heightened involvement and substantial realism in the choice of methods and targets seem to be disclosed. While fully 53 percent of the Southern Negroes felt that changing a bad local law was virtually impossible, only 20 percent of the Northern Negroes did so—a figure rather similar to that of Counterpart whites. The contrast in optimism was correspondingly great also between younger and older Negroes, with "virtually impossible" being the reaction of 28 percent and 47 percent, respectively, a substantially greater age difference than registered by white Counterparts.

As to whether they, personally, would actively try to change a bad local law if the occasion arose, sharp contrasts are found between North and South. More than half of the Southern Negroes felt it was unlikely they would ever try; only 27 percent of Southern Counterparts were so passive. Conversely, only 31 percent of the Northern Negroes felt they would never try to influence such a matter, but 50 percent of the Northern Counterparts admitted their probable inaction. For both Negroes and Counterpart whites, the younger age groups showed markedly greater propensities toward local political agitation. And when the question was posed, had any actual attempt to influence a local ordinance issue ever been made, 95 percent of the Southern Negroes said "never." On the same question, only 76 percent of the Northern Negroes had never tried, the same proportion as for Northern Counterparts.

THE LOCALLY CIRCUMSCRIBED POLITICAL WORLD OF AMERICAN NEGROES

In the study of American race relations today, intellectuals tend to assume that Negroes all along have felt oppressed and constrained at the mold of second-class citizenship, in 1895 as much as 1935 or 1965. Yet, little is known about their political socialization patterns, and a few cautionary points are pertinent. Ordinary Negroes lived mostly in the South. About 1890, open efforts began to disfranchise Negro voters and to impose Jim Crow circumscriptions with the force of law on Negro use of public facilities. By 1910 the political rules had been reformulated; the Supreme Court's "separate but equal" doctrine helped to quiet public concern about what was happening, while political realities ensured a steady deterioration in the public services and accommodations available in their home communities to Negroes. Incidental to this triumph of nasty-mindedness, much race hatred was preached and countenanced, apparently in part to reassure the poor whites that they were not the next target.

Frederick Douglass, the most militant national Negro leader, fought in vain after 1880 against the trend to disengage all national machinery capable of aiding the Negro. After his death in 1894, others founded the NAACP and the Urban League, conceived as instruments for rallying the racial elite, of training the "Talented Tenth" as race spokesmen and cadres for future struggles, of pursuing political goals not in political arenas but in academic, philanthropic, religious, and journalistic modes. Themselves the products of a selective social mobility process within the Negro world, most of the Negro publicists, lawyers, academics, and others on the national scene struggled to get and to keep open elite communication lines. Their efforts reflected a middle-class presumption that the Negro masses, when mobilized, would accept their lead. There is dignity and restraint, rather than anger and impatience, in the formulation of tasks confronting the NAACP by the militant leader, W. E. B. DuBois: "By every civilized and peaceful method, we must strive for the rights which the world accords to men."[2]

Nationally, the "accommodationist" style of Negro leadership was set by Booker T. Washington. The head of Tuskegee was a man of humble origins, a self-made man who had met the world on its own terms. He was realistic. Negroes lacked the skills and knowledge to succeed economically; education was the crucial resource needed, and education was provided by local governing bodies; Southern whites would only provide that crucial resource if the "products" were reliably docile.

Just when the use of governmental machinery to enforce disadvantages on the Negro was at its peak, Washington counselled submission. Work hard, in the service of the community, and you will become accepted in proper time. His advice and example were for Negroes to give up their interest in political power as a way of securing their rights. Industrial education and an appropriate station in the emerging industrial work of twentieth-century America, were the objectives he used.

De facto segregation in the North was not implemented by state laws and local ordinances as in the South; nor were prejudices so openly proclaimed by militant whites. But the Northern reception system has been a pale facsimile of its Southern prototype in many ways, and especially at the local community level.

Until the postwar years it can be argued that, North and South alike, Negro adults became politically socialized almost exclusively to

[2]Quoted in Charles E. Silberman, *Crisis in Black and White* (New York: Random House, 1964), p. 129.

the circumscriptions and indirect channels of the localities in which they lived. It was irrelevant to speak of national or even state-bestowed citizen status for Negro Americans. In the outlook of educated Negro elite figures, no doubt, an awareness of the life in the national and state superstructure of American politics existed. At the same time, it is quite understandable that most events occurring in the central institutional complex of American democracy would not touch the ordinary Negro American emotionally, nor arouse desires to participate. And for the Negro poor, during this whole century of segregation and lower-caste treatment, politics was white man's business; even in the local arenas of political life Negroes often could secure no electoral footing. The ambit of Negro influence was thus severely limited; it took only a primer to learn the rules of how to behave. Compliance with imposed norms was rudimentary but necessary, even when fellow-Negroes called it "Toming."

Myrdal's massive codification in 1942 of the circumstances of Negro life informs us about the extent to which Negroes of that and previous generations were a minority harder than Italians, Poles, or Jews to assimilate.[3] His study stressed themes that continue to preoccupy discussion today. Myrdal believed that Negroes were "exaggerated Americans," who believed in the American Creed more passionately than whites, and who should exploit their common bonds of belief with white Americans more effectively. It would not be possible for white Americans to sustain their corporate belief system unless those who asked their due were granted it, once heard. Negroes had not strenuously asked their due; avoiding scenes and temporizing had been the style.

The Negro community was dependent on the white community; whites were committed to their egalitarian, optimistic, democratic creed, as were the Negroes; by playing upon the beliefs of whites, Negroes could gain their objectives.

Did Negroes consciously or persistently aspire to full citizenship? Had they been politically socialized to want citizen status, but somehow left untutored in how to manipulate and persuade whites to grant them what was due?

Or had they undergone a harsher socialization process, one which left them not prepared to believe that the American political system, for all its protestations, would support them in their aspirations?

The argument here is *not* that Negroes were passive, apathetic, and for generations unable to protest effectively because they had become disenchanted with the American Creed—alienated from American society. Probably more commonly, Negro adults had never allowed themselves to become enchanted with "democracy" in the first

[3]Gunnar Myrdal, *An American Dilemma* (New York: Harper & Row, 1944).

place, so far as their own community and private lives went. Traditionally, Negro civic leaders occupying symbolic positions of respect were "tapped" by leaders in the white community as contact points. The influence of such "anointed" figures often depended more on their near-monopoly over liaison channels to the all-important white community's decisionmakers than on any spontaneous following within the Negro community which they might have generated. Undertakers, insurance men, bankers, teachers, a few professional men—above all, ministers of Negro churches: these were the men who traditionally were treated as spokesmen for their local Negro communities. Accommodationist, conservative, dignified, personally successful men: they have been for more than half a century the prime models for Negro children asking to be shown *local* "men of influence."[4]

With the mobilization of electoral strength, the decline of Negro ministers and leaders of fraternal organizations as sources for community leadership—whether in the liaison or symbolic sense—has steadily been taking place in Southern localities. "Street lights, sidewalks, and paved streets are more common in communities where Negroes vote in substantial numbers. Such things as Negro civic centers, bandshells, playgrounds, libraries, hospital annexes, and even swimming pools are found in increasing numbers."[5]

The dynamics of political *rapprochement* in Louisiana communities, according to Fenton and Vines, have occasionally involved an alliance of "shady white and underdog Negro" elements. Local politics centers around the sheriff's office. If a sheriff permits gambling, he is charged with corruption by middle-class residents of the community; to offset their electoral threat, the sheriff in such instances has catered to the marginal Negro vote for support. "The reward . . . is respect from the politicians and attendance at Negro political meetings, cessation of police brutality, and promises made and often kept regarding such matters as street improvements and better school facilities."[6]

Thus, in Southern communities where voter registration has progressed to a point sufficient to create a substantial potential bloc, a new, self-taught, and white-tutored breed of professional Negro politicians has begun to emerge. Specifically equipped with the organizing and

[4]See Silberman, chap. vii. Also M. Elaine Burgess, *Negro Leadership in a Southern City* (Chapel Hill: University of North Carolina Press, 1962); E. F. Frazier, *The Negro in the United States* (New York: Crowell-Collier-Macmillan, 1949), and G. Franklin Edwards, *The Negro Professional Class* (New York: Free Press, 1959).

[5]H. D. Price, "The Negro and Florida Politics, 1944–1954," *Journal of Politics* (May 1955).

[6]J. H. Fenton and K. N. Vines, "Negro Registration in Louisiana." *American Political Science Review* (September 1957).

campaigning skills appropriate to electoral politics, these new political journeymen bargain with some effectiveness among the rival white politicians anxious for their vote.

In Northern metropolitan centers, too, professional Negro politicians have emerged, men who work inside the party machine dominating their city, men who accept the terms of political life laid down by white counterparts who are scarcely less ethnic-minded—Irish, Italian, Polish, Jewish, and Puerto Rican "spokesmen" also judged by their readiness and reasonableness in making bargains, and by their ability to deliver votes as promised. Considerable variations remain, of course, in style, in methods used, and in results obtained.[7] In Chicago, Dawson's political strength within the Democratic machine, like that of other ethnic politicians, has depended on the historical "fit" between ward boundaries and Negro ghetto limits. Working in a solidly Negro area, he deals in tangible and divisible benefits, few of which pose clear moral questions. In New York City, on the other hand, Powell's role is also systemspecific, but here a much weaker and less unified alliance of politicians runs the dominant party apparatus. There is therefore scope for Powell's agitational style. He deals in moral questions, in intangible ideals and indivisible causes which must not be compromised. His dramatic skills link these to his personal leadership. Dr. Kenneth B. Clark, himself an occasional rival of Powell in Harlem, has this to say:

> In his flamboyant personal behavior, Powell has been to the Negroes a symbol of all that life has denied them. . . . The Negro masses do not see Powell as amoral but as defiantly honest in his protest against the myths and hypocrisies of racism. . . . He is important precisely because he is himself a caricature, a burlesque of the personal exploitation of power.[8]

The growth of militancy among Negroes—with the decline of "accommodation"—in the modal leadership style is a double-edged blade. On the one hand, it reflects a shift away from the habit of evaluating their social position primarily within the nonpolitical, "intramural" range of Negro rivals, and a shift toward evaluating it instead by explicit comparison to a counterpart group—their opposite numbers in the white middle-class.[9] On the other hand, it is a behavior pattern which, once initiated, generates its own reputation. It is far

[7]See James Q. Wilson, *Negro Politics* (New York: Free Press, 1960) for a comparative inquiry which develops these points systematically.

[8]K. B. Clark, *Dark Ghetto* (New York: Harper & Row, 1965), p. 210.

[9]Ruth Searles and J. A. Williams, Jr., "Negro College Students' Participation in Sit-Ins," *Social Forces,* 40 (1962), pp. 215–220.

more conspicuous than the older pattern of accommodationist leadership, and it is reinforced powerfully by the way in which other Negroes, both peers and elders, respond by endorsing and accepting it. The "accommodating" style is established by a sequence of occasions when aggressive confrontations were avoided; the "militant" style is more rhetorical, and tends to be *predicted* on the basis of of even a very small set of occasions when aggressive leadership options are used. Negro leaders drift into the former; they assert the latter kind of role.[10]

THE SKILLS AND HABITS OF CITIZENSHIP

Learning about political life, then, is not a simple, static, or finished process. Instead, it is highly complex; it is dynamic and changing; and, at best, it is imperfectly realized. Many Negro adults never become very effective at organizing and improving their daily lives. How much less likely that the methods used to socialize them to onerous predetermined political rules and arrangements should regularly be effective! Indeed, if Negroes had internalized the American dream and seriously wanted it for themselves, it is hard to believe they would not long since have been radically disenchanted and militantly alienated. Instead, it is only in recent years that a new generation of Negro youths begins to think seriously about claiming their birthrights.

In 1910, for a young Negro to study the program of the then-fledgling NAACP was not to review an impressive sequence of judicial victories, as the task is for his 1965 counterpart. The 1910 program was a recital of watered-down hopes and carefully worded aims. Even so, Booker T. Washington and William E. B. DuBois debated the proper goals and strategy for Negroes in polemical terms that made the former's call for self-improvement seem at odds with the latter's demand for Negro civil rights at once.

Today, also, there are rivalries and polemics among Negro leaders on the national scene, conflicts brought home to Negro citizens by television and radio rather than in exclusively Negro news media. But perhaps there is now a stronger sense of the need for a division of labor: the need for militant direct action protests, to arouse the Negro poor from apathy and self-hate, and the simultaneous need for persistent integrative efforts—through the courts, in union-management bargaining and in government personnel practices, in community service organizations, and through partisan political activities. Not only the symbolic struggles that eventuate in decisions to desegregate a

[10]See the insightful participant-observer case study by Allan P. Sindler, "Youth and the American Negro Protest Movement," prepared for the 1964 International Political Science Association Meetings in Geneva, Switzerland.

school, permit voter registration, make public accommodations equally accessible, or create job opportunities, but also the practical tasks of implementing and consolidating each such victory are coming to be seen by the young Negro of 1965 as part of the political world with which he must come to terms.[11]

But what does it mean to "come to terms"? One view expects each generation to produce a distinctive style, seizing new opportunities which older generations have yielded or neglected. Another view, not necessarily incompatible with the first, expects realism. Systematic adjustment to changing circumstances seems mostly to come from the older people, while youth refuse to come to terms and instead appear idealistic and unreasonable.

Not many studies of political socialization have yet been made, of Negroes or any other grouping. We have examined some systematic evidence about the attitudes and self-conceptions held by adult Negroes and their white Counterparts concerning American politics. But we know little of how those notions were first acquired, when today's adults were growing up and were gradually coming to understand their place in a white democracy. Neither for Negroes nor for other categories do we know much about the differentiation and attenuation of childhood attitudes and beliefs. Yet adults have to behave in response to situational insights, and adults have to acquire the experience and skills as well as the nerve and desire to mount fresh assaults on complacency and indifference.

Memorable experiences, for example, whether they arise in the midst of electoral campaigns, in moments of public crisis, or in the workaday context of civic co-operation, are hard to plan ahead of time. They tend to be memorable because of accidental and unexpected developments. The Montgomery bus boycott of 1965 began spontaneously when a weary Negro seamstress refused to yield her seat to a white. For more than a year, 17,000 Negroes refused to ride, cutting the bus line's patronage to a fourth of normal. From such unplanned rejection of roles and defiance of norms, in the ten subsequent years, boycotting has become a formidable political weapon for American Negroes. With notice spread by word of mouth or from the pulpits of Negro churches, the boycott has provided a community-level focus and has helped to create leadership-communication networks that are transforming Northern metropolitan slum areas as well as Southern colored quarters. In 1963, a third of a national cross-section of Negroes and more than two-thirds of a panel of Negro leaders

[11]See the sympathetic sketches by Howard Zinn, SNCC: *The New Abolitionists* (Boston: Beacon Press, 1964) and the careful case study of biracial cooperation and protest activities in a Southern community by Lewis Killian and Charles Gregg, *Racial Crisis in America* (Englewood Cliffs, N.J.: Prentice-Hall, 1964).

reported that they had boycotted certain stores in their local communities.[12]

The syndrome of dejection, self-contempt, a sense of worthlessness, and hopelessness is what Kardiner and Ovesey called the Negro's "mark of oppression." It has been repeatedly noted in studies since their work dealing with Negro psychological adjustment problems.[13] The problems of Negro personality formation are often traced to the "identity crises" through which Negro children perforce must pass: the color-bias they develop even in preschool play, often linked with a tense reluctance to acknowledge that they are Negro; the postpuberty estrangement of Negro youths from their white playmates, enforced by white parental racist fears of miscegenation; in young adulthood, too, after the relatively sheltered years of school and familiar neighborhood, "the full awareness of his social devaluation in the larger society" can cause severe emotional distress.[14]

Little is known about how the emotional wellsprings of love and hate, hunger and vitality are linked persistently to a set of socially "given" goals and goads. The levels of need achievement among Negroes vary substantially, perhaps as much as among whites, although the standards of behavior, lifeplans, and career objectives are manifestly different in the ghetto subculture into which most Negroes are born and in the American society which isolates them from awareness of those norms and denies them the rewards of compliance with those norms.

It is in interracial dyadic relationships that Negroes have usually learned manipulative strategies, situational tactics, and bargaining ploys. It has been in response to the emotional strain of interracial contacts that Negroes have generated double standards of fair play, humor, and even relaxation.

Almost every Negro adult—not only his organizational leaders— has been schooled in ways to get along in superior-subordinate relationships. Moreover, the picture he has acquired very commonly puts him in the latter role. The extent to which the mental outlook of oppressed people tends toward fantasies, childlike incompetence, and passive dependence is hard to measure; available evidence suggests that a pervasive pattern of such behavior has historically laid its imprint on Negro America.

[12]William Brink and Louis Harris, *The Negro Revolution in America* (New York: Simon & Schuster, 1964), p. 203.

[13]A. Kardiner and L. Ovesey, *The Mark of Oppression* (1951); see also the comprehensive survey by Thomas F. Pettigrew, *A Profile of the Negro American* (Princeton, N.J.: D. Van Nostrand, 1964).

[14]Kardiner and Ovesey, p. 8.

But when people acquire skills and sensitivities in how to sense the mood of superiors, how to parlay advantages, how to conceal their emotions, how to accomplish a thousand political artifices, they often find such assets portable to new circumstances and applicable in quite unexpected situations. American Negroes learned these skills under persistent conditions of duress. Perhaps many never have mastered techniques that could be used on anyone but a white superior; many have probably repressed all sensitivities to similar opportunities in intra-racial organizational relations. Even so, given this kind of schooling, American Negroes must often make very acute political followers, able to appreciate very well the difference between a leader's pretensions and his actual performances.

The Negro revolution in America has been manifest in headlines and news bulletins for more than ten years. It is tempting to speculate about the ways in which scenes of militant direct action, showing parental courage and group discipline in the face of mindless hatred, affect young Negro children today—in the choice of their ego ideals, in the games they play, the stories they read, the fantasies they have, the careers they want, the nightmares they endure, and in their heightened awareness of political rules and possibilities, now that such awareness carries an instrumental rather than an academic tag.

There is perhaps no single event that marks the watershed in American race relations better than the 1954 Supreme Court decision calling for "all deliberate speed" in desegregating the nation's schools. Yet it was ten years later, in the Birmingham riots of 1964, before the Negro poor entered the protest movement:

> The riots . . . were waged not by the disciplined cadres of relatively well-educated "middle-class" Negroes but by the apa-thetic poor who had previously remained completely on the outside, and whose potential for violence frightened Rev. Martin Luther King's lieutenants as much as the whites.[15]

Moreover, the nonviolent direct action methods of the new protest groups—CORE, SCLC, SNCC—represent also only part of a ten-year prelude to the far more fundamental revolution that is coming in the politics of neighborhoods and communities, of school districts and residential blocks, a revolution that began in scattered localities during the 1950s and received large financial and directional support from the 1964 Civil Rights Act and the resultant antipoverty program of the Office of Economic Opportunity. In states of the South as well as of the North, and at county and municipal levels, biracial area human resources councils are being formed, to co-ordinate and sponsor

[15]Silberman, p. 143.

programs for community action, establish and run youth job corps and urban centers, and encourage private nonprofit groups and universities to contribute to neighborhood improvement and adult education projects.

The importance of these experiences, both to acquire new skills and play new roles in civic affairs, can scarcely be overestimated. The full, genuine, and mundane "political resocialization" of American Negro citizens awaits the proliferation of such institutional scaffolding for public-spirited action.

10 Some Effects of Interest Group Strength in State Politics*

LEWIS A. FROMAN, JR.

. . . Generally, we would expect state constitutions in states which have stronger interest groups to reflect, in certain systematic ways, a greater amount of interest group activity than do the constitutions in states with weaker interest groups. More specifically, we would hypothesize the following relationships:

1. The stronger the interest groups, the greater the length of state constitutions.

This hypothesis follows in that states with stronger interest groups would be predicted to make greater efforts to achieve special advantage through constitutional provisions which refer to their activities. These efforts would result in longer and more detailed constitutions than in states with weaker interest groups. . . .

. . . the twenty-four states . . . classified as strong-interest-group states have constitutions which average 33,233 words in length; the fourteen states which are classified as moderate in interest group strength have constitutions which average 17,985 in length; and the

*Reprinted by permission of the author and publisher from *The American Political Science Review,* 60 (December 1966).

seven states which are classified as weak in interest group strength have constitutions which average 14,828 in length.

2. The stronger the interest groups, the greater the number of proposed amendments.

If the theory we have suggested is correct, then we would expect states with strong interest groups to have more proposals for constitutional changes than states with moderately strong interest groups which, in turn, would have more proposals for changes than would states with weak interest groups. This hypothesis would reflect a greater number of attempts to gain some special constitutional status. . . .

3. The stronger the interest groups, the greater the number of amendments which are adopted.

As with proposed amendments, we would expect stronger interest group states to have a larger number of changes in the constitution than in states with less strong interest groups. Once more, the data confirm the hypothesis. . . .

Additional support for this hypothesis, and for the theory being proposed here, is the following. We would also expect states with longer constitutions to have a greater number of changes in their constitutions. This follows if we assume, as we have been doing, that longer constitutions indicate a larger range of activities provided for in the constitution, and a greater specificity and detail. The greater constitutional comprehensiveness in states with longer constitutions would also suggest a greater need to revise the constitution as economic, social, and political changes occur. Hence we would predict that the longer the constitution, the greater the number of amendments. Table 1 provides data on this point.

TABLE I. RELATIONSHIP BETWEEN LENGTH OF CONSTITUTION AND NUMBER OF CONSTITUTIONAL AMENDMENTS ADOPTED

Length of Constitution	Average Number of Adopted Amendments per year	N[1]
Less than 10,000 words	.27	7
10,000–19,999	.67	18
20,000–29,999	.78	12
30,000 and over	3.04	9

[1]Michigan and North Carolina are excluded for lack of data.
SOURCE: The Book of the States, 1964–1965 (Chicago: The Council of States Government, 1964), pp. 12–15.

As Table 1 indicates, the average number of amendments adopted per year increases as the average length of the constitution increases.

Since states with stronger interest groups tend to have longer constitutions . . . and since states with longer constitutions tend to have a greater number of amendments (Table 1), hypothesis three, the stronger the interest group, the greater the number of amendments which are adopted, is directly derivable from these other hypotheses. The fact that this three-step chain of hypotheses is true at all three steps lends additional validity to the general theory being proposed here. It is also interesting to note that both strength of interest groups and length of constitution have an independent effect on the number of amendments adopted. When each is held constant the relationship with the other and number of amendments adopted is attenuated, but still present.

4. States with moderately strong interest groups will have the highest percentage of amendments adopted.

This hypothesis, although not immediately obvious, follows from the following argument. To this point our data indicate a positive relationship between strength of interest groups and both number of amendments proposed and number of amendments adopted. It is clear, however, that it is easier to propose an amendment than to get an amendment adopted. States with strong interest groups, then, would be expected to have a larger number of amendments proposed and a larger number of amendments adopted, but since it is easier to propose amendments than to have them ratified, their rate of success would not be expected to be the largest among the states.

Similarly, states with weak interest groups have the fewest number of amendments proposed and the fewest number of amendments adopted. But, again, since it is easier to propose than to adopt, weak interest group states would not have the highest rate of success. This reasoning would predict that states with moderately strong interest groups would have the highest ratio of amendments adopted to amendments proposed. Table 2 provides data on this hypothesis.

As Table 2 indicates, it is the states with moderately strong interest groups that have the highest percentage of amendments which are proposed adopted. States with strong interest groups have a ratio of adopted amendments to proposed amendments of 54.8 percent, states with moderate interest groups 62.8 percent, and states with weak interest groups 52.6 percent. Those states with the weakest interest groups have the lowest rate of success, but those states with the strongest interest groups do not have the highest rate of success. Indeed, their rate of success is much closer to weak interest group states than to moderately strong ones.

TABLE 2. RELATIONSHIP BETWEEN STRENGTH OF INTEREST GROUPS
AND PERCENTAGE OF PROPOSED AMENDMENTS ADOPTED

Strength of Interest Groups	Average % of Amendments Adopted	N[1]
Strong	54.8%	19
Moderate	62.8%	12
Weak	52.6%	5

[1]Politics in the American States (Boston: Little, Brown, 1965), p. 114.
SOURCE: The Book of the States, 1964–1965 (Chicago: The Council of State Governments, 1964), pp. 12–15; and Herman Zeigler, "Interest Groups in the States," in Herbert Jacob and Kenneth N. Vines, eds. Politics in the American States (Boston: Little, Brown, 1965), p. 114.

A POSSIBLE ALTERNATIVE EXPLANATION

Before accepting the above theory and hypotheses relating strength of interest groups to variations in state constitutions, it might be useful to explore a possible alternative explanation.

States also differ considerably in the extent to which it is easy or difficult to amend their constitutions. Some states, for example, require a two-thirds or three-fifths majority of the legislature and/or passage by two successive legislatures to propose and ratify constitutional amendments. All states but one also require a popular referendum after legislative action, but require differing majorities in the referendum. In addition, states also differ on whether they allow constitutional amendments to be proposed by initiative, and have different ways of calling together and proposing amendments in constitutional conventions.[1]

Given these widely varying practices in states, an index of difficulty of proposing and ratifying constitutional amendments was constructed. This index is derived from the three major ways in which the constitution may be amended and therefore reflects: (1) legislative difficulty, (2) presence or absence of the initiative, and (3) constitutional convention difficulty in proposing and ratifying constitutional amendments. One point was given to each state if a majority greater than a simple majority is required in the legislature, one point if approval by two sessions is needed, and one point if ratification by a majority vote in the election rather than a majority vote on the amendment is required. Additionally, one point is given if there are no

[1]For description of the differing state systems see *The Book of the States, 1964–1965*, pp. 13,15.

initiative procedures in the state. With regard to constitutional conventions, one point is given if greater than a majority in the legislature is required to call a constitutional convention, one point if approval is needed by two sessions of the legislature, one point if a referendum on whether there should be a constitutional convention is necessary, one point if a majority in the election rather than a majority on the proposition is required, one point if after the constitutional convention ratification of the amendment is required (one-half point is given if no provision is in the constitution for a referendum ratifying the amendment but the legislature may determine if a referendum is necessary), and one point if ratification requires a majority in the election rather than a majority on the amendment.

This index of difficulty of amending the constitution, then, can vary from 0 to 10. The median score was 4, the range from 1 to 9. Fifteen states had scores of 3.5 or less, sixteen had scores from 4 to 5, and fifteen had scores from 5.5 to 9.

Given this wide range in difficulty in amending state constitutions, we would expect that such variation might have an impact on the number of amendments which are adopted by the states. More specifically, we would hypothesize that the greater the difficulty in amending the constitution, the fewer the number of amendments which will be adopted. Table 3 provides the data to test this hypothesis.

Table 3 only partially confirms the hypothesis. Those states with the most difficult procedures to amend the constitution do have fewer amendments adopted, but the states with the easiest procedures do not have the greatest number of amendments adopted.

TABLE 3. RELATIONSHIP BETWEEN DIFFICULTY IN AMENDING THE CONSTITUTION AND AVERAGE NUMBER OF AMENDMENTS ADOPTED PER YEAR

Score on Difficulty of Amending Constitution	Average Number of Adopted Amendments Per Year	N[1]
Less than 3.5	1.29	15
4–5	1.32	16
5.5–9	.66	15

[1]Michigan and North Carolina and excluded for lack of data.
SOURCE: See Table 1.

This partial explanation of why states vary in the number of changes in their constitutions may be further explained, however, by variation in states in strength of interest groups. Consistent with our theory, it may be proposed that states would be expected to vary in ease or difficulty in amending their constitutions by strength of interest groups. That is, we would expect the following hypothesis to be true: the stronger the interest groups, the less the difficulty in amending the constitution. Table 4 presents data on this hypothesis.

TABLE 4. RELATIONSHIP BETWEEN STRENGTH OF INTEREST GROUPS AND DIFFICULTY OF AMENDING THE CONSTITUTION

Strength of Interest Groups	Average Difficulty of Amending the Constitution	N
Strong	4.21	24
Moderate	5.00	14
Weak	5.65	7

SOURCES: See note, Table 2.

The data from Table 4 confirm the relationship between strength of interest groups and difficulty of amending the constitution. States with strong interest groups have a difficulty score of 4.21, states with moderately strong interest groups have a score of 5.00, and states with weak interest groups have a difficulty score of 5.65. Hence we may say that even though the number of changes in the constitution is related to difficulty of amending the constitution as well as strength of interest groups, the reason why this additional explanation is at least partially true is because strength of interest groups is also related to difficulty of amending the constitution.

One further piece of data will also help to confirm the theory being proposed here. Since states with strong interest groups have longer constitutions, and since strong interest group states also have constitutions which are easier to amend, we would also expect there to be a relationship between length of constitution and ease of amendment. More specifically we would hypothesize the greater the length of the constitution, the less the difficulty in amending the constitution. Table 5 provides data on this hypothesis.

As can be seen from the Table, this hypothesis is for the most part confirmed. The states with the shortest constitutions have the most difficult amending procedures, and the states with the longest constitutions have the easiest amending procedures, although the two sets of states in the middle do not fall in the predicted order.

Summing up this section, then, there is a partial relationship between the difficulty of amending the constitution and the number of

TABLE 5. RELATONSHIP BETWEEN LENGTH OF CONSTITUTION
AND DIFFICULTY OF AMENDING STATE CONSTITUTION

Length of Constitution	Average Difficulty of Amending the Constitution	N^1
Less than 10,000 words	6.29	7
10,000–19,999	4.58	18
20,000–29,999	4.71	12
30,000 and over	4.11	9

[1]Michigan and North Carolina are excluded for lack of data.
SOURCE: See Table I.

changes made in the constitution. However, this relationship can be accounted for by the fact that there is also a relationship between strength of interest groups and ease of amending the constitution. The alternative explanation, then, may be rejected and the original explanation retained. Strength of interest group seems to be a major factor in explaining why states vary with regard to certain constitutional practices.

THE SECOND SET OF DEPENDENT VARIABLES

In the previous sections our concern was with the effect of strength of interest groups on some general features of state constitutions. In this section the focus will shift slightly to a combined constitutional-legislative variable, the method of selection of state officials. States differ widely in the number of office-holders who are appointed as opposed to elected to office. We will be concerned, in the following, with an explanation of this variation.

A priori one might predict that states with stronger interest groups would be *either* more likely or less likely to have a larger number of elected as opposed to appointed officials. the major political variable in either prediction is the ability of interest groups to influence the selection of personnel. Those who would predict that interest groups will have more influence if governmental officials are appointed rather than elected would suggest that interest groups would prefer the politics of dealing with the governor and, in some instances, the legislature, to the uncertainties of electoral politics. If this hypothesis is combined with the already-established hypothesis that strength of interest groups is related to political outcomes then this group would predict that states with stronger interest groups would have a greater number of appointed rather than elected officials.

TABLE 6. RELATIONSHIP BETWEEN STRENGTH OF INTEREST GROUPS
AND FOUR DEPENDENT VARIABLES

Strength of Interest Groups	Average Number of State Elected Officials	Average Number of State Agencies with Elected Officials	% of Elected State Public Utility Commissions	% of Elected State Courts of Last Resort	N
Strong	19.54	9.17	50%	79%	24
Moderate	14.64	7.14	7%	57%	14
Weak	7.71	5.86	0%	43%	7

SOURCE: The Book of the States, 1964–1965 (Chicago: The Council of State Governments, 1964).

On the other hand one could, with equal logic, agree that interest groups do want to maintain influence over the selection of governmental personnel but that such influence can better be established if personnel are elected rather than appointed. A governor is likely to be responsive to a wide variety of state interests. In some cases he may be a member of a political party which is less responsive to the concerns of certain interest groups. Gubernatorial appointment combined with legislative confirmation would provide some check on the governor, but interest groups, on balance, might be better able to influence the selection of personnel if such persons were elected in what, for minor positions, would be relatively low turnout elections rather than take a chance with governors. Proponents of this view would deduce an opposite conclusion from that previously advanced: stronger interest group states would have a larger number of elected rather than appointed officials.

How does one choose between these competing theories? Since the logic of each produces contradictory conclusions we might test those conclusions. Although this does not produce a direct test of the competing theories it does provide an indirect test, since the conclusions drawn from each are clearly contrary to each other. Evidence on these derivative hypotheses may support one theory as opposed to the other.

The relationship between interest group strength and selection of governmental officials will be tested in four different ways. First, what is the relationship between interest group strength and the total number of state officials who are elected? Second, what is the relationship of interest group strength and the number of state agencies with elected officials? This relationship will give us some idea of the range of offices which are subject to election.

Each of these variables gives an indication of the overall elective-appointive system within and among states. But what about specific instances? Third, then, what is the relationship between strength of interest groups and the selection of state public utility commissions? Fourth, what is the relationship of strength of interest groups with the selection of judges on state courts of last resort? Table 6 provides data to test these four relationships.

From Table 6 it is clear, in each instance, that states with strong interest groups rely more heavily on election of state officials than do states with weaker interest groups. The stronger the interest groups the greater the number of elected officials, the greater the number of state agencies with elected officials, the greater the likelihood that public utility commissions will be elected, and the greater the probability that judges on state courts of last resort will be elected.

The data, then, lend support to the second of the alternative theories. States with stronger interest groups are better able to isolate governmental agencies and officials from executive or legislative influence than are states with weaker interest groups, and are more likely to have agencies of government which are independent from the governor and legislature.

One further bit of evidence lends additional support to this conclusion. Given the evidence that elections rather than appointments are related to strong interest groups, it may also be inferred that those states with strong interest groups would have shorter terms of office than those states with weaker interest groups. This would provide additional control by interest groups by making governmental officials run for office more frequently and hence be less independent from outside influence. Table 7 provides data on terms of office of judges of state courts of last resort.

The data in Table 7 confirm this hypothesis. Length of term for judges on state courts of last resort decreases as strength of interest groups increases.

TABLE 7. RELATIONSHIP BETWEEN STRENGTH OF INTEREST GROUPS AND AVERAGE LENGTH OF TERM OF JUDGES ON STATE COURTS OF LAST RESORT

Strength of Interest Groups	Average Length of Term	N
Strong	7.58	24
Moderate	11.21	14
Weak	13.43	7

SOURCE: The Book of the States, 1964–1965 (Chicago: The Council of State Governments, 1964).

SUMMARY AND CONCLUSIONS

We began our discussion by suggesting that the literature on interest groups, generally speaking, lacks studies which attempt to test generalizations about interest group activity. The emphasis on theory and/or case studies we attributed to two factors: (1) difficulty in operationalizing theoretical concepts, and (2) difficulty and expense in collecting data for many interest groups or on many policies.

This study attempts to test several propositions about the relationship between strength of interest groups and variations among states with regard to structural and output variables centering on the constitution and the election of state officials. A theory was developed which explained why state governments would have such wide variations in their constitutions and the political processes surrounding them. More specifically, the following hypotheses about strength of interest groups were tested and confirmed:

1. The stronger the interest groups, the greater the length of the state constitutions.
2. The stronger the interest groups, the greater the number of proposed amendments.
3. The stronger the interest groups, the greater the number of amendments which are adopted.
4. States with moderately strong interest groups will have the highest percentage of amendments adopted.
5. The stronger the interest groups, the less the difficulty in amending the constitution.
6. The stronger the interest groups, the greater the number of state elected officials.
7. The stronger the interest groups, the greater the number of state agencies with elected officials.
8. The stronger the interest groups, the greater the likelihood that state public utility commissions will be elected.
9. The stronger the interest groups, the greater the probability that judges on state courts of last resort will be elected.
10. The stronger the interest groups, the shorter will be the terms of office of judges on state courts of last resort.
In addition, the following subsidiary hypotheses were also tested:
11. The longer the constitution, the greater the number of amendments which are adopted.
12. The longer the constitution, the less the difficulty in amending the constitution.
13. The greater the difficulty in amending the constitution, the fewer the number of amendments which will be adopted (partially confirmed).

All of these hypotheses confirm the theory which has been proposed here. Variation in strength of interest groups does have an impact on political systems. It was expected that states with stronger interest groups would be characterized by attempts by those groups to gain special advantages. Since constitutions are one of the vehicles through which advantages and disadvantages are distributed in political systems, these attempts would have an effect on the length of the constitution, the amending procedures within states, and the number of changes which are made. Since the selection of governmental personnel is also of primary concern to interest groups, it would be expected that differences in selection procedures would also vary by interest group strength. The data presented in this paper lend credence to these suppositions. . . .

11 Universities and the Pentagon*

GABRIEL KOLKO

If the Second World War brought the American military and universities together in an intensive manner for the first time, the permanent crisis of the cold war solidified that relationship and posed a basic threat to the very nature of the university by making it critical to the character of war and the global crisis of our generation. As World War II ended, President Truman's science adviser, Vannevar Bush, reflecting the interests of the new civilian scientific managers of the vast military research programs, urged a peacetime continuation of civilian-controlled military research centers. During the spring of 1946, General Eisenhower, on behalf of the Army, made the fundamental decision that "there appears little reason for duplicating within the Army an outside organization which by its experience is better qualified than we are to carry out some of our tasks." Modern warfare required a high level of scientific research, and the military would "find much of the talent we need for comprehensive planning in industry and universi-

*Reprinted by permission of the author and publisher from *The Nation,* October 9, 1967.

ties," via contracts and support to "broad research programs in educational institutions. . . ." There was never any illusion as to the rationale for such support, for the Pentagon often repeated in subsequent years that the Department of Defense would finance university research "in order to get results that will strengthen the national defense, and not as a contribution to higher education."

By fiscal 1964 Department of Defense grants to universities totaled $401 million, only twenty-five schools received more than three-quarters of the total, and the universities had become the heart of the Pentagon's expenditures for "basic research" designed to open the frontiers of science to new weapons systems and concepts. This critical dependence of the Pentagon and industry on the university over two decades means that the restoration of the university to its prewar role would cause a virtual revolution in U.S. military research structure.

As the nature of modern warfare changes from confrontations between technological powers in a state of mutual terror and unstable balance to wars against guerrillas, the Pentagon's needs have shifted increasingly from military hardware that has so far failed to bring victory in Vietnam to socio-economic "soft wares" that Washington hopes will compensate for the ideological and human superiority of guerrilla movements. And since only the university possesses the necessary social scientists for such research, it may fairly be argued that the Pentagon will increasingly need the university far more than the academy will require Defense Department funds.

The costs of military research to the university are of a very different magnitude, for the modern university is an enormously complex, incongruous and fragile institution: it embodies medieval corporatist notions of faculty control, Renaissance dedication to universality and truth, and big-business styles of operation and administration. It must still educate students, and without the cynicism which its inconsistent reality increasingly warrants. For all this diversity, the ultimate limitation on the conduct of a university in relation to the Pentagon or society is its obligation to create an educational environment and to honor the commitments of the majority of its faculty. For the university is not only the weakest part of the Pentagon's research apparatus; precisely because military research is inherently foreign to it, it is today the only vulnerable institution in the cold-war syndrome.

The critical weakness in the uneasy marriage between the American university and the Pentagon is the faculty and a set of humanistic obligations no one is willing formally to abandon for fear of destroying the very structure itself. Despite the general impotence of faculty consultative bodies, the real strength of the faculty in the top fifty or so schools rests with their highly favorable position in the academic market place, their relatively free mobility and their tenure. A faculty can apply pressures beyond the range and even the conception of students and they often get money and grants quite independently of the university. Their cooperation and morale is the very heart of the university, and no administrator can afford to treat it lightly. There are few great universities incapable of operating without military contracts, but none can exist without a faculty that alone determines that institution's standing and future.

If the one comprehensive study of the cost of government research to a major Ivy League school is an indication, the vast majority of faculty not engaged in contract research would gain appreciably by a divorce between university and Pentagon. Contract overhead allowances usually do not cover real but indirect costs difficult to measure, and it is primarily the teaching-heavy social sciences and humanities that make up the substantial deficit out of their tuition income and poorer working conditions. Beyond this, however, are the ethics and values which draw many scientists and academics to the university despite, quite often, banality, poor pay and hard toil. Most academics, including the scientists, do not care for the discipline and secrecy of government or business, and this group is the natural ally of those who seek a restoration of the university's independence and a reassertion of its ultimate dedication to humanist values in a manner that can remove the existing compromise with the cold war from a significant fraction of the university community. Such a process may go further in revitalizing the American university than any of the currently fashionable proposals for internal reform which assume that one can divorce the university from its structural setting.

The intellectual costs of Pentagon-sponsored research to the academic community are likely to increase with growing government dependence on the social scientists for "soft ware." Academic freedom is inherently incompatible with military research, and not merely because of the security clearance provisions which divide the faculty into those with and those without, or even because such research dissolves the concept of *community* into one of necessarily isolated, autonomous and secretive fractions, but because the essence of freedom and creativity is the ability of the scholar to decide, in the manner, place and time of *his own* choosing, what research to do and how to release the product of his efforts. The Pentagon has its own criteria, both for subject and faculty loyalty, and it imposes its priorities and decisions on the autonomy of the university. Academic freedom is based on self-motivation as well as freedom to publish, and requires a discriminating selectivity of problems of significance beyond those written into contract specifications. The classified research which comprises the most dangerous of Pentagon contracts by no means exhausts the threat to the university, for quite as critical is the matter of initiatives, possible external controls and, to an increasing extent, purposes.

Military research also violates the sensibilities of ever-growing numbers of faculty who see in the Vietnamese War and the general conduct and assumptions of American foreign policy a negation of their own attitudes and commitments. It is this group that has filled a vast number of costly ads in *The New York Times* and must now realize that there is almost a direct relationship between the size of their protests and escalation of the war. Numbers are purely speculative, but most university people abhor any hint of personal culpability for a war more and more of them oppose, and even if they are not united on what they would have the President do, they are quite certain that their university should not be a part of the miserable business of implementing American policy abroad. To some, myself included, the position is that one cannot hope or wait for Washington to alter its course in Vietnam before military exigencies leave it no alternative, and that America's ability to impose its design in Vietnam promises repetitions in Asia or Latin America that will define the relationship of men of conscience to the government and shape both the quality of our society and the peace of the world for decades to come. Given the utter futility of "positive" suggestions to Washington, the question has now been shifted from chimerical illusions about what one would like the government to do to what we would like to see it unable to do. Strong existential protests and rhetoric—which I fully favor—scarcely alter the ability of Washington to do as it pleases. The university is the one area of American institutional life in which there is any possibility of inhibiting Washington's disastrous course and refusing to abet it. And here, for all the reasons mentioned above, success *is* possible.

In fiscal 1964 the University of Pennsylvania ranked only eleventh in Defense Department university grants, but its Institute for Cooperative Research (ICR), by virtue of over a decade's experience, was a vital center of chemical-biological (CB) warfare development. Its work in creating total CB weapons and delivery systems made it critical to the overall work of the Chemical Corps. The ICR was the only university establishment in the country doing classified research in defoliation and herbicides. It was especially interested in the use of anti-crop chemicals in Vietnam, and it did other studies in psycho-chemical warfare and military technology. If its CB contracts in 1965 were less than $1 million, and its staff only about forty persons, the ICR's own research and subcontracts with Cornell involved such topics as target selection in Vietnam, from which it received much of its field data. Although its published reports revealed the contours of its work, not until September 1965 did the majority of the faculty and students realize such an institute existed on campus. Despite clumsy efforts by the ICR's executives and Penn administration to deny that ICR was working on classified research, much less CB warfare in Vietnam, by late October both student and faculty pressures were becoming too great to be ignored.

The students immediately released all the documents they had or could find and held several very large demonstrations, but by the end of 1965 they had essentially exhausted their levers for applying pressures. The faculty opponents to the ICR at first consisted only of four individuals—two from the sciences—ready to devote necessary time to the effort. They could call upon a larger group, but at no time was the faculty able to create a permanent protest committee. Despite the seemingly indifferent faculty response, these critics distributed a prodigious documentation on the ICR, secrecy in the university and the status of chemical warfare in general.

By early November this group forced the issue to the largest faculty senate meeting in many years. President Gaylord P. Harnwell proposed a resolution, which he described as a prohibition on contracts the results of which were not freely publishable. Obscure in terminology, he implied, but did not clearly state, that the policy would eliminate classified research at ICR. The senate passed the Harnwell resolution by a large majority, along with another asking the administration to apply it to the ICR, because most understood it to be a tactful elimination of the controversial research. What was significant in the vote was merely that the faculty opposed classified research, and when Harnwell several weeks later maintained that the ICR's work would continue, he hoped the faculty would forget the issue.

Given the nonbinding character and vagueness of Harnwell's own resolution, nothing at Penn changed. The original, uncompromising faculty opponents to the ICR continued to produce documentation for the faculty and cultivated the local and national press. The ICR's work was a matter of the Vietnamese War as well as classification, and the four key workers never ceased to regard it in this light. While the *Philadelphia Bulletin* followed the entire controversy in detail, in February 1966 *Scientific American* first gave it national coverage. By May 1966 the official leadership of the faculty senate had failed in their gentle efforts to create a meaningful review board to consider future classified contracts. Their caution was seemingly mocked by the renewal of the CB contracts in April and the persistently honest but tactless statements of the director of the CB research, Prof. Knut Krieger, that "the emphasis of the studies while originally very military in purpose have become even more so." Krieger proudly gave journalists and faculty the fine details of the ICR's work in Vietnam, as well as information on advanced projects in biological warfare, and faculty opponents discovered in Professor Krieger an unwitting and important ally. As he added fuel to the fire, the entire faculty became concerned that the controversy would irreparably damage Penn's national reputation and cause its teaching and research to suffer.

In August 1966 *Ramparts* published a detailed account of the work of the ICR, spreading its focus to the CIA's contacts with Penn's Foreign Policy Research Institute. *The New York Times,* national press services and numerous weeklies descended on what was now the most publicized campus in the United States. On September 4, in a release which made the top of page 1 of *The New York Times,* Harnwell announced the abolition of the ICR and the creation of a hand-picked review board to assure that "all research must be freely publishable." This time the attitude of faculty opponents was too mistrustful not to greet the announcement with reserve. What would happen to existing contracts? Would the review board's decisions be binding? The Pentagon immediately stated that Penn was still doing CB research, along with at least thirty-eight other universities. The faculty was horrified at the international publicity and the false claims of reform.

By this point it was clear to many faculty opponents that a final settlement would require a stand from the as yet unheard from trustees, and that only direct pressures on the university were appropriate. During January of this year, without informing the review board or the provost, Harnwell secretly renewed one of the controversial CB contracts until March 1969, information that was kept confidential for several more months. In mid-February, a group of at least twenty faculty members proclaimed that they would march in the forthcoming commencement wearing gas masks unless Penn abolished CB research work. If anything was representative of the total collapse of faculty-administration relations, this brilliant, perhaps decisive, gesture reflected it. On March 14, in a step designed to stop the masked faculty demonstrators, President Harnwell released a statement to the press indicating that Penn would not renew its CB contracts, which he claimed would expire within a year. The faculty agreed to call off their protest, and prematurely congratulated the president.

Within a few days a skeptical *Philadelphia Bulletin* reporter revealed the secret contract renewal, much to the distress of the entire faculty, students and a good portion of the key administrators who first learned of it from the press. The review board threatened to resign, Harnwell's vice president for government contracts offered to quit as a sacrifice, and by the end of March Harnwell offered to settle the problem by moving the research down the street to the Penn-controlled Science Center.

No one was satisfied, and during April it appeared indeed as if

Penn would soon be paralyzed. The faculty senate quickly convened and overwhelmingly passed a resolution, described by the moderate senate chairman as "one step below censure" of Harnwell, demanding an end to CB research. A faculty gas-mask protest was again threatened, and on April 26 more than 100 students organized a sit-in in the administration building, expanding it into a highly publicized sleep-in in Harnwell's office several nights later.

The inevitable followed shortly thereafter, for the university was sacrificing its entire academic life for chemical and biological warfare research which, *Science* had revealed the prior January, cost the university as much as $50,000 a year of its own funds and had now brought it near chaos. Unknown to most, however, was the fact that at least some departments were experiencing difficulty in hiring new faculty because of the ICR scandal and that a number of senior Penn faculty were openly threatening to leave. More than 100 alumni had written to the university protesting the existence of CB research, and the three local Quaker colleges had objected to moving the ICR's work to the Science Center, in which they were small stockholders. On May 4, the Penn trustees met and voted 39 to 1 to cancel or transfer chemical warfare research as soon as possible, but not to the Science Center. As of this time, no university or research center has agreed to take the Penn CB contracts, and the research has ceased.

The critical element in the abolition of chemical warfare research at Penn was faculty persistence and their refusal to quit once normal and traditionally ineffective channels of communication had broken down. The student pressure was of great assistance, but less durable, and there was little communication and no coordination between faculty and students. Publicity was vital, aided by the relation of the Vietnamese War to the controversial research, but the declining morale of the faculty (as well as the realization that hiring would become more difficult) was no less essential in widening the split in administrative ranks very late in the struggle.

To the Department of Defense the Penn experience was an unhappy one, but their only comment in 1966 was: "We could get along without Penn but we're not very anxious to try." During the House Committee on Appropriations hearings on the Defense budget last March, Congressmen confronted John F. Foster, Jr., director of Defense Research at the Pentagon, with questions on Penn and the possibility of its becoming a precedent, which revealed the military's need for all university research. Foster was "disappointed" that Penn was considering dropping the CB contracts, but hoped they might continue their unclassified contracts. "Have you given any thought to taking it all away from them if they will not do the classified part?" one Congressman asked; "I do not think that would help us. We need their help. . . . I am grateful for that which they are willing to do."

Rear Admiral J. K. Leydon, chief of Naval Research, was somewhat less tranquil several weeks later: "We have . . . been watching very carefully the manifestations that have been coming up in university circles . . . such as the recent publicity at the University of Pennsylvania." Foster, for his part, insisted there was no connection between the resistance to military research and the Vietnamese War, a point he stressed despite the repeated quotations of Penn faculty leaders on the subject in *The New York Times,* and the fact that the anti-ICR leaders were well-known anti-war activists. For the Pentagon to concede that anti-war activity could take this form was to open Pandora's box to the greatest challenge to military research it has confronted in two decades.

No cause is easier to advance than a respectable one. In calling for a return to traditional academic aims and commitments, *The New York Times* and McGraw-Hill's *Scientific Research* editorially praised the objectives of Penn's anti-war and anti-secret-research leaders. No strategy of direct interference with the Pentagon's work is likely to achieve such recognition—much less one that permanently alters the operations of an institution. Given this combination of relevance, respectability and the tactical power of the faculty, over the past year there have been similar manifestations of resistance elsewhere.

At Stanford, Montana and Cornell, to name a few, faculty members have already stimulated efforts to alter existing university-Pentagon relations over the past two years, and other activities are under way. Last November the American Anthropological Association (AAA) prodded by its former president, Ralph L. Beals, initiated a movement to prevent the CIA and Pentagon from continuing to exploit the profession. Dr. Beals insisted that anthropologists reveal not only the sponsorship but also "the purposes of their research," a formulation that goes far beyond mere classification. Early this year the AAA came out against classified research, as well as contracts not related to normal, self-defined research.

Stimulated in part by the revelations on CIA utilization of various contracts, the American Association of University Professors last April urged a comprehensive university reconsideration of all military contracts and their impact on the "autonomy and freedom of academic societies," and this year's session of the American Association for the Advancement of Science has scheduled a full-scale discussion of the

Above all, faculty protest over the relation of the university to the military is likely to grow because of the desire of many academics to resist the war and because the Pentagon has embarked on an important effort—"Project THEMIS"—to incorporate a much larger number of American universities into military research.

Every Defense Department-sponsored project relates to some military problem or system of interest to the Pentagon, and no scientist can assume otherwise. THEMIS' work, ranging from advanced explosives technology to military vehicles, includes the social sciences as well. The Pentagon hopes to find new universities with sufficiently large staffs to engage in these studies and "carry out high-quality research on problems related to national defense." It has allocated $20 million for THEMIS in fiscal 1967, and it has received 477 project proposals from 171 different universities, fifty of which have been selected for this year, with the Pentagon assuming their full costs the first two years and the universities two-thirds of the costs the remaining two. The Pentagon ultimately plans to grant 200 contracts over four years, mainly to hitherto uninvolved universities, all of which they can classify if necessary.

The nature of the university is such that even if a small number wish to accept military research the faculty can define the rules binding on the entire community. And since they need not direct their appeals on the matter to a historically indifferent Washington, but to university administrators who are naturally more responsive and, if necessary, vulnerable, such faculty power means that as they reject military research, whether for political or traditional reasons, they can hope to redefine the relationship of the university to the Defense Department.

When university administrators realize that there is a new breed of faculty willing to discomfit them—and themselves—with embarrassing questions and protests concerning the overall commitments of a school, and ultimately willing to boycott the worst offenders by refusing to stay or move there, then a basis will exist for the transformation of the American university, for many of the most distinguished and promising scholars oppose military research and the war in Vietnam.

The objectives of the resistance to military research should be to: (a) freeze and, where possible, eliminate existing contracts among the top twenty-five recipients; (b) exclude military research from those not already taking it, and in particular to prevent the implementation of THEMIS; (c) create a stigma and ethic among faculty and students concerning participation in military research in the university and outside of it, and ostracize those who insist on pursuing such research.

If the Penn experience is any indication, the faculty can convince or pressure many of the largest universities into giving up classified research, and for such centers as MIT, too economically committed to compromise, only refusal to work there will suffice. Once university administrators realize Pentagon research risks serious repercussions from the remainder of the faculty, they will carefully screen future contract requests before lightly undertaking to repeat the experience of Penn.

As a matter of routine, autonomous faculty-controlled review boards should scrutinize all contracts originating with or proposed to the Defense Department, State Department, CIA and Atomic Energy Commission. Such boards should have the power to survey and, if necessary, reject all contract proposals incompatible with the larger goals and assumptions of the university. This means far more than classified contracts, which is a convenient and easily exploited tactical lever that partially avoids confronting the basic issues of principle. All projects should be publicly explicit as to their purpose and ultimate end, and the Pentagon should indicate what use it intends making of unclassified research so that the scholar and his peers may evaluate its relevance and the commitments such work subsumes. Much social science "soft ware" is not secret, but insofar as military-sponsored research in all fields violates the scholar's values, he should never willingly permit his work to become a means of causing rather than curing, or even merely neutrally observing, man's physical and social ills, and such research should be discouraged. From this viewpoint, the *purpose* of research is quite as relevant as the security provisions and free publishability, and all Defense Department and CIA contracts must be disqualified.

Information on the military research activities in various universities may be obtained from the Pentagon's *Technical Abstracts Bulletin,* often in annual or institute reports to each university president, or from the administration itself. *All* faculty senates should endorse a firm policy on the matter to guide their administrators, most of whom would appreciate avoiding traps such as those that befell Penn's administration and who will confront a growing number of them in coming months. In finding such information, in taking such stands, the American university community may rediscover its own essential purpose and prepare the way for its own renaissance. It may also serve as the last important institutional refuge for the preservation of civilized values and conduct in America today.

PART III
DISTRIBUTION OF HUMAN VALUES: WELFARE

Introduction

Basic economic and social values—social-welfare values—have been the materials for much of the political controversy in American life. The just distribution of the benefits of the American civilization has been a critical matter several times in the life of the Republic: first, in the claims made by mechanics and farmers; second, in the assertions of labor and white immigrant groups within urban America, and currently by the non-Caucasian groups who reside in the core of our cities.

The ground covered by Charles Silberman and Milton Yinger in subsequent essays (Selections 12 and 13) is synthetic rather than original. In turn, they review the social processes of the unprecedented black migration to the urban North and West, and the accomplishments of federal efforts to provide more jobs, education, and housing since 1950. Moreover, their accounts highlight major stresses upon the private political economy and public welfare sectors in seeking to ameliorate human distress.

These stresses include the structural dislocation of semiskilled and unskilled labor in the modern economy. Politically, stress is multiplied by the institutional weakness that has retarded "self-help" propensities in the black community and the distinction between provisions for more individual opportunity and general guarantees of substantive social-welfare values without reference to individual achievement. Of course, the black does not receive anything approaching an equal distribution of our social wealth. Thus, the problems and genuine progress recounted in these essays use liberal guidelines to social-welfare distribution. These are: expanded opportunities (including desegregation), public resources to provide more social goods among black communities, and the use of mixed public and private incentives (for instance, job training and model cities) to provide new life within the fringe political economy permeating the urban black community.

Portions of the debate on the national open-housing bill presented in Selection 14 illustrate the use of federal action to expand the desegregated housing market. Although the proposal was passed only after the tragic death of Dr. Martin Luther King, Jr., its potential contribution was to the social welfare of middle-class blacks, who had already secured basic economic opportunities. Readers should find the opposing arguments of great interest, for they reveal the depth of values associated with the measure. Senator Bennett (R-Utah) stands with "property rights" against "human rights," a time-tested position used by every group seeking to preserve the social and economic status quo. Representative Waggonner (D-Louisiana) raises two other interesting points in his statement of opposition to national open housing: that the bill provides preferential treatment, not simply equal treatment, in its provisions and application, and that the series of civil rights bills under consideration by Congress during the mid-1960s was the product of increased social tension and civic disorder.

Both points should be carefully considered, because the American political economy has preferred and subsidized numerous interests. Oil interests, cotton, minerals, and airlines have been accorded special favors by the executive and the legislature. The difference here—a difference supported by the Kerner Commission's Report on the Causes of Civil Disorder—is that race rather than regional or economic preference is at stake. Moreover, the powerful, established, white-dominated institutions have the responsibility to support these interests that are under-represented in the marketplace of social justice. Waggonner's second point about the distribution of social welfare values as a product of accelerated social conflict is also important because it raises in modern guise an issue put forth by the Levellers of the seventeenth century: to what degree is political stability genuine and enduring without a high measure of equalitarianism in the allocation of social goods?

For more than a decade, the progressive segment of American society has viewed racial issues from the moral and political imperatives of desegregation and racial integration. Piven and Cloward (Selection 15) contend that for low-income blacks these are unrealistic options. The reasons are cogently advanced, and the authors subscribe to the view of black power advocates that housing, education, and other social values need to be made available wherever a group resides. In sum, the effective distribution of social-welfare values hinges upon the allocation of social and political power. Only when the latter forces are poured into the black community will structural changes be forthcoming in the allocation of social goods.

Part of the case against urban desegregation as an effective public strategy hinges on the role ethnic and class agencies play in providing community power and infusing a greater social product within their communities. The point is made clear by Richard Cloward:

> What the Negro needs are the means to organize separately and a heightened awareness of the distinctive goals to which his organizations must be directed. The Negro poor in our society do have interests distinct from, and more often than not, in conflict with those of other groups. Unless they organize along separatist lines, it is unlikely that they will have much success in advancing their interests.

This success requires a broad concept of social power in which many agencies participate. Roy Lubove (Selection 16) is aware that organized social work has never been geared to enhancing the redistribution of power and income among the poor. In his sketch of social work ideology, the public welfare system has been shaped in the image of private social work, with its concern for work, motivation, services, and enhanced individual productivity in lieu of collective economic support. Herein, proposals for family allowances and guaranteed minimum income are related to political strategies designed to strengthen ghetto communities. Social and political structures are importantly related to the revitalization of our cities and the shared power required to redistribute our immense social product.

12 The City and the Negro*

CHARLES E. SILBERMAN

It is the explosive growth of their Negro populations, in fact, that constitutes the large cities' principal problem and concern. When city officials talk about spreading slums, they are talking in the main about physical deterioration of the areas inhabited by Negroes. And when they talk about juvenile delinquency, or the burden of welfare payments, or any of a long list of city problems, officials are talking principally about the problems of Negro adjustment to city life. For the large city is not absorbing and "urbanizing" its new Negro residents rapidly enough; its slums are no longer acting as the incubator of a new middle class.

One reason for this failure is that city planners have been more interested in upgrading the value of the city's real estate than in upgrading the lives of the human beings who inhabit the real estate. They have tried to create middle-class neighborhoods by driving lower-class Negro residents out of the neighborhood being renewed,

*Reprinted from the March 1962 issue of *Fortune* magazine by special permission: copyright © 1962 by Time, Inc.

and bringing white middle-class residents in; Negroes bitterly refer to urban renewal as "Negro removal." (An estimated 80 percent of the families relocated by urban-renewal projects have been Negro.) The effort is doomed to failure. Driving the Negroes out of one area merely creates a new and frequently worse slum somewhere else in the city.

The city can be saved only if it faces up to the fact that "the urban problem" is in large measure a Negro problem. But the Negro problem is more than just an urban problem; it is also the problem of all the U.S., rural or urban, North or South—though it is in the large northern cities that the solution is most likely. Speeding the Negro's integration into American life—helping the big-city Negroes move up into the great American middle class—is the largest and most urgent piece of public business facing the U.S. today.

It is also the most difficult. There is a tendency among many well-intentioned Americans to underestimate this difficulty. Some people see the Negro problem as purely legal and social and assume that it will be solved automatically by desegregating schools, restaurants, bus terminals, and housing developments. Other people see it as purely economic, to be resolved by upgrading Negro jobs and incomes. And a good many Americans believe the problem would be solved if the Negroes would just decide to adopt white middle-class standards of behavior and white middle-class goals of economic success.

There are no cheap or easy answers to the Negro problem, however; it involves all these elements and a good many more besides. The problem's roots go back to slavery, whose impact is still being felt in the disorganization of the Negro family, and to the Negro's systematic exclusion from American society since slavery ended a century ago. These are sins for which all Americans are in some measure guilty and for which all Americans owe some act of atonement. Those who hesitate to act because of the magnitude of the problem should remember the stricture of Edmund Burke: "The only thing necessary for the triumph of evil is for good men to do nothing."

But the triumph of "good" in this instance (as in most others) requires a lot more than good will. To solve the Negro problem will demand difficult and occasionally heroic decisions on the part of civic and political leaders, and changes in the behavior of Americans in every walk of life: teachers and students; trade-union leaders and members; employers and employees. This article—the sixth in *Fortune*'s series on "The Public Business"—will document what is being done across the country, and what needs to be done, to speed the Negro's advance and thereby save the large city.

FILLING THE VACUUM

The Negro has come to the big city because it needed his labor, especially after the cutting off of European immigration created a vacuum in northern labor markets. The Negro population outside the Deep South has increased fivefold since 1910; it has nearly tripled just since 1940. Part of this expansion, of course, has come from natural increase rather than migration; but it is the migration of Negroes in the childbearing ages that enabled the natural increase to occur outside the South.

Most of the Negroes moving to the North have crowded into the slums of the twelve largest cities, which today hold 60 percent of the Negroes living outside the Deep South. Since 1940 the Negro population of New York City has increased nearly two and one-half times, to 1,100,000, or 14 percent of the city's population. In Philadelphia, Negroes have doubled in number since 1940, to 529,000, or 26 percent. The Negro population of Detroit has more than tripled, to nearly 500,000, or 29 percent of the city's population. And the Negro population of Los Angeles County has jumped a phenomenal sixfold since 1940, from 75,000 to 464,000.

The Negroes, to be sure, are not the only disadvantaged peoples coming into the large cities. In New York the Puerto Rican population swelled from perhaps 100,000 in 1940 to over 700,000 in 1960. And Cincinnati, Baltimore, St. Louis, Columbus, Detroit, and Chicago, among others, receive a steady stream of impoverished white hillbillies from the southern Appalachian Mountains. These Appalachian whites— of the oldest and purest U.S. stock—have at least as much initial difficulty adjusting to the city as do the Negroes and Puerto Ricans. But the Puerto Ricans and Appalachian whites affect only a limited number of cities, usually in only a limited way. There are a good many other city problems besides the Negro problem, in short. But the Negro problem is what city planners and officials are really talking about when they refer to The City Problem.

THE CRUCIAL DIFFERENCE

Migration to the large city has always involved a heavy cost in family dislocation, pauperism, crime, delinquency, and urban blight. Immigrants bring with them housekeeping and other habits that clash with city standards; and the impersonality of city life tends to erode the social relationships that regulated behavior in "the old country." Hence the U.S. middle class has always had the sense of being engulfed by uncultivated newcomers, and has always been on the move. As early as the 1840s, for example, New York City's Fourth Ward—the district in which George Washington had lived when he was inaugurated President—had become a slum so overrun by violence that even the police dared not enter except in parties of six or more. And by the 1870s New Yorkers were already lamenting the exodus of men of "moderate income to the suburban towns." With its "middle classes in large part self-exiled, its laboring population being brutalized in the tenements, and its citizens of the highest class indifferent to the common weal," a journalist commented at the time, "New York has drifted from bad to worse and become the prey of professional thieves, ruffians, and political jugglers." Measured against the backdrop of history, therefore, the gangs and crime and squalor of today seem almost benign, and some historians and sociologists have concluded that time and patience are almost all that's needed.

It will take more than that. The Negro is unlike the European immigrant in one crucial respect: he is colored. And that makes all the difference. The Irish, to be sure, faced job discrimination a century ago as severe as the Negro faces today. But the Irishman could lose his brogue; as soon as he was "Americanized," his problem was resolved. But the Negro cannot escape so easily. "All other slum dwellers, when the bank account permits it," James Baldwin has written, "can move out of the slum and vanish altogether from the eye of persecution." Not so the Negro.

There are other differences. The European peasant, no matter how depressed his position, had roots in a "whole society" with a stable culture and stable institutions and above all a stable family life. The Negro does not. Slavery made a stable family life (and a stable culture) impossible. Husbands could be sold away from wives, children from parents. Such family life as did exist centered almost entirely around the mother.

What slavery began, prejudice and discrimination have helped perpetuate. Family disorganization is endemic. Negro women frequently find it easier to get jobs—e.g., as domestics—than Negro men, thus making them the financial center of the family. The inability of Negro men to find jobs that confer status and dignity, together with the servility required of them in the South, have led Negro men to sexual promiscuity, drinking, and violence as means of asserting their masculinity. Embittered by their experience with men, Negro mothers seem to take more interest in their daughters' than in their sons' upbringing. Twice as many Negro girls as boys go to college. (Among white college students, the reverse is true.) And family disorganization is compounded by the overcrowding and dilapidation of Negro housing.

Hence the Negro, all too often, is trapped in a vicious circle from which he cannot extricate himself. Little in the Negro boy's environment is likely to give him any sense of aspiration or any direction; he has no male model to follow and little reason to assume that education offers a way out of the slum. His lack of education and aspiration, in turn, makes it virtually impossible for the Negro youth to find a job with dignity and status, even where discrimination is absent. All too often, therefore, he decides that there is no point to trying, and he loses the capacity to take advantage of such opportunities as do arise.

In the jargon of the social worker, he "develops a self-defeating mode of living" that keeps him trapped in the slum forever.

To make matters worse, the gap is widening between Negro education and training, on the one hand, and the requirements of the labor market, on the other. The Europeans immigrated during periods of rapidly expanding U.S. demand for unskilled labor; no great transfer of skill was needed to enable an Irish or Italian peasant to find a job on a construction gang. But in the U.S. today, the demand for unskilled labor is shrinking relative to the total labor force. Since 1947, employment of white-collar workers—executives, entrepreneurs, professional and scientific employees, clerks, and salesmen—has gone up 43 percent, compared to only a 14 percent gain in blue-collar and service-worker employment. By 1970 a substantial majority of workers will be in white-collar or highly skilled blue-collar jobs—in jobs that characteristically require real training and thought. Three out of four nonfarm Negro male workers, however, are in unskilled or semiskilled occupations, compared to only one in three among white workers.

In this new world of specialized skills, Negroes have more and more trouble finding and holding jobs. The unemployment rate among Negro men is more than twice that among white men. In some cities as many as one Negro male in three is out of work. The problem is particularly acute among Negro youths; in one northern Negro slum area surveyed by Dr. James B. Conant, 70 percent of the young men who had left school were out of work; in another the ratio was over 50 percent.

THE OTHER SIDE OF JORDAN

It would be a serious mistake to equate the Negro's apparent apathy and lack of motivation with a sense of contentment. It is a lot harder for today's Negro to bear his poverty and lack of status than it was for the European immigrant, who arrived at a time when the great majority of the population was poor. The Negro migration, by contrast, is occurring in an affluent society. Like the underdeveloped peoples everywhere, American Negroes have been fired by the revolution of rising expectations. In Harry Ashmore's phrase, Negroes have seen "the other side of Jordan"; they are in a hurry to cross. Among a good many Negroes, especially the college students involved in the sit-in movement, impatience with their rate of progress has conquered apathy and led to direct, disciplined, and frequently courageous action to improve the Negro position in American life. But among the great mass of working-class Negroes and a large part of the middle class, apathy exists side by side with a growing, festering resentment of their lot. These Negroes are more and more convinced that they should have a better life; they are less and less convinced that they themselves can do anything about it.

Impatience is greatest, perhaps, in the area of civil rights; the Supreme Court decision on school segregation raised expectations of a new era in race relations that has been painfully slow in coming. But Negroes are also impatient over their economic progress. During World War II and the early postwar boom, Negroes did make remarkable economic strides; the median income of urban Negro males shot up from less than 40 percent of white income in 1939 to 60 percent in 1952. Negroes have not been able to improve their relative position since 1952, however; the slowdown in the economy during the 1950s bore most heavily on the durable-goods industries, where many Negroes are employed. Thus the income of the average Negro male city dweller, which was 60 percent of the average white income in 1952, had gone up only to 61 percent by 1960. Outside the cities, average Negro income has actually declined since 1952.

As a result, impatience is turning into bitterness, anger, and hatred. The danger is not violence but something much deeper and harder to combat: a sense of permanent alienation from American society. Unless the Negro position improves very quickly, Negroes of whatever class may come to regard their separation from American society as permanent, and so consider themselves permanently outside the constraints and the allegiances of American society. The Negro district of every large city would come to constitute an American Casbah, with its own values and its own controls—and a deep hostility to the white community. In such a situation, communication between the races would become impossible. And life in the large city would become unbearable.

But the Negro advance depends on changes within the Negro community as well as within the white community. Understandably, Negroes have been reluctant to recognize this fact. They have assumed that an end to discriminatory practices will by itself solve the Negro problem. It will do nothing of the sort, although an end to discrimination certainly is a prerequisite to any solution. "If the color barrier could be eliminated overnight," Professor Eli Ginzberg of Columbia put the matter baldly in *The Negro Potential*, "that fact alone would not materially improve the position of the Negro."

The truth is that too many Negroes are unable—or unwilling—to compete in an integrated society. Because of the shortage of professional and technical personnel in industry and government, just about any qualified Negro can get a good job, but employers willing to hire Negroes have trouble finding Negroes to hire. Colleges and medical and professional schools eager to admit Negroes (and to give them scholarships) cannot find as many qualified Negroes as they are willing to admit; the National Scholarship and Service Fund for Negro

Students reports that there are five times as many places available in northern colleges as there are Negroes to fill them. Nor have Negroes been taking advantage of the professional and business opportunities that the growth of the big-city Negro population has offered. The number of Negro physicians in the U.S. has been static for fifty years. As the U.S. Commission on Civil Rights sadly concluded, a principal reason for continued Negro poverty is "the lack of motivation on the part of many Negroes to improve their educational and occupational status."

The Negro community also lacks the sort of self-help institutions through which the European immigrants climbed out of their slums. Negroes, as Professor James Q. Wilson of Harvard put it in *Negro Politics,* are "the objects rather than the subjects of civic action. Things are often done for, or about, or to, or because of Negroes, but they are less frequently done *by* Negroes." There is no tradition of Negro philanthropy. Because the Negro has no indigenous culture to protect, the Negro community has not seen the same need to organize itself that European ethnic groups felt. The paucity of Negro self-help organizations may also be due to the tremendous growth of public assistance during the past quarter-century. The fact that help now comes from the city or state or federal government, sociologist Nathan Glazer suggests, has tended to channel "social energies" into the formulation of demands for new governmental programs rather than into the establishment and financing of voluntary organizations among Negroes.

THE NEED FOR EXCELLENCE

This institutional vacuum must be filled. For one thing, charitable and social-welfare programs organized, staffed, and supported by Negroes are likely to have a much greater impact on Negro behavior than programs administered by government or by private white agencies, both of which tend to be viewed with suspicion and hostility. Then, too, as Professor Ginzberg has been reminding Negro audiences, freedom is only the precondition for equality, not its equivalent. The more Negroes get what they want in terms of formal rights—voting, education, desegregation, etc.—the more responsibility they will have to assume for their own well-being.

This fact is now beginning to get its due. Perhaps the most important single factor making for solution of the Negro problem is the emergence of pride of race among Negroes. This new pride is the product of many factors: the Negro gains during World War II, the independence of the African nations, the courage and dignity shown by the sit-ins and Freedom Riders. Pride, to be sure, is always a two-edged sword; among the Black Muslims it leads to hatred of everything white and to threats of anti-white violence. But overall, the new sense of pride is serving to raise the level of Negro aspirations and behavior; even the Black Muslims stress the importance of work, sobriety, chastity, and self-discipline.

A growing number of Negro leaders and spokesmen, moreover— particularly at the national level—are encouraging Negroes to assume more responsibility for their own fate. "All the intellectual arguments and sociological explanations in the world," the distinguished Negro journalist, Carl Rowan, now Deputy Assistant Secretary of State for Public Affairs, has written, "do not meet fully the need to do something about the fact that people are being killed and maimed, street gangs are spreading terror in big cities, young girls are bearing an increasing number of illegitimate children, and dope and gin mills are flourishing in our urban centers." Negro leaders must recognize, Rowan argues—and in fact, they are beginning to recognize—"that it is not enough to blame every Negro misdeed on segregation, or to pretend that integration will be a cure-all for every social problem in sight." . . .

The National Urban League, moreover, is shifting its emphasis from opening up new job opportunities to preparing Negroes for the job opportunities that are opening up. "It's one thing to eliminate barriers," Dr. Whitney Young Jr., the league's dynamic new executive director, observes, "and quite another to get a previously depressed people to take advantage of the new opportunities." Dr. Young believes that Negro family life must be stabilized if Negroes are to be able to take advantage of these opportunities, and he's looking for funds to finance an ambitious new program in which the league would recruit a number of settled, well-adjusted middle-class Negro families to "adopt" a newly settled family and facilitate their adjustment to urban life.

"MORE POWERFUL THAN APATHY"

There is reason to think that Negroes, even those living in the worst sort of slum, can be mobilized to help themselves. In many ways the most impressive experiment affecting the Negro anywhere in the U.S. is going on now in Chicago's Woodlawn area, an oblong slum running south of the University of Chicago campus and containing about 100,000 people, almost all Negro. Woodlawn's physical decomposition is more than matched by its social disorganization. It is the principal port of entry for Negroes coming to Chicago from the South, and so has had a large transient population. It also contains a flourishing traffic in gambling, narcotics, and prostitution. Woodlawn, in short, is a social chaos of the sort that social workers have always assumed can never produce a large, active organization.

It's producing one now. The guiding genius is a highly controversial Chicago sociologist and criminologist, Dr. Saul D. Alinsky, executive director of the Industrial Areas Foundation. (No one else in the city of Chicago, as two Woodlawn ministers have written, "is as detested or as loved, as cursed or blessed, as feared or respected.") Alinsky was one of the principal architects of Chicago's much-admired Back of the Yards Neighborhood Council, which has turned a white slum area that had been the locale for Upton Sinclair's *The Jungle* into one of the most desirable working-class neighborhoods in Chicago. Alinsky was asked by three Protestant ministers and a Catholic priest to organize Woodlawn; the project is being financed by grants from the Catholic Archdiocese of Chicago, the Presbyterian Church, and a private philanthropy, the Schwartzhaupt Foundation.

If Alinsky succeeds, it will be the first time a large, broadly representative organization will have come into existence in any Negro district in any large American city. Alinsky is trying to create an organization that, as one local leader puts it, "will be the most powerful thing in Woodlawn—more powerful than the political party . . . more powerful than the apathy that holds the community in its grasp." He eschews the usual appeals to homeowners' interests in conserving property values or to a general neighborhood spirit or civic pride—appeals, in his view, that apply only to middle-class neighborhoods. Alinsky, instead, uses the classical approach of trade-union organization. He appeals to the self-interest of the local residents and to their resentment and distrust of the outside world, and he develops a local, indigenous leadership.

"THEY'RE PAYING ATTENTION"

The issue that is principally animating Woodlawn now is the University of Chicago's proposal to annex a strip a block wide and a mile long adjacent to the campus. The Negro residents have no particular attachment to the strip in question, but they suspect that its annexation will be the prelude to bulldozing a large part of the area for middle- and upper-income apartment houses. There is ample basis for their fears; urban-renewal projects have been going on for some time under university sponsorship in the Hyde Park–Kenwood district north of the university, designed in good measure to clear Negroes out. To force the university and city-planning officials to bargain with the Woodlawn residents, Alinsky is mobilizing the residents into a group called the Temporary Woodlawn Organization; he had 8000 Woodlawn people enrolled in the TWO within six months of the project's inception. The TWO organized an impressive campaign to get the usually apathetic Woodlawn residents registered and voting; during the registration period last August, a caravan of forty-six buses took some 2300 members down to City Hall to register.

What makes the Woodlawn experiment significant, however, is not what it is doing *for* its members but what it is doing *to* them. "The most important thing to me about the forty-six busloads of people who went to City Hall to register," Alinsky says, "was their own reaction. Many were weeping; others were saying, 'They're paying attention to us.' 'They're recognizing that we're people.' " What is crucial, in short, is not what the Woodlawn residents win, but the fact that *they* are winning it. This fact seems to make the Woodlawn members see themselves in a new light, as people of substance and worth. While Alinsky's methods create a sense of militancy that could be misused, they create a sense of responsibility as well, and this is their most important product so far.

THE TWENTY-POINT DROP

The Negro problem is not just the responsibility of the Negro community, of course; its resolution requires drastically changed policies by a variety of governmental agencies. The social institution that touches the Negro problem most directly is the public school, which since the 1890s has been the principal means by which newcomers to the city, or their offspring, have been able to move out of the slums. The public school offers the greatest opportunity to dissolve the cultural barrier that blocks the Negro's advance into the mainstream of American life.

The opportunity is being muffed. Admittedly the problems encountered in the Negro (or for that matter, the white) slum school are enough to discourage the best-intentioned. Children entering school are ill-prepared, poorly motivated, and badly behaved; teachers must spend inordinate amounts of time maintaining order, and they are occasionally in danger of physical harm. Because families move from tenement to tenement with great frequency, pupil turnover is incredibly high—more than 100 percent in some New York slum schools; the standard quip has it that if a teacher is absent a week, she won't recognize her class when she returns. Under these conditions one might reasonably expect that cities would spend more per Negro pupil than they do per white pupil. The reverse is generally true; the schools in Negro slum areas are the most overcrowded, are manned with the least-experienced teachers, and have the highest ratio of students to teachers.

The results are predictably poor. Coming from semiliterate or illiterate backgrounds, which not only offer no incentive to learn but rather frequently regard the school as a hostile force, many children never learn to read properly. Their inability to read at grade level in turn makes them fall behind in every other subject, even vocational courses; for example, shop students can't learn carpentry if they can't read blueprints or calculate fractions of an inch. The result is that their learning ability itself becomes atrophied; IQ typically drops twenty points as the Negro child progresses through school. By junior or senior high, it is almost impossible to reach him or teach him; three out of five Negro youngsters drop out of school before completion— uneducated, seemingly uneducable, and virtually unemployable. And yet these children can be educated; New York City and St. Louis, in particular, as we shall see, have demonstrated the fact beyond doubt.

The question first is, what kind of education can they—and should they—be given? Unfortunately, the current discussion is being shaped by Dr. James B. Conant's recent *Slums and Suburbs,* which has been accepted blandly and uncritically by almost everyone concerned with the problem, Negro or white. Dr. Conant has performed a great public service in calling attention to the dimensions of the problem and to the need for immediate action. But he has prescribed the worst possible remedy: a great expansion of vocational education for Negro youth.

If Conant's advice were followed, it would doom the Negro permanently to the bottom rung on the economic ladder. "A generation or two ago," as Professor Eli Ginzberg put it in *The Negro Potential,* "a man with negligible formal education could become a skilled worker. Today, participation in the industrial process requires of the worker not only basic literacy but a fairly high level of ability to deal with words and figures." The worker must be able to follow written instructions, to read the bulletin board, to keep various kinds of records, to master considerable technical knowledge. And he must be able to learn new skills, for nobody knows what job skills will be needed ten years from now.

What the Negro child needs, in short, is the same kind of education the white child needs and is beginning to get: an education that teaches him how to learn, that gives him the intellectual discipline and depth of understanding that will enable him to meet new conditions as they arise. But it will take more than a return to the three R's to give Negro children this kind of education. To penetrate the environmental and cultural curtain that keeps the Negro child from learning, the school must take on a whole range of functions that lie outside its normal sphere.

A SUCCESS STORY

The most spectacular demonstration of what can be done to raise the aspirations and performance of Negro slum children is occurring in St. Louis, in the "Banneker group"—twenty-three elementary schools enrolling 16,000 children, 95 percent of them Negroes living in the city's worst slum. Dr. Samuel Shepard Jr., the assistant superintendent in charge of the Banneker district, decided to take action four years ago, when the city's high schools instituted a three-track system of ability grouping. Only 7 percent of the Banneker graduates were able to make the top ability track; nearly half were put in the bottom track. In three years Dr. Shepard has been able to triple the proportion of Banneker graduates admitted to the first track, from 7 percent to 21 percent, and to cut the number going into the bottom group to 21 percent. Last June, in fact, Shepard's eighth-graders actually exceeded the national norm in reading; three years before the Banneker eighth-graders had been a full year behind.

The results largely reflect the impact of Shepard's powerful personality and dedicated leadership. He has changed teachers' and principals' attitudes toward their students from one of condescension to one of sympathy and challenge. More important, he has changed the Negro community's attitude toward the school. He keeps up a steady fire of meetings and of assemblies, field trips, pep talks, contests, and posters, designed to inculcate a respect for learning. For the children, he sets up a very competitive athletic-like atmosphere, in which the kudos goes to "the achievers." For the parents, Shepard uses an extremely blunt approach. He shows them by slides, charts, and film strips exactly how poorly their children are doing and warns them that unless the children do better in school they'll be no better off than their parents. He explains that things *can* be different for children, he shows in great detail the relation between education and employment, pointing to specific jobs now open to Negroes in St. Louis for which no qualified Negroes can be found. He also explains at length how the school operates at each grade, what the parents should demand of their children, and how they can help. And through all of this he emphasizes reading as the key to academic—and vocational—success.

Shepard has achieved these results without the use of extra resources; the greatest strength of his program is the fact that it depends on the ordinary classroom teacher. But remedial-reading teachers, guidance counselors, psychologists, and social workers can also be used to good effect, as New York City has shown with its Demonstration Guidance Project and its Higher Horizons program. In the first year of the Higher Horizons program the city was able to cut third-graders' retardation in reading from six months to only one month. Under grants from the Ford Foundation's Great Cities School Improvement Project, other cities are experimenting with a variety of techniques. Detroit and Philadelphia, for example, are employing "school-community agents" in slum schools to try to break down parental suspicion and hostility and persuade parents of the importance of education.

The programs now in operation, however, affect only a minute fraction of the children needing special help. What must be done is to put these programs into effect on a mass scale. To do so will cost money, of course. But the cities will get the money back—and a lot more besides—in lower relief costs, decreased juvenile delinquency and crime, and increased income for its residents—not to mention a radical improvement in the whole quality of city life. "A community which made its schools rather than its central business district the tender object and physical center of its urban-renewal operations," Paul Ylvisaker recently suggested, "would be taking one of the noblest and shrewdest steps forward in the civic progress of this century."

THE UNDERDEVELOPED COUNTRY

The city, in short, must exercise "positive discrimination" in favor of the Negro if it is to enable the mass of Negroes to compete with whites on equal terms. The U.S. must learn to look upon the Negro community as if it were an underdeveloped country.

One thing that must be done—by industry and labor, as well as by government—is to develop long-range programs to educate workers who are already out of school, and whose lack of education makes them particularly vulnerable to technological unemployment. Armour's experience in trying to retrain workers made idle by automation has shown clearly that crash programs can provide only limited help. Of the 170 employees who applied for retraining when the company closed its Oklahoma City meat-packing plant, for example, 110 could not be given any training because they lacked the minimum skills in reading and mathematics. (See Labor, *Fortune,* July, 1961.)

There must also be a broadening of job opportunities for Negroes. There has been a significant reduction in job discrimination against Negroes in recent years, largely because of government prodding, but Negroes still find it very difficult to obtain jobs in the skilled trades, where union prejudice is a big stumbling block, and in clerical and sales jobs. It isn't enough for employers to make jobs formally available to Negroes; as a result of generations of discrimination, Negroes tend to assume that prejudice exists even where it has ended.

A special effort must be made, therefore, to publicize the new job openings; Negroes must be brought within the web of job gossip through active recruitment.

Meanwhile, cities must try to alleviate some of the disorganization of Negro family and community life. The city has a vast panoply of services designed to prevent, relieve, and cure problems of individual and family behavior and circumstance. But each service deals separately with the individuals involved, sometimes in bureaucratic competition with the others. As often as not, the Negro—or the white slum dweller, for that matter—sees the bewildering array of police, school, and welfare agencies as enemies to be played off one against another.

It is possible to close the distance between the individual and government, and to coordinate the activities of the agencies affecting him. Wayne Thompson, the young city manager of Oakland, California, has pulled together seven public agencies representing four levels of government into something called the Associated Agencies. Fortnightly meetings of the AA workers in each section of the city are held to coordinate their work. In dealing with one school marked by frequent violence, for example, the school superintendent allowed the police to seal off the school area and then clean out the guns and knives in the school lockers. The school, police, recreation, probation, and welfare workers then culled a list of troublemakers, letting each agency take responsibility for the children it already knew, or upon whom it had some particular claim. Out of 2800 pupils, only fifty-four turned out to be real troublemakers; when the whole job had been finished, only two had to be moved out of school and into detention. Since the Associated Agencies program started in the late 1957, Oakland has been relatively free of trouble. The city recently received a $2-million grant from the Ford Foundation to extend the program.

New York City is trying to accomplish somewhat the same thing through its Neighborhood Conservation Projects. The coordination is not as complete, and the emphasis is fairly heavy on conservation of real estate rather than of human beings. But several projects have gone beyond physical rehabilitation—e.g., in the Bloomingdale district on Manhattan's West Side. The projects, in a sense, are designed to create a modern-day (but honest) counterpart to the old Tammany district leader, who served a very important function for the European immigrant, in effect locating him in the city and providing a channel to its government.

THE HOUSING DILEMMA

More must also be done about Negro housing. Despite a remarkable improvement in the condition of Negro housing since the end of World War II, nearly half of all the houses and apartments occupied by Negroes are still classified as "dilapidated" or "deteriorating" in the census rolls, compared to only 15 percent of white homes. And Negroes live under far more crowded conditions. While good housing doesn't guarantee good behavior, bad housing does contribute to family disorganization and hence to delinquency.

The deterioration and overcrowding of Negro housing are due in good measure to the poverty of Negroes as a group. A study of the

Philadelphia housing market by Chester Rapkin and William Grigsby of the University of Pennsylvania, for example, disclosed that only about 5 percent of all Negro households had incomes sufficient to buy houses costing $12,000 or more—about the minimum price at which private builders were able to erect houses in that city. But discrimination as well as income robs the Negro of freedom of choice. Housing, as the U.S. Civil Rights Commission puts it, with only slight exaggeration, is "the one commodity in the American market which is not freely available on equal terms to everyone that can afford to pay."

Because economic and social factors bar Negroes from the market for new construction—and because Negro population is growing at an explosive rate in most large cities—Negroes are constantly looking for homes in the older, less expensive areas of the city. This pressure is as unsettling for the white community as it is for the Negro, for it leads to unstable and rapidly changing neighborhoods. To most white persons, as Eunice Grier of the Washington Center for Metropolitan Studies puts it, "there is no such thing . . . as a stable and permanent integrated neighborhood." Hence, when Negro demand appears in a neighborhood, the community either resists Negro entry—sometimes with violence—or it abandons the neighborhood completely. The latter usually occurs in any case. As Negroes start moving in, the whites start moving out—some because of prejudice, others because they fear that if they remain they will rapidly become a minority. Integration, as Saul Alinsky sardonically observes, "is usually a term to describe the period of time that elapses between the appearance of the first Negro and the exit of the last white."

There is considerable evidence to suggest that whites *will* live in integrated neighborhoods if they have some reassurance that they will not be swamped. For that reason a number of housing experts now advocate the use of "benign quotas" as the best—or only—means of solving the Negro housing problem. New York City's Housing Authority, for example, is using a quota system to try to integrate its low and middle-income housing projects, with fair success.

But the benign quota is no panacea and will work only where there is some authority able to decide how many Negroes will be admitted, and to determine which Negroes will be admitted. The authority must be powerful enough to enforce compliance after the quota has been filled. Enforcing a quota, moreover, frequently involves a painful conflict between two laudable objectives—housing integration and an increased supply of housing for Negroes. In order to maintain the desired racial balance, a housing authority frequently has to turn down qualified Negroes in desperate need of housing in favor of whites whose need is far less acute.

It's doubtful, in short, whether any simple, dramatic approach can solve the Negro housing problem. So long as the great majority of

Negroes have slum incomes, they are going to live in slums. In the long run, therefore, the only way to solve the problem of Negro housing is to solve the problem of Negro people—to raise the economic and social level of the Negro community.

THE COST OF DELAY

A new pride in self that is developing among Negroes is a powerful lever to raise Negro aspirations and achievements. The Negro's growing political activity is a powerful lever to force cities to face up to the problem; the Negro vote was decisive in last fall's mayoralty elections in Atlanta, Detroit, and New York.

And the U.S. economy itself should facilitate the Negro's advance during the 1960s. In a rapidly expanding economy employers will have to end job discrimination and upgrade unskilled and semiskilled Negro workers if they are to produce all their markets will demand. The training programs developed during World War II show what industry can do when the stakes are high enough. And with a shortage of skilled labor likely, unions will have far less incentive to restrict entry into the skilled occupations.

These trends will make solution of the Negro problem less difficult; but they will not solve it. If the Negroes are to take their proper place in U.S. society, millions of hard decisions will have to be taken by people of both races. And the longer the U.S. delays those decisions, the more painful this most urgent piece of public business will become.

13 Desegregation in American Society: The Record of a Generation of Change*

J. MILTON YINGER

Although some forms of segregation are accepted in all societies, other forms are opposed because they contradict basic values and disrupt the workings of the social system. Social change may transfer a particular form of segregation from the accepted to the opposed category. This has happened to racial segregation in the United States, where pressures toward desegregation have developed in virtually every aspect of social life. The extent of the change is briefly described and the probable future course of events is noted.

We have heard such terms as revolution and explosion so often in recent years that they have lost all shock value. This should not cause us to forget that this *is* a period of dramatic change—not least of all in the nature of intergroup contact. There are patterns of racial and

*Reprinted by permission of the author and publisher from *Sociology and Social Research*, 47 (July 1963).

cultural relations in the United States that were difficult to imagine twenty-five years ago. Although not without exceptions, the strongest trends have been in the direction of greater integration. An attempt will be made here to document that fact carefully and explore some of its significance for American society.

The term integration is used in various ways. In referring to an integrated society, this commonly implies one in which the members, regardless of race, religion, or national origin, move freely among one another, sharing the same opportunities and the same public facilities and privileges on an equal basis. Does the term imply also the absence of any barriers to purely private associations? Yes, if one is thinking of full integration; for we are dealing with a variable that can have many different scale values, from little to much.

Whereas integration is a state of affairs, desegregation is a process—a process of change within a society during which the degree of segregation is reduced. This too is a variable; desegregation can range from a small increase in the amount of interaction across group lines (three or four Negro children admitted to a formerly all-white school) to a major reduction in the number and height of the barriers to association. In this sense, it is not entirely meaningful to say that a factory or school or church as "been desegregated"—as if one were speaking of an either-or situation. But we shall occasionally use that phrase to mean that a formerly fully segregated situation has taken one or more steps toward integration. In most instances the first step is the most difficult and critical, thus partly justifying reference to it as desegregation.

It is important to ask how the process of desegregation is set in motion, sometimes breaking up stable patterns of segregation that have existed for many generations. There are varieties of segregation in all societies. To some degree it is the natural expression of group identity and function. Some forms of segregation are repugnant to a society, however, because they violate its basic values or because they create enormous problems.

Conflict over segregation may occur because the lines of separation that are taken for granted or approved in a society do not remain static. As a result of social change which creates new issues for the nation to handle, forms of segregation become unacceptable that formerly were allowed. But since the change hits individuals and regions in different ways and at different rates, there is often a period of sharp controversy during which some persons say, "the old way represents a desirable pluralism and a legitimate separation," while others say, "the old way represents a threat to the health of the society."

The United States is now in the midst of such a process of redefinition with respect to racial and religious segregation. It is no longer simply taken for granted; the older patterns of intergroup relations are rapidly being modified. Urbanization and industrialization, America's world position, and the growth in economic and political power among minority-group members strongly support the integration process. It is well also to note that desegregation has become a national, not simply a southern question. The economy is increasingly national in scope, as Arkansas businessmen painfully learned after 1957. And the migration of minority-group members has brought the question of segregation directly to the attention of almost every region of the country. Virtually all of the persons of Puerto Rican descent, many of the Mexican-Americans, and over forty percent of the Negroes in the United States now live in the North and West.

THE RECORD OF CHANGE

For two generations after the Civil War segregation was taken for granted by almost everyone. There were changes during this period, but the pace was so slow that even the cumulative effect over several decades was slight. Then, beginning perhaps in the early 1930s, there was a quickening in the rate of change, particularly in the South. Although it started from a lower base, the South has been industrializing and urbanizing more rapidly than the rest of the nation for the last twenty-five years. Among other things, this has meant a tremendous migration of Negroes away from the rural areas, most of them to northern cities. In the 1940s, 1,245,000 nonwhites (almost all of them Negroes) migrated to the North and West. In the 1950s migration was even heavier: 1,457,000 nonwhites, one out of seven of those living in the South in 1950, moved out of the region. At the same time, the colored population of southern cities increased at a rapid rate, a fact of great significance in understanding the process of desegregation; for interaction in the city, as sociologists have long observed, is significantly different from life on the planatation.[1]

It would be a mistake, in this account of desegregation, to forget the vigor and local effectiveness of the opposition. Since the purpose of this paper is to measure the steps being taken toward integration, however, I shall not record the evidence of this opposition—the schools that have been closed, the violence, the devices used to try to prevent colored citizens from registering to vote, and other signs that segregation is approved by some people. In some places, schools and parks have been closed rather than accept an order to integrate them.

[1] See J. Milton Yinger, and George E. Simpson, "Can Segregation Survive in an Industrial Society," *Antioch Review,* 8 (Spring 1958), 15–24.

A tiny amount of integration is being used in other localities in the hope that a token change will satisfy Federal courts and other agencies that are pressing for desegregation. Such facts are important for the student of American society. More important, however, are the evidences of change. It is not surprising that strong forces seek to preserve an established institutional pattern. It is more noteworthy that extensive change is underway in almost every aspect of national life. . . .

POLITICS

These developments can partly be understood as a result of changes in the United States affecting the political power of minority groups, especially of Negroes, who constitute over ten percent of the population. Three factors are of greatest importance in these changes: The elimination of the "white primary" in 1944 has been followed by a steady increase of Negro registration and voting in the South. In 1944 there were approximately 250,000 registered Negro voters in the South; in 1962 there were nearly one and a half million. (It should be noted that this represents only about twenty percent of the potential Negro electorate, compared with a registration of sixty percent among whites.) Inevitably the increased voting power of Negroes has resulted in competition for their support in some districts. In most areas where Negro voters are important they have won better police protection, more attention to their school needs, and in abatement in racist campaigns.

The second cause of the change has been the growth in size and importance of the white, urban middle class in the South. Their political interests do not all coincide with those of the landed gentry. Intra- and inter-party competition is developing. And where parties and politicians compete, they seek votes from formerly neglected groups. Urban voters are grossly under-represented in American politics, particularly on the state level, and particularly in the South. This important fact is beginning to change as a result of the Supreme Court decision barring practices that support gross inequality of representation among voters.

The third force affecting the political role of minorities in the United States has been the vast migratory movement of Negroes to northern cities. In at least eight industrial states, colored voters now hold strategic "balance of power" positions. To neglect their interests is to court defeat.

The effect of these three developments, supported by the increase in educational level and economic power of minorities, has been to give strong political impetus to the desegregation process. The 1960 election illustrates decisively the strategic importance of colored voters. The average shift from the Republican to the Democratic ticket between 1956 and 1960 was eight percent, just barely enough to elect President Kennedy. Among Negro voters, however, there was a shift of sixteen percent. Had the Democrats increased their vote among Negroes by only the eight percent that was the national average, Mr. Nixon would now be president. President Kennedy's margin of victory in Texas, South Carolina, Illinois, New Jersey, Michigan and several other states was far smaller than the number of votes he received from Negroes. These simple facts have not been overlooked by either party and will surely affect future campaigns.

THE ARMED FORCES

Closely related to the legal and political changes that we have discussed has been the desegregation of the armed forces of the United States since 1950. With only minor exceptions, all branches of the service segregated colored from white troops before and during the Second World War. This policy was abruptly changed when President Truman, after receiving the report of his Committee on Equality of Treatment and Opportunity in the Armed Services in 1950, ordered an immediate and rapid integration of all branches of the service. By 1954 the *New York Times* could write, perhaps only slightly prematurely, that racial integration in the armed forces is "one of the biggest stories of the twentieth century." In a period of three or four years, most of the barriers to the participation of colored Americans were removed. They are still vastly under-represented in the National Guard and in the officer corps, particularly of the Navy and the Marines. This latter fact is partly indicative of the lack of seniority and the lack of training. Only to a residual degree does it represent the lack of equal treatment. Integration of the armed forces has been accompanied by integration of government owned shore installations and other facilities for civilian employees and of schools for the children of service men. It has also meant that more Negroes are getting skilled training, some are receiving increased income, and throughout the services there has been an increase of equal-status contact across race lines.

EMPLOYMENT AND INCOME

In this brief listing I can only illustrate the changes affecting minority-group families that are taking place in the American economic system. Particularly since 1940 colored workers have made substantial gains in the income and skill levels of their jobs. Not all of the gains have been accompanied by desegregation; but the tendency is for the walls of separation to be lowered along with the lowering of income and skill differentials.

The average income of nonwhite families in 1930 was approximately thirty percent of the income of white families; by 1960 it had increased to sixty percent. Viewing these facts, one can remark the continuing large contrast or emphasize the extent of the reduction in the differential—and be correct either way. If the trend is of greatest interest, however, we should stress the closing of the income gap, roughly at the rate of one percent per year. If this trend were to continue, by the end of the century the average income of white and colored families would be equal.

Perhaps the most important aspect of the economic situation is the changing job pattern. Although still seriously disprivileged, the colored population has made important gains in the stable core of urban jobs for men—doubtless the best index of its place in the American economy. On the white collar level (professional, managerial, clerical, and sales jobs), the percentage of white males increased, between 1940 and 1962, from 30.3 to 41.2, while the percentage of nonwhite males in these jobs increased from 5.6 to 16.0. Although the latter change is slightly smaller in absolute amount (10.4 percent to 10.9 percent), it is a much larger relative gain for the nonwhites. On the semi-skilled and skilled job levels, colored men made steady gains during the same period. The increase among white workers was from 34.3 percent to 38.6 percent; among nonwhites it was from 16.6 percent to 32.7 percent. Most of these workers were recruited from the ranks of the unskilled and from among farm laborers, hence the new jobs represented significant improvement in their economic status.[2]

On the other hand, colored workers have persistently been hit much more severely by unemployment. Because their jobs are more often on the lower levels of skill, they are more seriously affected by automation. Participation in apprenticeship programs and skilled crafts has increased only slightly since World War II.

On balance, the forces have supported a slow trend toward job improvement for nonwhite Americans. Urban migration, improved education, industrial unions, state and local Fair Employment Practices laws, federal civil service and contract policy, and perhaps most importantly the high level of economic prosperity in the nation sustain the gains among minority-group workers. Some of these forces have had ambivalent results, to be sure, but their net effect has been to support the desegregation of the economy of the United States.

[2]United States Department of Labor, "The Economic Situation of Negroes in the United States," Bulletin S-3, Revised, 1962.

HOUSING

The extensive migratory movement of colored families into the cities of the nation and the improvement of their incomes, among other factors, have focused increasing attention on residential segregation. In many ways this is more a northern than a southern question, for the most numerous blocks of segregated houses are in the large northern cities. Many Yankees who critize the South for its segregated schools defend housing arrangements that have many of the same consequences for race relations and for personality development that school segregation has.

Housing desegregation has proceeded more slowly than almost any other phase of the process of change of the last generation. Most contractors and developers build for white families only; a few build for colored families; and a tiny fraction—a few score throughout the nation—build integrated projects. There are many integrated public housing units; yet there is a tendency among some of these to drift toward segregation. Even the process of urban redevelopment sometimes increases segregation: the deteriorated housing, often occupied by minority-group families, may be replaced by units too expensive for them. They are forced into the already overcrowded segregated areas, contributing to their further deterioration.

Some persons who accept integration in public facilities or in jobs resist the idea of desegregating housing because it represents a change near the "social" end of the scale of contact. This feeling is complicated by the fact the a house is a major lifetime expenditure. Housing costs are high; and for many years housing has been in short supply in most parts of the United States. The increase of the nonwhite population of the cities has been far more rapid than the increase in housing available to them—with resulting pressure and tension. In such a setting, powerful interests are able to profit by the sale of exclusiveness on one hand and by overcrowding on the other.

The Commission on Race and Housing has estimated that one-sixth of the American people are to some degree restricted in their choice of residence. Many of them, as a result, are forced into slums. These accommodations for minority-groups in the United States are probably an improvement over those previously available. But our national income and our national standards for minimum housing have also gone up, increasing the gap between what we have and what we accept as a national goal and policy.[3]

The consequences of residential segregation are severe, both for

[3]Commission on Race and Housing, *Where Shall We Live* (Berkeley: University of California Press, 1958).

those who experience it and for the total community. Housing segregation usually leads to other forms of segregation—in schools, parks, churches, hospitals, and public accommodations. It is often associated with discrimination in such forms as poorer police and fire protection, lower standards of sanitation, and lax enforcement of housing codes. Their lack of choice in housing makes colored Americans vulnerable to rental and purchase prices up to forty percent higher than white Americans pay for equivalent accommodations—a heavy overcharge for those least able to pay. Many slum residents are recent migrants to the city. They have a great deal to learn about how to live in a city, but their isolation blocks them from the pressures to learn. The group is turned in on itself, developing its own code of behavior in a context of frustration and hopelessness. The motivation and self-conceptions of segregated children are negatively influenced in a setting of separating subcultures and contracultures.

It is not only the minority-group member who suffers from this situation. The total community loses potential skills. Residential segregation creates conditions within which hostility and anti-social behavior can develop. It promotes the growth of slums, with a variety of negative effects on a community; and when the slums are cleared, the displaced population, often unable to afford the new housing, "piles up" into other areas, making new slums. Segregation created problems in the foreign relations of the United States. And by increasing distant and stereotype-laden contact, it promotes prejudices that tear the fabric of community life.[4]

Although segregation in housing is the overwhelmingly common fact, a close look will reveal even in this aspect of national life important tendencies toward desegregation. A new trend began—insofar as one can give a date to such a social process—about 1950, and in the last five years it has shown a significant increase in strength. The Federal Housing Authority and other governmental agencies concerned with housing at first considered segregated housing both natural and desirable. In the last decade, however, they have increasingly allowed and encouraged the development of integrated projects. In 1963 President Kennedy issued a long-awaited administrative order that all new governmentally assisted housing must be rented or sold without regard to race, religion, or national origin.

State and local laws, as well as federal actions, are beginning to restrict housing segregation. These laws are based not only on the constitutional grounds of due process (the illegality of being taxed without sharing equally in the benefits), but also on the police power of the community (the right to protect itself against blight and the

---

[4]See *Where Shall We Live* and Davis McEntire, *Residence and Race* (Berkeley: University of California Press, 1960).

unhappy consequences of residential deterioration). Several other forces are beginning to support the desegregation of housing. Some labor unions, with interracial membership, are entering the mortgage market. There is evidence for a general reduction in prejudice and a slight shift in attitudes toward integrated residential areas, perhaps based on the growing acquaintance with the favorable responses of those who live in such areas. A few score private builders are now explicitly developing interracial districts.[5] And a large number of churches have circulated open-occupancy covenants. These are the reverse of the restrictive covenants that extra-legally (but not yet illegally) segregate so many American neighborhoods along racial and religious lines. Thousands of church members have signed pledges similar to this: "I will welcome into my neighborhood as a resident any person of good character, regardless of race, religion, or national origin." Thus they seek to weaken the assertion that segregation persists only because residents will not accept integrated neighborhoods.

The total effect of such recent developments in the field of housing is difficult to assess. Supported as they are, however, by other pressures toward desegregation, it seems likely that they will grow in strength and that housing desegregation will proceed at a cumulatively more rapid pace.

EDUCATION

No aspect of the process of desegregation has received more attention than the changes in American schools. I need scarcely mention the strategic importance of education, both to individuals and to the whole group, in a society based on democratic political forms and diverse occupational skills. Those blocked from educational advance are kept in low status even if other influences favor their development. A group that is given educational opportunities has a powerful instrument with which to improve its status, even if for the moment other influences are unfavorable. Certainly the extent, if not always the quality, of our educational opportunities is an exciting and important part of the American resolve to maintain an open society.

The long run trend has been to make the educational ladder available to more and more groups in the United States. Desegregation is only the most recent manifestation of this trend. I shall not review here the series of Court decisions and the voluntary changes that have, since the late nineteen-thirties, slowly expanded the educational oppor-

[5]Eunice Grier and George Grier, *Privately Developed Interracial Housing: An Analysis of Experience* (Berkeley: University of California Press, 1960).

tunities of colored Americans and reduced the barriers of segregation. An important turning point was reached in 1954 when the Supreme Court ruled that any segregation in public schools was unconstitutional. This was followed in 1955 by an order that all school districts must proceed "with all deliberate speed" (for the Court recognized that there would be difficult problems to solve) to integrate their schools.

At the time of the 1954 decision, all of the schools in the Southern Region (17 states plus the District of Columbia) were segregated. By the beginning of 1963 over thirty percent of the biracial school districts (972 of 3058) had been desegregated to some degree; but the range was wide. The states can be classified into four groups. First are those which have had extensive integration (nearly half of the Negro children go to school with white children; and ninety percent of the biracial school districts have been desegregated): Washington, D.C., West Virginia, Delaware, Missouri, Kentucky, Maryland, and Oklahoma are in this group. One state, Texas, has had slight desegregation (174 out of 919 biracial school districts, involving two percent of the Negro pupils). There has been token integration in nine states, ranging from one student on the college level in Mississippi and South Carolina to several hundred in Tennessee. The six additional states in this group are Virginia, Arkansas, North Carolina, Florida, Louisiana, and Georgia. And in Alabama segregation is still nearly complete. In total, 7.8 percent of the Negro children in the southern region now go to school with white children.[6]

Desegregation of graduate schools and colleges began before the 1954 Supreme Court decision and has been carried farther than on the primary and secondary levels. Over half of the public colleges and universities of the South now admit colored students. Although the proportion is not large—is minute in fact in the Deep South—there are now perhaps seven thousand Negro students enrolled in institutions of higher education that were entirely segregated a few years ago. And there are white students in fifteen of the fifty formerly all-Negro colleges.

In terms of the number of persons involved, there has not yet been a major desegregation of schools in the South. The steps taken so far have been accompanied by extensive litigation, some merely token compliance with court orders, and, in a few instances, violence. In my judgment, however, the more important fact is that an essentially irreversible process has begun.

Although school desegregation is primarily a southern question, there are many quasi-segregated schools in northern and western cities produced by the concentration of nonwhite families in a few residential areas. A survey made by the American Jewish Committee in 1957 found that 20 percent of the public schools in Chicago, 43 percent in

Cincinnati, 22 percent in Cleveland, 21 percent in Detroit, 15 percent in Los Angeles, 20 percent in New York, 27 percent irf Philadelphia, and 7 percent in San Francisco had nonwhite majorities. This situation is not identical with one produced by total and officially enforced segregation; there is a substantial minority of white pupils in many of the schools mentioned above. Yet it cannot be denied that a· significant proportion of the colored children, and the Mexican and Puerto Rican children as well, in the large cities of the North and West attend schools in which intergroup contact is at a minimum. And the proportion attending such schools is likely to go up, as white families move from the cities to suburbs where few or no colored families reside.

Several procedures have been developed by school boards and administrative staffs to try to reduce the number of quasi-segregated schools. Skillful districting (gerrymandering in reverse) can sometimes be used to assign minority-group children to several schools. (The same procedure has been used, of course, and continues to be in some instances, to concentrate colored children in a few schools.) New York City transports several thousand pupils out of their districts in an effort to disperse heavy concentrations of Negro and Puerto Rican children in some schools. A few communities have shifted from the neighborhood concept for elementary schools to a plan calling for the assignment of all first and second grade children to one school, third and fourth graders to another, fifth and sixth graders to another. Although this increases problems of transportation, it can, at least in small and medium sized cities, reduce the tendency toward segregation in schools. It may, in addition, have significant educational advantages.

Such procedures as these, however, can only slightly reduce school segregation that rests upon the fact that many American cities contain large sub communities of nonwhites. Significant changes in the school pattern are dependent upon future developments in urban renewal programs, housing practices, and the economic position of minority groups. . . .

CONCLUSION

This brief catalogue of changes in American race relations during the last generation can only give a hint of the desegregation process. It is primarily a record of public acts and institutional changes, with little reference to the "tone" with which individuals have received and participated in those changes. Individual responses are important of course. The course of events when changes are accepted reluctantly, under fear of penalty, is different from the consequence of a new pattern that is accepted enthusiastically. Yet this contrast can easily be exaggerated, particularly if one is interested in long-run developments. Contemporary sociology emphasizes the extent to which the public definition of events, the institutional structure within which group interaction takes place, affects the individual's response. Within the last twenty-five years that public definition, as it applies to race relations, has been drastically changed in the United States. The extent of the change so far accomplished is reshaping individual attitudes in such a way that further change becomes more likely.

The fact that the present balance of forces is producing desegregation does not mean that the process is inevitable. We can say with some confidence that if present trends continue further desegregation seems likely. But present trends may not continue. Economic prosperity and growth have certainly supported the growth of integration. The rapid development of urban areas and the related heavy migration of minority-group persons, although their effects have been somewhat ambivalent, have lent support to desegregation. Without trying to list all the variables that affect the speed and direction of change, I would mention at least the following additional ones: The international situation, the presence of organized groups, the appearance of leaders with strategic skills, and the strength of the movement to extend and improve education. Most of these influences support desegregation now and seem likely to in the future.

There are some forces that may work in the opposite direction if they continue to operate: Although the concentration of Negroes in the rural counties of the South is much reduced, there is a strong tendency for them to be reconcentrated in the center of the large industrial cities. During the first 150 years of the nation's history, there was a steady decline in the proportion of the population that was nonwhite. Since 1940, this trend has been reversed and we can expect a small increase in the proportion of the population that is nonwhite (from 11.3 percent in 1960 to perhaps 14 percent in 2000). This does not seem to me to be a very important variable among those affecting desegregation, but if other factors were blocking further integration, the demographic situation might support them. And finally, the strength of "isolationist" and hostile movements among minorities—the Black Muslims are the most important current example—must be taken into account. Virtually all minority-group organizations now support desegregation, but this would not necessarily continue to be the case if the process of integration were to stop or significantly slow down.

What then can one say in summary regarding the prospects for continuing desegregation? It seems highly probable that further extensive desegregation will take place. The three hundred year era during which race symbols have been important in determining a person's life chances and in group relations in most of the western world is coming to an end. Its fundamental roots in slavery, in conquest, in colonialism and imperialism, in the sharp cultural differences often found, in plantation economies, and in the Civil War are all broken. (It is by no means impossible, however, that a reciprocal racism, already apparent in some measure, will develop, as more "nonwhite" peoples rise to military, economic, and political power. This would be one of history's bitter ironies were it to occur even as the European and European-derived peoples eliminated race from their perspectives. Lessons learned too late are not uncommon in human experience.)

Within the United States race lines are fading. That does not mean that a Negro will be elected mayor of New York, or of Birmingham, tomorrow (although the former may not be many decades away). Racial disprivilege will outlive the twentieth century, but in less and less extensive ways. If the United States takes as many steps toward full integration in the next twenty-five years as she has in the preceding twenty-five—and this seems fully likely—the country will have accomplished a major social transformation, deeply affecting the whole course of its development, within a half century. Seldom are such vital reorganizations accomplished so swiftly.

14 The Federal Open Housing Controversy*

MAIN FEATURES OF 1962 EXECUTIVE ORDER

Discrimination in the sale or rental of housing owned or assisted by the Federal Government was prohibited by an Executive Order (No. 11063) issued by President John F. Kennedy on November 20, 1962. The order also established the President's Committee on Equal Opportunity in Housing to promote non-discrimination in Federally assisted housing.

Main provisions of the Executive Order are as follows:

"Whereas the granting of Federal assistance for the provision, rehabilitation, or operation of housing and related facilities from which Americans are excluded because of their race, color, creed, or national origin is unfair, unjust, and inconsistent with the public policy of the United States as manifested in its Constitution and laws; and

*Reprinted by permission from *Congressional Digest* 45:11 (November 1966): "Controversy in Congress over Open Housing, Pro and Con."

"Whereas the Congress in the Housing Act of 1949 has declared that the general welfare and security of the Nation and the health and living standards of its people require the realization as soon as feasible of the goal of a decent home and a suitable living environment for every American family; and

"Whereas discriminatory policies and practices based upon race, color, creed, or national origin now operate to deny many Americans the benefits of housing financed through Federal assistance and as a consequence prevent such assistance from providing them with an alternative to substandard, unsafe, unsanitary, and overcrowded housing; and

"Whereas such discriminatory policies and practices result in segregated patterns of housing and necessarily produce other forms of discrimination and segregation which deprive Americans of equal opportunity in the exercise of their unalienable rights to life, liberty, and the pursuit of happiness; and

"Whereas the executive branch of the Government, in faithfully executing the laws of the United States which authorize Federal financial assistance, directly or indirectly, for the provision, rehabilitation, and operation of housing and related facilities, is charged with an obligation and duty to assure that those laws are fairly administered and that benefits thereunder are made available to all Americans without regard to their race, color, creed, or national origin;

"Now, therefore, by virtue of the authority vested in me as President of the United States by the Constitution and laws of the United States, it is ordered as follows:

"Section 101. I hereby direct all departments and agencies in the executive branch of the Federal Government, insofar as their functions relate to the provision, rehabilitation, or operation of housing and related facilities, to take all action necessary and appropriate to prevent discrimination because of race, color, creed, or national origin—

"(a) in the sale, leasing, rental, or other disposition of residential property and related facilities (including land to be developed for residential use), or in the use or occupancy thereof, if such property and related facilities are (i) owned or operated by the Federal Government, or (ii) provided in whole or in part with the aid of loans, advances, grants, or contributions hereafter agreed to be made by the Federal Government, or (iii) provided in whole or in part by loans hereafter insured, guaranteed, or otherwise secured by the credit of the Federal Government, or (iv) provided by the development or the redevelopment of real property purchased, leased, or otherwise obtained from a State or local public agency receiving Federal financial assistance for slum clearance or urban renewal with respect to such real property under a loan or grant contract hereafter entered into; and "(b) in the lending practices with respect to residential property and related facilities (including land to be developed for residential use) or lending institutions, insofar as such practices relate to loans hereinafter insured or guaranteed by the Federal Government."

Section 102 of the order directs the Housing and Home Finance Agency and other agencies to take appropriate action, including litigation where necessary, to promote the abandonment of discriminatory practices with respect to property as above.

Part II of the order instructs Federal agencies on procedures to be followed, regulations to be issued, and reports to be made in pursuance of the directive.

Part III, labeled "Enforcement," authorizes the President's Committee on Equal Opportunity in Housing to hold private or public hearings as deemed advisable for compliance, enforcement, or educational purposes.

Executive departments or agencies subject to the order are authorized to take steps to remedy violations of the order by various means, including: (a) cancellation or termination of agreements or contracts with individuals, firms, or agencies involving loans, grants, contributions, or other Federal aid; (b) refraining from extending further aid under any program affected by the order until it is satisfied that the affected individual, firm, or agency will comply with rules and regulations issued under authority of the order; (c) refusal to approve a lending institution or private lender as beneficiary under any affected program, or revocation of such approval if previously given.

Executive departments and agencies are directed to refer to the Attorney General violations of regulations issued pursuant to the order for such civil or criminal action as he shall deem appropriate.

Part IV establishes the President's Committee on Equal Opportunity in Housing, composed of the Secretary of the Treasury, the Secretary of Defense, the Attorney General, the Secretary of Agriculture, the Housing and Home Finance Administrator, the Administrator of Veterans Affairs, the Chairman of the Federal Home Loan Bank Board, a member of the staff of the Executive Office of the President to act as chairman, and such other members as the President may appoint from the public.

Part V details the manner in which the President's Committee is to function and lists its various powers. A final section, Part VI, defines terms employed in the order.

CONGRESS AND 1966 ADMINISTRATION PROPOSALS

In the first session of the 89th Congress, the single most notable action in the field of civil rights legislation was the passage of the Voting

Rights Act of 1965, signed into law (P. L. 89–110) by the President on August 6, 1965.

President Johnson, in his 1966 State of the Union Message to the Congress, called for additional civil rights legislation: "I recommend that you take additional steps to insure equal justice to all of our people by effectively enforcing nondiscrimination in Federal and State jury selection, by making it a serious Federal crime to obstruct public and private efforts to secure civil rights, and by outlawing discrimination in the sale and rental of housing."

Three and a half months later, on April 28, 1966, the President sent to the Congress a special message on civil rights, recommending further comprehensive legislation on the subject. With regard to "open housing," the President said: "I ask the Congress . . . to declare a national policy against racial discrimination in the sale or rental of housing, and to create effective remedies against that discrimination in every part of America."

The President's recommendations were introduced in the Congress as the "Civil Rights Act of 1966." H. R. 14765, an "omnibus" bill introduced on May 2 by Rep. Emanuel Celler, N. Y., D., was referred to a subcommittee of the Committee on the Judiciary. S. 3296, its counterpart in the Senate, was introduced on April 28 by Sen. Philip Hart, Mich., D., with the co-sponsorship of a number of other senators, and referred to the Subcommittee on Constitutional Rights of that body's Committee on the Judiciary.

House Action

In the House, H. R. 14765 was considered, together with approximately 50 other civil rights bills, by Subcommittee No. 5 of the Judiciary Committee, presided over by Rep. Celler, chairman of the full Judiciary Committee, and Administration sponsor of the bill in the House. Hearings were held on ten days during the month of May, followed by six additional days of executive sessions, during which several major amendments were adopted. The "open housing" portion of the bill, however, was unaltered by the Subcommittee.

The full Committee on the Judiciary then considered the bill for nine sessions, adopting an amendment offered by Rep. Charles McC. Mathias, Md., R. It would limit the prohibitions contained in the housing title to real estate brokers, lending institutions, and others specifically defined as being engaged in the business of building, developing, buying, selling, renting, leasing, or financing residential housing.

On Monday, July 25, 1966, House Resolution 910, seeking to discharge the civil rights bill from the Rules Committee under the 21-day rule, was taken up on the floor of the House. After spirited debate, the resolution was adopted by a vote of 200–180, and H. R.

14765, embodying the "Mathias compromise," became the order of business before the House.

Debate continued on the bill for more than two weeks, with Title IV, the "open housing" section, the center of most of the controversy. Finally, on August 9, the bill was passed, 259–157, after a number of amendments had been adopted. Among these were amendments to Title IV regarding "block-busting," rental to families with children, mortgages, rental of rooms, and trial by jury.

Action in the Senate

In the Senate, meanwhile, that body's version of the bill, S. 3296, had been taken up by the Constitutional Rights Subcommittee, chaired by Sen. Sam J. Ervin, Jr., N. C., D., of the Senate Committee on the Judiciary. Twenty-two days of hearings ensued over the period June 6-August 4; the Subcommittee subsequently voted to substitute the House-passed bill, H. R. 14765, for the Senate version which it had earlier considered. The Subcommittee adopted fourteen amendments of its own to H. R. 14765, most of them technical in nature, and none of which applied to Title IV.

The amended bill was reported to the full Committee on the Judiciary, where no further action was taken.

On September 7, 1966, a motion by Senator Hart to call up the bill, discharging it from the Judiciary Committee, was introduced on the floor of the Senate. Opposition to the bill, centering largely on its jury (Titles I and II) and "open housing" (Title IV) provisions, took the form of "extended debate" on the call-up motion, and a major effort was mounted to forestall Senate consideration of the civil rights bill itself.

Cloture Moves Defeated

Two attempts to invoke cloture were made. The first, on September 14, failed of the required two-thirds majority (of those present and voting) by 54 yeas to 42 nays. Five days later, on September 19, a second cloture attempt failed by 52 yeas to 41 nays, and the Senate Majority Leadership abandoned further attempts to consider the bill in the 89th Congress.

"OPEN HOUSING" FEATURES OF THE BILL

"Open Housing" provisions of the proposed Civil Rights Act of 1966 comprised Title IV of the bill. As amended by the House of Representatives in the course of that body's passage of the measure, these were principally as follows:

Policy

"Sec. 401. It is the policy of the United States to prevent discrimination on account of race, color, religion, or national origin in the purchase, rental, lease, financing, use, and occupancy of housing throughout the Nation."

Definitions

Sec. 402 lists various definitions of terms used in Title IV, including the following: "A person shall be deemed to be in the business of building, developing, selling, renting, or leasing dwellings if he has, within the preceding twelve months, participated as either principal or agent in three or more transactions involving the sale, rental, or lease of any dwelling or any interest therein.

"But nothing contained in this bill shall be construed to prohibit or affect the right of any person, or his authorized agent, to rent or refuse to rent, a room or rooms in his home for any reason, or for no reason; or to change his tenants as often as he may desire.

Prevention of Discrimination in the Sale or Rental of Housing

"Sec. 403. (a) It shall be unlawful for any person who is a real estate broker, agent, or salesman, or employee or agent of any real estate broker, agent, or salesman, or any other person in the business of building, developing, selling, renting, or leasing dwellings, or any employee or agent of any such person—

"1. To refuse to sell, rent, or lease, to refuse to negotiate for the sale, rental, or lease of, or otherwise make unavailable or deny, a dwelling to any person because of race, color, religion, or national origin or number of children or the age of such children.

"2. To discriminate against any person in the terms, conditions, or privileges of sale, rental, or lease of a dwelling, or in the provision of services or facilities in connection therewith, because of race, color, religion, or national origin or number of children or the age of such children.

"3. To make, print, or publish, or cause to be made, printed, or published any oral or written notice, statement, or advertisement, with respect to the sale, rental, or lease of a dwelling that indicates any preference, limitation, or discrimination based on race, color, religion, or national origin, or number of children or the age of such children or an intention to make any such preference, limitation, or discrimination.

"4. To fail to refuse to show any dwelling which he is authorized to show to prospective buyers, renters, or lessees, because of race, color, religion, or national origin, or to fail to submit promptly to his principal any offer to buy, rent, or lease because of race, color, religion, or national origin, or to fail to refuse to use his best efforts to consummate any sale, rental, or lease because of the race, color, religion, or national origin of any party to the prospective sale, rental, or lease.

"5. To represent to any person because of race, color, religion, or national origin that any dwelling is not available for inspection, sale, rental, or lease when such dwelling is in fact so available.

"6. To deny to any person because of race, color, religion, or national origin, or because of the race, color, religion, or national origin of the person he represents or may represent, access to or participation in any multiple-listing service or other service or facilities related to the business of selling or renting dwellings.

"7. To engage in any act or practice, the purpose of which is to limit or restrict the availability of housing to any person or group of persons because of race, color, religion, or national origin or number of children or the age of such children.

"8. To induce or attempt to induce any person to sell, rent, or lease any dwelling by representations regarding the present or prospective entry into the neighborhood of a person or persons of a particular race, color, religion, national origin, or economic status.

"b. Nothing in this section shall apply to an owner with respect to the sale, lease, or rental by him of a portion of a building or structure which contains living quarters occupied or intended to be occupied by no more than four families independently of each other if such owner actually occupies one of such living quarters as his residence.

"c. Nothing in this section shall bar any religious or denominational institution, or any charitable or educational institution or organization which is operated, supervised or controlled by or in conjunction with a religious organization, or any bona fide private or fraternal organization, from giving preference to persons of the same religion or denomination, or to members of such private or fraternal organization, or from making such selection as is calculated by such organization to promote the religious principles or the aims, purposes, or fraternal principles for which it is established or maintained.

"d. Nothing in this section shall affect, or be construed to affect, any liability for payment of a real estate or other commission by any person with respect to the sale, lease, or rental of a dwelling.

"e. Nothing in this section shall prohibit, or be construed to prohibit, a real estate broker, agent, or salesman, or employee or agent of any real estate broker, agent, or salesman from complying with the express written instructions of any person not in the business of building, developing, selling, renting, or leasing dwellings, or otherwise not subject to the prohibitions of this section pursuant to subsection (b) or (c) hereof, with respect to the sale, or lease of a dwelling owned by such person, if such instruction was not encouraged, solicited, or induced by such broker, agent, or salesman, or any employee or agent thereof.

Prevention of Discrimination in the Financing of Housing

"Sec. 404. It shall be unlawful for any bank, savings and loan institution, credit union, insurance company, or other person regularly engaged in the business of making mortgages or other loans for the purchase, construction, improvement, or repair or maintenance of dwellings to deny such a loan to a person applying therefor, or discriminate against him in the fixing of the downpayment, interest rate, duration, or other terms or conditions of such a loan, because of the race, color, religion, or national origin of such a person, or of any member, stockholder, director, officer, or employee of such person, or of the prospective occupants, lessees, or tenants of the dwelling or dwellings in relation to which the application for a loan is made."

Interference, Coercion, or Intimidation

Sec. 405 prohibits intimidation or harassment of any individual on account of his having exercised or encouraged others to exercise rights granted by sections 403 or 404.

Enforcement by Private Persons

Sec. 406 provides that rights granted by sections 403, 404, and 405 may be enforced by civil actions in appropriate U. S. district courts without regard to the amount in controversy, and in appropriate State or local courts of general jurisdiction. Upon application by any party in circumstances which the court deems just, a U. S. court may appoint an attorney for such party and authorize commencement of a civil action without payment of fees, costs, or security. The court may grant such relief as it deems appropriate, including a temporary or permanent injunction, restraining order, or other order, and may award actual damages to the plaintiff. Provision is also made preserving complainant's right to obtain relief in cases brought in State or local courts where laws exist prohibiting the above procedure.

Enforcement by the Attorney General

Sec. 407 provides that whenever the Attorney General has reasonable cause to believe that any person or group of persons is engaged in a pattern or practice of resistance to the full enjoyment of any of the rights granted by this title, he may bring a civil action in any appropriate U.S. district court by filing with it a complaint setting forth the facts pertaining to such pattern or practice and requesting such preventive relief, including an application for a permanent or temporary injunction, restraining order, or other order against the person or persons responsible for such pattern or practice, as he deems necessary to insure the full enjoyment of the rights granted by this title. Whenever an action under section 406 has been commenced in any court of the United States, the Attorney General may intervene for or in the name of the United States if he certifies that the action is of general public importance.

Enforcement by the Fair Housing Board

Section 408 establishes a Fair Housing Board of five members appointed by the President with the advice and consent of the Senate, no more than three of whom may be of the same political party, and who serve for staggered five-year terms. In addition, the section specifies the procedures for the organization and operation of the Board. The Secretary of Housing and Urban Development is authorized to investigate violations of sections 403, 404, and 405 of this title, and to file with the Board written complaints of such reported violations. The Board is authorized to serve such complaint upon the person charged, to hold hearings on such complaint in accordance with the same conditions, limitations, and appellate procedures as are provided for the National Labor Relations Board, and to treat violations in the same manner as an unfair labor practice under provisions of section 160 of title 29, United States Code.

Other Provisions

Section 409 assigns various administrative and reporting responsibilities to the Secretary of Housing and Urban Development.

Section 410 states that nothing in this title shall be construed to invalidate or limit any law of a State or political subdivision, but that any law that purports to require or permit any action that would be a discriminatory housing practice under this title shall to that extent be invalid.

Section 411 provides that cases of criminal contempt arising under the provisions of this title shall be governed by section 1101 of the Civil Rights Act of 1964.

Section 412 specifies that nothing in this title shall be construed to impair any right or authority of the United States under existing law to institute or intervene in any civil action or to bring any criminal prosecution.

SHOULD CONGRESS ENACT FEDERAL "OPEN HOUSING" LEGISLATION?

PRO: HON. NICHOLAS de B. KATZENBACH

U.S. Attorney General

From testimony given before Subcommittee No. 5 of the Committee on the Judiciary of the U. S. House of Representatives on May 4, 1966, opening hearings before that Subcommittee on H. R. 14765 and other proposed bills entitled "Civil Rights Act of 1966."

"The past 20 years have provided the country with millions upon millions of new dwelling units and have vastly changed the character of our urban residential areas. Suburbia has come into being around the boundaries of our cities and continues to spread.

"Except for our Negro citizens, virtually all Americans have had an equal opportunity to share in these developments in our national life. The Negro's choice in housing, unlike that of his fellow citizens, is not limited merely by this means.

"It is limited by his color. By and large, desirable new housing in our cities and suburbs is foreclosed to him, and, ironically, because of its scarcity, what housing is left available to him frequently costs him more, judged by any fair standard, than comparable housing open to whites.

"The result is apparent to all: impacted Negro ghettos that are surrounded and contained by white suburbia. The problem has arisen in metropolitan communities everywhere in the country.

"Segregated housing is deeply corrosive both for the individual and for his community. It isolates racial minorities from the public life of the community. It means inferior public education, recreation, health, sanitation, and transportation services and facilities.

"It means denial of access to training and employment and business opportunities. It prevents the inhabitants of the ghettos from liberating themselves, and it prevents the Federal, State, and local governments and private groups and institutions from fulfilling their responsibility and desire to help in this liberation.

"Through the years, there has been considerable State and private response to discrimination in housing. Seventeen States, the District of Columbia, Puerto Rico, the Virgin Islands, and a large number of municipalities have enacted a variety of fair housing laws.

"Volunteer efforts by private citizens also have been organized in many communities, such as Neighbors, Inc., in the District of Columbia.

"In addition, there has been a series of actions by the Federal Government.

"In the judicial branch, the Supreme Court acted decisively as early as 1948 when it held racially restrictive covenants to be unenforce-able in either the State or Federal courts.

"In the executive branch, President Kennedy's Executive Order 11063 of November 20, 1962, established the President's Committee on Equal Housing Opportunity and forbade discrimination in new FHA- or VA-insured housing.

"By now it should be plain that a patchwork of State and local laws is not enough. The work of private volunteer groups is not enough. Court decisions are not enough. The limited authority now available to the executive branch is not enough.

"The time has now surely come for decisive action by the legislative branch of the Federal Government. Durable remedies for so endemic and deep-seated a condition as housing segregation should be based on the prescription and sanction of Congress. This is all the more so as the issue is national in scope and as it penetrates into so many other sectors of public policy as the rebuilding and physical improve-ment of our cities.

"The extent to which the decisions of individual homeowners reduce the availability of housing to racial minorities is hard to estimate. But I believe it is accurate to say that individual homeowners do not control the pattern of housing in communities of any size. The main components of the housing industry are builders, landlords, real estate brokers, and those who provide mortgage money. These are the groups which maintain housing patterns based on race.

"I do not mean to suggest that the enforcement of segregation in housing is necessarily motivated by racial bias. More often the conduct of those in the housing business reflects the misconception that neigh-borhoods must remain racially separate to maintain real estate values.

"While there exist studies which indicate that segregated housing does not depress real estate values, many in the real estate business fear to take the chance. I have no doubt that they simply feel trapped by custom and the possibility of competitive loss. The fact is, however, that their policies and practices are what perpetuate segregated hous-ing.

"At present a particular builder or landlord who resists selling or renting to a Negro most often does so not out of personal bigotry but out of fear that his prospective white tenants or purchasers will move to housing limited to whites and that, because similar housing is unavailable to Negroes, what he has to offer will attract only Negroes. If all those in the housing industry are bound by a universal law against discrimination, there will be no economic peril to any one of them. All would be in a position to sell without discrimination. Indeed, experienced developers have stated that they would welcome such a law.

"Therefore, I think it would be a mistake to regard the most significant aspect of a Federal fair housing measure as its sanctions against builders, landlords, lenders, or brokers. What is more significant, rather, is that they can utilize this law as a shield to protect them when they do what is right.

"The same protection would be given an individual homeowner who privately has no reservation about selling his home to a Negro but who may be inhibited by the fears he could generate among the neighbors he is leaving. A uniform statute would outlaw segregation in all neighborhoods.

"There is a close parallel here with the impact of the public accommodations title of the Civil Rights Act of 1964. Restaurant or motel owners, willing to desegregate, failed to do so because of economic fears. Once the act was passed—and all of their competitors had to serve Negroes—many quickly complied.

"Title IV applies to all housing and prohibits discrimination on account of race, color, religion or national origin by property owners, tract developers, real estate brokers, lending institutions and all others engaged in the sale, or financing of housing.

"It also prohibits coercion or intimidation intended to interfere with the right of a person to obtain housing without discrimination—for example, the coercion of a mob attempting to prevent a Negro family from moving into a neighborhood.

"And it prohibits retaliatory action by real estate boards or associations against real estate agents who have refused to discriminate against Negroes or other persons of minority groups.

"Title IV provides a judicial remedy. An individual aggrieved by a discriminatory housing practice would be enabled to bring an action in either a Federal district court or a State or local court for injunctive relief and for any damages he may have sustained. In the court's discretion, he could also be awarded up to $500 exemplary damages.

"The title empowers the Attorney General to initiate suits in Federal courts to eliminate a 'pattern or practice' of discrimination, and to intervene in private suits brought in Federal courts.

"Title IV is based primarily on the commerce clause of the Constitution and on the 14th amendment. I have no doubts whatsoever as to its constitutionality.

"I have pointed out already how segregated living is both a source and an enforcer of involuntary second-class citizenship. To the extent that this blight on our democracy impedes States and localities from carrying out their obligations under the 14th amendment to promote equal access and equal opportunity in all public aspects of community life, the 14th amendment authorizes removal of this impediment.

"That there is official and governmental involvement in the real estate and construction industries needs little demonstration. Apart from zoning and building codes, there are the obvious facts of regulations covering credit, mortgages, interest rates, and banking practices, and there is the universal licensing of real estate agents.

"But there are more basic considerations.

"Are we to tell our Negro citizens that the Congress which has guaranteed them access to desegregated public schools and to swimming pools and to golf courses is powerless to guarantee them the basic right to choose a place to live? I would find this hard to explain, for I would not be able to understand it myself.

"To me it is clear that the 14th amendment gives Congress the power to address itself to the vindication of what is, in substance, the freedom to live.

"Congress can and must make the legislative judgment that without equal housing opportunity there cannot be full equality under law. Congress can and must determine that the enforcement of involuntary segregation through discriminatory housing practices is inconsistent with the words, spirit, and purpose of the 14th amendment.

"These are the human terms in which the Constitution speaks and cries out for quick response. There are also economic terms. The Congress is charged with the protection and promotion of interstate commerce in all its forms.

"I cannot doubt that housing is embraced under this congressional power. The construction of homes and apartment buildings, the production and sale of building materials and home furnishings, the financing of construction and purchases all take place in or through the channels of interstate commerce.

"When the total problem is considered, it requires no great leap of the imagination to conclude that interstate commerce is significantly affected by the sale even of single dwellings, multiplied many times in each community.

"There can be no doubt that anything which significantly affects the housing industry also affects interstate commerce. Discriminatory housing practices produce such an effect. They restrict the amount and type of new housing; discourage the repair and rehabilitation of existing housing; remove incentives to the purchase of new furniture and appliances, and frustrate the efforts of people to move from job to job and from State to State.

"Clearly the people, the money, the materials, the entrepreneurial talent which move in and to the housing market are not confined within single States. Rather they are well within the range of congressional regulation, and within this range Congress' judgment as to what problems need solving and how they should be solved is necessarily broad. Title IV identifies a national problem. It suggests an effective solution."

PRO: HON. EMANUEL CELLER
U. S. Representative, New York, Democrat

From the debate of July 25, 1966, on the floor of the U.S. House of Representatives on H. R. 14765, the proposed "Civil Rights Act of 1966." Rep. Celler is Chairman of the House Judiciary Committee which has jurisdiction over proposed civil rights legislation.

"By guaranteeing and insuring equality of opportunity to all people, regardless of race, color, religion, or national origin, we are not, like the lords of the manor, conferring a favor; we are dispensing justice.

"If we talked to a man from outer space, could you hear yourself say that here in the United States a man's life and way of life is determined by the color of his skin?

"Title IV seeks to end discrimination in residential housing. It prohibits discrimination on grounds of race, color, religion, or national origin by real estate brokers and agents and other persons dealing in the business of building, developing, buying, or selling of residential housing. This title provides for judicial and administrative relief and civil, not criminal, remedies in the event of violation of those prohibitions.

"The trouble in the ghetto areas is in part in response to a revolutionary spirit.

"That revolution is following a pattern, and that pattern existed in connection with the industrial workers of this Nation. It was not unlike the revolution of the farmers of this country. They likewise rebelled and they fought off the chains that bound them, and there was violence on the farms.

"It is not unlike the fight for the vote for women in the last century, that was a revolutionary mission. The vote had been withheld from the women for centuries, and they fought. You recall the terms of force which was used. Women threw themselves across the path of traffic, not only in this country, but in England, and there was violence—much violence—on the part of these ladies.

"I did not then, you do not now, condone violence, and I am sure you did not, and I do not condone it now, but I am just giving you some of the history of this country where we have had these waves of revolution. We are having them now.

"And just because we pass something here in Washington may not completely satisfy the militant voices. But what we do in Washington is quite different from what has happened in the localities where we have had this violence, where Washington has no control of the local police force or the local conditions that exist. These eruptions are most unfortunate, and it is hoped that temperate voices will prevail.

"However, if we do not pass this bill we would be encouraging those militant voices.

"The Negro is supposed to be free. But is he? Many rights have been denied and withheld from him—the right to be equally educated with whites, the right to equal housing with whites, the right to equal recreation with whites, the right to equality in labor with whites. We have accorded him some freedoms, but no opportunity to exercise them. That is like giving him an appetite but no food.

"It has be¢n said that we passed four principal civil rights bills; why another?

"The evil and scourge of not granting true equality among blacks and whites are pervasive, wide, long, and deep. It is like a prairie fire that cannot be extinguished save by long and patient effort. Great reforms do not just happen.

"The French Revolution was the accumulation of widespread evil of long duration. The English Reformation was preceded by decades of struggle and travail.

"Dr. Fleming worked hard for years before he came up with penicillin. The polio vaccine came to Dr. Salk after the greatest efforts. Insulin did not come in a day or a year, although the diabetic waited patiently and suffered agonies until it finally came upon the market.

"Similarly, Congress is the physician to rid the body politic of the disease of segregation. Segregation becomes a plague. No one is immune from its evil power. Plagues are not easily or quickly dissipated. It all depends upon whose ox is gored. Many civil libertarians have cried out against segregation. Now the warm winds of integration move northward and now all are feeling the heat.

"The bill before us, let me emphasize, operates equally in the North as well as in the South.

"In ancient Rome, bridgebuilding was considered a sacred duty. Note the name they gave to their priest: They called him Pontifex, which translated means 'bridgebuilder.' The Pope is called Pontiff, a bridge which unites that which nature divides. Civil rights laws unite those whom our society divides.

"This civil rights bill is a bridge, as it were, seeking to unite whites and blacks in recognition of human rights. It seeks to integrate them, according each equal rights.

"You cannot raze the slum, you cannot level the ghettos without what is known as title IV of this bill. Without title IV we shall continue to create new pales of settlement, new segregated areas, new ghettos and slums, placing us where we were years ago.

"The Negro is too often confronted with the equivalent of Hitler's 'verboten,' which means 'forbidden.' We must take out that word and destroy it as applicable in furtherance of segregation. They who believe in segregation are like those who seek to walk up a descending escalator.

"Especially dear to the white man is his home and his house. That spells to him happiness and dignity. It means also security. To deny him the right to own his house in an area where a white man can own one is to rob the Negro of his dignity and security and happiness. Whatever else you give him pales in value; whatever else you give him seems like a promissory note without collateral.

"Victor Hugo said that 'when the time of an idea has come, nothing can stop it.' The time of the idea of equality has come. To some of the Members I say that time is changing rapidly. Some can no longer be protected in their seats by the anomalous success. Already a number of segregationists have gone down under. Clouds are now on the horizon, 'clouds no bigger than a man's hand,' but they will grow to gigantic storm clouds and overwhelm.

CON: HON. WALLACE F. BENNETT

U.S. Senator, Utah, Republican

From an address on the floor of the U.S. Senate on September 15, 1966, during extended debate on a motion to proceed to the consideration of H. R. 14765, the House-passed "Civil Rights Act of 1966."

"I fully believe in protecting the rights of minority groups and that my record in support of prior civil rights bills in the Congress will substantiate this fact. However, we reach a point in the course of events where we must weigh the demands of minority groups against the constitutional rights of the majority of our population, and determine what is just and right as against that which might be socially desirable.

"The avocates of legislation such as that contained in title IV, argue that freedom involves the right to live wherever one chooses, or to buy whatever one wishes to buy. This is a fallacious argument and a tortured usage of the term 'freedom.' If I have the right to live wherever I might choose, then someone else must have the duty to permit me to do so. If I prefer my neighbor's home to my own, do I have the right to force him to sell to me? Obviously, I do not possess any such right in a free country under a constitutional form of government. Anyone who claims to possess any such right is patently wrong, and is talking about power not freedom.

"In a free country no one has a right per se to buy. What he has is a right to offer to buy. Likewise, if a proposed seller is a free man, he has the right to offer to sell or to refuse to sell as he may see fit. It is an elementary rule of law that a completed sales transaction occurs in a free country, only when a willing and able buyer bargains with a willing and able seller and they negotiate on terms which are mutually satisfactory. Such would not be the case under title IV. It would destroy the freedom of one man and place power in the hands of another by forcing the sale or lease of private property. To speak of this power as freedom is a gross distortion of the constitutional principles on which this great Nation was founded.

"Let us not misunderstand and let no one be misled into believing that this bill will satisfy the basic needs of minorities or of those who are in the ghettos. Their real needs are for jobs, or training for jobs, if they are not properly trained. Their real needs are proper education, ability to purchase adequate housing, and solutions to other basic problems of income. Measures like this bill are not going to encourage the basic individual initiative of all American citizens, including those who live in the ghettos, to get out and earn a living and to make a way for themselves in America. Private endeavor, not government compulsion has been the touchstone of greatness of our Nation.

"The fundamentals of our Nation's ghetto problem are not really dealt with in this legislation. Let us not try to fool anyone into believing that all civil rights problems are going to come to an end if this bill is passed, any more than they did when Congress enacted bills on civil rights in 1957, and 1960, 1964, and 1965.

"This bill will not in its present form accomplish its advertised objectives. This is not going to bring about the millennium or the solution of the plethora of problems relating to the ghettos today. This is not going to settle the riots.

"Title IV of H. R. 14765 is the most objectionable part of the bill.

"This title embraces the most dangerous attack on the right of private property which has ever been seriously attempted in this body.

"By enacting this title, we shall be seeking to deny large numbers of Americans the right to dispose of their own property as they see fit.

"Of course, this invasion of the right of private property would be made, under this bill, broadly speaking, only with respect to homes and living quarters. I fail to see where this makes the case any better. In a way, it makes the matter worse, because one of our most sacred traditions, which we inherited from and share with the British, is the idea that a man's home is his castle.

"Let no Senator be misled into accepting the idea that all the evils of title IV will be visited only upon those who are in the business of building, developing, selling, renting, or leasing dwellings. Of course, that is what the bill says; but the bill contains a section entitled 'Definitions' under which it is provided that anyone shall be deemed to be in this business of building, developing, selling, renting, or leasing dwellings if he has, within the preceding 12 months, participated as either principal or agent in three or more transactions involving the sale, rental, or lease of any dwelling or any interest therein.

"So, a woman who runs a boardinghouse and rents three rooms during the year is in the business; a man who gives up a job in one

State, and moves his family in a rented trailer to a job and home in another State, let us say a man employed in the construction business, and thus might actually have rented three buildings within a year, will be deemed under the language of this bill to be in the business of building, developing, selling, renting, or leasing dwellings.

"Most of the penal restrictions on property owners are contained in section 403, and this section has a subsection which says it shall not apply to any property owner with respect to the sale, lease, or rental by him of a portion of a building or structure which contains living quarters occupied or intended to be occupied by no more than four families living independently of each other, if the owner himself actually occupies one of these living quarters as his residence.

"Of course, if the right of private property is to be protected, then it must be protected for all men, whether or not they own one-family or four-family dwellings, and whether or not they live in such dwellings. But quite aside from that point, the exemptions provided in the subsection I just referred to do not really amount to as much as one might think.

"Not only does title IV seek to interfere unjustifiably and unconstitutionally with the right of private property; it goes further and provides for enforcement of this interference through a blanket authorization of civil actions in Federal district courts which cannot fail to bring with it, if this bill is enacted, the worst court congestion this country has ever seen.

"The proponents of H. R. 14765 state that title IV, the open housing title, is bottomed on the commerce clause and the 14th amendment. It is said that because building materials and home furnishings move across State lines, because people move their residence from one State to another, because mortgage money is borrowed outside the State, and because disputes and disturbances interrupt the interstate movement of persons and things, the business of buying and selling private dwellings is therefore interstate commerce and subject to regulation by the Federal Government, in spite of the fact that these dwellings are firmly fixed to a particular piece of land in a particular State. If this is so, then interstate commerce means something more than the courts have interpreted it to mean. Heretofore, the courts have said that interstate commerce ends when goods come to rest in the State of destination. While it is true that the Supreme Court in the recent case of Atlanta Motel against United States diluted that rule when it upheld the public accommodations title of the 1964 Civil Rights Act, it did so only with reference to commercial establishments which were using interstate goods for profitmaking resale. Here, we are talking about private dwellings where interstate goods have left the channels of commerce and have changed their status from personalty to realty. Only by the most devious and artful rationale can the interstate commerce clause be urged as a proper constitutional connecting link.

"Neither can the 14th amendment operate as a constitutional basis unless we are to ignore or repudiate its explicit language. That language reads ih part:

" 'No State shall make or enforce any law which shall abridge the privileges or immunities of citizens of the United States; nor shall any State deprive any person of life, liberty, or property without due process of law, nor deny to any person within its jurisdiction the equal protection of the laws.'

"In times past, the courts have uniformly held that the proscriptions of the 14th amendment apply to State actions only and not to actions by private citizens. Even the decision in Shelley against Kraemer, on which the proponents of this legislation rely most strongly, clearly states:

" 'That amendment erects no shield against merely private conduct, however discrimininatory or wrongful.'

"In the face of such plain constitutional language and such unequivocal interpretations by the courts, the proponents have strained mightily to have housing discrimination by a private citizen relate back to some action by the States. One sentence from their so-called constitutional memorandum illustrates their argument:

" 'Perhaps the principal impetus to housing discrimination . . . was legal recognition and judicial enforcement of the racially restrictive covenant.'

"Another sentence from the memorandum is revealing:

" 'A further reason for congressional intervention is that housing discrimination . . . is maintained today, not by a series of independent individual decisions, but by pervasive customs, practices, and attitudes that have the practical force of law. In these circumstances, the coercive effect of the custom may be treated as constitutionally equivalent to official action.'

"As I read that statement, it says there is no reason for a Congress, there is no need for State legislatures; all we have to do to create law in this country is to have a group of people in a particular community seem to be acting the same way, seem to be taking the same point of view on a particular problem, and the fact that they seem to be taking the same view, without any demonstration that there was an actual agreement among them, creates the situation, to use the words again, 'constitutionally equivalent to official action.'

"I cannot think of any way in which an idea can be strained and distorted more effectively.

"Not only is there nothing to be found in the Constitution to justify this change, there is much to be found which reasons against it. As Mr. Justice Douglas, hardly a conservative extremist, has said:

" 'The Bill of Rights, as applied to the States through the due process clause of the 14th amendment, casts its weight on the side of the privacy of the home.'

"Indeed it does. The third amendment protects private homes against the quartering of soldiers. The fourth amendment protects private homes against unlawful searches and seizures. The 9th and 10 amendments reserve to the people all unenumerated rights and all powers not delegated to the Federal Government.

"As a nonlawyer, I admit I am not qualified to give final and valid opinions on the constitutionality of such drastic revisions in basic law. However, it seems to me that the dangers are so obvious that even those of us who are not trained in the law can see them. Thus, it seems that the proposed change would strike fear in the hearts of every property owner in the United States of America.

"I hope this bill will be rejected, and that in the course of the discussion, the understanding of the dangers involved will become so clear to the American people that if and when it is brought up again in 1967, the will of the people will be made known to us more clearly and more swiftly than has been the case today. I hope that this bill not only will be overwhelmingly defeated, but also that it will be confined to that limbo which all such bills so richly deserve."

CON: HON. JOE D. WAGGONNER, JR.

U. S. Representative, Louisiana, Democrat

From an address on the floor of the U.S. Senate on September 15, 1966, during extended debate on a motion to proceed to the consideration of H.R. 14765, the House-passed "Civil Rights Act of 1966."

"Four times now in recent years, the Congress has chosen to override every lesson of history, and every law of commonsense by setting up separate standards of judgment and behavior for the Negro and the white races. You can see where the Nation is today as a result. These promises have all been proven false. I hope the past proponents of those so-called civil rights bills are proud of what they see when they look around the country today. The truth is they should hang their heads in shame.

"Let there be no mistake about it, the violence and threats of violence which are tearing this country apart have their roots in a single but massive error of judgment; an error that was consciously made in the face of naked political pressure and against the advice of those of us who opposed these bills in the past and oppose this one today. Any man who cannot say no and vote no when it is necessary does not deserve to serve the people. That mistake was in legislating, not equality before the law, which is every man's right, but special preference for the Negro.

"No American, and certainly not I, can oppose the philosophy of every man's right to equal treatment under the law regardless of the color of his skin.

"But I can oppose and I do oppose the destruction of one man's rights and privileges in order to spoon-feed another. And this is the crux of every civil rights bill which has ever come before this body. There is no better example than what is attempted by title IV of this bill before us now. Is this a proposal to give the Negro equality? No. It is a proposal to give the Negro preferential treatment by, among other things, taking away the rights of the property owner to sell to whom he pleases.

"Now you can couch this in any language you want, but you know the intent and the practical effect of it as well as I do. The practical effect is that no real estate agent will dare refuse to sell a house to a Negro instead of a white man if they both make him an offer, because he knows that the Federal Government will land on him with both feet. The same thing is true of the so-called fair employment practices which civil rights legislation has set up. This was not legislation to give the Negro equality in job opportunity. It was legislation to give the Negro preferential treatment by holding a Federal axe over the head of employers who choose a white man instead of a Negro regardless of their qualifications if they both apply for the same job. You know this as well as I know it and as well as the Nation now knows it. And you know, too, that the Nation is getting sick of it.

"The past civil rights bills were railroaded through Congress, often without even being read by many Members, partly because they were anti-South bills and it is a popular sport to lash the South. But the worm has turned, as you know.

"We tried to tell you that this was not just a southern problem; that it was the Nation's problem and now you know this is the case. When the 1964 and 1965 civil rights bills were being considered, violence was provoked almost entirely in the South. Now, in 1966, it is almost entirely in the North. I wonder if there is any conscientious observer who can say with any honesty whatsoever that this is mere coincidence. I doubt it.

"You know as well as I do that these incidents of violence are as well controlled as the ticking of that clock here in the well of the House. It is a matter of record that this violence is so well controlled that it could be, and was, turned off like a spigot during the presidential campaign of 1964.

"We who have been alarmed over this have said, over and over, that these mobs are activated by outside, professional agitators, but our words fell on deaf ears. But, pick up the newspapers today and see who is now saying that this is true. Some of the very men who cried, 'racist,' when we said this years ago are now reacting with alarm and panic when the obvious truth finally has sunk in. Of course these demonstrations are directed and controlled. Even though financial records have been produced to prove that certain civil rights groups are financed directly from Moscow, no one listened, or if they heard, they refused to believe. But now that the northern ox is being gored, there are many who are anxious to blame outsiders and Communists for their troubles because they refuse to admit that the appetite for special privilege is an insatiable one and that a tiger is stalking the streets.

"Follow the footsteps of Martin Luther King and the trail of bloodshed he has left in his wake wherever he has been. Even today in Chicago, as that besieged city poises on the brink of explosion, he smiles blandly to the corps of fawning sympathetic newsmen and says, 'We're not trying to start a riot.' But in the same breath he promises Chicago 'massive doses of creative tension.'

" 'Creative tension,' he says. Creative tension is another way of saying, 'You will either do what I say and give me what I want or I will turn mobs loose in the streets with bricks, bombs and Molotov cocktails.'

"At a time when the backbone of America was straighter than it is today, this man would be clapped in irons and charged with insurrection and inciting to riot. But what proposal do we have before us? One that lays down all the rules and regulations to protect King and his rioters. Not one stipulation do I see to protect policemen who are stabbed, shot, and beaten trying to enforce the laws of decent society.

"Title IV of this bill will reduce the American homeowner almost to the same level, propertywise, as a citizen of the Soviet Union, in that he, too, has practically no property rights. It opens up for unlimited Federal traffic an avenue which the Constitution has kept closed from the very day that document was signed by the Founding Fathers; the concept, rooted deep in the basic laws and traditions of our Nation, that a man's home is his castle.

"The English statesman, William Pitt, summed up this right in words of crystal, brilliant purity when he said:

" 'The poorest man may, in his cottage, bid defiance to all the force of the Crown. It may be frail; its roof may shake; the wind may blow through it; the storm may enter, the rain may enter—but the King of England cannot enter; all of his force dares not cross the threshold . . .'

"If ever there was an unassailable right of every free man in America, this has been it: that, in his home, every man has sanctuary from the oppression of his government. This right, inalienable, has played a vital role in the very development of the Nation, because it has been a heritage, a freedom, and a civilizing force giving us sober stability.

"But, under title IV every homeowner faces fines of unlimited amounts, judgments against him for causing a Negro, and I quote, 'humiliation and mental pain and suffering' if he refuses to sell his home to a Negro. Even prison is not ruled out since the bill authorizes the court to take steps to grant 'such relief as it deems appropriate,' and we know the record of the Federal courts in civil rights cases. The bill gives the Attorney General the power to haul a homeowner into Federal Court if he, the Attorney General, even thinks the homeowner might be about to discriminate against someone.

"As a practical matter, no homeowner could risk refusing to sell his home to any Negro applicant for fear of lawsuits and damage judgments that could strip him of all his property and his life savings and possibly send him to prison. If a Negro and a white man both offer to buy a home and if the owner sells to the white man, who can say he did not consciously or unconsciously discriminate against the Negro? In truth, no one can say. But the Federal courts will say, under the terms of this bill.

"Examine, if you will, the provision of this title that requires a salesman to use his 'best efforts' to sell a home to everyone who applies. This is probably the most ridiculous, but one of the most dangerous phrases in this entire bill. Who can possibly state what constitutes a man's best effort? The concept is asinine and would be laughable if it were not included in something that threatens to become the law of the land.

"In a Federal court, no man would be able to prove that he used his best efforts to sell a home to a Negro when he is challenged to prove it. Would he have to keep a tape recording of his sales pitch or a motion picture of his every gesture and every smile in order to vindicate himself? How much pressure would he have to exert on a potential buyer in order to qualify as doing 'his best'? Would the failure to shave the price a little be his downfall? What if his fountain pen ran out of ink at the time the papers were to be signed?

"Ridiculous you say? Look at the bill. This is what you are being asked to make into a Federal law. You are being importuned to place in judgment of every real estate transaction in the future, some bureaucrat who can, with a wave of his hand or the turn of his thumb, decide whether or not another man has used his 'best efforts' to sell a home.

"If that suggestion does not offend your sense of justice, examine the proposal in this title that says this same bureaucrat can sit in as a third party on every application for a home loan and substitute his judgment for that of the banker or lending institution involved. This provision negates the seasoned, experienced judgment of the lender and puts in its place a decision based on whatever sociological philosophies might exist in the bureaucracy at the moment.

"Ridiculous you say? Look at the bill. What banker or what lending institution would dare turn down a questionable loan to a Negro if this provision becomes law? Few or none, is the answer and you know it as well as I. You are being asked to enact legislation which will take away from the lender the right to make up his mind and lend his money and that of his associates or stockholders solely on the basis of his judgment of which of two applicants is the better risk. If this kind of law can be passed, how far away are we from another law that says the lender has to lend his money regardless of the applicant's ability to repay? The situation is exactly the same once you strip the lender of the right to make an economic decision based on economic considerations.

"While a limited governmental authority over private residences has always existed, it has, heretofore, been properly confined to regulating property so that its use did not injure the health or safety of others or destroy their use of their own property. Ownership has never been regulated before. Examples of these restrictions are many and include fire and sanitation controls, destruction of diseased trees, control of explosives, zoning, and in limited emergencies, rent control. However, each of these restrictions has involved a possible infringement upon public rights; not upon any individual's supposed rights.

"A law stating that an individual may not refuse a buyer's offer because his reasons for refusing are not satisfactory, is no different from a law saying that a buyer may not refuse a seller's offer because his reasons for refusing are not good enough. Nor is such a law more than a legal inch away from a law which would require a property owner to sell his home whether he wanted to or not if there is a buyer who wants it. Such is the Pandora's box this bill will open up if it becomes law.

"The party line among the civil rights leaders these days is 'cool it.' The very men who urged this tiger to take to the streets are now trying to calm the tiger down and we are all beseeched to help him back in the cage. This civil rights proposal is not the way to do it.

"The tiger is loose and he has tasted blood. He has tasted the heady brew of special privilege, and he will not give it up willingly and return to a responsible place in society. He has been taught that if he does not want to pay his rent he does not have to. He has been told that he need not work; that the Federal Government will take care of him on welfare and give him a guaranteed income. He has been exhorted to break any law he does not like without fear of punishment. He can loot stores before the eyes of police and know he will not be arrested for fear of 'starting an incident.' He has been taught that it does not make any difference if he marries the mother of his children or if he supports them. He can apply for a job alongside a white man and know he will get it, or else. He can dump an ashcan on the mayor of New York City, snipe at policemen in the streets, kill his fellow man, set fire to their property and know that his reward will be more civil rights from Washington.

"The truth is that the Negro has been used and he is coming to realize it.

" 'The world owes it to me' is the cry of the day, and I say the time has come, if this Nation is to survive, for us to stand up on our hind legs and say the one most needed verity of our times: 'No. The world owes you nothing. You work for what you get. You share duties and responsibilities with all men. You live by the common law of all. There will be no more special privileges for anyone.'

" 'Human rights; not property rights' is another cry from the streets, and, again, it is time for us to stand up and say: 'No. Where there are no property rights there are no human rights. The right to own and hold to oneself the product of your labor and sweat is the very seedbed of democracy. Without this seedbed there is no place for human rights to grow and flourish.'

" 'The end justifies the means,' the philosophy of the Communists, is still another cry and the answer of every American should be another loud and clear, 'No. It was just such a statement that produced the torture of the martyrs, the burning of witches and the crucifixion of Jesus Christ.'

"No problem can be solved better through socialistic processes rather than democratic ones.

"This annual outpouring of special privilege for the Negro is like the action of overly indulgent parents. The desired end will not be manhood and maturity, but perpetual childhood and dependence."

15 The Case against Urban Desegregation[*]

FRANCES FOX PIVEN
RICHARD A. CLOWARD

Although efforts at integration have produced significant gains in some areas, they have worked against the interests of urban Negro poor in housing and education. The authors discuss various approaches to housing and education desegregation that have been ineffective as well as measures that, in effect, have worsened ghetto conditions. The need is stressed for an improvement in ghetto conditions and the development of separatist institutions that can be the bases for developing political power and ethnic identity and advancing the specific interests of the Negro poor in our society.

For years the chief efforts of a broad coalition of liberals and reformers, in dealing with the problems of thhhe Negro, have been directed against segregation. Some significant gains have been made, particularly in the laws governing Negro rights in certain institutional

*Reprinted by permission of the authors and the National Association of Social Workers, from *Social Work*, 12: 1 (January 1967).

spheres, such as voting and the use of public accommodations. But in some areas the thrust for integration seems to have worked against Negro interests. This is especially true with regard to housing and education of the Negro poor in large cities.

There are two main reasons for this: (1) Efforts to ameliorate basic social inequities, such as deteriorated ghetto housing and inferior educational facilities, have been closely linked to the goal of integration and, since integration measures arouse fierce resistance, proposals to redress these social inequities have usually failed. It is for this reason that, after several decades of civil rights struggle, the lot of the Negro urban poor has actually worsened in some respects. (2) If the Negro is to develop the power to enter the mainstream of American life, it is separatism—not integration—that will be essential to achieve results in certain institutional arenas. Both of these points have implications for both public policy and political action.

DESEGREGATING HOUSING

Reformers oriented to the urban ghetto have generally sought two objectives that they have seen as closely linked—to promote desegregation and to obtain better housing and education for the poor. Restricted housing, they have contended, is the key factor in creating and maintaining racial barriers and, in turn, racial barriers force Negroes into deteriorated slums.

Efforts to desegregate housing, however, have been roundly defeated by massive white opposition. Indeed, residential segregation is increasing rapidly.[1] Moreover, because provision of decent housing for the poor has been tied to desegregation, this end also has been defeated.

Over the next decade or two many central cities could well become predominantly Negro, if the movement of Negroes into the city and the exodus of whites to the suburbs continue, and if the higher Negro birthrate persists.[2] Against these trends, the task of maintaining

[1]The proportion of nonwhites living in segregated census tracts in New York City rose from 49 to 53 percent between 1940 and 1950. In 1910 60 percent of the Negroes in that city lived in assembly districts that were less than 5 percent Negro. By 1960 62 percent were in districts that were over 50 percent Negro. "The Program for an Open City: Summary Report" (New York: Department of City Planning, May 1965). (Mimeographed.) *See also* Davis McEntire, *Residence and Race; Final and Comprehensive Report to the Commission on Race and Housing* (Berkeley: University of California Press, 1960), p. 41.

[2]Between 1950 and 1960—for the United States as a whole—the percentage gain in population was 17.5 for whites and 26.7 for nonwhites. The increase in the urban population was 27 percent for whites but 49 percent for nonwhites. In the same decade, the nonwhite population in central cities

racial balance in the cities seems insuperable. To offset them, huge numbers of families would have to be shuffled about by desegregation programs. This point has been spelled out by George Schermer who provides estimates of the number of people who would have to be moved each year in order to insure that a 50–50 population balance would exist in Washington, D.C., in the year 2000. (Washington is now 63 percent Negro.) Assuming that migration trends and birthrates remain constant, twelve thousand nonwhite families would have to be dispersed to suburban areas and four thousand white families induced to return to the District of Columbia *every year until* 2000.[3] Segregation between the suburbs and the central city is only part of the story. Even if whites could be induced to return to the city and Negroes could be accommodated in suburbs, residential integration would not result because Negroes and whites tend to live separately within the city itself. Any public program that would undertake to disperse growing concentrations of Negroes from the ghettos would have to shift formidable numbers to white neighborhoods and resettle whites in present ghetto areas.[4]

Approaches to desegregation have had little effect when the magnitude of the problem is considered. The most popular approach involves legal reforms coupled with education and information programs—legislation is sought to prohibit prejudicial treatment of Negroes, whether by deed restrictions, discriminatory actions of private realtors and landlords, or such governmental policies as the early FHA mortgage underwriting policy, which prescribed racially homogeneous housing developments. It is sobering to note, however, that many such reforms were won years before the civil rights movement but have failed completely to retard segregation.[5] Racial zoning ordinances, for example, were struck down by the courts in 1917.

Special agencies have been developed to hear complaints of

---

increased 63 percent while the white population continued to decrease. See *Our Nonwhite Population and Its Housing* (Washington, D.C.: Housing and Home Finance Agency, 1963), pp. 1–3. The nonwhite population in central cities reached 10.3 million in 1960 and may exceed 16 million by 1975, according to McEntire, pp. 4–5, 21–24.

[3]George Schermer, "Desegregating the Metropolitan Area." Paper presented at the National Housing Workshop, National Committee Against Discrimination in Housing, West Point, N.Y., April 1966.

[4]One report on desegregation concluded that housing and redevelopment programs directed to the goal of desegregation could at best only halt the spread of ghettoization. New York City's nonwhite population went from 9.5 percent in 1950 to 14 percent in 1960 and is expected to be more than 20 percent by 1975. (In 1900 it was 1.76 percent.) *See* "The Program for an Open City: Summary Report."

[5]The very proliferation of legal reform measures may account for the prevalent view among liberals that there has been progress in desegregation.

violations of antidiscrimination laws.[6] The procedures for achieving redress, however, ordinarily require knowledge and patience on the part of the plaintiff that cannot in fairness be expected of someone merely looking for a decent place to live. Moreover, these agencies are typically charged to negotiate grievances without sanctioning the landlord. Thus, although one apartment may be "opened" after torturous procedures, there is no deterrence to further violations—no carry-over effect. Each negotiated enforcement of the law remains an isolated event.

There are many programs that are designed to supplement the antidiscrimination laws by attempting to change the white community's discriminatory attitudes. Thus, "fair housing committees" have been established in receiving communities to overcome community hostility toward entering Negroes. Information and broker services are designed to overcome barriers to the movement of Negroes that result from communication gaps, such as a lack of information regarding housing opportunities outside the ghetto or difficulties in gaining access for inspection. Such programs as the Urban League's Operation Open City combine all these strategies to help Negro families find housing.

However, these efforts tend to reach only middle-class Negroes, because housing in outlying communities generally requires at least a lower-middle income. Moreover, even for the Negro middle class such measures do not result in broad-scale desegregation. Resistance in the receiving community varies directly with the number of Negro families who are likely to invade it. More important, the majority of housing opportunities are still controlled by the regular institutions of the private real estate market, and these agencies distribute information concerning available housing and provide access for inspection in accordance with class and racial neighborhood patterns that reflect the inclinations of the majority of housing consumers.[7]

---

[6]In New York City there are two such agencies: the New York State Commission on Human Rights and a parallel city commission. Both agencies recently announced a "great increase" in the number of complaints received. This increase, it turned out, resulted in a *total* of only 528 complaints over a six-month period. Needless to say, a complaint received is some distance from being acted on. "More Negro Families Are Utilizing Fair Housing Law Here and in Suburbs," *New York Times,* October 23, 1966, p. 117.

[7]A recent large-scale demographic study of the United States concluded, "Residential segregation prevails regardless of the relative economic status of the white and Negro resident." Karl E. Taeuber and Alma F. Taeuber, *Negroes in Cities: Residential Segregation and Neighborhood Change* (Chicago: Aldine Publishing Co., 1965).

HOUSING SUBSIDIES

Another general approach to desegregation takes the form of housing subsidies. Both the public housing program and the recent rent supplement program are intended, at least by some of their proponents, to promote integration as a by-product of rehousing the poor. However, it is found that when large numbers of tenants are Negro, low-income whites desert the projects or are reluctant to apply. Projects thus tend to become high-rise brick ghettos rather than outposts of integrated living. Programs to further integration by locating projects in outlying white communities have provoked even more serious opposition. Only when white tenants predominate has any degree of community tolerance resulted.[8] The political tension produced by this issue has contributed to the shaky political life of public housing. Indeed, this form of housing subsidy seems to be expiring in many cities.

The new rent supplement legislation so far also shows signs of accommodation in its provisions that enable outlying communities to veto a proposed invasion by low-income and minority groups. In any case, current appropriations are adequate only for a few showpiece programs throughout the nation and are likely to be decreased in the next session of Congress. If experience with public housing is any predictor, the opposition that the rent supplement program aroused in Congress, which almost defeated it, will be repeated more fiercely in local communities as efforts are made to implement the plan. Public subsidies, in short, have failed to reverse the trend toward segregation in urban areas.

EDUCATION AND JOB TRAINING

A third general approach to desegregation is based on this country's hallowed belief in individual mobility. Once Negroes have better jobs and higher incomes, it is asserted, they will be able to bid competitively for housing beyond the ghetto.

However, programs intended to advance Negroes economically by education and job training have only tenuous bearing on their housing. These programs currently reach merely one poor person in ten. But even if the scope of these programs was vastly expanded, millions of today's poor would not be helped by attempts to equip them for better

[8]In the city of Newark, N.J., the racial balance in projects is regularly graded from over 90 percent Negro for projects located in the central ghetto ward to over 90 percent white in outlying "country club" projects. Coincidentally, Newark has been able to obtain much more public support for public housing and to build more units per capita than most other cities.

jobs. Of the 35 million people below the federal poverty line (i.e., an annual income of $3100 for an urban family of four), several million are aged; they are permanently out of the labor force and can be lifted out of poverty only by the direct redistribution of income. One third of the poor are in families headed by females, and it does not seem reasonable to expect this group to raise itself out of poverty by entering the labor force. Many of the remaining poor are ill and others are permanently unable to compete for a host of additional reasons.[9]

It must also be recognized that a stretegy of enhancing economic mobility—even if it succeeded in lifting large numbers of people somewhat above the poverty line—would not greatly improve their capacity to procure decent housing. In urban areas, adequate housing is difficult to obtain for families with annual incomes of less than $7000.[10] Indeed, even middle-class whites have required and obtained huge governmental subsidies to bring adequate housing within their reach (e.g., urban renewal, low-cost government-insured mortgages such as FHA, special tax advantages allowed by federal law for builders and realtors, and real estate tax abatements allowed by local governments).

WORSENING OF GHETTO HOUSING

While efforts to get people out of the ghetto have been ineffective, a variety of other measures put forward in the name of desegregation have substantially *worsened* housing conditions within the ghetto itself. Under the general public mandate of meeting the nation's housing needs and redeveloping the urban core, huge subsidies have found their way into the middle-class market and the business community, and have had widespread and devastating effects on low-income residential areas. Urban redevelopment has resulted in the destruction of low-rental housing and low-income communities, so that many poor people

[9]*See* Mollie Orshansky, "Counting the Poor: Another Look at the Poverty Profile," *Social Security Bulletin,* Vol. 28, No. 1 (January 1965), pp. 3–29.

[10]Nationally, it is estimated that an income of over $7000 (which only 3.4 percent of nonwhites possess) is required to purchase new, privately constructed housing. Housing costs are much higher in urban areas. Schermer, "Desegrating the Metropolitan Area."

[11]In most metropolitan areas nonwhites pay slightly lower rentals than whites in each income group but get vastly inferior housing. McEntire, pp. 135–147. In New York City, for example, there are three times as many substandard units occupied by nonwhites as whites at each income level.

are pushed farther into the ghetto.[12] Moreover, in the process of redevelopment, owners and tenants on sites scheduled for clearance are placed in a prolonged state of uncertainty and often become either the agents or the victims of quick exploitation. Relocation programs designed to mitigate the effects of redevelopment on low-income people and small businesses are ordinarily inadequate.[13] The stalemate now seen in some urban renewal programs may be considered as an achievement in that the poor have finally been spurred by the accumulated abuses of years of dislocation to protest against the further destruction of their homes and communities.[14]

In the housing act of 1949 Congress asserted a national responsibility to provide a decent dwelling for every family. This, however, has not progressed very far. In New York City, for example, Mayor Lindsay's housing task force recently reported that there were half a million unsound units currently occupied (roughly the same number reported through years of new public assaults on the slums) and that the number was on the increase even though *the number of low-rental units* has decreased more than 30 percent since 1960.[15] In Boston, the last family-size public housing unit was built in 1954; the city's nationally acclaimed urban renewal effort diminished by 12 percent the supply of low-rental housing (less than $50.00 a month) between 1960 and 1965.[16] The federal public housing program has produced only 600,000 low-income dwelling units in the three decades since it was initiated. The federal urban renewal program and the federal highway

[12]Criticism of urban renewal has been launched from both the right and the left. See Martin Anderson, *The Federal Bulldozer* (Cambridge, Mass.: MIT Press, 1965); Herbert J. Gans, "The Failure of Urban Renewal," *Commentary*, Vol. 39, No. 4 (April 1965), pp. 29–37; and the replies to Gans by George M. Raymond and Malcolm D. Rivkin, "Urban Renewal," *Commentary*, Vol. 40, No. 1 (July 1965), pp. 72–80.

[13]For a review of experience with relocation see Chester Hartman, "The Housing of Relocated Families," *Journal of the American Institute of Planners*, Vol. 30, No. 4 (November 1964), pp. 266–268.

[14]James Q. Wilson analyzes the political dilemmas created by renewal programs in "Planning and Politics: Citizen Participation in Urban Renewal," *Journal of the American Institute of Planners*, Vol. 29, No. 4 (November 1963), pp. 242–249.

[15]"An Analysis of Current City-Wide Housing Needs" (New York: Department of City Planning, Community Renewal Program, December 1965), p. 67. (Mimeographed.)

[16]Michael D. Appleby, "Logue's Record in Boston: An Analysis of His Renewal and Planning Activities" (New York: Council for New York Housing and Planning Policy, May 1966), p. 43. (Mimeographed.)

program have together demolished close to 700,000 units, most of which were low rental, in less than half that time. Meanwhile, private builders, spurred on by federal tax incentives and mortgage programs designed to encourage construction, have made still further inroads on the supply of low-income housing by reclaiming land to erect middle- and upper-income units. The cheap accommodations that remain in large cities are in buildings that have been permitted to run down without maintenance and repairs or in which rents are pushed to the limit the captive market can afford. High-minded public policies notwithstanding, the dimensions of housing needs among the nonwhites in big cities have, in fact, enlarged.

In summary, attempts to provide better housing for the Negro have failed not because anyone has denied the moral imperative of desegregation. Rather, they have failed under the auspices of this moral imperative. It seems clear, therefore, that if the poor are to obtain decent housing, massive subsidies must be granted for new and rehabilitated housing in the ghettos and slums. The Negro is far from possessing the political power to gain subsidies for integrated low-income housing. The more relevant question is whether he can even mobilize sufficient pressure to house himself decently wherever he does live.

DESEGREGATING EDUCATION

To emphasize the importance of upgrading ghetto housing is also to accept racially homogeneous elementary schools in large cities, at least for the foreseeable future. Integrated education has been one of the central goals of reformers, and few seem prepared to relinquish this objective. However, the demographic and political realities in large cities cast grave doubts on the feasibility of achieving anything resembling integrated education at the early grade levels.

As a result of the housing patterns described earlier, Negroes are rapidly becoming the largest group (in some cases, the majority) in the central areas of many large cities. Furthermore, they represent an even greater proportion of the school-age population because Negro families are usually younger, larger, and without the resources to place their children in private schools.[17] The white youngsters with whom Negro children presumably are to be integrated are slowly vanishing

[17]Negroes already comprise over 50 percent of the school-age populations in Chicago, Philadelphia, and Washington, D.C. (where they comprise more than 80 percent). In other cities they are rapidly approaching the majority— Detroit, for example, has well over a 40 percent population of school-age Negroes.

from inner-city areas, and there is every reason to expect that these demographic trends will continue.

The issue of integrated education is also complicated by socioeconomic factors, particularly in the cities. Recent evidence suggests that diverse economic backgrounds of pupils may be more important than racial diversity in the education of the Negro student. One study of American education, for example, shows that mixing middle-class students (either Negro or white) with lower-class students (either Negro or white) usually has a decidedly beneficial effect on the achievement of the lower-class student and does not usually diminish the middle-class student's achievement.[18] By contrast, the integration of poor whites and poor Negroes does not seem to yield an improved achievement of either group.[19]

But the number of middle-class whites available to be mixed educationally with lower-class Negroes is rapidly declining, and of the whites left in the city with children who attend public schools, an increasing proportion is poor. (As for middle-class Negroes, their numbers are very small to begin with, and many send their children to private schools.) If mixing along class lines is to be achieved, therefore, educational arrangements in which suburban and ghetto children are brought together will be required. Such arrangements are improbable. The defense of the neighborhood school is ardent; it reflects both racial and class cleavages in American society. Efforts to bring about racial mixing, especially when coupled with the more meaningful demand for economic class mixing, run head-on into some of the most firmly rooted and passionately defended attitudes of white families.

Bussing Versus "Educational Parks"

Two schemes have been advocated for achieving racial integration while minimizing political resistance. One involves reshuffling children to achieve a racial balance by bussing them to distant schools. Aside from the enormous logistical problems this poses, bussing usually

[18]James R. Coleman *et al.*, *Equality of Educational Opportunity* (Washington, D.C.: U.S. Government Printing Office, 1966).

[19]Several studies show that by no means do Negroes do uniformly better in integrated schools. They either do better or worse than in segregated schools. One intervening variable appears to be the degree of bigotry exhibited by whites: the greater the bigotry, the more likely that Negroes will achieve less than in segregated schools. Poor and working-class whites have traditionally held the most prejudiced attitudes; integrating them with poor Negroes may actually hurt Negroes. Coleman, especially pp. 330–333. *See also* Irwin Katz, "Review of Evidence Relating to Effects of Desegregation in the Intellectual Performance of Negroes," *American Psychologist*, Vol. 19 (June 1964), pp. 381–399.

has met violent opposition from all sides.[20] The second scheme is the development of massive "educational parks," which would centralize upper-grade facilities for children from a wide area. The superiority of these new plants, it is argued, will help to overcome the opposition of white parents to integration. However, even in such plants segregation is likely to persist on the classroom level as a result of the "tracking system," particularly because educational parks are intended only for older children, whose academic levels already reflect wide inequalities in home environment and early schooling. Equally important is the fact that the cost of such educational parks would be enormous. It is improbable that many such parks would be built, and the merits of such an investment must be weighed against alternative uses of funds for the direct improvement of program and staff in ghetto schools.

Improving Ghetto Schools

The lower-class school, particularly in the large-city ghetto, has always been an inferior institution. Recently the physical facilities in many ghetto schools have improved because of new building programs; but the lower-class Negro school still reflects significant inequalities when it is compared to its white middle-class counterpart. For example, the quality of the teachers has been shown to have a critical influence on the child's learning—lower-class schools, however (especially ghetto schools in large cities), have inferior teachers and are generally characterized by higher staff turnover. To overcome historic inequalities of this kind would be no small achievement.[21]

The authors conclude, in short, that although schools that are racially and economically heterogeneous are probably superior, removing class inequities in the quality of teachers and programs is also an important goal—and a far more realistic one. Such educational im-

---

[20]There seems to be a somewhat easier acceptance when numbers of Negro children are assigned to white schools than when white children are assigned to ghetto schools. This has not been tried on a sufficient scale to put white tolerance to a genuine test, however. It is also true that Negro parents do not want their children to travel far either.

[21]There have been many studies—including the work of Allison Davis and subsequent studies by August B. Hollingshead—on class biases in the intelligence test and the differential response of the school system to children of different socioeconomic backgrounds. Many other studies document the sharp differences between the low-income school and its middle-class counterpart. For a recent study of inequalities by class in a large northern urban school system, see Patricia Cayo Sexton, *Education and Income: Inequalities in Our Public Schools* (New York: Viking Press, 1961). *See also* Coleman *et al.*

provements in the ghetto will require public action and expenditure, and these are likely to be achieved only if massive political opposition to demands for class and racial mixing is avoided. As in the case of housing, the coupling of measures for integration of education with measures to improve existing conditions in large-city ghettos must lead to the defeat of both. The choice is between total defeat and partial victory; to many, it may appear a difficult choice—but at least it is a choice.

PRIVATE SOCIAL WELFARE: SEPARATIST INSTITUTIONS

In discussing housing and educational reforms for the urban ghetto, the authors have stressed the political futility of integration measures. It is not only the feasibility of integration that is open to question; it is also far from clear that integration is always desirable.

Liberals are inclined to take a "melting pot" view of American communities and to stress the enriching qualities of heterogeneous living—however, the history of ethnic groups in American society belies this view. There have always been ethnic institutions, and these, as has been widely observed, have served important functions in the advancement of different groups. An important precondition for the establishment of such separatist institutions—particularly when the members of the ethnic group are poor—has been the existence of substantial aggregations of people in residential proximity. The current emphasis on integrating people physically in schools and neighborhoods thus deflects attention from a fundamental problem confronting the Negro—the lack of organizational vehicles to enable him to compete with whites for control of major institutions that shape the destiny of the ghetto (housing and educational systems, governmental bureaucracies, corporate economic complexes, political parties, and so forth). Without separatist institutions the Negro is not likely to come to share control in these various spheres, and the powerlessness of the ghetto's population will persist.

The value of separatist institutions is revealed clearly in the field of social welfare. There is, of course, considerable precedent for ethnically based social welfare institutions, which symbolize for many the highest values of self-help. Networks of agencies have been formed by Jews and white Catholics; even Protestants—under the impact of a pluralism that has made them act like a minority as well—have formed essentially white ethnic welfare institutions to advance their interests. Throughout the country these voluntary agencies raise a huge amount of money, which is directed to the less fortunate in their respective ethnic and religious communities (and sometimes to those in other communities as well).

POLITICAL INTERESTS

The point that is not generally recognized about private agencies, however, is that they are as much political as they are social welfare institutions; they serve as organizational vehicles for the expression of the ethnic group's viewpoints on social welfare policy and also as the institutional means for other forms of political association and influence. Religio-ethnic welfare institutions—from hospitals to child care facilities—command enormous amounts of tax money. In New York City, for example, they are now routinely paid over $100 million annually from the municipal budget (exclusive of antipoverty funds). Thus, these agencies are important political interest groups that, in acting upon their own organizational needs, serve the interests of their controlling ethnic and religious constituencies as well.

Exerting pressure for various forms of public subsidy is only one of the political functions of private agencies. They maintain a deep interest in many forms of governmental policy and actively seek to influence the shaping of policy in ways consistent with their interests. These political activities tend to be overlooked because private agencies exert power chiefly at the municipal level—not at the more visible level of national politics. However, large areas of public service *are* controlled locally and, even when programs are initiated and supervised by federal or state authorities, it is primarily at the municipal level that services are organized and delivered to their intended consumers. Public welfare, education, urban renewal, housing code enforcement, fair employment, law enforcement, and correctional practices—all of these are, in large part, shaped by local government.

Nowhere is there a Negro federation of philanthropy—and there are few Negro private social welfare institutions. Consequently, the Negro is not only without an important communal form but also lacks the opportunity to gain the vast public subsidies given for staff and services that flow into the institutions of white communities. In effect, to advocate separatism in this area means to insist that the Negro be given the prerogatives and benefits that other ethnic and religious communities have enjoyed for some decades.

If the Negro expects to influence the proliferating social welfare activities of government, he will need his own organizational apparatus, including a stable cadre of technical and professional personnel who can examine the merits of alternative public policies, survey the practices of governmental agencies, and activate their ethnic constituencies on behalf of needed changes.

COMMUNAL ASSOCIATIONS

Ethnic social welfare institutions serve another important function. This country has faced the problem of assimilating poverty-stricken minority groups into its economic bloodstream many times in the past, and religio-ethnic institutions of various kinds have played a significant part in that process. One of the ways by which such groups effect their rise from deprivation is to develop communal associations, ranging from fraternal and religious bodies to political machines. These communal associations provide a base from which to convert ethnic solidarity into the political force required to overcome various forms of class inequality. They are, therefore, an important device by which the legitimate interests of particular groups are put forward to compete with those of other groups.

The Negro community lacks an institutional framework in private social welfare (as well as in other institutional areas), and the separatist agencies of other ethnic and religious communities are not eager to see this deficiency overcome. When the Negro is concerned, they resist the emergence of new separatist institutions on the grounds that such a "color conscious" development represents a new form of "segregation." This view has frequently been expressed or implied in behind-the-scenes struggles over the allocation of antipoverty funds. In one city after another private agencies have either fought against the development of Negro-sponsored programs or have sat by while Negro groups argued in vain with municipal, county, or federal officials over their right to form autonomous, ethnic institutions to receive public funds.[22]

By and large, private agencies have contended that race is an irrelevant issue in deciding who should mount programs in a ghetto. Existing agencies, it is argued, have the proved professional and organizational competence to operate new programs, and many have succeeded in obtaining public funds to do so. In the end, however, this form of "desegregation" is destructive of Negro interests. Although coalitions of existing ethnic and religious agencies may provide services to the ghetto (especially with the financial incentives of the antipoverty program), these services do not strengthen the ghetto's capacity to deal with its own problems. Rather, they weaken it. Through the "integration" of Negroes as clients in service structures operated by others, political control by outside institutions is extended to one more aspect of ghetto life. Furthermore, the ghetto is deprived of the resources that could encourage the development of its own institutions or bolster them. Existing voluntary agencies could serve the ghetto far better if they lent political, technical, and financial aid to the development of new social welfare institutions that would be under Negro management and control.

[22]Some OEO funds have been used to stimulate the growth of Negro welfare institutions. Bitter conflicts have inevitably followed—as in the case of New York's HARYOU-ACT and the Child Development Group of Mississippi. Neither of these embattled agencies has received appreciable support from established social agencies.

Class power in the United States is intimately connected with the strength of ethnic institutions. Powerlessness and poverty are disproportionately concentrated among minority groups—Negroes, Puerto Ricans, Mexicans, and so forth. The success of traditional ethnic and religious social agencies in resisting the emergence of Negro institutions is a reflection of class power differentials. But it also reveals that class power is produced and maintained in part by racial and ethnic power differentials.

NEED FOR SEPARATIST ORGANIZATIONS

A new system of voluntary social welfare agencies in the ghetto can hardly be expected to produce the collective force to overcome the deep inequalities in our society. Ethnic identity, solidarity, and power must be forged through a series of organized communal experiences in a variety of institutional areas. In housing, for example, energy should be directed not only toward improving ghetto conditions, but also toward creating within the ghetto the organizational vehicles for renovating buildings and, more important, for managing them.[23] Similarly, educational reforms should mean not only improvements in facilities and staff but also arrangements under which the local community can participate in and influence the administration of the schools.[24]

What the Negro needs, in short, are the means to organize separately and a heightened awareness of the distinctive goals to which his organizations must be directed. The Negro poor in our society do

[23]In a tentative way, this possibility is now being explored by some groups (e.g., churches), which are receiving loans to rehabilitate ghetto buildings under the federal low-cost mortgage program. These groups form local corporations to rehabilitate and later to manage houses.

[24]Parent groups in East Harlem recently boycotted a new school (P. S. 201); they abandoned earlier demands for school integration to insist that the Board of Education cede a large measure of control to the local community. The ensuing controversy brought to the fore certain issues in professional and community control. As of this writing, a final resolution has not been reached. Without some administrative arrangement to insure greater involvement by the ghetto community, the schools will continue to be responsive to other, better-organized religious, ethnic, and class groupings that traditionally have been powerful enough to assert the superiority of their claims for educational services and resources over that of the ghetto. There is some indication that such arrangements may also bring educational benefits. A recent study showed a high correlation between the achievement of Negro children and their feeling that they can control their own destinies. *See* Coleman *et al.*

have interests distinct from and, more often than not, in conflict with those of other groups. Unless they organize along separatist lines, it is unlikely that they will have much success in advancing these interests. Judging from the history of those ethnic groups that have succeeded in gaining a foothold in our pluralistic society, it seems clear that ethnic separatism is a precondition for eventual penetration of the ruling circles and the achievement of full economic integration. Minority groups will win acceptance from the majority by developing their own bases of power, not by submerging their unorganized and leaderless numbers in coalitions dominated by other and more solidary groups. Once they have formed separatist organizations, participation in coalitions (whether councils of social agencies or political parties) can then be a meaningful tactic in bargaining for a share of power over crucial institutional processes in the broader society.

In a recent essay David Danzig observed:

It is, to be sure, a long step from the recognition of the need for power to the building and strengthening of indigenous social and political institutions within the ghetto from which power can be drawn. The Negro as yet has few such institutions. Unlike most of the other religio-ethnic minorities, he lacks a network of unifying social traditions, and this is why he must depend on political action through color consciousness as his main instrument of solidarity. That solidarity entails a certain degree of "separatism" goes without saying, but the separatism of a strengthened and enriched Negro community need be no more absolute than that, say, of the Jewish community. There is no reason, after all, why the Negro should not be able to live, as most Americans do, in two worlds at once—one of them largely integrated and the other primarily separated.[25]

In these terms, then, physical desegregation is not only irrelevant to the ghetto but can actually prevent the eventual integration of the Negro in the institutional life of this society. For integration must be understood, not as the mingling of bodies in school and neighborhood, but as participation in and shared control over the major institutional spheres of American life. And that is a question of developing communal associations that can be bases for power—not of dispersing a community that is powerless.

[25]"In Defense of 'Black Power,' " *Commentary*, Vol. 42, No. 3 (September 1966), pp. 45–46.

16 The Welfare Industry: Social Work and the Life of the Poor*

ROY LUBOVE

Much has been written lately of social work's "disengagement from the poor," and what Saul Alinsky has termed the "welfare colonialism of the social welfare industry." But has it ever been otherwise? That is, has the social work system ever been geared to enhancing the political power of the poor, or to encouraging decisive measures of income redistribution? The ideological and institutional heritage of American social work has not equipped it for many of the tasks demanded by the war against poverty. A dove cannot be expected to become a hawk— at least not overnight.

The problem, historically, is not simply the literal detachment of social work from the poor, but a reluctance to concede (implausible as it sounds) that the commodity desperately needed by the poor is money. The main thrust of social work, especially before the 1930s, must be understood in the context of the American work culture and a

*Reprinted by permission of the author and publisher from *The Nation*, 202 (May 23, 1966).

commitment to private and voluntary support of charitable enterprise. These decisively influenced the response of social work to the poor, and blocked efforts to deal with poverty as an issue of income maintenance and redistribution.

Organized social work emerged in the 19th century to reinforce, not to protest against, the imperatives of the work culture. Private relief and charitable agencies attributed poverty in a land of opportunity to character defects—notably, to improvidence, ignorance and intemperance. Their mission was to rehabilitate the character of the poor through personal influence and service. The first requirement of the poor was "not alms, but a friend." It was not merely the right but the civic duty of the successful to help acculturate the immigrant and working-class poor. Otherwise class, ethnic and religious differentiation would undermine the stability of the republic. The primary responsibility for socialization, however, belonged to private agencies; public welfare could only pauperize and demoralize through the prospect of readily obtained material assistance. Robert W. de Forest, noted philanthropist and president of the influential New York Charity Organization Society, thus explained: "If the duty of helping their less fortunate neighbors were taken off the shoulders of those who are able to help by having the city or state assume that burden, much of the neighborly intercourse between the poorer and the richer would cease. Public outdoor relief makes for a class separation and the enmity of classes. Private charity makes for the brotherhood of men."

Brotherhood, for all practical purposes, meant the assimilation by the poor of work incentives and disciplines. Their salvation, and that of American society, depended upon the diffusion of middle-class behavioral norms which assured economic mobility: thrift, sobriety, ambition, zeal for self-improvement and, not least important, fear of the consequences of dependency. Far from dedicating itself to the goal of economic security, American social work throughout most of its existence has embraced a deterrent psychology which expected work motivation to arise from fear and the "despair of unemployment, disease and underfeeding." As a social worker at the turn of the century observed: "The working classes are willing to provide for themselves if an unwise charity does not offer a bonus for incompetence."

Few Americans probably realize that long before the depression of the 1930s the American Association for Labor Legislation tried heroically but futilely to institute a comprehensive social security program. The movement flourished in the decade following 1911, when the first workmen's compensation statutes were enacted in this country. Inspired by the achievements of Bismarck and Lloyd George, it attempted to establish income maintenance programs which operated independently of the unpredictable, penurious and humiliating poor laws, not to mention the genteel friendly visitor from the private charities.

Sponsors of the American social insurance movement sought, through a vast enlargement of the public welfare sector, to provide protection against the long- and short-term risks which affected the worker's income—accident, sickness and maternity, old age and invalidism, unemployment and death (resulting in dependent widows and children). Contrary to conventional wisdom, social insurance experts presumed that income security was the pivot of any modern welfare system, and that it was necessarily a public responsibility. Their logic was simple. Survival depended upon work, but work was not always available. Although income could be interrupted at any time, financial obligations remained constant, or might even become heavier in times of adversity like sickness. It was necessary, therefore, to create new welfare institutions which guaranteed a measure of income continuity, and which did not expose the individual to the indignities of private or public charity. It was not a question of character, morality, incentive or the other traits prized by social work, but of the realities of poverty in a wage-centered, capitalistic society.

Apart from workmen's compensation and mothers' assistance legislation, the first social security movement failed miserably. The constraints of the American work culture proved too powerful. Equally important, the work culture was rooted in a broader value complex suggested by the term "voluntaryism." By this was meant the right of citizens to define and pursue their goals in free association. Voluntaryism made possible limited government, maximum liberty and free enterprise. Social security, statist in orientation, was incompatible with voluntaryism and, therefore, with democracy itself. Private social work, which viewed itself as a vital expression of the voluntary tradition, usually favored minimal government initiative in its own sphere.

Social work is criticized today for having adapted its service structure in recent years to a middle-class clientele. Yet if poverty is interpreted as a problem of income redistribution requiring substantial changes in the institutions and power relationships of American society, social work has never identified with the poor. Its detachment from the economic realities and pressures which pervaded the lives of the poor was reinforced in the early 20th century by a growing preoccupation with professionalism. This ultimately made psychiatry the key to social work knowledge and function. Professionalism and psychiatry did produce one major change. Intervention in the lives of clients had been justified in the 19th century on grounds of an assumed personal superiority; in the 20th century it was justified by the expert techniques, allegedly acquired through formal education. What remained the same over the years was the emphasis upon case work and counseling services, now geared to the agency's image of itself as a repository of psychiatric wisdom. Since the needs of the poor are often concrete, immediate and material, it is not surprising that the traditional social work system and the poor have experienced a breakdown in communication.

But the detachment of American social work from the economic realities of poverty explains only half the story. Dissident social workers and others who did struggle for public income maintenance programs in the past confronted opposition as well as indifference. Isaac M. Rubinow, the social insurance expert, writing on the eve of the great depression, complained that "social workers almost dread to admit that they deal with poverty—only with maladjustment, which, we are glibly told, may just as frequently arise in any economic stratum."

If poverty did not exist, or if it was rooted in personality problems, there was no need for government programs which might shift the balance of power and influence from the private to the public welfare sector. We could continue, as Rubinow put it, to "sweep away the ocean of human misery with a charitable broom." The depression finally made clear that voluntary institutions had been assigned a responsibility they could not meet—"to serve as a substitute for, and to the exclusion of, a broad program in dealing with poverty, misery, distress, and economic maladjustment." Until the 1930s voluntaryism was the American substitute for a genuine social policy, and long delayed the establishment of public programs in income maintenance, housing, medical care and other fields—programs instituted decades earlier in Europe.

The Social Security Act of 1935 and subsequent developments greatly enhanced the role of the public welfare sector, but the influence of the old traditions remained potent. Indeed, the most masterful achievement of the Social Security Act was to provide a small measure of economic security for selected risks, with a minimum of income redistribution. We have no better authority on the limited purpose intended for the social security system than Edwin Witte, director of the technical staff of the Committee on Economic Security. Social security, Witte explained, was not designed to "modify the distribution of wealth and it does not alter at all the fundamentals of our capitalistic and individualistic economy." The absence of government contributions to old-age and unemployment insurance suggests the act's fiscal conservatism, limited conception of function and emphasis upon keeping the program as closely work-related as possible.

Today, no less than in the 1930s, our social security system is best understood as an effort to provide some economic security without significantly affecting income distribution; it is thus to some degree an exercise in futility. Excluding education, public social welfare expenditures in 1962–1963 totaled $43 billion, approximately 7 percent of the GNP. In dollar volume ($25 billion) and in percentage (4.5), expenditures for social insurance programs overwhelmed the rest. Health and medical services, and veterans' programs, followed at 1 percent each; then public assistance at 0.9; and miscellaneous welfare programs at 0.3. In effect, the American social security system is predominantly organized around the contributory social insurances, which are comparatively regressive in terms of the tax burden imposed upon lower income brackets.

On the other hand, private benefit plans have advanced rapidly in the United States, and these are the most regressive social welfare measures of all because of their links to employment stability, seniority and upper echelon personnel. Finally, the United States does not compare favorably with other industrial countries in the percentage of its GNP devoted to welfare purposes. These considerations, quite aside from the circumscribed benefits provided by the statutory programs, suggest that the American welfare state is woefully underdeveloped by income-maintenance criteria.

The public welfare system has, in large measure, been shaped in the image of private social work, with its traditional concern for work motivation, rehabilitation and "services" in lieu of economic support. A good example is the Economic Opportunity Act of 1964 and the general tendency of the war against poverty to concentrate upon measures which will enhance the individual's productive potential. Public welfare has inherited from the voluntary sector, and the American work culture, a suspicion of any direct income-maintenance function. Since the days of the mothers' pension struggle in the early 20th century, public officials have parroted the therapeutic rhetoric of private social work in order to justify their role. Income maintenance was not seen as sufficient reason for a public welfare system. The public sector also had to perform the superior tasks of case work and rehabilitation (as encouraged, for example, in the Public Welfare Amendments of 1962). The result is a public sector that lacks the funds and resources for either function, but whose frustrated personnel is nonetheless expected to combine the roles of investigator, clerk and case worker.

The American social welfare system—private and public—has never been equipped to deal with the poverty that is a product of income deprivation, pure and simple. The poor might benefit if private social work devoted more effort to financial therapy, and if public agencies became less apologetic about the income-maintenance function as an end in itself. To face up to the economic realities which govern the life of the poor, however, is to confront the hard questions of power and income redistribution which have been evaded historically by a stress upon social work's service role. It may even be unfair to ask a dove to become a hawk.

PART IV
DISTRIBUTION OF HUMAN VALUES: ENLIGHTENMENT

Introduction

The politics of enlightenment are critical to the well-being of a democratic system. It ought to be clear that the urban school, the multiversity, and the research and development center are all saturated with political meaning. Yet it is probably still true that the distribution of skills and enlightenment are not often viewed in a political context. The first two contributions to this section explore some American myths about the degree of closeness between knowledge and power. In the process, some matters of critical import for the quality and distribution of skills and reason are raised.

First, the editor sketches (Selection 17) the history of political education in its relationship to the purposes and structure of the American educational system. It is his thesis that the ideology and practices of formal political education have been congruent with the political and educational systems in which they came to fruition. Two models of official civic education, namely the "rational-activist" model and the "integrative-consensual" model, have dominated teaching materials and guiding concepts of civic education. However, neither form retains the general support, the functionality, or the control of educational institutions that existed in an earlier period. Indeed, the tendency for them to be absorbed by an emerging third model, namely the "segmented-organizational" educational apparatus, accounts for the frequency with which formal education appears unrelated to genuine political participation and to the maturation of democratic attitudes.

Robert H. Salisbury examines the relationship between political and educational systems at the local level in Selection 18. Using concrete cases, he finds that arguments on behalf of the school's professional independence from partisan politics helped to create the myth of the unitary community in which the schools performed an apolitical function. He explores changes in practices that represented labor and ethnic groups in the educational processes because it became apparent from time to time that when educators treat the community as a unitary phenomenon, they are less able to offer programs and facilities which serve the differentiated needs and values of particular subgroups in the city. From this perspective, and aware that the urban poor and black communities no longer accept the unitary myth, he explores a realistic alternative. That alternative includes the big city mayor as the chief organizer of the important educational interests within the community, for the mayor and federal or state agencies can protect the school system when its apolitical stance is greeted by intense political pressures. Behind these first two contributions is the realization that the processes of education and enlightenment are intimately related to the totality of political issues in city and nation.

The personal and political significance of education is presented in a more intimate mode by the editor in Selection 19. Therein, he examines the chasm between the operations of a midwestern school system (wedded to the unitary myth explored by Salisbury) and the life styles of black adolescents at the time of the "black revolution" before the death of Martin Luther King, Jr. In particular, the psychic energy drained into the protection of self-esteem ought to concern us. The experiences of these young citizens makes it clear that the school's relevance to social and political life is of utmost importance.

The relevance of school to social and political life applies to the higher learning as well as to the inner city schools. In his review of education's political impact (Selection 20), the editor calls attention to the structural and personal factors that have been politicized in the era of the federal-grant university. This analysis leads to Christian Bay's empirical examination of student political activists in Selection 21. From this evidence, which the reader should inspect for himself, Bay concludes that more conservative views among students or adults are likely to be less rationally and less independently motivated, compared to more radical-liberal views. His position is that while every new human being is potentially a liberal animal and a rebel, yet every social organization he confronts, from the family to the state, is likely to seek to "socialize" him into a conventionally pliant conformist. The problem of creating genuine centers of political learning and personal development directly confronts all those concerned with public policy and civic enlightenment. The modes of analysis offered here are dedicated to the stimulation of the political will to translate ideas into political deeds within the educational structure of our highly developed society.

17 Education and Political Enlightenment in America*

EDGAR LITT

Formal political education has developed distinct ideologies and practices congruent with political and educational development. It is the thesis of this essay that two models of official civic education, namely, the rational-activist and the integrative-consensual, have dominated teaching materials and concepts. Neither form retains the general support, the functionality, or the dominant educational institutions that did exist in an earlier historical period. Indeed, the tendency for them to be absorbed by an emerging third model, namely, the segmented-organizational educational apparatus, is one of the major reasons for the frequency of "null" findings relating formal education to political participation and attitude-formation.

"The educational and the political role of social science in a democracy is to help cultivate and sustain publics and individuals that are able to

*Reprinted by permission of the author and publisher from *The Annals of the American Academy of Political and Social Science,* 361 (1965).

live with, and to act upon adequate definitions of personal and social relations" (C. Wright Mills, *The Sociological Imagination*).

"The task is a strategy of escape to freedom by undoing the residue of past socialization" (Harold Lasswell, *The Future of Political Science*).

SOME CRITERIA OF CIVIC EDUCATION

An inquiry into the politically relevant content of formal education— what the schools teach about such matters as participation and citizenship—should begin with clear intellectual premises that set forth the substantive foundations of our study.[1] This is necessary because the extant civic education research contains a variety of traditions, a diffuseness of substantive and methodological assumptions. Some writers set forth utopian treatises about the good life and the model citizen; other scholars report findings about participation and political attitude change in a most abstracted way, assuming a kind of timelessness to their results; and other men insist that teaching and learning of public consequence can only be understood in relation to broader contexts in which educational and political systems interact to form the subject matter of the classroom. Unfortunately, those studies which do exist are so disparate in approach as well as subject matter that it is difficult to make generalizations about their findings. To find that political participation cannot be taught by verbal and social cues in the large introductory political science course of a contemporary, metropolitan university has a different meaning than such an observation at Choate or Williams in 1920.[2] To discover that the sons and daughters of Irish-American immigrants were taught a bland, consensual view of American government in 1910 varies significantly from the fact that their assimilated and allegiant grandchildren receive a similar civic

[1] I have learned much from two unpublished papers which Professor Fred Greenstein of Wesleyan University made available to me, namely, "Political Socialization," prepared for the *International Encyclopedia of the Social Sciences,* and "Memorandum to the UCLA Civic Education Project," December 30, 1964, and from conversations with Professors Kent Jennings, University of Michigan and Bradbury Seasholes, Lincoln-Filene Center, Tufts University, about their national study of civic education.

[2] See A. Somit *et al.,* "The Effect of the Introductory Political Science Course on Student Attitudes toward Personal Political Participation," *American Political Science Review,* 52 (December 1958), pp. 1129–1132; Marvin Schick and Albert Somit, "The Failure to Teach Political Activity," *American Behavioral Scientist,* 6 (January 1963).

education in 1963.[3] The research findings do not "add up" to an account of civic teaching in the schools—much less do they innately suggest theoretical concepts with which to assimilate them. Such findings and concepts receive only such meaning as we impute to them. Three premises seem especially appropriate to the task of this essay. One is that politically relevant learning is most likely to occur when formal curriculums, and the self-concepts of teachers, are congruent with the educational milieus, and when the educational process itself meets the expectations of the larger political system. For instance, the legitimate rule of the nineteenth-century British elite is enhanced by the unity of a classical curriculum in their history and culture, a segregated "public school" experience providing subtle class learning by peers and headmasters, and forums in which the skills and responsibilities of leadership are shaped.[4] A second premise is that both the content and expectations of formal civic education can best be understood within specific historical periods of a nation's political development. The key question to focus on is the anticipated political effect of this education on those students who will probably play assigned political roles as adults. My third premise is that the effects of formal political learning are publicly found in an enhanced or diminished scope of human reason and competence in political decisions fundamentally affecting one's life chances. This third premise is normative, although I do not believe it is any more value-laden than treating civic education as an instrument to secure a stable, socialized polity, or as a key element in the modernization of human resources.[5] Indeed,

---

[3]The pattern of consensual-integrative education, stressing adherence to democratic norms without participatory or realistic political instruction, is evident in "Gamma," a lower middle-class school district discussed in Edgar Litt, "Civic Education, Community Norms, and Political Indoctrination," *American Sociological Review,* 28 (February 1963), pp. 69–75.

[4]Note Richard Rose, *The Politics of England* (Boston: Little, Brown, 1964), chap. 3; R. Wilkinson, *Gentlemanly Power: British Leadership and the Public School Tradition* (London: Oxford University Press, 1964).

[5]Compare James Coleman: "We endeavored to formulate a neutral, nonculturebound concept of political development" [but] specification of the traits of political modernity, however, leads one inescapably to two polar patterns of political development, one that derives its capacity through coercion and rests upon a subject political culture, and one that generates its capacity through consensus and a civic political culture"—in his *Education and Political Development* (Princeton, N.J.: Princeton University Press, 1965), p. 540. See also the lucid discussion by two developmental economists, Frederick Harbison and Charles A. Myers, *Education, Manpower, and Economic Growth* (New York: McGraw-Hill, 1964), especially pp. 160–185.

it seems a highly urgent assumption to make about the conduct and interpretation of civil research in a polity that is already highly stable, highly developed, and highly participatory. Moreover, there is another reason for imposing this criterion on the politically significant content of the schools. The carriers of civic education, namely, the social scientists and other professional educators, are key intervening variables in any research paradigm that asks about civic learning. The scholar conversing with the neophytes of a professional class, the secondary school teacher coping with the multitudes in search of education's secular religion, the Institute's researcher reporting the political survey's results to and about the sample class he has never seen before and will never see again—these relationships may have deep significance on what the schools do and do not teach about the political order.[6]

The application of these premises seems especially fruitful because the schools, as cultural institutions, provide legitimation, expectation, and a protopolitical context. The official status of the schools is strategic in transforming the interests and aspirations of interest groups and social classes from a basis of power to one of authority. The "natural condition" obtains when business gains after the Civil War became industrial statesmanship, when the dominance of a Southern oligarchy is related to a peculiar historical account of the Reconstruction, and when approval of partyless, independent voting is linked with a concern about the articulation of urban-ethnic demands. Legitimized interests are sanctioned by official textbooks and expanded to discuss the bases of their position or their techniques of power. So, too, do school textbooks and classrooms provide forums for debunking or altering authoritative relationships, as in the reconstruction of the Negroes' role and power in urban politics.[7]

Expectation refers to the anticipated political roles envisioned by a society and its authoritative educational system. Is this model student

---

[6]Low situational feelings of power and self-esteem are often reported in studies of secondary school teachers in America. Note National Educational Association, Research Division, "Teacher Opinion on Pupil Behavior, 1955–56," *Research Bulletin* (April 1956), pp. 51–107; Fletcher G. Watson, "The Hero Image in Education," *Harvard Graduate School of Education Association Bulletin* (Fall 1962), p. 1 ff.; Ralph B. Kimborough, *Political Power and Educational Decision Making* (Chicago: Rand McNally, 1964). On the university level, a strong relationship between educational permissiveness and apprehensiveness among social scientists during the McCarthy period is shown in Paul F. Lazarsfeld and Wagner Thielens, Jr., *The Academic Mind* (New York: Free Press, 1958), pp. 152–158.

[7]See the report of a conference sponsored by the Lincoln-Filene Center for Citizenship and Public Affairs, Tufts University, *Negro Self-Concept: Implications for School and Citizenship* (New York: McGraw-Hill, 1965).

to be a member of a mass who does not question the rule of a superior and ordained elite, an industrial worker who needs the skill and understanding to know his role in modern society, or a child of the Enlightenment expected to participate in the voluntary mosaic of parties, interest groups, and informal circles of political opinion-formation?

The context of education refers to the opportunities available for learning alternative civic roles. This latent curriculum may be congruent with expected political roles as in an "Oxbridge debate" preparatory to a governmental career, or it may be unrelated to such expectations as in participating student conventions that do not link with voluntary associations having dispersed power and political relevance. So, too, the educational permissiveness of a searching, "democratic" curriculum may be unreinforced in a large educational bureaucracy, functionally segmented, and sharply hierarchical in its distribution of authority. These, then, are matters for exploration.

AMERICAN CIVIC EDUCATION: THE RATIONAL-ACTIVIST MODEL

In a speculative frame of mind, I propose to deal with these issues. My thesis is that the substance, the ideology, and the institutions of American civic education have been substantially changed; that, in the process, old expectations of political learning acquire legitimacy in a formal curriculum meeting political demands of specific periods. Three working models of civic education seem most dominant in the American experience and provide the basis for comparative exploration.[8]

One is the rational-activist model. Both the classic ideology and the institutions of American civic education are strongly influenced by the liberal ethos of this model. Its focus is on the mastery of the political environment by the application of reasoned, voluntary effort. Reflecting the dominance and ego-ideal of an autonomous professional class, it stresses the belief that harmony and political compromise are fundamental to civic education. "The bourgeois mind is," as Mannheim saw it, "intellectualistic in so far as it attempts solely through thought, discussion, and organization to master, as if they were already rationalized, the power and other irrational relationships that dominate."[9] Its

[8]Elitist-ascriptive and political-indoctrination types are less applicable to American civic education. Note Richard R. Fagan, *Cuba: The Political Content of Adult Education* (Stanford, Calif.: Hoover Institute on War, Revolution, and Peace, 1964); Jeremy R. Azrael, "Soviet Union," in Coleman, pp. 233–271.

[9]Karl Mannheim, *Ideology and Utopia* (New York: Harcourt, Brace, and World 1936), p. 175.

language is that of law and history articulating the discourse of rights, duties, and obligations.

The good citizen is essentially a product of character training who participates responsibly in the affairs of society.[10] Girded by denominational zeal, sensitive to the expectations of their social class, linked to the political responsibilities of the State Department and the civic association, the graduates of preparatory schools and strong liberal arts colleges provide the models of civic training. Civic training puts strong emphasis on the moral component of civic duty, on public responsibility, and on voluntary participation. These virtues of the Protestant Ethic found their way into public school civic textbooks and thus provided the guidelines for other aspiring groups. The proponents of this model saw no need for specialized, formal instruction in citizenship:

> Ours is a college preparatory curriculum [at Phillips Academy, Andover]. So far as the program educates for citizenship it does so in the sense that a college liberal arts program does. We offer a few elective courses . . . for example a minor course open to seniors called social problems.[11]

> The vitals of a prep-school are not located in the curriculum. They are located in a dozen other places, some of them queer places indeed: in the relations between boys and faculty; in who the boys are and where they come from; in a Gothic chapel or a shiny new gymnasium; in the type of building the boys live in and the sort of thing they do after supper; and above all in the headmaster.[12]

Clearly designed for an ascending bourgeosie, nurtured by independent professions and *laissez-faire* economics, visible in the pluralism of ethnic, regional, and class politics, this liberal ethos and its rational-

---

[10]The transformation of university education from an instrument of character-training to instruction and research is traced in Walter P. Metzger, *Academic Freedom in the Age of the University* (New York: Columbia University Press, 1961).

[11]Letter from John M. Kemper, Headmaster, Phillips Academy, Andover, Massachusetts, quoted in Franklin Patterson, *The Adolescent Citizen* (New York: Free Press, 1960), p. 117.

[12]C. Wright Mills, *The Power Elite* (New York: Oxford University Press, 1959), p. 67. A general relationship between the formation of pretechnocratic elites and selective exposure to humanistic and legal studies is suggested by the distribution of college enrollments presented by Coleman, p. 530.

activist curriculum provide a *general* citizen role. Moreover, it is learned in harmony with the norms of an academic community, diverse in power and culture, that itself fits into a political system based on interest-group bargaining and the broker state. Alongside the federalism of quasi-autonomous states, the economics of the family firm, and the community politics of the homogeneous middlesized city, there stand in the center stage of American education relatively small, high-quality institutions perpetuating a congruent political belief system. The belief system is congruent with the nineteenth-century liberalism because it includes an emphasis on rational deliberation in the formation of public policy, an open exchange of opinion in face-to-face meetings, and strong confidence in the ability of self-governing men to decide for the good of the community.[13]

The intellectual ghost of John Stuart Mill and his model parliament hovers beneficially above the informal devices that link the formal and informal curriculums. These include the self-governing faculty, the equalitarian atmosphere of the seminar, the tutorial, the individual scholar, the informal initiation into professional-class life style—those techniques by which a professional class transmits to its young the pleasures and responsibilities of public service and interest. In the era of pluralistic liberalism, the liberal arts college, the preparatory school, and the selective public high school are the dominant educational institutions.

The withering away of pluralistic liberalism and the social structure supporting it suggests the anachronism of the type of civics education, with its emphasis on legalistic and humanistic studies and on the conventional learning of governmental forms and institutions. The forum *par excellence* for the teaching of this national model was the small liberal arts college. Since 1951, private institutions' share of the college-student population has declined from about 50 percent to 39.6 percent.[14] The nationalization of the American educational system and

[13]Empirical evidence of such permissiveness among small, private-college, social science faculties (although not those of denominational and teacher-training institutions) is found in Lazarsfeld and Thielens, p. 128.

[14]Projections of the Ford Foundation's Fund for the Advancement of Education forecast that public institutions' share will rise to 70 percent by 1970 and 80 percent by 1985. See "Public Colleges Swell Enrollment as Private Schools Limit Growth," *The Wall Street Journal,* May 8, 1965, pp. 1, 17. Rather than painting an idyllic picture of the private, liberal arts college, I am trying to relate its meaning to the strength of the rational-activist mode. Its decline in one educational milieu is described by Harold Taylor, former president of Sarah Lawrence, in "Freedom and Authority on the Campus," *The American College,* ed. Nevitt Sanford (New York: John Wiley & Sons, 1964).

its political order affect both the content and the efficacy of civic instruction.

THE INTEGRATIVE-CONSENSUAL MODEL: CREATING THE GOOD CITIZEN

The crucial fact about the development of American secondary and collegiate public education is the extent to which the liberal ethos of the self-cultivating, participating citizen was adapted from model private schools. In the Progressivism of Dewey, in the writings of George Counts, in the missionary zeal of other great schoolmen, the civic role of the school is clear—it is to reconstruct society and to train a responsible citizenry. In operational terms, this meant that the belief system and self-concept of the urban, immigrant mass must be changed. *No longer could it be assumed that a liberal education subsumed socialization for voluntary participation in a pluralistic political system.* Civic education became an overt, although poorly articulated, instrument of state policy. "Americanization" meant that the schools must create an allegiant and integrated citizenry. Beyond obtaining political loyalty, the schools explicitly sought to alter the normative and cognitive dimensions of politics. In essence, it was a strategy of inducements and deprivations. In order to succeed, to obtain the fruits of social mobility and political respectability through education, the immigrant must change the nature of his political ethos, the core referents of his political vocabulary. Nonpartisanship, not the urban political machine; merited public achievement, not patronage and familial loyalties; a harmony of community interests, not the overt "selfishness" of interest-group conflicts—these were the signs of the good citizen.

The official political culture of the "melting pot" school system did appear to transmit political identification and allegiance. But, in its fundamental differences with the political institutions of ethnic politics and cohesion, it failed to change the style of urban politics radically. In historical perspective, the major accomplishment of the new civic education was to promote fundamental consensus, to use conventional information about American history and institutions as a damper to "dysfunctional" radical political ideologies and intense subcultural loyalties. Perhaps in their transmission of the small-town political ethos, the schools did not overcome the realities of emerging urban political forms. But they did play a role in reinforcing basic Americanization, teaching primary skills of civic literacy, and fusing socialism with the technology of industrial progress. Dewey's ideas of progressive education did not liberate the child from the local restraints of the

Vermont small town—those restraints were irrelevant in the urban core. But they did liberate and nationalize education—from parish to nation in Riesman's useful terminology—and initiate recruits into the emerging industrial order.[15]

It is from this experience that a new vocabulary of civic education developed. The child is to be socialized, adjusted, acculturated to the prevailing political order. Indeed, as Theodore Lowi has documented, the normative imperatives of primary civic allegiance, of creating an integrative and consensual citizenry, remain interspersed with functional analysis in contemporary American government textbooks.[16]

Moreover, the retardation of "realistic" political analysis of conflict and dissentual public behavior is related to the kinds of "social problems" occasioned by both mass education and universal politicization. While the American polity itself underwent an enlargement of scale, an increase in centralized federal power, and corporate bureaucratization, the norms of the pluralistic liberal society were adapted to the era of the welfare and garrison state. One reason for what appears to be merely a "cultural lag" in the concepts of civic textbooks and instruction was an effort to adjust rational-activist expectations to political nationalization. This fusion wedded older expectations of voluntary, deliberative politics with the newer demands of a highly allegiant citizenry. The infusion of political realism, the new perception of party politicians, and the sensitivity to minority-group demands were devices by which the formal agencies of civic education legitimized the public policies stemming from the New Deal.[17]

To recapitulate, the integrative-consensual model arose from the creation of an integrated political system reducing parochial loyalties and providing social services. The central problem of this civic training is to alleviate xenophobia, authoritarianism, and other evidences of mass intolerance stemming from the dislocations of the old pluralistic order and to replace them by rationally functional public and private institutions of enormous wealth and power. The comprehensive high

[15]I have drawn extensively on the comprehensive and astute review of civic education programs by Carol H. Quinn, in her unpublished manuscript, "Is Citizenship Education Creating the Measure of Social Competence Necessary for Democracy?" (January 14, 1965); Michael Walzer, "The American School," *Dissent,* 6 (Spring–Summer 1959), pp. 107–121, 223–236.

[16]Theodore J. Lowi, "American Government, 1933–1963: Fission and Confusion in Theory and Research," *American Political Science Review,* 58 (September 1964), pp. 589–599.

[17]This appears to be a reasonable interpretation of the social-class and political-community factors influencing the existence of civic education approximating the rational-activist or consensual-integrative typologies in Litt, "Civic Education, Community Norms, and Political Indoctrination."

school and the public university are the dominant educational institutions in this transitory period.

THE SEGMENTAL-ORGANIZATIONAL MODEL

While the schools may teach political material conforming more or less to several civic models at the same time, a third major adjustment among the political system, its educational apparatus, and the young is most compelling. The representative citizen in the third model is the person with analytic, technical skills highly trained to perform an intellectualistic, specialized task. In such civic learning, participatory and allegiant norms are fused with highly concentrated instruction focusing on narrowly defined career tasks, including those of political management. The language of the liberal ethos (rights, duties, civic obligation), and the discourse of the period of nationalization (adjustment, consensus, equilibrium) are increasingly replaced by a technorationalistic syntax (systems, tooling up, stabilizing mechanisms) reflecting the dominance of bureaucratic and scientific political elites. In the process, the moralistic and the analytical or "realistic" forms of political instruction are replaced by more abstract and impersonal conceptual units. The central instructional units are the national federal-grant university and the highly developed or prototype research institute.[18] Loyalty to place and class and national allegiance are operatively supplanted by skill-group identification. The premises of this civic model are essentially Burkian and organic. The bases of substantive judgment are those of the managerial and analytic skills (including political "models"), rather than secularized moral premises or adaptation to new sociopolitical structures.[19]

CONCLUSION: EFFECTIVE CIVIC EDUCATION FOR WHOM?

It follows from this analysis that both the question of analytical content and the question of public expectations of the schools are

[18]The rationalization of the educational system signifies the declining utility of civic integration by diffuse instruction. See Ronald Gross, "Toward a Technology of Teaching," *Dissent*, 11 (Winter 1964), pp. 99–103; a stimulating, but as yet inconclusive discussion about the linkage of the segmental-organizational model with the dominance of scientific-technocratic curriculum is presented by Coleman, pp. 527–540.

[19]It should be noted that one conceptual limitation of civic education appraisal is the tendency to think in terms of unadjusted or partially socialized citizens. I am suggesting that the weakness of the integrative-consensual model is its lag behind the immediate and societal structures in which it operates.

fundamentally influenced by the stage of political development, including the relationships obtaining among the neophyte citizen, the educational institution, and the political system. There is nothing inevitable about this process, no laws of political inevitability that negate, for example, the efficacy of the rational-activist model. However, the effectiveness of civic education does depend on a theory of power. It is such an abstracted notion of the rational citizen, appropriate to the era of pluralistic liberalism, that accounts for the intellectual flaw in the processes of civic education. Similarly, the perpetuation of the consensual-integrative model and the assumptions on which it is based are also likely to be less meaningful than they were at a time when the existence of a culturally diverse population was a matter of primary political concern. Neither the limited broker state nor the assimilative, open society exists to provide realistic content to the two historical models of civic education. The outlines of the segmented-organizational mode are clear enough, yet they provide no basis for either peaceful change or substantive enhancement in civic creativity. It would seem more appropriate to create a civic culture, rather than to perpetuate those elements of one no longer germane to public experience. And in this fusion of public policy with cultural and human development (which is not quite human resource development) lies the best hope of returning to the schools the civic mission that many feel erodes when, as in past experience civic educators call utopian whatever differs from their present milieu.

18 Schools and Politics in the Big City*

ROBERT H. SALISBURY

We know that many big-city school systems operate with substantial formal autonomy. They are not run by the political or administrative leaders of the city, but are insulated from those leaders and the interests they represent. In part this autonomy is a consequence of various formal features of local government which give to the schools the authority to run their affairs with little or no reference to the demands of other city officials. Perhaps in larger part, however, the insulation of the schools may be a function of the ideology, propagated by schoolmen but widely shared by the larger public, that schools should be free from "politics," i.e., the influence of non-school officials. Insofar as this view is shared, it has made formal independence a less relevant variable, and most of what evidence we have suggests that the formal structure of school-city relations does not matter very much: the schools are largely autonomous anyway.

*Reprinted by permission of the author and publisher from *Harvard Educational Review*, 37 (Summer 1967). Copyright © 1967 by President and Fellows of Harvard College.

It has been argued that autonomy for the schools means that professional educators would be free to carry out educational policies which they, as professionals, deem most effective without the intrusion of conflicting and educationally deleterious demands from nonprofessionals. But autonomy and insulation may also result in other things. Autonomous schools may be unresponsive to important groups in the community whose interests are not effectively served by the dominant values of professional schoolmen. Autonomy may mean a fragmenting of efforts aimed at solving community problems because of inadequate coordination and planning. And autonomy may also bring vulnerability as well as insulation. If the schools are separated from the rest of the community's political system, they may be more easily exposed to the protests or demands of groups which are disaffected from that system, unable to work their will within its often labyrinthine structures, but able to organize direct popular support. And if they attempt direct protest action, they can make life most difficult for schoolmen who are unable to retreat into positions of mutual support among city officials with many programs and agencies and client groups. Unable to trade off one group against another, the schools may be and often are the targets of protest which may well have its roots in other facets of the city's life, but are directed against the schools precisely because they are autonomous and vulnerable.

The argument that the costs of "political control" far exceed the costs of autonomy needs re-examination. I have been struck by the frequent reference in that argument to the allegedly baleful effects of Big Bill Thompson's 1927 campaign for election as mayor of Chicago in which he concentrated much of his flamboyant oratory on the issue of control of the public schools. Big Bill promised to sack the superintendent who was, said Thompson, a lackey of King George and the British. Educators have ever since been agreed that a mayoral campaign subjecting the schools to this kind of educationally irrelevant attack was ample evidence of the need for protection from big city politics. Thompson's rhetoric was, of course, so blatantly demagogic that he makes an easy object lesson, but behind the rhetoric the issue has other features which make its moral much less clear.

In a most interesting book, called *School and Society in Chicago*,[1] George S. Counts examined the 1927 election soon after it happened. Counts' assessment is one of considerable ambivalence. On the one hand, he has no sympathy for Thompson's tactics of catering to his anti-British constituents by threatening to "punch King George in the snoot." Yet Thompson, in denouncing Superintendent McAndrew, was

---

[1]George S. Counts, *School and Society in Chicago* (New York: Harcourt, Brace and World, 1928).

exploiting a very real conflict within the schools which had already engaged major socio-economic sectors in the community.

William McAndrew had come to Chicago in 1924 in the wake of a series of political scandals and convictions affecting members of the school board. McAndrew was looked to as a reformer who would use his office more vigorously than had his predecessors. Particularly, he was expected, apparently by all the most interested parties, to establish the superintendency as the center from which the schools would thereafter be run. Professional educational criteria were to prevail. No more politics!

McAndrew interpreted this mandate to mean that *he* would select the criteria; the classroom teachers would not. He believed that *professional* educators should embrace teachers and administrators in the same organizational units, so he effectively discouraged the previously vigorous teachers councils in the Chicago schools. Chicago had a strong and long-standing set of teacher organizations including units of the American Federation of Teachers, and McAndrew's unsympathetic view of their status led to abiding tension. Counts reports that the teachers' groups provided effective support for Thompson's election.

In addition, McAndrew had alienated organized labor in general. Not only had he rejected the propriety of the teachers' unions. He had introduced the junior high school. Chicago labor spokesmen construed this to be a step toward separate vocational training for working-class children. They viewed the junior high as an early breakaway from an equalitarian curriculum and this, they feared, was aimed at producing a docile, cheap labor force. Finally, McAndrew was a champion of the platoon system, or, as it was generally referred to, the Gary Plan. He favored the alleged efficiencies of the Plan and justified them quite frankly in a business-oriented way. Moreover, he actively and often consulted with representatives of the Chicago Association of Commerce; never with spokesmen of labor.

The result was a fairly considerable class conflict over McAndrew and his policies, both inside the school system and in the community. William Hale Thompson exploited these tensions and, in a way, helped resolve them. At least, after Thompson won, McAndrew was fired.

The important morals of this story seem to me to be the following: First, McAndrew provoked a severe conflict among the schoolmen themselves. The alleged intrusion of "politics" into the schools was really more the widening of a breach that already existed. Breaches among the schoolmen have been rather exceptional, from McAndrew's time until very nearly the present. Educators have proclaimed their fundamental unity of purpose and interest; and to a remarkable degree, they have lived up to it. But as teachers' unions grow strong and make demands and, occasionally, strike, and as community-wide controversies develop over the location, programs, and financing of the schools, the myths and practices which lead educators to maintain a united front in facing the outside, nonprofessional, world cannot survive. And, if there are conflicts, they will be exploited. The only question is, "By whom?"

The second lesson of the Chicago case of 1927 relates to the ultimate problem-solving machinery. McAndrew and the schools became a central issue in a partisan political race. Was this an appropriate mechanism for resolving a virtual class conflict involving the largest category of public expenditure? If it was not, then what is the regular political process for? Why are educational issues not properly determined in this arena? Why not indeed, except, perhaps, that Big Bill made the final determination. This dramatic fact has been enough to cinch the argument whenever some hardy soul could be found to play devil's advocate.

Later in this paper I shall explore further the two features I have drawn from the Chicago case; the political significance of unity among the schoolmen, and the possible consequences of determining school questions within the regular political processes of the community. Before I do, however, I would like to consider further what seems to me an important element of the context of school politics, in Chicago and every other city, then and now. This is what I shall call *the myth of the unitary community.*

George Counts concludes his analysis of the McAndrew affair by calling for "the frank recognition of the pluralistic quality of the modern city. Such recognition would involve the extension of a direct voice in the control of education to the more powerful interests and the more significant points of view."[2] The recommendation troubled Counts. He believed that it would really only "regularize practices already in existence," since these groups were already actively engaged in the struggle for influence over the schools. Still Counts recognized that he was making a "radical" proposal. It went directly counter to an historic perspective which has long pervaded the thinking of educators: namely, that the city is a unity for purposes of the school program. That is, regardless of ethnic, racial, religious, economic, or political differences and group conflicts in other arenas of urban life, education need not, and should not if it could, recognize or legitimize those differences. Education is a process that must not be differentiated according to section or class. Learning is the same phenomenon, or should be, in every neighborhood. Physical facilities and personnel should be allocated without regard to whatever group conflicts might exist in the community.

[2]Counts, p. 357.

Schools have not always been run this way in reality. In the nineteenth century, some concessions were made to such prominent ethnic groups as the Germans by providing special classes in the German language; but in St. Louis, these were discontinued in 1888, or just about the time that ethnic heterogeneity really blossomed in the city. In recent years, a good many departures from the norm can be observed. In many cities, ethnic representation on the school board has been accepted as a hostage to the times, though the tendency is generally to deplore the necessity of special group recognition. Representatives of labor, of Negroes, and of Catholics hold big-city board memberships today and their constituents would complain if they did not. But the prevailing doctrines have not altered as much as the practice, I suspect, and the perspective which denies the legitimacy of group conflicts over school policy is certainly still widely held.

Surely an important element of this view of the city was the egalitarian democracy espoused by a large portion of professional education's intellectuals. The common school, later the high school, and now the community college have been urged and supported as mechanisms for equalizing the life chances of everyone in the community. To introduce programs for one group that were not available to another, or to build different kinds of school buildings for different neighborhoods, would cultivate group and class differences in the twig-bending stage which would lead to deeper socioeconomic cleavages in the adult community. Most people, it seemed, never considered the possibility that the have-not groups might receive *more* and *better* education than the middle class.

It looked like the poor could only get short-changed in a system of differentiated education and a caste system would result. This was the position not only of educators but probably of most actively concerned lay citizens too. It was an operative theory to guide education policy, and it was linked to a view of the community beyond the school system. For a consensual, integrated, organic community was and is an abiding standard for many American intellectuals. A proper city should manifest no deep-seated social or economic cleavages. Groups and classes with opposing interests are considered dangerous to the continued tranquillity of the polity. When they exist, as they increasingly did in the industrial city of turn-of-the-century America, it becomes necessary to adopt programs, such as universal education, and institutions, such as nonpartisan local government or at-large elections, that overcome the threatening heterogeneity.

But burgeoning immigration, the rise of the urban political machine, the emergence of corporate economic interests, and the enormous increases in scale of the urban community were parallel and closely connected phenomena of the 1880–1910 era. The metropolis which emerged threatened to erupt in group conflicts that would engulf the schools unless defenses could be found. The unitary-community perspective, more or less accurate as description a generation before and still serviceable for many smaller communities outside the metropolis, from that time on has been primarily a myth for the big city.

Still, it is a useful myth, and its uses were and are many. First, it served as a sharp contrast to the "political" world. Urban politics in the muckraker era was plainly a politics of group conflict and accommodation. The boss was a broker of social and economic tensions, and part of his brokerage fee to the community was the heightening of group consciousness. Ethnic identity for many Europeans was first achieved through the processes of American ward politics. Irish, or Italian, or Czech nationalisms, for example, were much promoted in the cities of this era, as candidates and parties sought ways to secure the loyalties of the urban electorate.

With the political arena patently corrupt and marked by the conflicts of a myriad of "special" interests, the unitary-community perspective of education could justify the institutional separation of the schools from the rest of the political community. Independence from "politics" would keep out the selfish aims and corrupt tactics of the politician.

Independent school systems were not new of course. Institutional separation had always been a prevailing pattern. But in the larger cities, until the end of the nineteenth century, the structure of the independent school systems had been highly political.[3] Many school boards were chosen by wards. Some were selected by the city council, some by direct and frequent election. Ward representation was not originally viewed as a way of representing diverse group interests in the city as much as it was a means of keeping the board in close touch with the electorate. It resulted, however, in highly "politicized" school boards, sensitive to neighborhood pressures, particularly in the area of school-building. The ward system promoted log-rolling among sections of the city over many components of the school program. Neighborhoods sometimes traded off advantages, thereby probably facilitating rapid construction in many cities. Wards might also block one another, however, and thus retard the whole system.

The development of the professional educator to fill the newly created position of superintendent of schools inaugurated a different approach to education in which lay control would operate in increasing tension with the professional expert. With ward representation, this tension might well have been unbearable, at least to the professional

---

[3]See the discussion in Thomas McDowell Gilland, *The Origin and Development of the Power and Duties of the City School Superintendent* (Chicago: University of Chicago Press, 1935), esp. Chap. vi.

educator. But parallel to the rise of the superintendency came the elimination of the ward system, and at-large election systems were rapidly adopted for the selection of school-board members.

The unitary myth was and is of great use in justifying an at-large school board. If the community is an organic whole with a single public interest in education, the board member should be protected against local, "selfish," interests by giving him a city-wide constituency. Moreover, since there are no legitimate "special" group interests in education, any responsible citizen can serve on the board, and there is no reason to give particular groups in the community a seat. To give a seat to labor, for example, would be wrong because it would constitute recognition of a special-group perspective on educational policy. Indeed, in a unitary community, there is really no such thing as representation on the school board, since there are no interests to represent. If, as George Counts and others found, urban school-board members were drawn predominantly from middle class, WASP, business-oriented strata of the community, it was a fact without significance in a unitary community.[4] In a recent study of school desegregation in eight northern cities, Robert Crain found that business and professional persons who serve on the school board, do so as individuals, not as class or elite spokesmen, and that such "nonrepresentative" individuals have been more acquiescent to integration than Board members elected by party or ethnic constituencies.[5]

The myth has thus been important in underwriting equalitarian educational programs, in separating the school systems from the main political process of the city, and in validating middle-class control of the schools. In addition, it was a useful adjunct to the emergence of professional expertise in education and school administration. Expertise rested on the assumption that valid ways and means to run the

[4]George S. Counts, "The Social Composition of Boards of Education: A Study in the Social Control of Public Education," *Supplementary Educational Monographs,* XXX (July 1927), p. 83. See also the more recent findings of Roy Coughran, "The School Board Member Today," *The American School Board Journal,* 6 (December 1956), pp. 25–26, reprinted in August Kerber and Wilfred R. Smith, eds., *Educational Issues in a Changing Society,* rev. ed. (Detroit: Wayne State University Press, 1964), pp. 284–287. W. W. Charters argues cogently that whatever the political significance of middle-class membership on school boards may have been, there is little empirical basis for concluding that membership really has meant policy control anyway. See his "Social Class Analysis and the Control of Public Education," *Harvard Educational Review,* XXIII (Fall 1953), pp. 268–283.

[5]Reported in "Educational Decision-Making and the Distribution of Influence in Cities," (paper presented to the American Political Science Association, September 7, 1966).

schools existed and were independent of the particular interests and values of particular groups. A good school system is good for everyone, not just a portion of the community. Experts, those people with professional training in the field, are qualified by their specialized training to tell good from bad, and laymen, if they are sensible, should defer to this expertise. If the unitary assumption is undermined, however, then no one, however well trained, can identify or administer a "good" school system. One may then ask only, "Good for whom? For which groups?"

Apart from a social scientist's perverse interest in exploring the myths we live by, is there any point to this discussion of the unitary-community myth? I believe the answer is "Emphatically, yes!" When educators treat the community as a unitary phenomenon, they are less able to offer programs and facilities which are differentiated to serve the diverse needs and values of particular subgroups in the city. It is an indictment of educational political theory that head-start projects for the urban poor only began on a large scale in 1965. Not that schoolmen did not often recognize the differential needs of slum children and sometimes tailor programs to fit those special needs. Rather, they had to do it in an inarticulate, often *sub rosa,* fashion since such programs went counter to the main stream of schoolmen's thinking. And so the programs were generally ineffective in meeting a problem of such magnitude.

The unitary-community idea was not simply for the guidance of educators. As we have seen, it helped protect the independence of the schools from the community's political processes. Or did it? Raymond E. Callahan has argued that the independent urban schoolmen were, in the period from about 1910 to 1930, extremely vulnerable; not, perhaps, to partisan political pressure, but to the dominant socio-economic interests of the community.[6] In this period, business was pretty generally dominant, and Callahan attributes the rise of the "cult of efficiency" in educational administration to the desire of vulnerable schoolmen to please the influential businessmen. In a way, Counts's story of Chicago confirms this point; during the relatively "nonpolitical" period when McAndrew was exercising full authority, the Association of Commerce occupied a very influential place while labor was excluded from school affairs. The "intrusion of politics" under Thompson meant the return of the teachers and other nonbusiness interests to active and influential positions.

Independent schools, operating according to the myth of the unitary community, were and are rather feeble instruments for seeking public support, and this weakness is one key to the business domination

---

[6]Raymond E. Callahan, *Education and the Cult of Efficiency* (Chicago: University of Chicago Press, 1962).

Callahan has described. School-tax rates and bond issues and, in some states, the annual school budget, may require specific voter approval in a referendum. How are the schoolmen to persuade the electorate to say yes? They have relatively little of what in urban politics is sometimes called "clout." They have no network of support from groups and interests for whom the educators have done favors in the past and who now can be asked to reciprocate. They may sometimes get the teachers and the parents and the children to ring doorbells, but such efforts are often ineffectual compared to the canvassing a strong party organization might do. Since approval of a school referendum invariably costs the taxpayers money immediately—there is no intervening lapse of time as there is between the election of a candidate to a city office and the possible future increase in taxes—a sizable negative vote may normally be assumed. Where is the positive vote coming from? Educators have gone on the assumption, quite probably correct, that the benevolent patronage of the business leadership was necessary if they were to have a chance of referendum success.

Today, in the big city, the structure of the situation has not changed. Only the interests which effectively make demands upon the schools have changed. Negroes, the poor, middle-class intellectuals, and teachers have partially, perhaps largely, displaced the businessmen. The unitary-community myth is still used as a defense of the schools. In order to persuade predominantly Catholic, lower-middle-class voters of Irish or Polish descent to support higher taxes for public schools, it is very important to emphasize the undivided benefits which all residents receive from an undifferentiated educational program. The difficulty is that today the pitch is no longer believed. It is evident, for example, that Negroes do not buy the myth that the community is unitary. They know better. Moreover, even though a school board with a unitary-community perspective may permit integration, Negroes demand a differentiated school program with compensatory facilities to help them fight prejudice and poverty, to help them reach a high enough level so that equal educational programs will no longer leave them behind. Meanwhile, those ethnic groups whom Wilson and Banfield have shown to be comparatively unwilling to vote for public expenditures for *any* purpose are especially unenthusiastic about putting high-cost programs into Negro slum schools.[7] Unions are anxious about job competition from the products of improved vocational programs. And although property taxes for schools may be only a minor problem for large corporate business, they are often severe in their effect on smaller business and on small householders. The latter

[7]James Q. Wilson and Edward C. Banfield, "Public-Regardingness as a Value Premise in Voting Behavior," *American Political Science Review,* LVIII (December 1964), pp. 876–888.

groups, especially, are potential city dropouts; that is, they may move to suburbia if taxes go up, and the result may be to depreciate further the city's tax base while its educational needs increase. The unitary-community myth no longer serves to quiet the demonstrations or to pass the tax increase. It has largely outlived its usefulness. Yet it is still frequently articulated by schoolmen and lay supporters of the schools, perhaps because, as the inveterate gambler said in explaining his continued patronage of the crooked card game, "It's the only one in town."

There is another dimension in which unity has been emphasized with respect to schools. Educators have tried very hard to achieve and maintain consensus among all those engaged in the educational enterprise. Unity is a prerequisite to a reputation for expertise, and it thus adds to the bargaining power of schoolmen as they seek public support. Unity inside the school helps justify independence from "politics." In the Chicago case of 1927 and again today, in Chicago and elsewhere, the vulnerability of the schools to group pressures from the community depends heavily on the extent to which the board, the superintendent and his administrative associates, and the teaching staff remain as professional allies rather than splitting into conflicting camps. . . .

There is, obviously, the now genuinely optimistic prospect of federal funding, especially rich for urban schools serving slum populations. I shall not explore this dimension in detail, but I want to note an important point: urban interests have for years done much better at the federal level than in the state capitol. The reasons are complex and not very well understood, but among them is the strong, warm, and skillfully administered relationship between city political leaders and federal officials. Federal officials in all the relevant branches and agencies have come to be responsive to political leaders and politically skillful administrators in the cities. Mayors, urban-renewal directors, and local poverty-program administrators are especially skilled, individually and through their national associations, at bringing their points of view to the sympathetic attention of Washington. The newspaper accounts of the federal treatment of the Chicago schools in 1965 suggest to me that, as Mayor Daley salvaged Superintendent Willis's federal school money from the fire, so the help of political leaders in other cities may be necessary to maintain satisfactory relationships with this newly opened source of major financial assistance to big-city schools. Indeed, the requirement, which Washington officials seem to be taking seriously, that poverty programs and the new educational programs be closely coordinated may, in turn, force the schools into closer relationship with many other agencies of city government and thus, inevitably, into the mainstream of urban politics.

Earlier I raised the question of the significance of deciding the McAndrew affair within a partisan electoral process. Let us return to that dimension of our general problem. I have suggested that autonomy and isolation have serious disadvantages for urban schools. What is to be said on the other side? What would it be like if the schools were a more integral part of the urban political system; if, for example, they were made a regular line department of the city government with a director appointed by the mayor to serve at his pleasure? How would such a process work? What would be the substantive effects on educational policy and on the city generally?

To examine this issue directly, we need to be clear about how city political systems actually function. No single formulation will do justice to the complexities of the question but at least three points seem especially pertinent. First, political scientists generally have found that in large cities, and some of the smaller ones too, influence is rather widely dispersed, specialized, and exercised in a discontinuous fashion. That is, one person or group will be active and influential on one set of issues while quite a different array dominates the next set. This tendency is perhaps accentuated when a specialized set of issues, such as education, is determined within a specialized institutional framework. But the institutional framework is primarily reinforcing, not by itself determining. A second, related, finding of political scientists' examinations of the urban community is that great pressure is generally exercised in questions of substantive policy program (though not so much on elections or top level personnel appointments or tax rates) by the program's professional and administrative experts. In urban renewal or public health and hospitals, to take two examples from regular city government, the professional personnel run the programs about as completely as schoolmen run the schools; perhaps, more so.

A third finding is rather different from the first two, however. In many cities, though by no means in all of them, a critical and continuing role of substantial import is played by the mayor. He is the chief organizer of the dominant coalition of interests and the chief broker among them. He is the chief negotiator in balancing not only the disparate and often conflicting groups in the city but also in representing city needs to state and especially to federal agencies. More than that the mayor is the single most important problem-solver. He is committed, out of sheer re-election necessity if for no other reason, to rebuilding the slums, attracting new business, renovating downtown, implementing equal rights and opportunity and, as federal money is at last making it possible, improving the life chances of the urban poor. Not all mayors face the same circumstances, of course. Some are weak in formal authority to control even their governmental environment; many are lacking in the fiscal and human resources to get the necessary leverage on the social and economic environment. Nevertheless, there is a substantial similarity in the orientation and role of big-city mayors, and this convergence has been especially pronounced during the past decade. In style or substance, mayors of today have little in common with Big Bill Thompson. Actually, mayors might not relish taking more direct responsibility for the schools. Why should they take on another large problem area when they too can fall back on the argument that the schools should be nonpolitical? If they were to accept a more active role, it might be because they really want to resolve the complicated difficulties of urban life, and solutions *must* include effective use of the schools.

These three generalizations are all relevant to my question but in somewhat different ways. They suggest that if the schools were integrated with the urban governmental system, the educators would continue to make most of the technical and administrative decisions but the mayor and his coalition of community support would play a major role in giving over-all program and fiscal direction. The schools would compete more directly than now with other city programs for available money. Their programs might be more differentiated among different segments of the community, as the mayor tried at once to solve problems and ease tensions and to please the major elements of the coalition that elected him. Their top administrative personnel might be more vulnerable to the vicissitudes of electoral fortune, though mayors might be only slightly more effective in breaking through the defenses of the educators' bureaucracy to choose (or fire) their own men than are independent school boards now. Educators might find themselves and their programs more often subordinated to other agencies and programs than is presently the case, but this subordination might be more a difference in perception than reality; an independent school system already must compete for money and support, but in an indirect and segmented manner. It is not clear that mayor-directed schools would be more generously financed from the local community but neither is it inevitable that they would be poorer.

In my judgment, the principal difference between the existing arrangements for the government of urban public education and this hypothetical control by the mayor would be in the schools' relationship with the increasingly pluralistic and tension-filled community. An independent school system asks for community support directly, unprotected by any of the confusions of mandate that attend the election of political officials. The schools are naked against community pressures except as their unitary-community ideology and whatever rational citizen demand there may be for their services may shield them. I have argued, and so do the protest demonstrations and the negative votes in referenda, that these are not sufficient protection if the urban schools are to perform the extraordinarily difficult, high cost, tasks of educating the urban poor. It is not coincidence, I think, that recently the schools have been so often the target of the alienated and disaffected elements of society. Whether protesting against *de facto* segregation, double taxation of Catholics, or alleged Communist infiltration, the pickets know that the schools are vulnerable to direct assault. No other programs or interests get in the way. No other issues or loyalties intrude.

But the processes involved in electing a mayor and a council, especially on a partisan ticket, but also in a large, heterogeneous city with nonpartisan government, do mute these kinds of pressures. Mandates *are* vague; constraints on the specific policy choices which the officials. will subsequently make are loose. And the protection afforded to the professionals is considerable. They may administer their programs while someone else takes the heat, and diffuses it. . . .

In all that I have said thus far, my principal points appear to be as follows: (1) more direct and effective political (mayoral) control of the schools will be difficult to engineer because of the resistance of schoolmen, regardless of formal governmental structure, to "nonprofessional" direction; and (2) big-city school interests might get a more receptive hearing in state and national capitals and be partially screened from local direct action protests if they merge their interests more fully with the over-all city administration. But would this type of result lead to more effective education? This, in my judgement, is precisely the *wrong* question. In the urban center, there is no education which is separate from the issues of race, poverty, housing, crime, and the other human problems of the metropolis. The issue we need to face is whether greater mayoral control would lead to changes in school policy (e.g., better coordination and cooperation with urban renewal, recreation, and poverty programs) which would make the educational program more effective in solving the larger complex of community problems. In a simpler era, one could argue that Big Bill Thompson may well have done just this in Chicago. And, forty years later, one might well feel that, in the same city, Mayor Daley might have achieved more effective integration than Superintendent Willis seemed disposed to provide had the mayor chosen to violate the educators' code of independence and exert more direct control of the situation.

At the same time, there should be no mistake about the fact that greater administrative integration of schools with city would, in many cases, mean subordination of the schools to the city government. Moreover, such subordination might often mean that the schools were being used as instruments to achieve policy goals which extended well beyond more narrowly defined educational objectives. To some extent, of course, this is happening anyway, and indeed it has always been so. But the issue of political control forces us to be explicit about the question of how the many goals we wish to achieve in the city can best be approached. If it turned out that education was not at the head of the list, educators would be compelled to acknowledge that fact in a situation where they had to bargain for their share of the local resources against the direct competition of other programs as well as against the fiscal prudence of the electorate.

Direct competition for local money; subordination of educators to other public officials with other interests and programs; the self-conscious use of the schools as instruments to fight poverty, improve housing conditions, or fight city-suburb separation: these have been virtually unthinkable heresies to devoted schoolmen. Yet, are they much more than an explicit statement of steps and tendencies already being taken or implicit in present practices? I think not; we are already moving this way, to some extent we always have been doing so, and the real question to be faced is: How might we do these things better? A greater measure of local political leadership in education and coordination of the schools with other portions of the community might well contribute to this end.

19 Political Survival in the Big City School*

EDGAR LITT

Every school system contains a set of political values designed to determine the lives and attitudes of the young. These values are built into the patterns of authority, behavior, and curriculum within the school. Although there are many ways to comprehend patterns of political learning, a microscopic approach prevents us from taking refuge in abstract concepts about society and the schools. For almost a year this writer and several associates conducted classes in "civic education" with a group of twenty black male adolescents. Weekly meetings were held on the premises of a social agency in a Midwestern city. Most of these young men were members of the sponsoring organization; they came from stable families; and, with few exceptions, they were enrolled in an "inner core" black high school.

Resentment about the quality of the schools and the uses of university research presented a problem. It was therefore necessary to create trust as well as rapport, and this meant providing instrumental

*This article was prepared especially for this book.

values to the participants. We could have provided money or whatever status gratification black young men would consider desirable from the constant attention of white social scientists and their graduate students. Yet, these considerations seemed trite and mechanical in the present case. It may be a romantic illusion, but what still seems to differentiate social scientists from other equally frail beings is that the former possess some professional knowledge about the operation of political institutions.

It was this social exchange of knowledge for responses to our questions that, in our opinion, propagated the climate of affection in which our endeavors proceeded. Moreover, our information had to be relevant to the felt needs of the participants. In the political climate of the city in which our work progressed, as in so many northern cities, the relevant information was explicitly political. Our exploration centered on the political processes of the city: how key decisions were made, how a precinct is organized in an election, what the political party structure is, and what relevance voting had to public policy formation. We also discussed the structure and operation of governmental agencies important to the lives of these young men and their families. Information concerning welfare agencies, the several extant programs charged with the elimination of poverty, and community pressure groups was examined.

Moreover, in each "lesson" we used concrete examples of community action on social space familiar to our young participants. Here we used survey materials about their section of the city and its relationship to broader political processes in the community. It was Karl Mannheim who argued that one should have a say in the determination of one's life fate, and that social knowledge is necessary to improve the skills and knowledge ordinary men require for that task. In that spirit, our workshops sought to relate the concrete personal needs of black adolescents to the political processes of their community and, beyond that, to the sketches of behavioral theories guiding our themes.

The thrust of the inquiry turned in time to the significance of education. In hours of questioning and probing, designed to discover the structures of social thought of the twenty young men who, often at personal sacrifice, faithfully attended our "Civics Club," several themes continually reappeared. Our inquiries about the most visible community actors, such as the mayor and the city council, yielded only nebulous responses. Divorced from either intense support or hostility, city hall and its inhabitants appeared, in the eyes of our respondents, to be merely "there." They were part of the political landscape, unendowed with salient personal or role qualities, and disconnected from the life experiences and concerns of these young men.

The story was different when other authentic public figures, such as the police, were mentioned. Yet it was the educational system, with its profound and intensely held problematic nature, that most often held the attention of the young men. To be sure, our attention to these responses may reflect our own concern with political education, yet the frequency and intensity of collated responses suggests that we are reporting something other than the selective perception of social scientists.

Faith in education as the golden road to secular salvation and, more pragmatically, as the necessary prerequisite to any decent job and life is etched deeply on the consciousness of all these young men. "I mean without education you cannot get anywhere in life," said John, an intense, slender member of his high-school basketball team. And the others verbally assented to his forcefully spoken comments. Education, they believe, unlocks the key of personal fulfillment and ends the discrimination and poverty that plagues their parents and relatives.

The best evidence for the proposition that education is good for man and that higher education is valuable in solving society's ills is found in the responses of a rare breed among our assembly: the high-school dropout. Henry has been through the school system in a particularly revealing way. He began at "North," a high school with a good academic reputation, then was transferred to "Central," a problem school in the city's core. His continuing and mounting disciplinary problems led him in a fatal way to the city's vocational school. (Incidentally, these boys are very perceptive about the status hierarchy within the city's high schools.) As Henry comments: "I was so bad that they sent me to Vocational, and that is really the end of the line." (The other boys nod and verbalize agreement.) After much effort he managed to free himself of even this lowly scholastic status and to be dropped completely from man's effort to salvage his fellow man through grades and credits and the rationale of compulsory school attendance.

Yet—and this is the significance of Henry's contribution to our dialogue—his rebellion marks a deep personal concern for education. Not only does he assent to the general value of education, but he can recall precisely the names of every teacher and the subject matter of each course in his odyssey through the city's high schools. No mark of apathy or rebellion can cloud Henry's abiding faith in education. While complaining about the white, middle-class expectations of some teachers (but not all), he knows what he has lost and weighs his fate accordingly. Just as one may say in traditional Catholic theology that the Church temporal errs while the Church eternal remains omnipotent, so, too, in the mind of this young citizen the sanctity of education remains despite the behavior of its all too human representatives.

The mystique of the curriculum also looms large in these discussions. We had expected in the course of our discourses to find the problems of the schools in interpersonal relations, in the conflict between black and white, in the disputations between the expectations of adults and the probings of youthful behavior. Yet, while we uncovered traces of these tensions with others and with authority, a more subtle, persistent process proved to be at work. When I asked Smith, who is normally articulate and responsive, about a particular history course we had been discussing—a subject made relevant by our previous investigation of the city's budding programs in the welfare fields and the origins of newly created efforts to eradicate poverty—he fumbled for an answer. "I don't know—the history they teach us is about olden times. It seems that I don't find myself a party to it." No mention was made of Martin Luther King and the civil rights movement or the insights to be gained by comparing the Athens of Socrates with the Black "core city" of contemporary freedom fighters.

What occurred here, and what reappeared so often in the remarks of the other boys, was bewilderment about the rationality of the subject matter (especially in the humanities and social studies) taught in their schools. It may be said with some truth that these are the observations of semiliterate, semieducated black urban youth. After all, minority status and powerlessness are not eternal virtues that, in the nature of things, point up the inadequacies of the existing system. Yet this interpretation misses the point, because in discussions ranging from community politics to the social structure of American society these young men have shown previously untapped capacities to grapple with the implications of social thought. Smith is plainly puzzled by his experiences with formal education: "I don't know—the truth is that I have no notion of what I am supposed to take away with my schooling, what it is saying to me as a black and a man."

It is precisely here in the absence of understanding about processes so patently critical to one's fate in life that behavior patterns acquire a larger significance. Just as no one explained the "natural order" of the plantation system to black slaves, no one (except in the crisis atmosphere of a "Freedom School") has explained the rationality of the school program to contemporary black youths. The vitality of these expressive young men is treated as antisocial behavior and a threat to the educational process. To defer impulses for a known, if distant, goal is one thing; to act as if the curriculum spoke to them is, in their eyes, a self-denying act, and since they are not ashamed of their bodies and feelings, a calculated response is forthcoming.

It is in this context, I believe, that the responses to authority of socially integrated young black men can be understood. Deprived of a comprehensive explanation for their own program of studies and its meaning to their own behavior, they see the petty testing of principal and teacher authority in larger proportions. A natural openness to exploration, evident in our discourses with these young men becomes stunted when threatened by the incongruity between the curriculum and their personal style. The problem is that the meaning and rationale of "civilization," in so far as it appears in the authoritative school system, are not communicated by those who carry the teacher's college burden to the city's inner core.

The result is a partial withdrawal by urban youths from the experiences and problems that could enliven them. It would seem that these young men are asking to be included, not in the formal sense of curriculum making, but in the sense of having their feelings and movements included within the learning processes. The rigid ordering of seats, the endless bells and rules that make more vivid the marginal differentiation between the roles and life styles of teacher and student, avoiding the class material, styles of dress and speech, and their threat to the teacher's status are constantly in the foreground of controversy and discussion. The accompanying motive for so-called antisocial acts lies less in race problems or, in the case of these young men, in the rejection of education, than in the protection of self-esteem.

This protection of self-esteem underlies so much of student and school behavior that the motto "thou shalt not cut on me" is an apt one for the dynamics of urban education. In light of the nonrational perception of school processes and teacher-student relations, its urgency is heightened in classroom and school assembly. "I wish he would stop cutting on me so," responded Frank when asked about his relations with his major teacher. "I walk into the room [attired in pegged pants] and right away he says, 'Look, the troublemaker is here again.' Man, I don't want no trouble so I wish he wouldn't get on me for everything." Beyond social difficulties and the temperaments of generations, the absence of a meeting ground in subject matter and its relation to self enhances the "cutting up" view of teacher roles that these young men perceive. In this context, there is little rational behavior that remains, except to protect self-esteem with the varied (and often disturbing) means at their disposal. Feeling themselves rejected in educational processes, the young men make school into the forum for acting out these problems between students and teachers.

Except for Henry, who had given up and dropped out of the system, the behavior of these young men was more prudent, a more self-rewarding response to education's ambiguities as expressed in the urban core school. If a student values education as an ideal endowed with almost magical qualities, the symbiotic patterns of teacher-student relations that lack personal trust and meaning often become destructive. These young men are not fools because they are aware of education's influence on their lives. Thus they "cut up at the margins," testing teacher authority boundaries while carefully refraining from going too far and being dropped from the only system able to provide them the credentials to the adult world of work and status. This prudential strategy testifies not only to their reality-bound orientation;

it also argues against an alternative view, namely that these young men cannot defer gratification of their impulses. On the contrary, cutting-up at the margins is an effective device for protecting their self-esteem and adapting realistically to adult requirements. This behavior permits the young men to graduate and yet to protest the lack of pertinence of all they have learned to their personal life situations.

However, in drawing a balance sheet, the costs involved should not be ignored. First, much time, energy, and emotional feeling go into the marginal disputations between the formal educational system and its young charges. There is a kind of petty industrial sabotage at work in these processes. It is not an effort comparable to achieving worker control over management or even an effort to secure higher wages. Rather, it is an effort to be included within the system so that the rationale of the operations involves, in a human sense, the needs and life styles of those involved.

Second, the costs of the prudential marginality described include those values of insight and sensibility that have always been the fruits of a liberating education. Despite the disadvantages of their racial plight, the young men described herein do survive the school system and become partially functioning members of the adult world. But they do not know—no one has taught them to know—what can possibly be involved in the term "liberal education." And this loss must be weighed against the brave efforts of an educational system to prepare everyone for life.

20 Public Knowledge and Private Men: Political Impact in the Post-Kerr Era*

EDGAR LITT

When, however, we enter the realm of politics . . . a new type of knowledge seems to emerge, namely, that in which decision and standpoint are inseparably bound up together. In these realms there is no such thing as a purely theoretical outlook on the part of the observor.

—KARL MANNHEIM[1]

THE NEW RELATIONS OF EDUCATION AND POLITICS

In an agrarian society trapped in a cycle of poverty and ignorance, available public knowledge is carefully guarded in the special education provided the sons and daughters of the ruling strata. In a populist society, knowledge becomes personalized at a mass level and often infused with a plebian hostility toward those who claim the credentials

---

[1]"Prospects of Scientific Politics" in Karl Mannheim, *Ideology and Utopia: An Introduction to the Sociology of Knowledge* (New York: Harcourt, Brace and World, 1936 ed.), p. 116.

*Reprinted by permission of *The Harvard Educational Review,* 38 (Summer 1968), pp. 495–505.

of a special intellectual (and political) competence. In a postindustrial society, itself a contradictory mix of democratic procedures and highly centralized organizations, knowledge becomes the key instrument of development and progress, the touchstone of social mobility and national power. Moreover, the institutions of knowledge are in constant tension while they constantly transgress their own principles. Political men use them to disseminate skills and ideas and to promote research in the name of corporate and governmental interests. In these institutions knowledge can be speedily converted from a resource for human liberation into a primary device for tightening social controls among a vibrant and mobile citizenry. In private terms, education bears an intimate relationship to the life style and opportunities of the citizen. In public terms, knowledge and the agencies of knowledge (specifically, scientific discourse and public universities) become the master instruments in the creation and distribution of human valuables. Once the ornament of a frivolous aristocracy and infused with a mélange of ethnic and regional interests, higher learning now seems too politically significant to be left to the behavior of boards of regents, faculty guilds, and student pressure groups. In fact, as the relation between public policy and the products of abstract learning becomes more explicit, the ability to order and present public knowledge itself becomes the critical instrument of power and mastery over men and events. Its co-option by political agencies unites the spirit of the enlightenment with the nightmare of contemporary American policies in Southeast Asia:

> The CIA in Vietnam prides itself on being more catholic in its real affinity with ex-leftists and psuedo-leftists of all stripes, as well as with the radical right. It likes intellectuals, which is natural, first because they are walking repositories of information, and second because the CIA sees itself as a lonely master-mind, the poet and unacknowledged legislator of the government. Finally the CIA, collectively speaking, is an auto didact which never had time to get its Ph. D. and yearns to meet real, motivated political theorists and oddballs and have a structured conversation with them. The relentless resort to academic jargon about the war in Vietnam, on the part of half-educated spokesmen and commentators, doubtless reveals the CIA influence on people who may be unaware of it.[2]

Increasingly it is in terms of such a "knowledgeable culture" that public issues and private sensibilities are defined, for no resource of

[2]Mary McCarthy, "Vietnam III: Intellectuals," *The New York Review of Books,* 8 (May 18, 1967), pp. 8–9.

modern life—not wealth nor numbers nor conventional political power itself, to each of which the higher learning is intimately related—more powerfully determines our private aspirations and our public life. Let discontent appear among young intellectuals, and students and plenary conferences are held to diagnose and cure the incipient alienation. Let the demands of new social movements become sufficiently strident, and some segment of our corporate knowledge system will probably respond by creating appropriate "programs." Let war efforts increase, and universities will devote increased resources to biological research and also serve as the forum for sustained antiwar protest and study.

The linkages among formerly distinct educational, corporate, and governmental realms are vividly present in many forms. For instance, the "public vocational university," a pure type of knowledge service institution, has been created by the federalization of education. The public vocational university serves the political knowledge complex in a significantly different way than the land-grant university aided agrarian interests or than the urban universities aided labor-union members. While the land-grant and urban universities served specific private interests, the public vocational university is itself a product of the national power structure that creates and applies knowledge throughout the public realm. While the pursuit of national influence based on specialized expertise transformed major private universities from centers of classical undergraduate education to bastions of scientific research and graduate training, the public vocational university underwent no shocks of adaptation and role conflict.[3] While earlier knowledge centers had a cultural base in either the ethos of a social class, the philosophy of scientific rationalism, or the needs of a particular ethnic or occupational group, the public vocational university was born without any independent heritage. As the product of the national political economy, it represents the total fusion of public knowledge with public power, of applied with basic learning, and of scholarship with service to the state. Using the technique of federally financed contract research, and practicing selective inattention to embarassing public issues, this novel institution embodies Bismarck's concept that service to the state is the highest calling of academic men.

The public vocational university is a functional blend of knowledge and power in the service of the national state. The university's role is vocational insofar as it concentrates on the application of knowledge to concrete social problems. The university's role is public to the extent that it is defined by the central political economy rather than by local interest groups or the disadvantaged. Thus the academic

---

[3]The public vocational university and its political significance is discussed in Edgar Litt, *The Public Vocational University: Captive Knowledge and Public Power* (New York: Holt, Rinehart and Winston, Inc., 1969).

culture loses its social class, regional, and equalitarian emphasis. The culture of the public vocational university is formed in the corporate power of national firms and governmental agencies. Despite historical differences, the public vocational university of modern America closely resembles the Bismarckian notion of knowledge united with power in the collective service of the national state.

A second strand in the web of education and national politics is the effort to redefine the significant rules and human processes involved in the formulation and presentation of politically significant knowledge. The growing bonds between centers of ideas and the centers of national political, economic, and military power have produced many efforts to redefine norms governing the new relation between knowledge and power, norms never articulated by the classic schoolmen, interest-group theorists, or civic educators such as Charles Merriam and John Dewey. For instance, to modernize the description of American social folkways whose archetypes William Graham Sumner once located in the strivings of acquisitive businessmen, Robert E. Lane has articulated a new set of arrangements appropriate to the nature-knowledgeable society.[4] In such a society the expansion of knowledge creates power as a result of its usefulness in remedial policy changes. Thus a probable description of the new relation between knowledge and power would involve a policy-forming cycle beginning with the public linkage of specific values to an awareness of new knowledge, continuing with its growth and development among the policy professionals in government and the academy, and ending with its eventual application to the social and psychological maladies of specific groups. In a functional correspondence between academic and political man, between university research teams and government agencies, knowledge and what is regarded as knowledge tend to be shared without external pressures to make sure the groups keep in touch with each other. Although researchers, agencies, and institutions continue to seek more rewards within the traditional knowledge sector, the social norms for converting knowledge into public policy are gaining general acceptance.

There is no longer any need for reference to a guiding set of ideas toward which men should strive in an undefined future. Now the social processes of knowledge rather than appeals to folk wisdom, specific elite expertise, or bonds among a beleaguered community of scholars themselves increasingly influence public policies. As opposed to traditional logrolling or influence, criteria of objective truth and

[4]See Robert E. Lane, "The Decline of Politics and Ideology in a Knowledgeable Society," *American Sociological Review,* 31 (October 1966), pp. 649–662; see also Daniel P. Moynihan, "The Professionalization of Reform," *The Public Interest,* 2 (Winter 1966), pp. 23–35.

documented evidence, which were formerly only of academic or professional import, must now be among the bases of policy selection. Thus there is a new ideology of a knowledgeable society: information must be public; its sources must be indicated; and policy choices based on appeals to older ideological premises or personal experience must be put aside.

The changing sociology of public knowledge sketched here explains the political prominence of the multiversity and the creation of the public vocational university as an applied mechanism for policy research. Such a description no doubt spells out the rationale of individual intellectuals who seek to ameliorate social ills by the systematic utilization of behavioral science. While it understates the potentially irrational uses of public knowledge, the "knowledgeable society" thesis certainly highlights the hopeful rationalism dominant in the current relations between educational and more traditionally political institutions.

One result of this growing interrelation is the critical response from some intellectuals who contend that indeed professional skills are becoming dissociated from humane concerns and from actions that could improve the quality of our political life. As Theodore Roszak summarizes the case for the loyal opposition:

> We do not have an intellectually respectable politics in America principally because the single largest intellectual interest group in our society, the learned professions, has opted out of politics. It has felt no professional obligation to relate the life and work of its members to the problems of justice and survival which dominate our times.[5]

In recognizing the declining influence of political publics unrelated to specialized knowledge, such social criticism reinforces a description of the integration of education with both the bureaucratic means and policy ends of dominent political and economic institutions. Behind the critiques of specific policies lies the realization that the heritage of independent literary and political intellect has been absorbed first in the multiversity and second in the interconnection between the univer-

[5]Theodore Roszak, "On Academic Delinquency," in Theodore Roszak (ed.), *The Dissenting Academy,* (New York: Pantheon, 1967), p. 38. See also Robert Engler's "Social Science and Social Consciousness: The Shame of the Universities," in the same volume, pp. 182–207. The consequences of switching from an opinion leadership to expert role in confrontations about American foreign policy are cogently weighed by Joan W. Scott, "The Teach-In: A National Movement or the End of an Affair?" in L. Menashe and R. Radosh (eds.), *Teach-Ins: U.S.A.* (New York: Praeger, 1967), pp. 190–193.

sity and the government. The decline of the pluralistic formation of opinions as a political force complements the new emphasis on research expertise. Thus, as liberal education and the social sciences are overshadowed by preprofessional training and a behavioral science in which the perspectives of policymakers—not the publics with whom they deal—are prime considerations, new public consequences of knowledge both encourage and follow internal educational changes.

POLITICAL SOCIALIZATION AS MYTH AND REALITY

The interplay of structure, norms, and consequences within the political knowledge system has most recently been studied under the rubric of "political socialization," that is to say, the institutions and forces that shape individual and collective learning of the political culture. Drawing on antecedents in child-socialization research and social psychology, the formal study of political socialization has already produced a second generation of scholars for whom the subdiscipline, despite its eclecticism, conveys a firm sense of academic legitimacy and a guide to comprehending empirical causality. However, the changing and evolving relation between education and politics requires that we at least examine the preconceptions that may be confining the current research and that were designed to illuminate precisely that relation.

This examination is necessary because the political problems of knowledge complement intellectual problems that have been widely ignored in the rush to stake out a new field of inquiry. It seems clear that political-socialization studies contribute to an organically conservative and static view of American political life.[6] In countless studies young adults are found to acquire norms of stable allegiance to the governmental regime, to base their political attitudes on nonrational and apolitical factors, and generally to support a working distinction between a benevolent, problem-solving policy elite and a mass that has learned to accept the realities of an ongoing political system. Moreover, the main lines of inquiry have been more directed toward understanding political attitudes than political behavior and have been pitched at such conceptually abstract levels (system support or responses to distant political figures) as to confirm self-fulfilling claims about generalized political loyalty and allegiance. If there is any single thread that unravels the body of work under review, it is the gestaltist position

[6] I have drawn on James Coleman (ed.), *Education and Political Development* (Princeton: Princeton University Press, 1965); Jack Dennis (ed.), *Recent Research on Political Socialization: A Bibliography of Published, Forthcoming, and Unpublished Works, Theses, and Dissertations, and a Survey of Projects in Progress* (Medford, Mass.: Lincoln Filene Center for Citizenship and Public Affairs, 1967). (Mimeographed.)

in which "background responses" from strata of the citizenry are tapped in order to further highlight the ongoing political institutions and their key actors in the foreground of the field.[7] There may be a touch of professional ideology here (in the name of anti-ideology), but the essential point is that recent work indicates the powerful effect on the child of more overtly political forces than has been previously thought to be within the mainstream of political-socialization inquiry. Further, this work suggests that primary factors, such as family background and personality characteristics, do not greatly help to explain the acquisition of varied political attitudes and behavior—assumptions that are central to the basic concept of political socialization itself.[8]

In large measure, the guiding gestaltist view has been found in those inquiries specifically directed at the educational system as a contributor to learning about the seamless fabric of American political norms and behavior. Neither the formal curriculum nor faculty influence nor the gyrations of "student culture" have been very satisfactory in explaining the new politics of education and knowledge, although studies of all three have reduced our ignorance about the life styles of student activists and about the political attitudes of diverse educators.[9]

Thus far I have tried to remain faithful to the body of empirical evidence accumulated during the last decade, but now the mythology accompanying this "reality" needs to be articulated. It may be comforting to think that individual political socialization cumulates within the tight framework of an ongoing and highly absorptive political system. But what appears to be significant political socialization is a result of a

[7]See Christian Bay, "The Cheerful Science of Dismal Politics," in *The Dissenting Academy,* pp. 208–230, and his "Politics and Psuedopolitics: A Critical Evaluation of Some Behavioral Literature," *American Political Science Review,* 59 (May 1965), pp. 39–51.

[8]This point is developed in Edgar Litt, "Education and Political Competence: A Prescriptive Approach," paper presented to a Conference on Politics and Education, University of Oregon, June 1966. Compare these recent studies: Fred I. Greenstein, "The Impact of Personality on Politics: An Attempt to Clear Away Underbrush," *American Political Science Review,* 52 (March 1968), pp. 169–184; and in the same volume, Roberta S. Sigel, "Image of a President: Some Insights into the Political Views of School Children," pp. 216–228. Representative studies in which the assumption of organic and cumulative political supports dominate are David Easton and Jack Dennis, "The Child's Image of Government," *The Annals of the American Academy of Political and Social Science,* 361 (1965), pp. 40–57; and their "The Child's Acquisition of Regime Norms: Political Efficacy," *American Political Science Review,* 61 (March 1967), pp. 25–38.

[9]See, for instance, the excellent comparative review, "Students and Politics," *Daedalus* (Winter 1968).

failure to place the individual consequences of education within a suitable political context. Attention to the individually cumulative aspects of political socialization has overshadowed the importance of distinct systemic contributions of knowledge systems that are themselves changing under the impetus of political forces within American society. Consider the tendency toward greater "liberalism," which is usually found to be correlated with increased formal education and advanced education at certain types of institutions (liberal arts colleges as distinct from teachers' colleges and high-quality graduate schools as distinct from technical or applied scientific training institutes). In operationally defining *"liberalism"* as "openmindedness," "political consciousness," or "heterodoxy toward ideas," most research treats the educational institution—like the broad political system overshadowing it—in neutral terms. Yet it is certainly possible for American collegians to become more liberal while matriculating at Cornell, Michigan State, or American University. Meanwhile, the institutions themselves become more illiberal through internal bureaucratic rigidities, academic jingoism in Vietnam, and sponsorships of Camelots that exploit the people in underdeveloped nations. The amazing ability of the American system to compartmentalize applies to the campus as well as to the personal liberalism of educated whites who reside in systematically segregated suburbs or to the learned racial prejudice of union members who are nevertheless members of a highly integrated industrial union. It is only when the cumulative and institutional dimensions are closely related, as in small-scale liberal arts colleges, that the political consequences of education can approximate the norms and behavior of the institution itself.

Adding an emphasis on the systemic context to investigations of the personal consequences of educational institutions also makes us less likely to treat such political activism as student protest movements or similar involvement among social science and humanities professors as individual aberrations due to status deprivations (in the case of students) or professional marginality (in the case of faculty and administrators). What has been so often missing in the burgeoning political socialization studies has been any overt emphasis on the political context within which civic education (individual development), socialization (adjustment to system requirements), and political learning (skill and organizational development) occur. The Free Speech Movement on the Berkeley campus of the University of California was as much an issue of the institution's changing social role as described by former-President Kerr's term "multiversity" and of the role of its activist students in the civil rights movement as it was an expression of the realities or fictions of personal alienation and the absence of stabilizing fraternities and dormitories in student life. The realities of American policy in Vietnam have accentuated the diverse patterns of political response among the campus interest groups, variations that earlier would have been found in the less critical political realms of department and collegian life.

All of this has developed in an overtly political era in which federal aid to education is no longer primarily guided by efforts to placate diverse interest groups or to advance a basic economic or theological creed. Rather, the American knowledge system has been seduced into dealing explicitly with issues of public policy, issues to which the received doctrine of academic freedom and custodial care of collegians is dissonant. On one hand, the university as educator was the incubator of the model political citizen, the dutiful social member, or the trained technician. On the other hand, the university as an ongoing institution was thought to represent particular interests or to serve as a counter against anti-intellectualism. In contrast, a revised and more useful view of the university would show it to be the microcosm of those social and political concerns current in the larger society. From this more realistic perspective much of what has passed as political socialization must be seen as an effort to muffle conflict in the name of gentility and to repress those concerned with effecting changes either in the university or in the larger political community that it increasingly mirrors in function and process. Overt political learning, in the formal curriculum or in informal teach-ins and discussions, must be viewed in the context of university efforts to influence policy changes. The older, passive view of the institutional foreground is unrealistic and must be abandoned since, in fact, it is precisely foreground matters—that is, major social and political concerns of the society—that are being decided in miniature in the developments within the American university system.

A fascinating point of entry for further study along these lines, and one that revives the ancient doctrine of political education as the core of university life, would be to focus on an issue such as racial militancy or Vietnam, in order to determine how the contours of institutional, professional, and political life shape its resolution within the university communities as well as in the broader political realms that campaigning students have traversed along the paths cleared by consulting professors and fund-raising university presidents. Education's true political impact is defined by the personal and systemic claims for human development and resources, which in turn produce the stuff of political conflicts and coalitions. In such an expanded view, the State Department's academic apologist and the SDS leader moved by millennial urges are part of the same holistic paradigm, as are the university's managerial corps and its "apolitical" professionals. Participation in the articulation and judgment of claims on political knowledge by the entire university community are the essence of genuine political learning.

Past emphasis upon cumulative individual responses to political education was highly appropriate when the roles of citizen, activist, opinion former, and intellectual had a major impact on the political knowledge system. But as we have seen, the main thrust of political socialization is to emphasize the seeds of purely cognitive training, which will be useful in policy analysis. Such an emphasis, if it persists, signals the end of politics as conflict and human striving, in the name of a conservative, computerized order. Yet the realities of those issues upon whose resolution the life of the republic depends demand something in addition to such a rigid and fixated perception. Studying the cumulative political consequences of both personal *and* systemic development forces us to puzzle about the multiversity's role in exacerbating or repressing politics within the educational sector as a miniature polity. It also will lead to examination of the learned professional and methodological approaches that desensitize our awareness of the significance of the new knowledge polity. Thus when knowledge was a scarce commodity it made sense to rigorously exclude social and political values from scholarly work. When higher education was isolated from national political currents, it seemed reasonable to see the political consequences of education as by-products of more fundamental and basically nonpolitical forces. But a new awareness means that the problem is to select for a fresh synthesis the most relevant knowledge about personal development, institutional redirection, and political life within the public knowledge system itself. No longer is it a case of student politics versus administrative neutralism or self-contained campus issues being played out against a backdrop of high-level national and international politics.

The nationalization and absorption of the American university system create a highly politicized situation for its several constituencies. Dominant political ideologies may seek to obscure these facts as well as to propagate the sectarian causes of a particular group. Indeed, a reluctance to acknowledge these altered conditions of personal and systemic political education is a critical problem, whether it is located in the professed neutrality of behavioral science research or within the supposed bureaucratic neutralism of a policy administering class.

The failure of universities to impart the life style, of Dewey's concerned citizen, Goodman's communitarian, or Descartes' rational, public man has left a legacy of privatism among educated men. Today such privatism is further encouraged by the typical middle-class view of knowledge as either above or below the political realm.[10] But whatever our lingering doubts, we have all become objectively politi-

---

[10]See Edgar Litt, "Education and Political Enlightenment in America," *The Annals of the American Academy of Political and Social Science,* 361 (1965), pp. 32–39.

cized in our roles to the extent that scholarly life and educational institutions themselves have become emerging political realities. The politics of midcentury America with its fusion of knowledge and power will not let Clark Kerr's neutral technician reside in peace and retain his intellectual self-consciousness at the same time. The public path of all educated men winds between seats of knowledge and the more traditional governmental repositories of political power. So do the activities of men who thought they remained engaged in the usual academic business, untouched by developments in the urban centers, in Southeast Asia, or in American political institutions themselves. The time is surely ripe for thinking in terms of multiple personal and systemic political consequences rather than in organic terms that were better suited to earlier and more clearly bifurcated periods of university-governmental relations. It is also required that we put away our outmoded talk of pluralistic-interest balance and our end-of-ideology rhetoric and take at face value the realities of education's politicization and its impact upon the roles demanded of political men who rely on evidence and reason for the logic of their public contributions.

21 Political and Apolitical Students: Facts in Search of Theory*

CHRISTIAN BAY

Why do students active in protest movements tend to do better academically, and be more intelligent and intellectually disposed, compared to more apolitical students? There is a wealth of data to show that this is so, but an astounding absence of efforts to make theoretical sense of it. Moreover, for decades we have known that more liberal or radical students have, statistically speaking, been more intelligent or academically able than more conservative students; and similar relationships have been found with a corresponding regularity in studies, though fewer in number, of adult populations. How can we account for this apparent preponderance of intelligence and intellectual resources on the left of the political spectrum? . . .

*Reprinted by permission of the author and publisher from *The Journal of Social Issues,* 23: 3 (1967).

RECENT WORK ON STUDENT ACTIVISTS

I shall not attempt an exhaustive survey of all available data on student activism or student leftism generally. The reader is referred to several of the articles in this issue for a summary of these data; the articles by Trent and Craise and by Flacks are particularly relevant. Of especial importance to the line of argument which I have been developing are the following findings.

Berkeley 1957 — Selvin and Hagstrom Findings

Hanan C. Selvin and Warren O. Hagstrom in December 1957, while things were still fairly quiet on the Berkeley campus, did a study of the views on civil liberties in a sample of 894 Berkeley students (Selvin and Hagstrom, 1965). Anticipating that abstract statements favoring the Bill of Rights would sooner indicate conformism than liberalism, these investigators elicited responses to specific civil liberties issues involving conflicts with other values. On the basis of these responses they constructed a Libertarianism Index. They divided their sample into three groups: highly libertarian (34 percent), moderately libertarian (46 percent), slightly libertarian (20 percent).

Of interest here are the data comparing the highly libertarian students with the Berkeley student body in general. In a linear relationship, again, the proportions of highly libertarian students on the Berkeley campus ascend from freshman to senior and graduate level: 21 percent–29 percent–34 percent–40 percent–54 percent. The relationship between libertarianism and grades is inconclusive in the lower division but clear in the upper division: among A to B + students 54 percent are "highly-libertarian," compared to 37 percent among B to C + students and 25 percent among students at C level or below.

Children of blue collar workers among Berkeley students are libertarians more often, by a wide margin, than are children of parents better able to support their offspring financially through college; this is true in spite of the fact that blue collar parents average lower educational attainments than other parents and are likely to be relatively non-libertarian themselves. "Greater economic independence, in the sense of self-support," conclude Selvin and Hagstrom, "is strongly associated with having more libertarian attitudes than one's parents" (Selvin and Hagstrom, 1965, p. 504).

Among male students the social science and humanities majors were by a wide margin found more libertarian than the rest, with engineering and education (a field that has recruited low achievers in Berkeley) and business administration at the bottom. Among female students, social welfare majors were most libertarian, while life science majors shared the next level of libertarianism with social science and humanities majors, and with education majors once again at the bottom. And, finally, fraternity and especially sorority students—who are least likely to get to know well people with unorthodox ideas—are least likely to be libertarians, compared to students with other living arrangements.

Berkeley 1964 — Somers' Data

In November 1964, when the student rebellion at Berkeley was under way, Robert H. Somers interviewed a carefully drawn sample of 285 Berkeley students. He found 63 percent to favor the goals of the Free Speech Movement, while about 34 percent approved of the FSM's tactics; clearly favoring goals as well as tactics were 30 percent, and Somers calls this group the *militants,* while the *moderates,* again 30 percent, clearly supported FSM's goals but not the means used, and 22 percent *conservatives* were opposed to the ends sought as well as the tactics used (Somers, 1964).

For my purposes the crucial findings of this study are summarized as follows by Somers: "it is hard to overlook the fact that in our sample there is a strong relation between academic achievement and support for the demonstrators. Among those who reported to our interviewers a grade point average of B+or better, nearly half (45 percent) are militants, and only a tenth are conservatives. At the other end, over a third of those with an average of B- or less are conservatives, and only 15 percent are militants." If the FSM represented a minority of students, Somers concluded, it would be "a minority vital to the excellence of this university" (1964, p. 544).

Berkeley 1965 — Heist's Findings

Early in 1965 Paul Heist did a study of a sample drawn from a list of more than 800 persons said to have been arrested in the Sproul Hall sit-in (Heist, 1965). On advice of their legal counsel, about 50 percent of the 33 percent sample refused to return the questionnaire but the rest cooperated, 128 in all; an additional 60 FSM activists were recruited subsequently as subjects for the study. In addition, a random sample of 92 seniors (class of 1964–1965) were given the same two questionnaires. Also, Heist had access to the same attitude inventory data from 340 seniors (class of 1962–1963) and from "2500+" entering freshmen, all at Berkeley. Further details of this study by Heist plus other related work are presented by Trent and Craise in this issue.

Heist developed an Intellectual Disposition Index on the basis of six of the twelve scales in his attitude inventory, and with this instrument divided his FSM sample and his three general student samples according to eight "degrees," from low to high Intellectual Disposition. Here is what he found:

For the total FSM group we find almost 70 percent in the top three categories and none in the bottom three, and it is to be remembered that a large proportion, in fact, the majority, of the FSM persons were freshmen, sophomore and juniors. The number of persons in these upper categories in the senior sample amounts to 25 and 31 percent. The Free Speech Movement drew extraordinarily larger proportions of students with strong intellectual orientations, at all levels (freshmen through graduate) (Heist, 1965, 21-22a).

Watts and Whittaker and FSM

William A. Watts and David N. E. Whittaker's study of FSM activists compared to Berkeley students generally started with this hypothesis: "We expected that FSM members would be more flexible as defined and measured by personality tests of flexibility-rigidity . . . than their counterparts who were less committed, neutral, or even opposed to the Movement" (Watts and Whittaker, 1966, p. 43).

Their study was based on questionnaires administered to a chance sample of 172 participants among the 1000-1200 students who "sat in" at Sproul Hall in the afternoon of December 2nd, 1964, (and who were on this occasion not arrested, or not yet, except for the two thirds who stayed on all night). In addition, the same questionnaire was given to a random sample of 182 Berkeley students at about the same time; 146 of these cooperated. The instrument included a 27-item rigidity-flexibility scale. The most important result of this study, for present purposes, is its indication of "strong support for the prediction of greater flexibility among the FSM members" (1966, p. 59). The authors conclude that this latter finding is of particular interest considering the purported rigidity of the FSM members in negotiations with the University administration, and suggests the necessity of distinguishing between a trait of rigidity as psychologically defined and commitment.

Two other findings of the study by Watts and Whittaker should be noted in passing. First, with an additional sample of 181 students drawn from the District Attorney's arrest list for December 3, and 174 names drawn at random from the Student Directory, they failed to establish greater academic achievement on the part of the FSM'ers compared to other students, and concluded that these activists were quite typical or average with respect to grade point averages (1966, p. 52). While Watts and Whittaker's objective check is more trustworthy than the data on grade point averages reported in the Somers study which were based on respondents' information, I am inclined to discount, until substantiated by further research, this particular finding by Watts and Whittaker, because it appears to run counter to so many other findings discussed in this article. It may well be valid for the 773 who were arrested, though I would have liked to see a replication of the study, which can easily be done; if it is valid for this group, I would still doubt that it is valid for FSM activists generally. It is possible, for example, that the most *academically* as distinct from *intellectually* oriented students among FSM activists felt greater anxiety than the rest about their academic credits, and were more likely to shrink from taking the most extreme risks.

Secondly, the FSM students were far more likely to have parents with advanced academic degrees, compared to the cross-section sample: "approximately 26 percent of the fathers and 16 percent of the mothers of the FSM sample possess either Ph.D. or M. A. degrees compared to 11 percent and 4 percent respectively in the cross-section" (Watts and Whittaker, 1966, p. 53 and Table 4). This finding does not contradict Somers' finding that student militants were more likely than the rest to have blue-collar fathers. Among several factors that could be taken into account here, I would emphasize the difference between having militant attitudes and being prepared to jeopardize academic achievements; the value of academic credits may well loom somewhat larger to the self-supporting student from a working class background, than they do to students from families in which academic proficiency or intellectual gifts or future financial safety tends to be taken for granted. The latter category among the militants may be more likely to risk jail and expulsion for their beliefs.

I have confined this brief inquiry to activists on the Left, who are far more significant than those on the Right, both by their numbers (at least in the better universities), and by their tendency to persist in political activities disturbing to the university "image" desired by most administrators and trustees. In so far as rightist student groups, the most important one among them at the moment being Young Americans for Freedom, have staged demonstrations, they have usually been *ad hoc* counter-demonstrations, directed *against* issue-oriented protests by liberal or leftist student activists; there have been no protracted campaigning or even articulate political programs; and while student leftists have tended to be fiercely independent of older leftists, or of the "generation over thirty" generally, there has been no evidence of a corresponding intellectual independence among organized rightist students.

TOWARD A PSYCHOLOGICAL THEORY OF RADICAL VERSUS CONSERVATIVE ATTITUDES

The most promising approach to theorizing about the psychological nature of liberal and radical versus conservative political attitudes, I believe, is to consider what kind of functions political opinions may serve for those who hold them, in terms of their personality and social needs. It is quickly apparent that the function of serving a rational, realistic understanding of the political world is one but only one possible function of a person's "politics."

Types of Motives Underlying Political Opinions

The over-all function of any political or other social opinion, write M. Brewster Smith, Jerome S. Bruner and Robert W. White, (1960, p. 275) is to strike a "compromise between reality demands, social demands, and inner psychological demands". Daniel Katz (1960) distinguishes between rationality (or reality-testing) motives, value-expressive motives, social acceptance motives, and ego defense motives. These are suggested analytical categories; specific opinions usually serve a mixture of needs or motives. The relative weight of each type of motive varies from person to person, from attitude to attitude and from time to time; few of us, if any, are free of neurotic ego defensiveness, and none of us are free of social acceptance needs or desires for consistency and for realistic understanding of the world in which we live.

In their 1954 paper, Irving Sarnoff and Daniel Katz applied their three categories of motives in a discussion of a clearly *undesirable* type of attitude, namely anti-Negro prejudice; and one of their main concerns was to show how a better understanding of the motives of attitudes could facilitate processes of attitude change. Thus, to the extent that prejudice is rationally founded—on the basis, say, of the limited knowledge available to many a Southern American white boy or girl, it presumably can be influenced by new knowledge. To the extent, however, that prejudice is based on social acceptance motives, it will take evidence of an entirely different kind of influence or do away with it—namely evidence that such a change of opinion would not reduce a person's acceptance in whatever groups he wants to be or become part of. To the extent, finally, that ego defensive motives determine the prejudice, it may take psychotherapy to reduce it.

Ego Defensive Motives

There is evidence, wrote Gardner Murphy more than twenty years ago, "that functional intelligence can be enormously enhanced, first by the systematic study and removal of individual and socially shared autisms, second, by the cultivation of curiosity, and third, by the art of withdrawal from the pressures of immediate external tasks, to let the mind work at its own pace and in its own congenial way" (Murphy, 1945, p. 16).

The most fundamental obstacle, of course, to the "freeing of intelligence" is the active presence of ego defensive motives. Severely repressed anxieties about one's worth as a human being, which may well be the result of a childhood starved of affection, may predestine a person to become a "true believer" in Eric Hoffer's sense—a person who seeks a new collective identity because he cannot live with his own self (Hoffer, 1951). Such anxieties, if unresolved, may predestine a person to become an authoritarian or an anti-authoritarian personality (cf. Bay, 1965, p. 207–217), a bigot, a rightwinger, or, more rarely, a left-winger. This type of person is not psychologically free; his views may keep his anxieties and fears manageable but contributes no realistic understanding of the external political world.

Some of the data discussed previously can be understood in this light; Adorno *et al.*, Rokeach and McClosky all found right-wing views statistically associated with indices of neurosis of one kind or another. But what of McClosky's finding that, for example, "liberals" appeared less hostile than "moderate liberals," and what of the data on student activists?

Social Acceptance Motives

To account for such data we need to consider the prevalence of social acceptance motives, too, as obstacles to the freeing of political intelligence. To the extent that a person is deeply worried about his popularity, his career prospects, his financial future, his reputation, etc., he will utilize his political opinions not for achieving realistic insight but for impressing his reference groups and his reference persons favorably. These processes of obfuscation may be conscious or, more likely, subconscious, but they are above all pervasive in our society, and in every other society, too—above all in highly competitive and socially mobile societies, in which the difference between "success" and lack of it may make for vast differences in prospects for the satisfaction of physical and self-esteem needs, and perhaps for many other kinds of needs as well. Social acceptance-motivated political beliefs serve the individual's desired image, status and career, etc., but contribute little toward a realistic understanding of his political world—at least in so far as it extends beyond his immediate reference groups and persons.

Social acceptance-motivated opinions may well tend to be liberal in some university faculties, as charged by some conservative writers, including conservative students wishing to explain why liberalism increases with amount of education (cf. Naylor, 1966 for a discussion of this). But by and large, in every stable social order, they tend to be conservative, or at most mildly liberal, firmly within the established framework of constitutional objectives and processes. In every stable society there are rich and poor, strong and weak, privileged and underprivileged; and not only political power and influence but social status and respectability are associated with seeing political problems through the eyes of the former rather than the latter, in each paired category.

Statistically speaking, therefore, *more conservative views, among students or adults generally, are likely to be less rationally, less independently motivated, compared to more radical-liberal views.*

I am by no means arguing, of course, that liberal and radical views cannot be neurotically motivated. The point is a more modest one: the frequency of neurotic motivations—now including not only deeply repressed anxieties about the individual's own worth but also milder ego deficiencies such as constant worry about popularity or career prospects—is probably higher the further away the politically active person is from the left side of the political spectrum (I did not say left *end*).

The statistical data surveyed make good sense if viewed in this perspective. With reference to the Berkeley data, surely one should expect ego defensiveness to be manifested by a fear of anarchy and equality, and lead the individual to detest both the style and the objectives of FSM-type movements. And the more intensely or neurotically one is preoccupied with career worries, the less one would be disposed to mingle with the student rebels; these students, more typically, appear to have decided that certain values are more dear to them than conventional career prospects. The articles by Keniston and Flacks make this same point. As rebels they are more likely to have made a choice and to have marshalled the intellectual and emotional resources, at some point, to stick to it, also in situations of severe stress. Obviously, some will for spurious or chance reasons pursue neurotic social acceptance needs with FSM-type groups as their reference systems; but this happens in almost every group, and is likely to occur with less frequency in a rebellious political action group than in less demanding and socially more homogeneous groups like, for example, fraternities and sororities.

"Only Rebellion Can Expand Consciousness"

As Albert Camus saw, only rebellion, on some level, can expand consciousness; "with rebellion, awareness is born." Awareness of being human—of being more than an aspiring carpenter, merchant, lawyer, educator or military officer. Or dutiful son or daughter.

In our daily trials rebellion plays the same role as does the *"cogito"* in the realm of thought: it is the first piece of evidence. But this evidence lures the individual from his solitude. It founds its first value on the whole human race. I rebel—therefore we exist (Camus, 1958, pp. 15 and 22).

Camus' portrait of the rebel presents a normative ideal in persuasive terms: to become fully human, a constant tendency to be revolted by and to rebel against oppression and injustice is required. While I admit to sharing this normative position, my present argument is empirical, though speculative: I submit that it will help make sense of all the data reviewed in this paper if we consider Camus' rebel a developmental model—a *probable* type of person to develop *to the extent that* not only ego defensive but more mildly neurotic social acceptance anxieties are resolved or successfully faced up to.

This kind of theory is bound to be speculative if only because such social anxieties are so pervasive. Yet it is possible to argue that the various data associating leftism with academic competence, intelligence, psychological and socioeconomic security, etc., may be seen as tending to support this theory. Further research in this area is desirable and feasible, and can be usefully focused by this kind of theory.[1]

The more secure and sheltered a person's infancy and childhood, and the more freedom that educational and other social processes has given him to develop according to his inner needs and potentialities,

---

[1]One Polish study by Hannah E. Malewska, for example, ought to be followed up: she found that children's notions of moral norms become more responsible (less formal and superficial) the less severely disciplinarian their parents and the more urbanized their surroundings (Malewska, 1961). Work on children's politics is on the increase, but often restricts itself unduly to cognitive aspects. An exception is the work of Fred J. Greenstein (1965).

Patricia Richmond and I a few years ago found that among liberals in a pacifistically oriented organization, the more "extreme" supporters of rights of specific unpopular minorities tended to be somewhat less dogmatic · in Rokeach's sense, than the more moderate supporters of such rights (Bay and Richmond, 1960). More work is needed to improve on instruments like Rokeach's Dogmatism scale, and to develop additional instruments to measure neurotic obstacles to rationality in the general population, so that we might discover how widely and in what types of contexts it is true that resolution of anxieties and reduction of other psychological burdens stimulate tendencies toward rationality, political activism, leftism and related phenomena.

Let me in conclusion mention the valuable, still small but apparently growing literature that seeks in-depth understanding of the political views and their motivations in particular individuals, whether prominent or humble, and whether dead or still living. A masterly political biographical study in psychological terms is *Woodrow Wilson and Colonel House* by Alexander and Juliette George (1956). Justly famous is Erik H. Erikson's *Young Man Luther* (1958). Arnold A. Rogow's *James T. Forrestal* is particularly valuable for its searching analysis of the issues associated with possible mental disorder in high office (1964). Among psychological studies of the politics of humbler individuals, who are left anonymous, reference has been made to *Opinions and Personality* by M. Brewster Smith *et al.* (1960), a study limiting its scope to attitudes toward the Soviet Union. Three other very useful works are Robert E. Lane's *Political Ideology,* a study of fifteen "average" New Englanders, mostly working men; David Riesman's *Faces in the Crowd,* dealing with "average" Los Angelese; and an excellent Australian study of five more or less politically active individuals,—*Private Politics,* by Alan F. Davies (1966).

the more likely that a capacity for political rationality and independence will develop, simply because the likelihood of severe anxieties is relatively low. In addition, again converting Camus' ideal into empirical-theoretical currency, the better the individual has been able to resolve his own anxieties, the more likely that he will empathize with others less fortunate than himself. A sense of justice as well as a capacity for rationality is, according to this theory, a likely development in relatively secure individuals, whose politics, if any, will therefore tend toward the left—toward supporting the champions of the underdog, not the defenders of established, always unjust, institutions. And young people, with the proverbial impetuousness of youth, are likely to seek extremes of social justice, or militant means, simply because their emotions, and more particularly their sense of elementary morality and justice, have not yet been dulled by daily compromises and defeats to the extent that most older persons' emotions have been.[2]

Let me sharpen my own position as follows: *Every new human being is potentially a liberal animal and a rebel; yet every social organization he will be up against, from the family to the state, is likely to seek to "socialize" him into a conveniently pliant conformist.*

Many parents and some schools are child-oriented to the extent of trying to give children the security and freedom to develop according to their own inner needs and potentialities. With a good start of this kind, such children may, when they approach adulthood, be able to resist the socializing of privilege-defending states, universities and other established institutional pillars of the *status quo*; if so, they become the student rebels, the civil rights workers, and the peace activists: a small minority, but a growing one in terms of influence among young people.

[2]Now there are some older persons, too, who for all the toll of many years of practical experience, seem to have remained able to share the basic moral and political outlook (if not necessarily the views on tactics) of militant student activists. As I read some of Erik H. Erikson's recent work, he appears to conclude that man's sense of social responsibility and his degree of social sensitivity depend on his maturation beyond the Freudian psychosocial stage of genitality; he calls this hypothetically higher developmental stage *generativity:* "I refer to man's *love for his works and ideas as well as for his children,* and the necessary self-verification which adult man's ego receives, and must receive, from his labor's challenge. As adult man needs to be needed, so—for the strength of his ego and for that of his community—he requires the challenge emanating from what he has generated and from what now must be 'brought up,' guarded, preserved—and eventually transcended" (Erikson, 1964, pp. 130–132). Erikson describes parenthood as "the first and for many, the prime generative encounter" but argues that those who approach or reach the generative stage of psychosocial development to that extent *need* to teach, to instruct and influence, and in other ways actively work for the good of not only their own children but of their community and their society, or mankind, as well.

References

Adorno, Theodore W., Frenkel-Brunswik, E., Levinson, D. J. and Sanford, R. N. *The Authoritarian Personality.* New York: Harper and Row, 1950.

Bay, Christian. *Structure of Freedom.* New York: Atheneum, 1965 (1958).

Bay, Christian, and Richmond, Patricia. Some varieties of Liberal experience. Unpublished paper, 1960.

Camus, Albert. *The Rebel.* New York: Vintage, 1958.

Davies, Alan F. *Private Politics.* Melbourne: Melbourne University Press, 1966.

Erikson, Erik H. *Young Man Luther.* New York: Norton, 1958.

Erikson, Erik H. *Insight and Responsibility.* New York: Norton, 1964.

George, Alexander, and George, Juliette. *Woodrow Wilson and Colonel House.* New York: John Day, 1956.

Greenstein, Fred J. *Children and Politics.* New Haven: Yale University Press, 1965.

Heist, Paul. Intellect and commitment: The faces of discontent. Center for the Study of Higher Education, Berkeley, 1965. (mimeo)

Hoffer, Eric. *The True Believer.* New York: Harper and Row, 1951.

Katz, Daniel. The functional approach to the study of attitudes. *Public Opinion Quarterly,* 24, 1960, 163–204.

Lane, Robert E. *Political Ideology.* New York: Free Press, 1962.

Lindner, Robert. Political creed and character. *Psychoanalysis,* 2, 1953, 10–33.

Malewska, Hannah E. Religious ritualism, rigid ethics, and severity in upbringing. *Polish Sociological Bulletin,* 1, 1961, 71–78.

McClosky, Herbert. Conservatism and personality. *American Political Science Review,* 52, 1958, 27–45.

Murphy, Gardner. The freeing of intelligence. *Psychological Bulletin,* 42, 1945, 1–19.

Naylor, Robert W. Why intellectuals are liberal. *Western Politica,* 1, 1966, 33–37.

Newcomb, Theodore M. *Personality and Social Change.* New York: Holt, Rinehart and Winston, Inc., 1943.

Riesman, David. *Faces in the Crowd.* New York: Free Press, 1952.

Rogow, Arnold A. *James T. Forrestal.* New York: Crowell-Collier-Macmillan, 1964.

Rokeach, Milton. Political and religious dogmatism: An alternative to the authoritarian personality. *Psychological Monographs,* 70, 1956, 1–43.

Rokeach, Milton. *The Open and Closed Mind.* New York: Basic Books, 1960.

Sarnoff, Irving, and Katz, Daniel. The motivational bases of attitude change. *Journal of Abnormal and Social Psychology,* 49, 1954, 115–124.

Selvin, Hanan G., and Hagstrom, Warren O. Determinants of support for civil liberties. In Seymour M. Lipset and Sheldon S. Wolin (eds.), *The Berkeley Student Revolt.* New York: Anchor, 1965, 494–518.

Shils, Edward. Authoritaranism: Right and Left. In Richard Christie and Marie Jahoda (eds.), *Studies in the Scope and Method of "The Authoritarian Personality."* New York: Free Press, 1954.

Smith, M. Brewster, Bruner, Jerome S. and White, Robert W. *Opinions and Personality.* New York: Wiley, 1960.

Somers, Robert H. The mainsprings of the rebellion: A survey of Berkeley students in November, 1964. In Seymour M. Lipset and Sheldon S. Wolin (Eds.), *The Berkeley Student Revolt.* New York: Anchor, 1965, 530–557.

Stouffer, Samuel A. *Communism, Conformity, and Civil Liberties.* New York: Wiley, 1955.

Watts, William A., and Whittaker, David. Free speech advocates at Berkeley. *Journal of Applied Behavioral Science,* 2, 1966, 41–62.

PART VI
DISTRIBUTION OF HUMAN VALUES: THE POLITICS OF RESPECT

Introduction

The impact of modern politics influences the basic life chances and self-respect of the citizenry. The "politics of respect" is critical in modern politics because deprivations produce a spiral of personal frustration and political outburst. Historically, the politics of respect has ranged from populist movements, such as Agrarian Populism or black power, to ameliorative programs of political welfare, such as the New Deal and the "War on Poverty" by the Kennedy-Johnson administrations. This historical perspective convinces us of one point—the distribution of psychic and political respect is critical to the public order. Factors such as individual and group esteem are closely related to attitudes about and behavior within political channels. Of even greater importance is the contemporary realization that the disruption of dignity and self-respect itself is a basic political value.

The role of self-respect and dignity-values within American politics has changed markedly. The moral equality of man, the

Protestant ethic awarding individual dignity and responsibility, and the constitutional system of checks and balances once provided the political framework within which individual respect could be achieved. The development of the modern welfare state led to a second major emphasis, namely the articulation of respect through interest groups and programs designed to remove structured disadvantages in personal opportunity, education, and political repression. Developments in the underdeveloped world, and in our own racially torn society as well, have led to the realization that respect is earned by government when individuals participate in decisions about their lives. This Jeffersonian concept has never had more vitality than in contemporary American politics, for within the political party, the urban core, and the university campus it is no longer healthy to drain human energies into the pseudopolitics that evade major issues.

The importance of respect as a basic political value has profound implications for our public life. Values about personal advantage or disadvantage in the social order are linked to the networks of social and political identifications created by individuals. Moreover, as Joan Moore's contribution to this section (Selection 22) makes clear, the distribution of advantages and disadvantages influences the type of politics engaged in by diverse strata of the citizenry. Thus, disadvantaged groups, such as blacks and the poor, conceptualize politics in specific terms that are based on the channels of political-party and interest groups available to them. By contrast, advantaged groups and individuals generalize about political life and the expectations of politicians in a more "rational" and abstract manner. Selection 22—a careful blend of conceptual and empirical work—indicates that a narrow, private political style is a consequence of accrued disadvantage and disrespect.

If the distribution of disadvantaged social positions is inimical to the Republic, then public programs designed to eradicate such conditions ought to be studied carefully. The politics of respect is fought in an arena of competing interests. During recent decades the executive-centered Democratic party has dominated the positions and benefits of national political control. William Haddad, a former staff member of the Office of Economic Opportunity, describes the political problems of the Office of Economic Opportunity and its professional staff. Caught between the institutional power of urban mayors and congressmen and between the assertiveness of the black and poverty revolutions, Office of Economic Opportunity director Shriver maximized the professional independence of his staff. This strategy, and Shriver's political leadership, helped the antipoverty programs to survive and prosper in Washington. However, the community-action phase of the program was tied to a states'-rights doctrine that gave local and state political organizations ultimate control of the program. Haddad's tempered criticism (Selection 23) concerns the limited participation actually awarded to blacks and to genuine poverty groups. Herein the power for the disadvantaged promised in the community-action program was tempered by political forces. The writer's concern and the realities of the political life of OEO under Shriver are based on the process by which "the 1936 liberal has learned to compromise with city halls. As far as the poor are concerned he is as much a part of the Establishment as big business."

Sidney Lens (Selection 24) views the assorted poverty programs undertaken during the Kennedy-Johnson administrations from an even broader perspective. Lens's analysis is that these programs were essentially adaptations of New Deal welfare liberalism to novel situations. In fact, the poverty programs were designed to alter only the distribution of social disadvantages, not the political structure feeding social disadvantages. If the goal is to eradicate poverty rather than to merely reduce the number of poor people, then the relationship between the politics of respect and the distribution of political power must be clarified. Mr. Lens makes the point in his article,

> When all is said and done the essence of a war against poverty is power—power to force through economic concession and to hold out hope, power to desegregate segregated communities, power to achieve equal education, power to abolish job discrimination. . . . and to break patterns of dependency and the degrading practices of relief and welfare agencies.

Robert Levine acknowledges these realities of the politics of poverty and respect (Selection 25). His concern is that the stalemate between the poor and the "Liberal Establishment" will cripple the effective delivery of massive amounts of jobs, education, and community services to the poverty groups. Therefore, he seeks politically effective administration of poverty programs. This means facing two related problems: the problem of control over policy and the problem of control over the actual administration of programs. Levine argues for a dominant federal role in setting down meaningful and professional guidelines to aid the poor. However, the absence of sufficient professional skills in the field (not to mention the political realities described by Haddad and Lens) renders ineffective the central administration of policies. A revised version of "creative federalism" is needed in which national standards are implemented in the pluralistic arena of urban and state politics. Levine hopes for creative conflict between the poor and those local bureaucracies that are capable of imaginatively translating their demands into reality under federal guidelines. The trouble is that the federal government itself often holds the balance of power between the assertive poor and black communities, as do local agencies, who may not respond to Levine's plea for creative administration.

It is clear from these selections that the problems of the politics of respect are significant. Only effective intervention by other forces can avoid the politics of despair when deprived groups confront a cautious Establishment. Herein lies the question for the next decade of Americans, namely, whether any combination of black leadership, white middle class, and enlightened private corporations can ameliorate conflict by dealing constructively with the plight of the "other America." Henry Pratt shows how complex is the process of social change within major institutions (Selection 26). His analysis of liberal movement within the American clergy pays attention to personal, social, and ideological factors. Yet more than the goodwill of churchmen will be required because of the determination among the disadvantaged never to forfeit their claims to political respect, never to return to the slumbering passivity of an earlier day.

22 Social Deprivation and Advantage as Sources of Political Values*

JOAN W. MOORE

In a recently published paper, V. O. Key, Jr., and Frank Munger comment as political scientists on sociological research on voting. They complain of the sociologist's propensity to explain political behavior in terms of voters' nonpolitical roles, in particular the ethnic, social-class and religious roles. They ask:

> Is there some sort of political order . . . more or less independent of the identification of citizens and electors with those non-political groups to which we have an index in their social charac-teristics? . . . If there is no political community, if citizens, or many of them, have no political role more or less autonomous from their other roles, a good many centuries of political specula-tion . . . have been beside the point. . . . There may well be, for part of the electorate at least, roles, identifications, and prefer-

*Reprinted by permission of the author and the University of Utah, copyright owner.

ences of a purely political nature with quite as much reality as his "social characteristics."[1]

Among the topics mentioned for further research by these authors is "the individual's . . . comception of his role as a voter."[2] Although this seems like the kind of problem that would have been tackled at the outset of sociological interest in political behavior, data on voters' self-concepts are curiously rare.[3] Most research on voters and voting has looked for the covert, rather than the overt meanings of voting to the voter, concentrating on the latent, rather than on the manifest level. It may be that both the elusive nature of the social structure of the American political system and the ambiguities and incoherencies in the political aspects of our culture encourage such an approach.

It is the purpose of this paper to explore the conscious values that individuals have about themselves as voters. In ideal-type fashion, we will attempt to extricate those values which seem "purely" political from those which seem to be blurred diffusions from other, non-political social roles. Into this "social-political" framework, we will then attempt to fit a more traditional kind of data—attitudes toward elected officials as they vary by social characteristics of voters.

SOURCES OF DATA

Although the purpose of this paper is conceptual clarification, we will present data illustrative of the points made. These data were collected in the course of a study of a campaign for Congress held in 1956. The Congressional District studied, one of the most heterogeneous in a large and heterogeneous metropolitan area, was sampled in such a fashion that the sample could be called representative, with random sampling of households in a stratified sample of precincts. Approximately one hundred voters were interviewed, first in early October and later in mid-November.

[1]V. O. Key, Jr., and Frank Munger, "Social Determinism and Electoral Decision," in Burdick and Brodbeck (eds.), *American Voting Behavior* (New York: Free Press, 1959), p. 299.

[2]Key and Munger, "Social Determinism and Electoral Decision."

[3]See Robert E. Lane, *Political Life* (New York: Free Press, 1959), and Burdick and Brodbeck for current reviews of the literature. Even Lane's comprehensive review of "Conscious Needs Served by Participation" overlooks this topic.

The interview was extremely broad,[4] each round lasting over an hour, and placing the congressional campaign in the context of the voters' perceptions and attitudes toward the presidential campaign under way and the local political structure. Both interviews were aimed at exploring the full dimensions of the voters' experiences during the campaign, and specific questions about the congressman formed a relatively minor part of the interview.[5]

The small size of the sample limits the study to the generation of hypotheses, and precludes conclusive statements. The data reported here, then, are illustrative only. (Numbers in tables below vary because of non-response.)

VALUES ABOUT THE SELF-AS-VOTER

A priori, we would expect the components of the voter's self-concept to stem from two sources: first, from his political training during childhood and adolescence, and second, from his participation in the on-going political structure. (Analogously, if we wish to understand an individual's concept of himself as, say, a professional artist, we look first at the values offered to him in art school and second at the values offered to him in the typical commercial-art studio.)

Unfortunately for *a priori* analysis, both of these sources present inconsistencies. Early political training in our society gives the typical voter little guidance in the acquisition of a political self-image that is

[4]Both prestructured and open-ended questions were asked, and a variety of techniques used. The following topics were touched on in the first round: awareness of the local (ward) political structure and opinions of its officials, awareness of the total slate of candidates running, awareness of and ideals about the congressmen, perception of major issues, sentence-completion items on issues and parties, open-ended and pre-coded questions on the presidential and vice-presidential candidates, the voter's voting and party history, his interaction with various others about politics, and his social characteristics. In the second round of interviewing, a similarly broad approach was taken; issue items and some sentence-completions were repeated, actual voting and voting switches were examined, along with the voter's interaction with precinct workers, his attendance at rallies, etc.

[5]We were, for example, concerned about the effects on Negro and white voters of one candidate's liberalism toward Negroes, which was probed only in the sentence completion items. "The best thing about Candidate's stand on Negroes. . . ." Where we elicited only a "don't know" response, there was no further probing. These items were set in a group of sentence completions dealing with both national issues and presidential candidates.

both culturally legitimate and realistic. Family, peers, and teachers—in that order—influence the young person's conception of the political world and of himself in it.[6] The teachers and schools—representatives of the larger society—exhaust formal political training, which tends to be limited on the one hand to implanting an attitude of reverence toward the semi-sacred national heroes,[7] and on the other hand to the general injunction to the prospective voter to be active, moral, wary, rational, and impersonal in his political evaluations.[8] The norms seem to demand that the voter focus on the official and the candidate, either as an object for reverence, or as an individual to be judged much as an employer judges a prospective employee—objectively, with a minimum of personal involvement or prejudice.

The lack of congruence between the reverent and the bureaucratic political selves held up as ideals in the school is exacerbated by sub-group political socialization. Ethnic or social-class groups tend to demand loyalty to the group, and provide social support for the development of a political self remote from both of the ideals held up in the schools. Not only loyalty, but group and self-interest may be taught. To put it briefly, there is little consistency, and apparently increasing competition[9] between the various ideal political selves held up to the voter in the course of political socialization.

These problems are only poorly resolved by later life-experiences. (Inconsistencies in other facets of socialization, e.g., sex-role socialization, do tend to wash out in adult experience, for example, by the increase in distinction between adult sex roles.) First, the voter is rarely an active participant in a continuous political structure (such as a political party) that could clarify the dimensions of his political self. Second, the sporadic political events—campaigns and elections—in which he does participate (or, at least, during which his values about himself come up for re-examination) offer equally inconsistent cues. The local candidate, in talking to a small and presumed homogeneous

---

[6]Herbert Hyman, *Political Socialization* (New York: Free Press, 1959), pp. 107–109.

[7]The consequences for the political-social self of establishing such national heroes as sacred figures are well detailed in W. Lloyd Warner, *American Life* (Chicago: University of Chicago Press, 1953), and in his *The Living and the Dead* (New Haven: Yale University Press, 1959).

[8]See Lane, *Political Life,* pp. 157–161, for a summary of research on differences in the extent to which citizens feel morally bound to participate in political affairs—one dimension of socialization.

[9]Data presented by Hyman, *Political Socialization,* pp. 63–65, suggest an increase in social-class differences in political values with the onset of maturity.

audience, does give out clear cues, reminding the Negro voter, e.g., to vote *as a Negro* and the worker to vote *as a worker*.[10] However, the voter is exposed not only to local candidates, who can make such distinctions, but, more continuously and more reliably, to a full slate of speech-makers, many of whom employ a wide range of symbols in a shot-gun attempt to hit some responsive chord in their heterogeneous mass audience. In campaigns in which the total society participates, i.e., the Presidential campaign, the voter's exposure to the candidates gives him few strong cultural supports for one or another self-

We have posited two types of ideal political self held up in the schools: the "rational-bureaucratic," and the "reverent." We have further suggested that home and neighborhood experiences offer another political ideal—group identification in the cause of group advancement. This analysis provides the basis for a typology of voter-self-concepts. These range from specifically "political" (in Key and Munger's terms) to totally non-political, where the voter's self-definition and orientation are totally derived from other social roles. (This is an "ideal" typology, not an empirical one; it is an attempt to state alternative "pure" role-patterns which the political system permits and may encourage.)

In this ideal-typical scheme, there are two types of "compartmentalized" political behavior, i.e., behavior that is self-conscious to the point where the political is compartmentalized and distinct from the voter's other roles.

1. First, there is the type of compartmentalizer who believes himself to be a rational voter, with a consistent ideology in terms of which he holds himself responsible for evaluating political events. For the Rational Compartmentalizer, compartmentalization of political evaluations is a continual act of will, a disengagement of the political from other aspects of the self. It is this Rational Compartmentalizer that Key and Munger seem to refer to as "purely" political, whose political role is relatively autonomous of his other roles. It corresponds to the "rational" ideal held up in the course of early political training.

2. Second, there is the Interest-group Compartmentalizer, member of a group or social category[11] with such strong political significance that its advancement colors all political events. Here, the total self is equated with the political self, in a compartmentalizing, specifically political fashion. The Interest-group Compartmentalizer places a

---

[10]This process is detailed in J. Gerasimo, J. Moore and J. Smothers, "Amateur vs. Professional: Study of a Political Campaign" (unpublished manuscript).

[11]See the distinction between these two concepts made by Lane, *Political Life*, p. 189, following David Truman.

high value on politics and is highly selective in his perception and evaluation of political events. A consistent approach is made to all political phenomena, and where this approach is irrelevant, the voter tends not to perceive the "extraneous" event.[12]

3. For many voters, however, there is only the most generalized, moralistic orientation to politics. The principle motive of the Generalizers is to select the "Best," and the vagueness of the criterion means that idiosyncratic principles are given free play. The basic assumption of the Generalizer is that in every political affair there is a "best"—not "a best for a given office," or "a best for a given situation in the world," just a "best." Such a voter defines himself as moral and his task as the evaluation of political events and officials in *general* moral terms.[13] The Generalizer has focused on the evaluative aspect of his political role, deriving criteria for evaluation diffusely from other social roles. This type corresponds to the hero-seeking, reverent aspect of political socialization.

There is one notable omission from this typology—that of the party-identifier voter. This omission is deliberate. Very few people have continuous relations with a party—as precinct workers, for example, or Young Republicans. For those few, there are continuous social pressures to hew to the "party line," allowing little room for ambiguity in their political self-definitions. For such people, the party seems to replace all other social sources of political identity.

But the majority of party-identifiers do not have direct social

[12]This type corresponds to ethnic and social-class political ideals offered in childhood and adolescence. An illustration of this high degree of selectivity was noted in our interviews. Many Negro respondents actually failed to perceive, or at least to mention the Suez or Hungarian crises in 1956 at any place in this long interview. Further, when respondents were asked to chose three "most important" issues from a list of nine, only 19 percent of the Negro respondents chose "foreign affairs," as compared with 44 percent of the white respondents. On the other hand, 78 percent of the Negroes chose the issue of "desegregation" as compared with only 33 percent of the whites.

[13]An account of a Rational Compartmentalizer confronting a Generalizer was reported as follows: "Ald. Seymour F. Simon (40th), acting Democratic committeeman in his ward and now a candidate for election, got a letter from a 20-year-old University of Chicago co-ed stating: 'A gentleman came to my parents' home this morning with a petition for your nomination as ward committeeman. I asked this man just what this petition was, who you are, what you have done for this ward, and what you intend to do; in general, why you deserve a vote. This gentleman answered that he represented you *because you are a good man.* I again asked, what is a good man, why is Seymour Simon a better nominee than the Republican candidate?' She complained that Simon's representative, a precinct captain, gave no adequate answer." *Chicago Daily News,* January 30, 1960.

relations with their official parties. The party cannot exert a direct constraint upon them, because they have no "real" social role in the party. Their reasons for identification with one party or another seem to depend upon such role factors as are discussed above,[14] and hence have not been dealt with separately here.

Using these abstract ideal types in the qualitative analysis of our interviews proved fruitful. An intense focus on the personal characteristics of the candidates seemed to be a hallmark of a Generalizing approach. When it was accompanied by a partisan predilection, this interest in the candidates' goodness and badness was diffused into an interest in the *party's* goodness and badness, and in the moral attributes of the members of the parties. The *social* and not only the political universe came to be divided into Democrats and Republicans— absolute good and evil coinciding with party divisions. For example, the woman whose evaluation of one candidate was: "I think Eisenhower has the most qualities next to the Lord. He always takes care of his job, never once did what he shouldn't. He's the head of his country and the head of his family; his wife and children respect him," made the following comments on the parties:

> Republicans are people who believe in the right thing to do. Republicans have a clear conscience. There are a lot more selfish people among the Democrats; I don't know any Republicans who are selfish. I could never make a mistake judging Republicans from Democrats. People that are *really Republican inside* are more understanding and give you a chance. I never make a mistake about them.

For this woman, the political was inextricable from the general morality; "real Republicans" and "real Democrats" become moral and not political types. The candidate similarly is evaluated morally, as a whole person, and not as an officeseeker. It is the voter's whole self which enters into his political actions.

Although such intense involvement in politics as the above quotation implies is rare, diffusion of moral values—almost intact—from the non-political to the political sphere seems to be encouraged during the course of a campaign. Existing partisan predisposition, diffuse and moralistic, finds strong expression in attachment to particular candidates, who are evaluated more as persons than as political figures. The

---

[14]There has been a proliferation of proto-party groups since the end of the second world war, the ADA, the John Birch Society. Such groups probably exert the same degree of pressure on their members as does the party on its active members. An analysis of the active members of such groups, and a comparison of them with active party members, might prove very illuminating.

Generalizer applies little more rationale in rejecting candidates of opposing parties than he uses in rejecting slight personal acquaintances.

Interestingly, among many Generalizers, political discussion was disapproved. It, like personal gossip, was felt to be "not nice." The private quality of political attachments seems part and parcel of the Generalizing approach to politics.

On the other hand, many poorly educated Negroes in our sample displayed startling political knowledge and sophistication, combined with a very low interest in the candidates as individuals. This phenomenon became more understandable when we viewed them as Interest-group Compartmentalizers, either as Negroes or as workers. An initially clear, and *politicized* total identity provided a basis for high interest in politics and for evaluating issues, candidates, and parties in terms of group (and individual) advantage. These evaluations are validated and sharpened by continual interaction with like-minded individuals. Everyone in this necessarily closed group perceives the campaign selectively, and the sum of such perceptions is a high level of awareness and knowledgeability, even though its scope is narrow. Specific features of the social identity become a basis for political identity, continually reinforced, refined, and amplified by interaction with people in the same social situation.

Apart from facilitating a holistic analysis of interview data, these ideal types were used in an attempt to explore quantitatively the relationship between such self-defining values and social characteristics. After the election three questions were asked of the voters:

> 1. "Suppose you could get to talk to the head of the Democratic party. What would you tell him he should have done to get more votes of people like yourself?"
> 2. "Now, how about the Republicans? What do you think they should have done to get more votes of people like yourself?"
> 3. "Now, thinking back over the campaign and the election, what would you say were the most important things that made you vote the way you did?"

These questions were designed to elicit the voter's self-definition, or better, his self-definition as it emerged in his explanation of his own behavior. Responses were, of course, on a conscious level; the questions do not probe the depth of voter motivation nor did we analyze them for consistency with other expressed attitudes. Responses to these questions were taken as indicators of the respondent's own presentation of himself, and coded in terms of the abstract typology just presented. Specifically, they were coded in terms of which two of the following four themes predominated:

1. The respondent identifies himself with a group that has political interests. (Interest-group Compartmentalizer.)

2. The respondent "rationally" assesses the needs of the situation and weighs the candidates' merits accordingly. (Rational Compartmentalizer.)

3. The respondent expresses emotional and personal attachment to one or more of the leading candidates. (Generalizer.)

4. The respondent declares that the other party is repellent and/or that his own party is superlatively good and that he could never vote for any other party's candidate. (Generalizer.)

For empirical purposes candidate attachment had to be separated from party attachment.

The final tally of the two leading responses[15] of each individual (Table 1) is far from conclusive support of the validity of the typology offered above, but it has suggestive aspects.

TABLE I. SELF-CONCEPT THEMES, BY RACE AND OCCUPATION[1]
(in percentages)

| | Whites | | Negroes | | |
| | Non-Manual Workers | Manual Workers | Non-Manual Workers | Manual Workers | |
Theme					
I. Rational Compartmentalizer	64	54	50	11	
II. Interest-group Compartmentalizer	4	8	69	89	
III. Candidate Attachment	64	77	25	11	
IV. Party Attachment	50	46	50	84	
(Number of individuals)	(28)	(13)	(16)	(19)	(76)

[1]Two highest-ranking themes for each respondent.

The most striking feature of the table is the almost complete absence among whites, of both socio-economic levels, of interest-group identification. Negros of both levels, on the other hand, chose this more often than any other. Most Negroes in our sample viewed political phenomena through the lenses of what politics could do for them. Candidate attachment was very low. The lowest status Negroes were almost all coded in the Interest-group and Party Attachment categories.

Higher status Negroes continued to vote "as Negroes," but they

[15]Coding entailed a ranking by two investigators of the relative importance of all four themes. Coding reliability was maximized by taking the top two, rather than one theme.

also tended, rationalistically, to view situational exigencies as more important in affecting their political behavior than did lower status Negroes. Compartmentalization of the political from other selves, whether on a diffuse partisan or more rational basis, characterized the caste-bound Negroes of both social levels.

White respondents of both social levels stressed situational rationality and Candidate Attachment far more frequently than did the Negroes.[16] Whites of both socio-economic groups are more alike in political identity than like either of the Negro groups, even though the two groups of Negroes differ substantially. The caste boundary thus seems of striking importance in political self-definition, and class differences within the white caste seem less important than they appear in the Negro caste.

It is also notable that the "purely political" theme—rational stress on situational factors—appears with more frequency in the higher status groups. We might perhaps conclude that the tendency in the white group is to start from a generalizing approach, which can be "refined" into a more rationalistic "purely political" approach. Whereas the Negroes, starting with an Interest-group approach, may add this rationalistic "political" approach without abandoning their interest-group identity.

VALUES ABOUT THE CONGRESSIONAL ROLE

There are some political offices for which the general culture and the political system provide relatively clear-cut criteria for voters to use in evaluating candidates. People are at least roughly aware of the nature of the requirements for such offices as president, governor, and mayor. This awareness may be far from adequate in terms of political theories about the enlightened citizenry, but it provides at least some kind of measure for the voter to hold up against particular candidates.

This is not the case for the congressman: the voters we encountered were ambiguous about the scope and content of the congress-

[16]Data presented by Alfred de Grazia, "The Limits of External Leadership over a Minority Electorate," *Public Opinion Quarterly*, 20, 113–128, are similar to these, although his interpretation of them is different. Comparing Negroes and others on why their most memorable election was important to them, he found that Negroes were coded predominantly in two of the seven categories: (1) "because of a man whom I wanted . . . what he would do, would give us," (2) "because of myself (my first election, meant my job)," p. 121. De Grazia interprets Negroes as focusing on *"personal leadership and father-like qualities"* of the candidates, whereas my interpretation stresses *"what the candidate would give us,"* in a more rational sense. De Grazia's data are from a Chicago mayoral election, mine from a national election, which may account for the difference in focus.

man's activities and about principles to be used in evaluating any particular candidate. In an effort to pin down elements perceived in the office and the manner in which they are evaluated, we submitted a set of statements to our respondents[17] that in essence asked them to choose whether they wanted a congressman to follow a "local-oriented" or a more idealistic pattern of values. Specifically, we asked them if they preferred a congressman who:

> (1) is a good lawmaker or (2) is a man you can turn to.
> (3) helps people or (4) does his job.
> (5) is independent of his party or (6) is loyal to his party.
> (7) votes according to his conscience or (8) votes for his people.
> (9) is outstanding in his community or (10) is hard-working.

(These statements represent dilemmas, in this case not mutually exclusive, each requiring the respondent to choose between a congressman who is committed to "his groups" or to his office.) Table 2 presents a tally of the "localistic" choices of our respondents, broken down by race and occupation.

TABLE 2. CHOICES OF "LOCALISTIC" VALUES ABOUT THE ROLE OF CONGRESSMAN, BY RACE AND OCCUPATION (in percentages)

| Pattern Variable | Whites | | Negroes | | |
	Non-Manual Workers	Manual Workers	Non-Manual Workers	Manual Workers	Total Number of Individuals
2. is a man you can turn to	24	43	50	68	(80)
3. helps people	32	43	78	80	(79)
6. is loyal to his party	46	73	83	84	(80)
8. votes for his people	47	64	55	77	(81)
9. is outstanding in his community	30	29	33	16	(81)

On only one of these dilemmas is there general consensus. This is on the final one, where most people, regardless of race or socio-economic level, prefer a congressman who is hard-working to one who is outstanding in the community. Being a congressman appears to most people as a job in and of itself. Whatever the bases to which people attribute local eminence, they are apparently not felt to be adequate for this new, and separate status.

[17]Adapted from Parsons' pattern variables. See Talcott Parsons, *The Social System* (New York: Free Press, 1951), chapter 2, for a discussion of the pattern variables.

On all other issues, however, localistic values about the congressman become commoner in the lower status groups. (In this instance, we consider all Negroes, regardless of occupation, as in a lower social status than all whites.) There is a certain selectivity involved, however; it is only in the lowest status Negro (manual-worker) group that a majority values a "man you can turn to" more than a "good lawmaker," whereas a majority in all categories except the highest (white non-manual workers) values a man who "votes for his people" more than one who simply "does his job." In effect, then, the lower the status of the group, the more it is believed proper to make demands—personal as well as categorical—of the elected official.

There is nothing really new about this finding; it has been demonstrated in both attitude surveys and case studies of lower as compared to higher status voters. It seems reasonable to conclude that there are some values about political phenomena which are based in voters' perception of their own group situation of social, political and economic deprivation. Particularly for the Northern Negro, whose social and economic situation is clearly one of deprivation, the demands that can legitimately and effectively be made in the political sphere assume substantial importance.[18]

On the other hand, social, political, and economic advantage can permit the voter to cope with and value a higher degree of political complexity—to depart from the need to view the candidate as unequivocally "good" or "bad," "for him" or "against him," and to view him as good or bad only in the context of particular political goals. Such people value a high differentiation of candidates and officials from each other and from party "label" (cf. the high value on party independence in Table 2), even though they may not fully be able to follow through on such values. These values do not involve the voter's assessment of his own or his group's political and social needs as much as is the case for the deprived groups.

DISCUSSION

The only surprise in the data on values about the congressman comes when we juxtapose these values with the values about the self presented above. In particular, it seems paradoxical that Negroes, who do not regard themselves as interested in candidates, should show such a demanding attitude toward officials. This seeming paradox can be interpreted as indicating a system of sub-cultural priorities. Among Negroes, categorical political interests are primary; when individual

---

[18]See references cited in Lane, *Political Life,* p. 253, on the Northern Negro's high sense of political efficacy.

officials or candidates are the focus of concern, it is felt legitimate to make both categorical and individual demands of them.

We have attempted here to explore the social concomitants of "purely" political behavior, and to suggest that a situation of either unusual social deprivation or unusual social advantage can become the basis of specifically political values. Each situation (with its attendant sub-culture) tapped in this study has different consequences. Deprivation appears to produce a strong identification with the group, which in turn legitimates the making of demands upon the elected official who can implement the group's political needs. Advantage, on the other hand, tends to produce more traditional "rationality," along with a value on independent and moralistic officials. It is only among the most advantaged group that an "autonomous" political role (in Key and Munger's sense) seems to emerge. A larger sample, permitting finer gradations of social advantage or deprivation, would offer a test of these conceptions.[19]

Values about officials, it is argued, cannot be meaningfully extricated from values about the self on the one hand and the objective social situation of the group on the other hand. Although statements made in this paper must, by the nature of the data, be tentative, and although they refer specifically to minority groups within the society, they attempt to offer a sociological formulation of political roles that is congruent with the traditional thinking of many political scientists. They suggest that the use of more refined techniques to assess and explore interrelations between values held about the self and a series of culturally ranked political objects might begin to fill in some of the conceptual gaps in our thinking about the political institutions of this society.

It may well be that the "centuries of political speculation" are applicable to only a small, but specifiable part of the electorate: it would seem to be the sociologist's job to specify the social characteristics of that part of the electorate. In a broader perspective, Key and Munger highlight the sociologists' neglect of rationality in politics, and of the social factors that facilitate or inhibit the exercise of rationality in the political sphere.

---

[19]The sociological concepts of "relative deprivation" might prove very fruitful in such analysis. Our findings may have been different if we had interviewed "relatively deprived" manual workers, instead of the relatively prosperous ones in our District. See Robert K. Merton, *Social Theory and Social Structure* (New York: Free Press, 1958), pp. 225–386.

23 Mr. Shriver and the Savage Politics of Poverty*

WILLIAM F. HADDAD

Behind the high-minded purposes of the Poverty Program, two groups are locked in a ruthless struggle for power. A report from the hidden battlefield, by an ex-general fresh from combat.

The War Against Poverty represents jobs and money, the historic cement of organizational politics. The federal agency in charge, the Office of Economic Opportunity (OEO), has over a billion and a half dollars this year to spend in cities, towns, and hamlets across the country in the first great surge of federal welfare largess since the New Deal.

Many of the nation's Mayors, Governors, and Congressmen remember the PWA, the WPA, and the other Roosevelt programs that lifted the dead weight of the Depression and, incidentally, built the great urban power bases of the Democratic party. When the War on Poverty was announced, here it seemed, was more of the same.[1]

To be sure, the vocabulary was new. In the 1930s, no one talked of dropouts, disadvantaged children, the problems of the aging, or school integration. But the ingredients of the program seemed familiar enough: contracts to be let; favors to be granted; jobs to be filled, ranging from the top $25,000-a-year administrative posts to thousands upon thousands of "subprofessional" slots designed to involve the poor themselves. It was through such instruments in the 1930s and 1940s that the Democrats built a constituency among the poor and eventually wrested local and national political power from the business elite that had long run the Republican party and the country. In the Poverty Programs, today's city halls and statehouses see the means to reinforce their position.

If they should succeed—and the outcome is as yet by no means clear—then the Poverty Program will be a disastrous failure.

This is a many-front war. About half of OEO's funds have been allocated to programs in which the chain of command runs directly to Washington—such projects as the Job Corps; the preschool Head Start program; and VISTA, the domestic Peace Corps. These programs have gotten under way with no more than what might be considered a normal amount of political infighting.

The rest of the money is earmarked for something called the Community Action Program (CAP). It provides financial support for specific local anti-poverty efforts in rural and urban areas—everything from birth-control clinics to neighborhood law firms where the poor can obtain free legal service. In themselves these seem innocuous endeavors. But Congress wrote into the law a proviso which converts Community Action into a powder keg. Local programs, says the law, must be "developed, conducted, and administered with maximum feasible participation of residents of the areas and members of the groups served."

What this meant in political terms was soon apparent to members of Congress, to Governors and Mayors, and to the established social agencies whose power and influence had long been based on their beneficences to the poor. If now the poor were to be given not merely the money but a voice in expending it, would not their leaders become competitors for power?

[1]OEO has grown so rapidly that few Americans have been able to keep track of all its activities. The cost of OEO-sponsored projects actually represents only a small slice of the nation's poverty budget, which runs annually to some $35 billion in public and private expenditures. Established welfare programs, such as social security, unemployment insurance, and aid to slum schools, cost more than $18 billion a year in federal funds.

The issue became concrete and explosive as the Poverty Program moved into the field. Typical was one West Coast Congressman who found himself besieged by two rival groups contending for control of the local Poverty Program. One included all the respectable social agencies of the area; the other was a collection of radicals—"people from the valley no one ever heard of." When OEO said the latter were more representative of the poor, the harassed Congressman exploded.

"I've known these Community Chest people all my life," he shouted. "They've been helping the poor for generations. They're the best people in town. Who the hell ever heard of the other group?" Nonetheless, OEO insisted on a merger of the two factions.

Philadelphia's Mayor Tate suffered a similar and even ruder shock. When the War on Poverty was announced, he organized a thirteen-man task force—of whom eleven were city officials—to direct it locally. As a starter he asked for $13 million in OEO funds and invited a hundred local civic groups to submit ideas on how to spend the money. The operating agency was to be the Philadelphia Council for Community Advancement, a group financed by the Ford Foundation which was about to close up shop and had already been sharply criticized for its lack of grass-roots support.

Soon Mayor Tate and his plan were under the same fire—from the ADA, CORE, the NAACP, and the press. It seemed, one writer cynically observed, that the plan was "for the poor to be on the payroll at election time." Mayor Tate, however, ignored the protests and took his proposals to Washington, confident that the Johnson Administration would smile on a Democratic Mayor who had moved so speedily to implement the program.

He was stunned when OEO coldly told him that not more than a third of his board could be made up of city officials. Tate pushed all the traditional political buttons but no one jumped. By October, a month before the 1964 election, it was clear that Mayor Tate was coming home empty-handed, and his plight was intolerable. He had promised to help the poor. Now he was charged with letting political and patronage considerations override his humanitarianism. Actually, Mayor Tate was only guilty of doing business as usual. No one told him the rules had been changed.

There was, in the end, nothing to do but compromise by setting up an independent board. It includes five Mayoral appointees, the Presiding Judge of the County Court, twelve representatives of religious, racial, and labor organizations and social agencies, and twelve representatives of the poor. The last were chosen through unique elections in which, as it turned out, only 3 percent of the city's 500,000 poor actually voted. (The poor later complained that they were not informed about the election.) This was a feeble showing—no more than the token emergence of a new power bloc which has only begun to feel its political identity and whose future direction is unknown.

Still it has an unpredictable potential. Sensing this, and smarting from OEO's support of the poor, the U. S. Conference of Mayors last June came close to adopting a resolution accusing OEO of "trying to wreck local government by setting the poor against city hall." (The resolution they adopted contained less explosive language, but the warning was clear.)

This is, in many respects, an ironic charge to be leveled at OEO, which is directed by Sargent Shriver—as political an animal as any Cabinet member in the Johnson Administration. He is, to be sure, many other things besides a politician.

HANDSHAKER WITH A VISION

I have worked with Shriver for over four years—as his Associate Director in the Peace Corps and as his Assistant Director and Inspector General in the Poverty Program. And I still don't know precisely what makes him run.

Like President Johnson, he uses the levers of power with one eye on the press—of which he expects too much objectivity—and the other on Congress, whose moods and necessities he understands to perfection. In the Kennedy style, he dislikes weakness. Signs on his door at the Peace Corps read, "Nice guys finish last," and, "Good guys don't win ball games."

Shriver drives himself and his staff relentlessly. When someone suggested an early-morning meeting "about ten" he shook his head. "By ten o'clock the day is half over," he said.

His liberal social philosophy is rooted in Catholicism. He is both a devout Catholic and one of the Church's most prominent laymen. He is also a highly pragmatic politician, equally comfortable chewing a cigar with a Senator and delivering an inspirational talk to Peace Corps volunteers. He has an insatiable appetite for new ideas.

"That's a great program," he will say. "Now find me the man to run it." In this fashion, for example, the idea of starting in March a preschool program to involve over half a million children in 13,000 centers by July was woven into the incredibly complicated fabric of the Program. It promises to be one of its most popular ventures.

No one doubts that Shriver's concern for the poor is both deep and real. Yet one of his most faithful lieutenants only half-humorously told a reporter, "Shriver doesn't give a damn about people. He uses them. He uses me. When I can't produce, out I go. You don't get two chances here."

This was not said in anger. For Shriver's ability, personal charm, and his quick, Kennedy-esque humor command a rare loyalty. But he runs his office like a big-business corporation. Occasionally he may bestow lavish praise. More often he forgets who accomplished what.

These qualities made him the ideal leader of the Peace Corps. The cause was good, the time was right, and each worker was secure in his own talents. No one in the Peace Corps ever dreamed he could do the job as well as Shriver.

But the Poverty Program was something else again. In the Peace Corps, Shriver set up his own independent sources of information to keep him precisely informed about what was happening in the field, down to the lowest level. Now, in another highly controversial and visible program, he decided to do the same thing. This was my job as Inspector General. "I want to know about our problems before the press or Congress," he said. And, because in fact he so often succeeded in doing this, he was often able to deal with crises before they became catastrophes.

But the organization over which he presided was not made up only of tough, able young men fanatically devoted to their chief. The top layer of his staff were public figures chosen not merely for their competence but because they possessed the impressive credentials which would guarantee Congressional approval. Among them were some who soon had no hesitancy in saying to anyone who would listen that they could do a far better job than Shriver if given a chance. They told the press they resented his constant probing, his reversal of their decisions, his opening to overall staff debate their most sensitive issues. They fought his private line of information.

Shriver certainly appointed no one whose qualifications he did not respect. But personally he seemed more at home with his second-echelon staff—a group of young men in their thirties still full of hope and ideas. When he was working with these Young Turks,[2] trying to get a new project started or a program expedited, the sweet smell of the Peace Corps success lingered on. He is given to inviting the juniors to stir up a competition of ideas within his staff. For some, these methods didn't seem like orderly procedures. Nor were his eighteen-hour days and seven-day weeks conducive to the relaxed cameraderie which makes for harmonious relations on Capitol Hill.

"You know why I really voted for the Peace Corps?" a powerful member of the House Rules Committee told me. "One night I was leaving at 7:30 and there was Shriver, walking up and down the halls of the House Office Building, by himself, looking into all the doors. He came in and talked to me. I still didn't like the program, but I was sold on Shriver. I voted for him.

"Now I can't get him on the phone and we don't see him walking the halls anymore."

[2]They included: Dick Boone, who was trained in Chicago's Back of the Yards; Edgar May, a young Pulitzer Prize-winning reporter; William Mullins, Edgar Cahn, Sam Yette, Chris Weeks, Bob Clampitt.

THE FINE ART OF SAYING NO

Inaccessibility was, of course, only a minor reason for the inevitable hardening of Shriver's relationship with Congressmen and other political leaders. In the Peace Corps he was not dealing in any valuable political currency. None of the politicians showed any eagerness for jobs to teach in Malaya or to build roads in Tanganyika. But the Poverty Program could be translated into political power, if not for them, perhaps for their political opponents. Although Shriver was realistic enough to know he needed the support of the Congress, and could not stir up too many Mayors and Governors, he also knew that the program would fail in its goal if it became—or even appeared to be—a political pork barrel.

So he guarded the independence of his staff, many of whom took a certain pride in saying no to politicians. This was not easy for Shriver. One House leader, for example, sent over the names of thirty-nine "acceptable" candidates for high-level jobs. Not one was accepted. After repeated phone calls from the Hill, Shriver assembled his senior staff. "Isn't there at least one man on that list you can hire?" he asked. The answer was no.

Early in 1965 OEO authorized a grant of $132,000 to the state of Louisiana. Governor John J. McKeithen promptly announced the names of a half-dozen appointees who would run the program. Almost at once the OEO office in Washington was flooded with letters and phone calls from Louisiana complaining that some of the McKeithen appointees were mere political henchmen, and that many were rabid segregationists. White supremacists and civil-rights leaders, labor and business, Negroes and white citizens joined in the protests. But the Governor stubbornly defended his choices. There would be no changes, he said.

While other Southern Governors awaited the outcome with intense interest, Shriver—as is his practice—decided to find out the facts for himself. He sent to Louisiana a team of investigators borrowed from the Internal Revenue Service. These men do not have access to tax records while on a special assignment of this sort. But nonetheless McKeithen cried foul. He appealed to Congress, the White House, the Vice President. Finally he came to Washington to beard Shriver in person. Their appointment was on a Saturday. Because of a sudden heavy snowstorm, Shriver arrived an hour late, an accident which rubbed salt in the wound.

"He [Shriver] obviously didn't like me," McKeithen reported when he got home. "And within thirty seconds after we met, the feeling was mutual. . . . In the first place, he was ten minutes [sic] late. And when he got there, he started looking down his nose at me as if he were trying to shut out some odor that was offensive to him."

Shriver, of course, had no power to tell a Governor whom to appoint. But he was and is free to withhold a grant if he felt it would not be administered effectively. Shortly after their confrontation, McKeithen "reluctantly" sent his hand-picked staff home. A new group was appointed, and some of those most severely criticized were not on it. Poverty money has begun to flow into Louisiana and into other Southern states where OEO's policies have been similarly tested.

WHERE IS THE VICTORY?

Though the War on Poverty can chalk up many victories in the cities and the more industrialized areas, it is stalemated in some rural counties of the South—notably in Appalachia, where the local politicians could teach big-city bosses a trick or two.

In one Appalachian county, for example, the "boss" is a woman Superintendent of Schools. (The school system represents one of the few sources of jobs and contracts in depressed areas.) She is also the wife of the Judge of the Circuit Court, an aunt of the County Court Judge, and mother of the Assistant School Superintendent and State Senator. Another relative runs the county newspaper. The chairman of the Poverty Program is a cashier at the family bank. The executive director of the program was fired recently and replaced by a nephew of the "boss."

This family, according to a local newspaper editor, controls not only school and courthouse patronage, but also highway, parole, probation, and welfare jobs. They also own some school buildings and the garage where the school buses are repaired. To pour poverty funds into this county would merely strengthen the status quo which needs a poverty-stricken constituency just as a Negro politician needs a Negro ghetto as a power base. Unless the Poverty Program can somehow change this pattern, Appalachia will not break out of the cycle of poverty.

There is a dim prospect that this may one day come about. VISTA volunteers and others on the fringes of the Appalachian Poverty Program report that opposition is forming. Some men have lost their livelihood in retaliation.

Meanwhile, of course, the people of Appalachia need help. So do uncounted thousands of young and old, whose plight and existence the Poverty Program has brought to public view.

"I don't get to eat but one time a day," one young woman wrote. "I am so glad when night come [sic] I do not know what to do."

At Camp Catoctin, Maryland, a young Job Corps enrollee failed to eat for several days. When a counselor questioned him, the young man broke down and cried.

"My teeth hurt so much when I eat that I was afraid you would find out and send me home."

A dentist removed seventeen teeth. He found the infection had spread throughout the young man's body, affected his ears and eyes, his weight, his view of life.

In Jacksonville, Florida, the medical examinations for the Head Start (preschool) program revealed that 52 percent of the 1055 children tested were anemic; 45 percent needed dental care; 31 percent had hearing defects; 25 percent had eye troubles; and 5 percent were partially blind.

Programs that disclose needs like these and do something to remedy them are valuable of course. But they do not represent any major victory in the war against poverty. For the fact is that the poor have lost confidence in the traditional "servants of the poor." They no longer follow the leader nor graciously accept the dole society provides them. They intensely dislike the way they have been handled and are beginning to sense that, finally, they are in a position to do something about it.

FINDING A VOICE

This realization is the heart of OEO's Community Action Program. It holds that the poor themselves must identify their problems, devise solutions, and execute these decisions. The main advantage does not come from the school built, or the program successfully completed. It comes from participation, from the use of their own power. It also comes from making mistakes and learning from them.

The Achilles' heel of the Community Action Program is the concept of states' rights—a cliché beloved by aging politicians. For the poor don't fear federal control or centralization. In times of crisis, it has been the federal government that produced for them, not the local authorities. It was so during the depression decade and it continued to be so during the civil-rights decade. On the family farm, in Appalachia, on the Indian reservations, with the Mexican-Americans, with the Negro, with the migrant worker, what little has been done has been done by the federal government, after local authorities failed.

And now, it is only when the federal government—through OEO—injects itself into the local decision-making process, that the poor can again have a real voice in the Poverty Program.

Republicans, in general, find this doctrine wicked if not subver-

WAR ON POVERTY

Cost for First Year: $800 million
Estimated Cost for Second Year: $1.5 billion

	Activities	Scope	Administered by
Youth Programs			
Job Corps	Remedial education, job training for men and women, 16–21, who are out-of-school and out-of-work; provided in residential rural and urban centers where enrollees live, work, learn. The most successful centers are run, under contract, by major industries.	First year: 10,241 in 48 centers Second year: 50,000 in 121 centers	Office of Economic Opportunity (OEO): with staff help from Depts. of Agriculture and Interior
Neighborhood Youth Corps	Part-time hometown work for teen-agers who are (1) out-of-school, or (2) in-school and need money to stay in. Work in newly created jobs in non-profit or municipal agencies. Out-of-school, about 30 hours; in-school, about 15 hours; both at $1.25 an hour.	First year: 278,000 Second: 280,000 (200,000 year-round; remainder in summer programs)	Dept of Labor
College Work Study	Part-time employment for college and university students from low-income families; 15 hours, $1.25 an hour.	First year: 37,482 in 674 schools Summer: 46,000 in 766 schools Second Year: 105,000 in 1,100 schools	Office of Education (Dept. of HEW)
Adult Programs			
Adult Basic Education	Diversified programs for adults 18 and over whose illiteracy impairs ability to get or retain employment.	Two-year total: 105,000	Office of Education: to states
Rural Loans	Loan assistance, management advice to low-income and non-farm rural families and cooperatives not able to get credit elsewhere.	First year: 11,000 indiv. loans, 82 to cooperatives Second year: 15,500 indiv., 350 co-ops.	Farmers Home Administration (Dept. of Agriculture)

WAR ON POVERTY (continued)

Adult Programs	Activities	Scope	Administered by
Small Business Loans	Small Business Development Centers to provide loans and management advice to small businesses which cannot get conventional financing. Emphasis on minority groups.	16 SBDCs have been funded; 10–15 under way	Small Business Administration
Work Experience	Work and training for unemployed heads of families and others, to prepare them for regular employment and self-sufficiency. Usually for people on relief rolls.	First year: 88,700 (276,700 dependents) Second year: 109,300 (327,900 dependents)	Welfare Administration (Dept. of HEW)
Community Programs			
Community Action Program	The major component of the War on Poverty. Financial support for local anti-poverty programs in urban and rural areas, on Indian reservations, etc. Local programs vary but usually include child development, remedial education, literacy courses, day care, legal aid, neighborhood services, consumer education, services for aged. Some birth-control programs.	First year: 3,169 grants Second year: 4,200 grants	OEO: to local community
State Technical Assistance	Community Action funds to states to assist smaller communities to plan programs.	First year: 47 states Second year: 50 states	OEO: to states
Head Start	Most successful undertaking to date. Summer preschool child-development centers providing education, medical care, nutrition. Will become year-round under local Community Action boards.	Summer, 1965: 561,000 children 13,344 centers Second year: no estimate	OEO: to Head Start centers

WAR ON POVERTY (continued)

Community Programs	Activities	Scope	Administered by
Migrant Program	Special needs of migratory agricultural workers and families: housing, sanitation, education, day care.	First year: 100,000 people Second year: no estimate, funds increased	OEO: to local community or organization
Indians	Programs for improving conditions on reservations.	Grants to 25 reservations	OEO: to tribal councils
Legal Services to the Poor	Neighborhood legal firms to provide free legal help to indigent. Will come under Community Action Program.	Being developed	OEO: to local community
Aged	"Foster grandparents" for infants, older children, and the retarded in institutions. Home health aides and home-makers for bedridden old people and broken homes.	18,000 old people in 20 states working average of 4 hours a day 5 days a week	OEO: to local community
Consumer Education	Provides information on how to shop, to avoid exploitation. Will come under Community Action Program.	Being developed	OEO: to local community
Research and Demonstration	Moneys made available for experimental ideas.	First year: $14,600,000 Second year: $75 million	OEO: to local community or university
Volunteer Programs			
VISTA	Domestic Peace Corps: one-year service for men and women 18 to 80.	First year: 1,000 in 59 projects Second year: 4,000 in 1,400 projects	OEO

MAJOR FEDERAL WELFARE PROGRAMS OUTSIDE OF OEO

Estimated Annual Cost: $18,378,000,000[1]

Cash Payments ($14 billion)	Food ($268 million)	Education ($2 billion)
Social security	Stamps	Aid to slum schools
Old-age assistance	Distribution	Teacher corps[2]
Unemployment insurance		Aid to impacted schools
Aid to dependent children		Federal scholarships
Medical		Manpower training
Relief		

Housing ($110 million)	Regional ($2 billion)
Rent subsidies[2]	Economic development
Public housing	Appalachia

[1] Expenditures by state and local governments and private philanthropy run to an additional $15 billion annually.
[2] No funds as yet appropriated by Congress.

sive. To them the Poverty legislation sounded like a computerized version of the New Deal, and they reacted accordingly. Equally bewildered though not hostile are the graying 1936 liberals who can't quite figure out what is happening. They still hold the charter of liberalism but, like the toothless Legionnaires of World War I, they have lost their troops. The Poverty Program has driven the final wedge between what is happening in the streets and what is happening in the plush offices of the labor unions, in the higher echelons of government, and in the remoteness of the university.

The 1936 liberal has learned to compromise with city hall. As far as the poor are concerned, he is as much a part of the Establishment as big business. And today the minority poor picket the blatant racial segregation of some unions.

The liberals still invoke the names of their heroes (my heroes). But there is little applause. Their children have their own heroes.

Not long ago, Shriver visited the Job Corps camp at Kilmer, New Jersey, and, as is his custom, he began inviting the enrollees to express their opinions. "Shriver was great," a reporter told me later. "He had a tremendous rapport with the kids. He lost them only once."

"When?"

"When he began asking them who they thought should come to visit their camps. They named Cassius Clay, the disc jockey Murray the K, and people like that.

"Shriver then suggested some well-known liberals. He asked if they would like to see A. Philip Randolph. 'Who's he?' the kids asked.

"Shriver told them, but it was obvious that they had never heard of the fight for unionism. Whitney Young. No. He kept naming people, but he lost the crowd. He was speaking a language they didn't understand."

Rejecting the liberal heroes of the past, the poor have so far not developed strong or noteworthy leaders of their own. Their society is wrapped in frustration and disappointment and they are cynical, hostile, turbulent. Many have been chased from slum to slum by the liberal Urban Renewal Program. Even young men who arrive hopefully at Job Corps camps feel the Poverty Program will disappear after the news stories have been written and the pictures are taken.

The poor are wary of new programs and offers of help. They've had their hopes raised before, only to find the liberal programs were for someone else. Now they're determined to make their own mistakes with their own leaders.

It is easy to romanticize the poor, but, in fact, poor Negroes can be exploited by their own as easily as by "whitey" downtown. Some are as reckless with power as were some of the Italian and Irish leaders who first captured the Democratic party at the local level. For example, this fall, when New York's District Attorney Frank Hogan subpoenaed the books of Haryou-Act, the multimillion Poverty Program in Harlem, and the New York *Herald Tribune* printed the story, Negroes from Harlem promptly picketed the newspaper, condemned Hogan, and threatened violence.

"There has never been a grand-jury investigation in Harlem when black babies were cremated in tenement fires," said Livingston Wingate, the program's highly paid director. "This investigation is a smear tactic by forces opposed to the War on Poverty. The only thing that stands between the black youth of Harlem and the guns of the outer society is Haryou-Act. Remove Haryou-Act and you're asking for a holocaust."

The poor are the newest minority, maybe the last minority, to be melted into the pot of democracy. If they follow history, they will first maintain a separationist policy. Next they will press against the Establishment. Soon they will have a wedge and later a slice. Eventually they will become part of the Establishment and defend its goals and their position.

For all the irritation the Poverty Program is causing, the social revolution it is bringing about has narrow, almost middle-class horizons. It has its roots, as Professor Richard A. Cloward of Columbia said, "in relatively moderate ideologies—self-help, local autonomy, democratic collective action, and the importance of ethnic separation. The struggle, in short, is in the tradition of urban politics and nothing more."

Shriver maintains that "involvement of the poor must mean giving them effective power, a respected and heeded voice, and genuine representation in all aspects of the program and at all stages in the significant decision-making processes."

In its first year, the Poverty Program has held off the other contestants of power so the poor could gain their voice, so they could become involved, so their needs can be met by their decisions. From here on in, it cannot aristocratically rise above politics and hope for the best. It must enter the struggle and win the battle.

24 Shriver's Limited War: How Much Has It Altered the Social Structure?*

SIDNEY LENS

"The national war on poverty," wrote Sargent Shriver recently, "is now in its eighteenth month. And we are winning that war. Not as rapidly as we would like to but faster than we thought possible. . . ." We have taken, he says, "the first giant stride . . . of the journey." This is flawless institutional advertising, sturdily supported by round-number statistics.

In this year and a half jobs have been provided for a half million teenagers through Neighborhood Youth Corps projects; 5000 grants have been made for Community Action Projects; 600,000 pre-school youngsters have benefited from the Head Start program; more than 30,000 people of various ages have indicated a desire to join Volunteers in Service to America (VISTA); 300,000 teenagers are trying to get into the Job Corps and 20,000 are actually in the process

*Reprinted by permission of the author and publisher from *Commonweal,* June 1, 1966.

of being trained. All-told this initial effort "has reached more than three million poor people directly with jobs and other kinds of services they did not have before." Together with the improvement in the economy it has resulted in a decrease of the number of poor in this short time by a whopping 2.2 million.

The figures are impressive, indicating that Shriver has squeezed quite a bit out of a $2 billion expenditure. But what does it really add up to? The 300,000 jobs made by the Neighborhood Youth Corps are temporary. And so is the status of those added to payrolls only because of the additional $12.8 billion spent on the Vietnam war, and the 300,000 more drafted into the armed services. How many of the poor who have become "un-poor" as a result of these exceptional circumstances will remain that way, Mr. Shriver does not discuss. Furthermore, welfare community action projects, youth work, job training and similar activities are nothing particularly new. If they are being increased and accelerated that is all to the good but, as Christopher Jencks observes in the *New Republic* the whole effort "consists almost entirely of old programs aimed at traditional objectives." In a sense what is happening is that certain services and charities are being nationalized. As of 1964 only one out of every five poor 7.3 million, was getting public assistance payments. The anti-poverty program, therefore, has a large field in which to graze. But is it really abolishing poverty or offering a few palliatives to 34 million poor whose poverty is becoming hereditary?

Unemployment among the Negro poor, for instance, is twice that of the whites, and teenage Negroes in particular are finding it so difficult to find work that almost a quarter of them lack jobs. Shriver's figures would be more convincing if they told us how much of this problem has been whittled away. Instead of questionable statistics it would have been wiser to concentrate on *social patterns*. How much social change has the anti-poverty program brought about? How much has it altered the *structure* of a society that has bred poverty all these years?

As of last year the one-fifth of the population at the bottom of the ladder, those earning less than $2500, received only 4.1 percent of the national cash income while the one-fifth at the top, with incomes of $10,000 a year or more, hauled away 51.3 percent. The share of the lower fifth has actually declined somewhat. How does the anti-poverty program propose to reverse this trend? A simple solution would be to drastically re-distribute income so that the share of the lower fifth would be, say 12 percent and the upper fifth 43 percent—that would be a true anti-poverty program. But that is not at all what Mr. Shriver or the President is contemplating.

Mollie Orshansky, writing in the *Social Security Bulletin*, claims that it would take only $12 billion to bring the poor up to $3000 a year per family, and if you add the "near-poor" (those earning less than $78 a week for a family of four), the total would be $21.5 billion. Last year the gross national product went up by $48 billion. Why then doesn't the government *redistribute income* so that more of the Gross National Product would accrue to those in need?

The answer of course is that this runs counter to President Johnson's philosophy. The President is willing to spend a billion and a half a year for the poor, but he evidently has no intention of changing the *relationship* between poor and rich. The $11.5 billion tax cut of 1964, for instance, provided a boon of $2.5 billion for business (in addition to tax benefits in previous years of $5 billion annually), plus large savings for affluent individuals. Those in the $2000 to $4000 bracket were given a reduction of 13.6 percent; those in the $200,000 bracket, 23 percent. The one-eighth of the taxpayers who earn $10,-000 a year or more harvested 45 percent of the tax cut. A little for the poor, a lot for the rich seems to have been the underlying motif. But what sense did it make to introduce an anti-poverty program when far more could have been accomplished not only for the poor but the economy as a whole by giving the *whole* tax cut to the lower-income groups. Not only would many millions of those below $60 a week have raised themselves above the poverty level, but because most of the saved taxes would have gone into the purchase of consumer goods (instead of winding up in bank vaults or investment funds) the economy itself would have been given a much greater spurt.

Other measures that could have relieved poverty include:

1. Covering the two million agricultural workers with the benefits of the National Labor Relations Act, so that they could organize into powerful unions.

2. Abolishing the "secondary boycott" provisions of the Taft-Hartley Act so that strong unions could come to the aid of farm, service, retail and other poor workers.

3. Raising the minimum wage law appreciably—say to $2 an hour—and above all including not seven but all 17 million of those not covered.

4. Raising unemployment compensation to 80 or 100 percent of average wages (a measure once contemplated by members of Rex Tugwell's team during the New Deal), and making compensation indefinite as long as unemployment lasts.

5. Guaranteeing those incapable of work an adequate annual income as a matter of right without the degrading tests of local welfare agencies.

6. Providing service jobs at union wages for the four percent of the work force still unemployed.

7. Improving social security so that the aged could live at their previous living standards.

The effect of such measures of course would be to redistribute income, to make our society more egalitarian. This would be a real "first giant stride . . . of the journey," but neither Mr. Johnson nor Mr. Shriver are thinking in these terms. Their sights are focused on *ameliorating* want, not extirpating poverty.

Mr. Shriver is certainly not, as some extremists say, a capitalist ogre, nor has President Johnson failed to deal with some of the points raised here, such as increasing minimum wages, widening the coverage, adding to social security. But philosophically they are wedded to the idea of improving the lot of the poor without disturbing the prerogatives of the rich.

Such a philosophy presents many pitfalls. First of all there is the matter of economic downturn. The present boom, mostly fed by the fuel of military expenditures, can come to a quick end if peace should "break out," or for other reasons. History proves that in recessions (or depressions) the burden is shifted on the powerless poor. There is no guarantee that this won't happen again, for there are no mechanisms in our social structure—such as guaranteed jobs or guaranteed incomes— that offer the impoverished a floor of protection.

Secondly, it is not clear how the anti-poverty program proposes to alter the patterns of dependency that are now such a distinguishing characteristic of being poor. The man in want who now depends on social workers from his welfare office will soon be depending more on social workers and others subsidized by the national government. Theoretically the poor themselves are supposed to be a major part of the decision-making process in the war against poverty. But in reality they are almost universally excluded. They remain, as before, powerless—dependent.

Here, alas, is a pivotal point that the federal administration will not, perhaps cannot, grapple with. When all is said and done the essence of a war against poverty is power—power to force through economic concessions and hold onto them, power to desegregate segregated communities, power to achieve equal education, power to abolish job-sharks, power to break into high-paying skilled jobs, power to unionize service and agricultural jobs, power to enforce housing codes and eliminate slums, power to break "patterns of dependency" and the degrading practices of relief and social agencies. To gain such power the poor find themselves arrayed against the local political barons—the very elements who are sheltered under the President's wing. Here, unfortunately, is the ultimate contradiction of the anti-poverty program, that it buttresses local power elites whose power must be weakened if the status quo is really to be changed.

Consider Chicago, where the Chicago Committee on Urban Opportunity has received more money per capita than any other major city. Here the program is squarely locked into Mayor Richard J.

Daley's politics of the status quo, and is headed by a "safe" Negro named Deton J. Brooks. Brooks sees to it that jobs with his agency are doled out as patronage to Daley's machine and that the more militant groups representing the poor are screened out of decision-making. The Woodlawn Organization (TWO), a coalition of 104 organizations representing 33,000 Negro families, was left out of the steering committee that presumably guided CCUO's destiny. So was JOIN (Jobs or Income Now), a project of the Students for a Democratic Society, which works among poor whites. So were other forces. On the original steering committee of 25, only two were Negro and no one active in the civil rights movement. Most were either businessmen or representatives of public agencies.

The bitterness of many poor at Chicago's program is reflected in TWO's paper. "The Chicago Committee on Urban Opportunity," it says, "is the colonial power, and we black people are its 'natives.' " Millions of dollars, TWO claims, are going into programs that "do nothing to break up Chicago's ghetto. Little jobs are being handed out by the thousands, with the obvious intent of making people more content with staying exactly where they are. Is any poverty money being spent to crack the segregating housing market? Is any poverty money being used to crack segregated school boundaries? Is any poverty money being spent to force the craft unions to admit Negroes? No, the men who make the decisions about where poverty money goes in Chicago do not want to break up the ghetto. The program handed down to Chicago Negroes really robs us of our dignity and manhood. The ghetto gates are barred shut."

TWO experts ask why the anti-poverty program does not take aggressive action to move large numbers of Negroes into white areas, or why there is not more work available for them in skilled union crafts. A few jobs or job training, they say, is meaningless unless the *pattern of power* in a city like Chicago are broken down. But that is precisely what CCUO and Daley have no intention of doing. The anti-poverty program, instead of adding to the power of the poor Negro and the poor white, makes him even more dependent on those who have kept him in second-class status for decades. "The so-called War on Poverty," says TWO, "is actually a war against the poor."

Perhaps it was not meant to be this way. Perhaps Mr. Shriver—certainly some of the people around him—intended it to be otherwise. But the poor are not gaining political power through the anti-poverty program; on the contrary they are becoming even more frustrated. And without political power they cannot batter down the facade of slums, miseducation, job discrimination, that keeps them in want and inferior status. As one JOIN leader puts it: "The anti-poverty program is just another form of handout." It does not foster social change; it has become another device for sustaining the status quo.

25 Rethinking Our Social Strategies*

ROBERT A. LEVINE

I

As one reflects on the troubled history of the "war on poverty" and
other social programs of the Great Society, it becomes clear that the
problem is not so much the nature of the programs as it is difficulties
of administration. What has been happening, in fact, is that new goals
and new programs are proliferating faster than improvements in
administrative procedures. More dismaying, they are increasing far
faster than the number of competent administrators and planners. This
proves that good ideas are relatively easy to come by but are not easily
incarnated in workable programs—especially large programs involving
millions of people.

Given the fact that we do not want to abandon the goals, what we
have to do is to design a system which is sensitive to defects in
administration—a system which is likely to work even with imperfect

*Reprinted by permission of the author and publisher from *The Public Interest,* 10
(Winter 1968). Copyright   1968 by National Affairs, Inc.

planning and less than perfect managers. What this may mean is that a substantial portion of the *operation* of the Great Society programs could be turned over to private organizations and local communities, while *policy guidance* and the setting of conditions which will bring private and local operators to operate in the interests of public policy remain in the hands of the national government. If "creative federalism" has any meaning, it should proceed by this kind of division of labor.

II

To some extent, "creative federalism" has been confused with decentralization. In fact, even for many liberals decentralization has become a new slogan, if not a new panacea. But the problem is not decentralization as such, but the kinds of incentives one can offer people and institutions to carry out programs which are socially desirable. The argument has been made that decentralized operations move decision-making closer to the place where decisions are applied. It implies that such decisions will be more responsive to particular conditions and cases. But this is not always so. Some of the worst bureaucratic systems are the most decentralized. A major problem with the Public Assistance structure, for example, is that decisions are made by the caseworker, case by case, and often in quite arbitrary fashion.

Nor is there much of a case for simply turning over federal programs or federal funds to the states. Some states simply might not be interested in going along with a policy, even if this policy is approved by a national majority. Categorical grants of federal funds, giving the states wide discretion so long as they use the money for designated purposes, may be possible for certain limited areas, as in education; but block grants for purposes as broad as getting rid of poverty, for example, will be relatively ineffective in states which are not terribly interested in getting rid of poverty—and these are by and large the poorest states.

The key, then, may be not decentralization as such, but the design of a system in which people make decisions for themselves in their own best interests, but in which the sum total comes out as a net increment to the social good—something like Adam Smith's "invisible hand." And if incentives or rules can be designed to induce the many "prime movers" in business, the states, and the localities to move in the same socially desirable direction at the same time, the cumulative impact of this movement would surely be greater than the power of the federal government to accomplish the same ends by administrative means.

III

In considering the Great Society programs, let us distinguish two approaches which we shall call simply *the more* and *the less* administrative approach. Both require national planning, because the results have to be aggregated to national levels. But they diverge substantially in the way they are carried out.

The highly administrative approach is one in which programs are planned in detail. A master plan sets forth the levels of programs, this is supplemented by subordinate plans, and these in turn are supplemented by plans at the operating level—in industries, plants, states, cities, school districts, local communities, etc. All these plans must be coordinated with one another to insure consistency. And all this takes many planners—probably more than are available, certainly far more than can be used economically, given other demands on planning capabilities.

The less administrative approach sets general rules to guide decisions, and then counts on existing "natural" economic and social forces—such as market conditions, incentives, and bargaining power—for their execution.

By and large, those programs which have stressed detailed planning and detailed administration have either not worked, or have worked only on a scale which was very small compared to the size of the problem. Consider the following examples of the highly administrative approach:

The National Recovery Administration

Probably the most detailed and comprehensive attempt to make the economy work by elaborate plans and rules was the NRA, initiated by Franklin D. Roosevelt in 1933. Under the NRA, each industry was to prepare compendious structural, operating, and pricing plans which were to be ratified by the federal government. Until NRA was declared unconstitutional in 1935, it attempted to do just that. Its major impact on American economic and social policy was Section 7A, which was translated into the National Labor Relations Act. But in no other respect did the detailed regulation of prices and market policy work at all.

Price Control and Rationing

These devices, during the Second World War, undoubtedly did keep price levels below where they would otherwise have been (given the other policies of the time); but the exigencies of detailed administration encouraged such abuse that the whole system became completely unworkable after the end of the war.

Public Assistance

Public assistance, which started out with high hopes of designing aid to fit individual needs in the 1930s, has become a brutal system of degrading investigation and "big brotherism," as well-meaning social workers have tried to apply detailed rules to individual cases.

Public Housing

Public housing has created and perpetuated ghettoes while replacing old slums with new ones. The major reason for this is that the designers of public housing would not—*and could not*—think through all the implications of their carefully planned idea.

MDTA Training

Training under the Manpower Development Training Act has worked in many cases to retrain those affected by structural economic change, and in fewer cases to give initial training to those needing basic skills. But because it has depended on a detailed system of negotiating the setting up of institutional courses and On-the-Job-Training slots, it has had to remain quite small relative to existing needs. There are simply not enough administrators to set up the number of small projects adequate to reach a major portion of those in greatest need with the types of programs that they require.

By contrast, the examples of the less administrative approach— the setting of general rules within which people can move freely in their own interest—show substantially more success. For example:

Fiscal and Monetary Policy

There can be little doubt that the sophisticated use of fiscal and monetary policy in ironing out economic fluctuations has worked far better than the price control—wage control—rationing systems of wartime. By controlling the aggregate demands on the economy, but allowing millions of individuals to "reallocate" their own choices, fiscal and monetary policy have been able to maintain prosperity with sufficient price stability.

The Income Tax

The income tax system, with all its loopholes and abuses, is an effective way of collecting revenue by setting general rules, and allowing people to apply them to themselves. To the extent that the system has not worked, it has been because of the many specific exceptions written into the law, and—in the case of higher incomes— because of the move toward an "administered" system. The income tax system shines particularly in contrast with the local property tax systems, which have depended upon detailed administration—individual assessment by external authority—and which have been badly abused and have provided insufficient revenues.

The NLRB

Finally, there is the National Labor Relations Board, which illustrates either the difficulties of the more administrative approach or the advantages of the less administrative, depending upon what one considers its major objective to be. The Wagner Act set up an administrative system to enforce industrial justice. This worked moderately well, but was subject to substantial abuse because of its detailed administrative rulings. As a result, it was drastically amended by the Taft-Hartley Act of 1948, which complicated the administrative system considerably. As administrative attempts to deliver justice, both laws were mixed in their effects. But as attempts to change the structure of industry by changing the rules of collective bargaining in the marketplace, they were outstandingly successful. For the laws pushed the parties to set the conditions of a "just" bargain between themselves, rather than laying down the outlines of a "just" (or "unjust") contract by government fiat. They did affect the outcome of the bargain, but only by shifting the balance of bargaining power—Wagner toward labor and Taft-Hartley toward business.

These contrasting set of examples argue strongly and pragmatically for the more general approach. The detailed administrative approach does not work for clear enough reasons—which start with the impossibility of writing detailed rules to fit every case, and end with the lack of highly trained people to administer every case, assuming even that an administrative solution is possible.[1]

Let us consider then, the characteristics of a less administrative approach to current problems:

1. Programs should be wholesale rather than retail. Public administrators should not set up many small carefully-designed programs;

---

[1]Some counterarguments however, should not be ignored. The less administrative approach may have all too visible "wastage." A historical example of this comes from the land grant system of encouraging railroad building in the last half of the 19th century. Huge profits were made at the public expense—but the railroads were built. One argument against income maintenance programs is that some people will "abuse" the system by sitting on their porches and living on the dole when they "should" be working. And they might. The question is whether these abuses are more or less tolerable than the alternative—a system of detailed investigation of the public assistance type.

individual "operators," large and small, should be encouraged to set up programs which conform to the general rules.

2. Programs must provide incentives for such operators to set up individual programs in their own self-interest. Indeed, such incentives for individuals to do voluntarily what is socially desirable is central to any general system.

3. These incentives should work largely through the market. This does not mean that business enterprise is in some sense superior to public officialdom. On the contrary; the advantage of working through the marketplace is that you don't need superior people and superior plans to achieve your goal.

4. The "market" need not be understood merely as the competitive market of classical economics. The concept of the market here is a broad one, which includes the "bargaining markets" discussed by John Kenneth Galbraith as well as the "trading markets" discussed in standard economic texts. A very powerful tool which can be used by government is to set up conditions which strengthen the bargaining power of designated groups, as was the case with the trade unions under the Wagner Act.

As to the kind of rules necessary for operation:

1. They should be, as far as possible, self-applied rules. As with the rules of the income tax system, they should be set up in a way which makes it reasonable to expect that people will apply these rules to themselves. Self-applied rules are doubtless subject to abuse; the self-employed evade taxes more frequently than do those whose income is withheld by their employers. But the alternative of detailed snooping is worse than a certain amount of tax evasion.

2. In order to minimize abuses, the general rules will have to be enforced—but they can be enforced as the tax rules are, by exception. That is, we assume that most people comply, and we check up only on a random sample basis. Together with strong penalties for noncompliance, such a system keeps the tax system workable.

3. Rules are more workable if they are of the "don't" variety rather than of the "do" variety. Individuals will more readily tolerate rules—or limits—on what they can't do than specific directions on what they have to do. An example here—a perverse one—is the recent political failure of many open housing laws. Although these laws are essentially of the "don't" variety, the campaigns against them have been cleverly designed to make them appear as "do" laws. The open-housing opponents have contended that such laws would force people to sell or rent homes to others chosen by the government. This charge is false—the laws are "don't" laws preventing a certain kind of behavior rather than directing another kind—but the proponents of open housing have not been able to make this clear.

Finally, an additional characteristic of a general system is that where sophisticated and detailed rules are necessary, these should apply to a small group of controlling interests, rather than to the populace at large. Monetary policy, for example, does not limit what any single individual can spend, but its operation does depend in part upon a detailed set of rules applied to a sophisticated set of people, the bankers. Where necessary, strategic groups can be singled out for detailed application of rules, but this should be the exception.

IV

The setbacks of the War on Poverty arise, in part, from the difficulties of applying a specific and administered program to more than 80 million poor individuals.[2] The resources of welfare workers, teachers, trainers, community organizers, have been insufficient. The ends have also been limited.

Had vastly larger sums been available, the distinctions between more and less administered programs would have tended to disappear, simply because it would have become possible to overwhelm the problem of poverty with waves of money. This is the story of American defense policy. What if billions are spent on programs which would be considered "wasteful" by the standards applied to the War on Poverty? The remaining billions still buy an awful lot of defense.

Lacking such sums, however, what we might be able to achieve is a long-run redesign of the Poverty Program to reduce the amount of detailed administration, and to provide more incentives for individuals to develop their own programs.

Such a redesign would begin not with a specific service-providing program, but with a specific application of a general principle relevant to any program. Public decisions in the United States are arrived at in large measure by a political bargaining process, and one reason for the past lack of services of all sorts to the poor has been their weakness in this bargaining process. The influence of the poor has not been felt in the education process, therefore poverty-area schools have been treated poorly; the poor have not been felt in legal circles, therefore justice for the poor has been unequal; and so forth. Typically, until recently, the constituents of any government agency consisted of its clientele and its own bureaucracy. Since the poor were not the major

[2]It should be made clear that the War on Poverty and the programs of the Office of Economic Opportunity are not identical. The funds budgeted for OEO, about $2 billion, form less than 10 percent of the total $25 billion requested for the War on Poverty with the remainder ranging from education to old age assistance. Many rules discussed here have already been applied to OEO programs as such, particularly in the Community Action area.

clientele of any agency, their bargaining power was negligible. The creation of an independent anti-poverty agency, the Office of Economic Opportunity, and the Community Action Agencies, which are its analogs at the local level, has begun to change this situation. An independent agency, with the poor as its sole clientele, and with a bureaucracy which is still relatively new and idealistic, is a *sine qua non* of an effective war on poverty. Hopefully, as the bureaucracy hardens with age (as it inevitably will) the bargaining power of the poor themselves will increase to the point where the additional bargaining power of the new bureaucracy will not be necessary. Until that time—and it has not yet been reached—independent poverty agencies at the national and at the local levels, with their independence maintained through independent sources of funding, are essential.

The service-delivery programs of the War on Poverty are divisible into four major categories: job programs; individual improvement programs, primarily educational; community betterment programs and income maintenance. This is how they might be redesigned:

1. *Jobs* A tight economy, providing jobs for anyone who can be trained, is essential to any anti-poverty program. Given this, more training and better provision for those who cannot be trained are needed. Instead of a training program which depends upon specific small-scale projects and which is never likely to reach the bulk of those in need, we should encourage business through profit incentives, as well as through exhortation.

a. Such programs have been rejected in the past because, in addition to subsidizing training, they provide a direct subsidy to business. Nevertheless, such a subsidy seems to be the only way to provide enough training really to reach the population in need. To distinguish this from proposals to subsidize training in general through a tax credit, the subsidy should be confined to trainees who declare themselves poor by affidavit, who have inferior employment records, or who otherwise can be identified by a simple system. Broad training programs, not focused specifically on the poor, we have found, help the poor but little. A variation on the subsidy theme might be a training insurance program, to insure those firms who train the poor against losses due to turnover of trainees before the company has had its training investment returned.

b. A general "mobility subsidy," workable through tax credits, should be given to anyone moving to take a new job. Rather than the current types of experimental mobility programs, which use a social-work approach—taking someone in a depressed area by the hand and leading him to a skill-shortage area—these would be simple but substantial money allowances to people who move. Money would inevitably be provided to those who don't need it and who would have moved anyway; but the alternatives are either the program remaining far too small or a vast bureaucratic organization.

c. A public employment program for those who could not get jobs any other way. A substantial portion of the hardcore poor are not likely to be able to get jobs in the competitive market *even after absorbing all the training they can.* A public job is a preferable alternative to income maintenance for those who can work and need work for their own self-respect. Such a proposal—that the government be the "employer of last resort"—was made last year by the President's Commission on Technology, Automation and Economic Progress. It found that more than five million useful jobs—in schools, museums, hospitals, and parks—could be filled if the money were made available to these institutions. Under this system, the government would not "employ" the poor, but make the monies available to nonprofit public institutions to do so.

What we are eliminating here are all the current anti-poverty training programs which have been laboriously negotiated, employer by employer, and substituting for them broad financial incentives for training and mobility. The one detailed program which might be retained is the small-scale, high quality program such as the Job Corps, which has been shown by cost-benefit analysis to work; such a program is directed at a crucial target and group—eligible boys number no more than 200,000 at a given time.

2. *Individual Improvement—Education* We do not really know how to aid the poor educationally. This is not to say that we should not continue to experiment. But the payoff is likely to be very long in coming. Two general programs are suggested.

a. A substantial expansion of federal funding for slum schools. Whatever else they need, most school systems need much more money to do anything for the underprivileged. Such funds might be provided through the broad unstructured approach of Title I of the Elementary and Secondary Education Act; or they might be provided by the "Follow-Through" approach, in which kids who have been in Head Start get additional aid in their early school years. The latter has the virtue of reinforcing the gains which Head Start has already demonstrated it can bring about. In any case, however, the real payoff may be a generalized "Hawthorne" effect wherein the schools, children, and teachers all improve because they know the nation as a whole is interested and committed. This commitment, however, must continue to be expressed by directing such broad aid toward poor children and their schools, as Title I now does, rather than diluting the commitment by a program of general federal aid to all schools, rich and poor.

b. Parallel to this, in higher education, would be a GI Bill type of scholarship program. Unlike the GI bill, this would be limited to those with low incomes, but it should apply to all those capable of doing college work.

The major change here is in the de-emphasis of the search for the "right" educational program which will solve all of the educational deficiencies of the poor. We do not abandon evaluation of alternatives, but we do abandon the effort to direct the money in the "precisely right" direction concentrating instead on the task—difficult enough—simply teaching the poor.

3. *Community Improvement* This portion of the program would be redesigned in the following respects:

a. In the housing field, we want to provide more and better housing, and to desegregate. The first objective could be achieved by substantial incentives to private business to build better housing for the poor. The current "turnkey" pilot projects in which public housing is built by private firms, who then turn the key over to public housing authorities provide an example. As to desegregation, there is little doubt that compulsory open housing has slowed down. We should still seek open housing laws, but failing that we can seek legislation compelling realtors and commercial sellers to deal on a nondiscriminating basis. (Such an approach to the realtor is an example of a measure applied to a small group of controlling interests, rather than one applied to the entire population.) This approach would substitute for massive public housing projects—which have not worked well in providing decent housing and not at all in ending desegregation—for urban renewal, and for detailed "planned growth" (which still seems to mean Negro removal).

b. A major part of the War on Poverty has been, and should continue to be, the creation of self-controlled and self-directed community institutions among the poor. A continued and expanded neighborhood center program could bring people and services together, and create the "nodes" around which community institutions could be built. Such a concentration could avoid the dilemma inherent in current programs which give the appearance of using federal money for the direct creation of new local political power groups. Political power is implicit in such organization, but so far as federal programs are concerned, it should remain implicit. Such institutions and such political power constitute "black power" in the constructive, self-help, coalition-politics sense.

c. Legal programs to help the poor understand their rights.

d. Health programs would be created around the neighborhood center, by holding out financial incentives for doctors, nurses, technicians, etc. to enter the center.

e. Family planning programs, making information and devices available to whomever wants and needs them.

4. *Income Maintenance* In our nonbureaucratic program there would be an income maintenance program of the negative income tax or family allowance type. This may be the single most important part of the program. For half or more of poor families, work opportunity has little meaning; the family head is usually aged or disabled or a woman, or suffers from some disability or other. Yet a simple system

of income maintenance for these families can mean opportunity for their children. The same is true for the children of families of the working poor. Money helps. But current public assistance systems are spotty, cover only a quarter of the poor, and discourage work incentives by taking away a dollar of assistance for a dollar earned. They represent the worst in highly administered systems, from the investigation of the "man in the house" to the social worker's decision about whether the family should or should not buy a new blanket. What is needed is a national income maintenance system—a system which covers all the poor, one which works by simple affidavit (enforced, as are the income tax laws, by exception), which separates services from income maintenance, and above all allows retention of part of earnings, as an incentive to earn and thus get off welfare. Working through the tax system or the social security system, it could substitute rules for administration, and simplicity for insane complexity.

What is being suggested is a "liberal" program in that it works for the abolition of poverty. But it is "conservative" in that it seeks to do this largely by financial incentives and avoiding as much as possible detailed administration. From 1933 to 1940, the social needs of this country were so great that almost any program could prove effective. From 1940 to 1960, there were few new social programs, but the general progress of the economy achieved many of the social goals of the time. In 1960 and 1964 the country resolved to clean up many of the residual social problems left over in a prosperous economy—but we are now witnessing a reaction against the administration of such programs. Perhaps we can continue to move toward the same goals, but to do so in a way which is more agreeable to the still powerful urge of Americans toward individual liberty.

26 The Liberalization of the American Churchman*

HENRY PRATT

It came as a surprise to many when the National Council of Churches, apparently without disruptive stresses, entered one of its most liberal and militant phases in the early 1960s. Breaking with its traditional "educational" strategy for confronting social problems, the council took an outspoken position in favor of civil rights legislation. In a move without precedent in its fifty-year history, the council endorsed and helped organize the 1963 March on Washington, designed as a dramatic way of indicating support for the new civil rights legislation. It boldly resolved through its general board that the time had come to set aside timorous hesitations based on "organizational survival" and address itself to the roots of the race crisis.

Moreover, the council authorized establishment of a new commission in religion and race, which overlapped and partially superseded an existing department, and granted it a mandate of unprecedented scope. In the summer of 1964 the council took the key role in organizing a "Freedom Summer," which involved large expenditures of

*This article was prepared especially for this book.

money in order to recruit, train, transport, and maintain young civil rights workers in the Deep South. The NCC's Delta Ministry Project began in Mississippi on a small scale in 1963, but its scope was expanded, and it was active in 1967 despite its militant character and unpopularity among many white people in its constituency.

The voting patterns of Protestant clergy and laity and the normal social responses of organized Protestantism do not account for such militant liberalism. Indeed, the churchmen could have legitimately fashioned other organizational responses more suited to past behavior.

If, in the early sixties, the NCC's leaders had been timid about pushing beyond the minimal consensus then emerging at the grass-roots level that the churches should "do something" about the race problem and related matters, they easily could have confined themselves to issuing a new pronouncement on civil rights and, at most, authorizing someone to testify in favor of the Kennedy administration's pending bill. There was ample precedent for this, and it would not have conflicted with the council's customary strategy of exerting moral leadership through "education" and the more routine forms of political representation.

Thus, to arrive at a more satisfactory explanation of the council's behavior, one must probe for deeper levels of causation. A clue as to where to begin is contained in a recent article by Harvey Cox:

> The bureaucratization of religious organizations is [one] factor contributing to the entrance of church groups into the political arena as forces to be considered. Although this may sound unlikely to some church members, there can be little real doubt that it is true. . . . At the upper levels of governmental and private bureaucracies one sees today the development of a group of people who are in command of information and technical competence that goes considerably beyond the views of the people they are supposed to represent.[1]

From Cox's perspective the "managerial revolution" in the churches has significantly intensified the tendency toward social involvement by providing a pool of men who are "somewhat more insulated from direct lay control."[2] A disproportionate number of the Protestant clergy who participated in the 1965 Selma March, for example, were of this variety. Thus, by studying the social backgrounds of the kinds of people whom the council recruits to staff positions we may gain an important clue to explaining its pronounced liberal bias.

[1]Harvey G. Cox, "The 'New Breed'" in American Churches, *Daedalus,* (Winter 1967) p. 141.

[2]Cox, pp. 141–142.

SOURCES OF RECRUITMENT OF STAFF PERSONNEL

Sanford and his associates have demonstrated that students in a typical liberal arts college develop in the direction of increasing social responsibility and declining ethnocentrism and authoritarianism during their four years in residence.[3] In like manner, undergraduates in a large university who elect to major in the arts and sciences (that is, the liberal arts) have on the average become significantly more politically liberal by graduation than students with majors in vocational subjects, the change being partly attributable to self-selection (the initially more "liberal" students selecting the more "liberal" fields to major in), but more importantly to subject matter and classroom atmosphere.[4] The prevailing ethos of the liberal arts college, especially as mediated through peer-group relationships, exerts strong pressure upon students to adopt more liberal views, and once adopted these views are likely to persist for indefinite periods after graduation.[5]

It seems reasonable to assume that those theological seminaries which resemble the liberal arts college in emphasizing a broadly humanistic orientation (as opposed to seminaries with a predominantly vocational or sectarian tendency or both) would similarly tend to inculcate liberal policy preferences among their students, especially among students already predisposed in this direction by virtue of undergraduate training. This is, of course, not to suggest that seminaries engage in overt political indoctrination, but simply that a liberalizing in social values is an important latent consequence of being exposed to such an atmosphere at an impressionable age.

An analysis of the higher educational backgrounds of thirty-one top staff personnel presently (1967) serving in the NCC was undertaken to see whether colleges and seminaries of this type were more prevalent than one might have expected on a chance basis. The persons selected for study occupied what were rather arbitrarily classified as "policy relevant" posts, specifically those executives attached to the office of the General Secretary, the heads of the four divisions in the council (all with the rank of "associate General Secretary"), and the twenty-two heads of departments except those situated in the office of administration.[6]

[3]Nevitt Sanford, *Where Colleges Fail* (San Francisco: Jossey-Bass, Inc., 1967) p. 7.

[4]Nevitt Sanford, *The American College,* (New York: John Wiley and Sons, 1962) p. 568–569.

[5]Theodore Newcomb, *Persistence and Change: Bennington College and Its Students After Twenty Five Years* (New York: John Wiley and Sons, 1967) p. 37, (Table 4: 13)

[6]The exclusion of the six departments in this office was based on the premise that their functions were chiefly of a managerial or "housekeeping" character and did not have sustained impact on broad policy.

TABLE I. EDUCATIONAL BACKGROUNDS OF 31 TOP STAFF PERSONNEL
IN NCC, 1967[a]

	Number of Persons	Number of Degrees	Number of Institutions
College			
Private, nonsectarian	9		
Church-related	11		
Public	8		
Not ascertained	2		
No college	1		
Total	31		
Graduate Degrees			
Ph.D.	5		
Th.D.	1		
Candidate for Ph.D.	1		
M.A.	7		
Total	14		
Institutions granting B.D. degree or equivalent[b]		9	
Union Theological Seminary			
Yale Divinity School		4	
Harvard Divinity School		1	
Pacific School of Religion		2	
10 denominational seminaries		12	
Total		28	
Type of Seminary[c]			
Interdenominational only	14		
Denominational only	5		
Both types	6		
No seminary	6		
Total	31		
Location of Seminary[d]			
Northeast			17
Midwest			3
West			2
Border			1
Foreign			2
Total			25

[a]Includes all executive staff attached to Office of General Secretary; heads of divisions; heads of departments. Omits heads of "offices" and units engaged chiefly in "housekeeping activities."

[b]Totals include some individuals who attended more than one seminary.

[c]Multiple counting for individuals with more than one seminary degree. Of the twenty-five seminary graduates, twenty-one subsequently became ordained clergymen. SOURCE: Personnel Department, Office of Administration, NCC.

[d]Individuals who received bachelor-level degrees from more than one seminary are here classified by the institution attended last.

As indicated by Table 1, certain seminaries stand out as contributing a disproportionate share (roughly 60 percent) of all bachelor of divinity degrees earned by these NCC staff members. Since several individuals earned more than one degree at the bachelor's level and at different institutions, it appears that only a rather small proportion of council staff executives have had theological training wholly within their own particular denomination. The predominance of interdenominational and nondenominational seminaries (Union, Yale, Harvard, Pacific School of Religion) is perhaps not entirely unexpected in view of NCC's own interdenominational character, but this does not rob the finding of interest and significance. Equally interesting is the breakdown of seminaries by region, with the Northeast (usually considered the most liberal region) far ahead of all others combined. Again, the fact that the NCC itself has its headquarters in a major eastern city (New York) and is immediately adjacent to its largest single source of staff, Union Theological Seminary, no doubt has something to do with the pattern. Finally, and again perhaps not surprisingly, the group of thirty-one is noteworthy for its achievement of graduate degrees—the thirteen earned doctorate and master's degrees were obtained by ten individuals. A variety of fields are represented and a number of leading graduate schools. As students, our panel had more than a routine exposure to university life.

Three institutions (Union, Yale, and Pacific School of Religion) have granted more than half of the bachelor of divinity degrees conferred upon the thirty-one individuals in our panel. What, if anything, do these institutions have in common? A few statistics may help to give perspective before confronting the question directly.

In 1965, according to the *Statistical Abstract of the United States,* there were 50,000 persons enrolled in "independently organized professional schools of religion and theology".[7] While no breakdown was offered, it is believed that the vast majority of these were enrolled in schools closely identified with one particular sect or denomination. More precise data are available on the 127 institutions that collectively comprise the American Association of Theological Schools (AATS). In 1965 total enrollment in the association's member schools was 21,529. As indicated by Table 2 the students in nondenominational seminaries may be considered atypical, since they represent only about one out of seven of the total AATS student enrollment. The Yale Divinity School and Union Seminary, which between them account for almost half of those in top NCC staff posts, had a combined 1965 enrollment of 1049 or only about one-twentieth of the AATS total.[8]

[7]*Statistical Abstract of the United States,* 1966, Washington, D.C.: Bureau of the Census, Department of Commerce, p. 131.

[8]*Yearbook of American Churches,* 1967, p. 223.

TABLE 2. ENROLLMENT IN INSTITUTIONS AFFILIATED WITH AATS, 1965[a]

Type of Institution	Number of Institutions	Total Enrollment
Denominational—affiliated with NCC member church	16	11,837
Denominational—affiliated with church not in NCC	95	6,986
Nondenominational or interdenominational	16	3,156
Total	127	21,529

[a]Statistical Abstract of the United States, 1966, Washington, D.C.: Bureau of the Census, Department of Commerce, p. 131.

SOURCE: Yearbook of American Churches, 1967 (New York: National Council of Churches, 1967) pp. 222–224.

Striking resemblances exist among the four interdenominational seminaries most prevelant in the backgrounds of the thirty-one persons. One resemblance is their location in or near large urban centers (Union in New York, Yale in New Haven, Harvard near Boston, and Pacific School of Religion near San Francisco) and their status either as an organic part of or a cooperating institution with an immediately adjacent university, namely Columbia, Yale, Harvard, and the University of California at Berkeley, respectively. By virtue of their location the four schools not only reflect the intellectual and liberal ethos of a great university,[9] but are also more likely to be affected by the existence close to their very doorsteps of urban social problems. Union's deep commitment to the East Harlem Protestant Parish is perhaps the best-known example of how urban seminaries have sought to relate to such issues. Most Protestant seminaries are not like this. Many were deliberately located in areas away from city life and universities. As Littell puts it:

A long line of denominational seminaries followed [the split of Andover Theological School away from Harvard in 1808], many of them deliberately set out in the countryside to spare the young men the perils of encounters with "pagan learning" in the liberal university and temptations in the city. With the highest proportion of Protestant clergy coming from village and farm, the dislocation

[9]Benton Johnson has made this point in another connection: "Ascetic Protestantism and Political Preferences," *Public Opinion Quarterly*, 26 (1962) p. 39.

of many seminaries simply served to blind seminarians further to the main direction of American thought and social direction.[10]

These four seminaries also resemble one another in terms of the degree to which they are willing to accept radical social and political views among their students and faculty. Partly by virtue of their location in cosmopolitan urban centers and partly (presumably) by their relative freedom from the constraints imposed by any one sponsoring denomination, the four have been noteworthy in the extent to which their contribution to social thought has taken the form of radical analysis of society and openness to political dissent.[11] While the faculties of these institutions have had a pronounced liberal cast throughout the twentieth century, it seems highly significant that the faculty's radicalism was especially pronounced in the 1930s, when many present NCC executives were presumably enrolled as students. After mentioning the importance of seminaries, one writer at that time insisted that "practically every radical leader of consequence in the present [1934] American scene was originally inspired by religious conviction, however anxious some of them may be to hide or deny that fact now."[12] Another offered a representative list of twelve of the "foremost religious radicals" as of the year 1937, which, upon examination, turns out to contain no fewer than eight persons who were then teaching or had recently taught at three leading interdenominational seminaries: Yale Divinity School, Chicago Theological School, and especially Union Theological Seminary.[13]

CHANGES IN POSTSEMINARY CAREER PATTERNS

The discussion thus far helps toward a better understanding of why NCC career-staff personnel are, by virtue of their seminary back-

[10]Franklin H. Littell, "Protestant Seminary Education in America," in *Seminary Education in a Time of Change*, James M. Lee and Louis J. Putz, editors (Notre Dame, Indiana: Fides Publishers, Inc., 1965) p. 545.

[11]The fact that such criticism is sometimes, as in the case of Reinhold Niebuhr, couched in terms of "Christian orthodoxy," in opposition to what Niebuhr regards as liberal sentimentality and naiveté, does not essentially change the fact that it is criticism from the "left" rather than the "right."

[12]"Religion as a Source of Radicalism," *Christian Century*, LI (April 11, 1934), pp. 491–494. According to Donald P. Mayer, *The Protestant Search for Political Realism*, 1919–1941 (Berkeley: University of California Press, 1960), "Union Theological Seminary led in the production of young radicals in the early 'thirties" (No. 53, p. 451).

[13]Herman Reissig, "Homeless Religious Radicals," *Christian Century*, LIV (August 4, 1937), p. 972.

grounds, mostly liberals. The preceding data on seminary backgrounds shed some light on why NCC staff personnel are typically liberals, but they do not help to explain the *increasing* militancy of the staff referred to earlier.[14] It is possible, however, that differences exist in the career patterns of the earlier and the most recent personnel in terms of their careers subsequent to graduation from seminary. If one could show that NCC executives at an earlier time typically served a number of years in a "conservative environment" while their more recent counterparts have not done so, we should have a clue toward an understanding changing policy views.

It has been noted that the typical "main-line" Protestant clergyman is not a political "liberal" as that term is commonly used today. Pastors of churches, it was suggested, largely share the views of their middle-class portion of the laity when it comes to public policy matters, even though on balance they may be slightly more liberal. Pastors tend to share the political values of the white middle class, since middle-class people are the ones whom they interact with most extensively.[15] If a council of churches were to recruit its staff randomly among Protestant ministers, a very high percentage of the staff would have parish backgrounds, given that the overwhelming proportion of ordained clergymen are found serving in local churches. Only a small fraction are to be found in one of the various nonparochial ministries (hospital and military chaplaincies, seminary faculties, and so forth), although a larger proportion no doubt have served in such ways at one time or another in their professional lives. *Only a minute proportion of all ordained clergy are staff personnel in denominational (judicatory) offices or interdenominational agencies such as the National Council of Churches.* The figures in Table 3, taken from a recent study of how ordained clergy are deployed in the Episcopal Church, are presumably fairly typical of the situation prevailing in most "main line" Protestant bodies. In an analysis of the most recent seminary graduates (1961–1966) the same survey found no substantial change of a recent nature in the relative numbers going into the various occupational categories.[16]

---

[14]The same seminaries which now contribute heavily to NCC personnel did so in the past.

[15]Lenski, *The Religious Factor,* (New York: Doubleday, 1965) p. 276.

[16]Taylor, *Ministry for Tomorrow,* Report of the Special Committee on Theological Education of the Protestant Episcopal Church, (Greenwich, Connecticut, Seabury Press, 1967) p. 77. This pronounced preference for the parish ministry may be undergoing substantial modifications, however. One recent study has revealed that only 30 percent of seminaries intend to stay in the parish ministry: Keith R. Bridston and Dwight Culber (eds.) *The Making of Ministers* (Minneapolis: Augusburg Press, 1964), pp. 193–194.

TABLE 3. DEPLOYMENT OF ORDAINED CLERGY IN THE PROTESTANT
EPISCOPAL CHURCH, 1966

Status	Number
Bishops	186
Parish Ministry	7,342
Overseas missionaries	180
Nonparochial staff officers (ecumenical and others)	18
Other nonparochial ministries	1,503
Retired	1,155
Occupation unknown	356
	10,740

SOURCE: Charles P. Taylor, Ministry for Tomorrow, Report of the Special Committee on Theological Education of the Protestant Episcopal Church. (Greenwich, Connecticut: Seabury Press, 1967) p. 62.

In an earlier period of time the career backgrounds of staff personnel in the NCC apparently mirrored this heavy preference for the parish ministry. Instead of working their way up a career ladder in the council (or in the headquarters staffs of member churches), those recruited tended to enter staff posts at a high level through lateral means after having served for some time in a local church. There were, of course, exceptions to this, but the tendency is quite pronounced. In a typical year for the council, 1931, only three out of nine staff executives were without parish experience.[17] Two-thirds of the executives at the time had parish experience, averaging 18.5 years.

On the other hand, breakdown of the thirty-one "policy related" executives in 1967 reveals a sharply contrasting pattern. The council's office of personnel made available to the author dossier summaries containing extensive information on all thirty-one persons. The summaries indicated that only three of this group had had parish experience, on the basis of some specific reference to that effect in the summary. While this could be somewhat misleading, especially since many seminary students serve as assistants in parishes during summers, it seems quite unlikely that any substantial parish experience was omitted from the information on the other twenty-eight persons. The

[17]Although a depression year, 1931 did not differ much from the 1920s in terms of composition of the council's staff. The council succeeded in riding out the Depression with relatively little reduction in personnel. Dr. Samuel McCrea Daveart, the executive director in that period, informs the author that no changes in executive staff attributable to lack of funds were made at this time. (Interview with Dr. Daveart, 1967).

relative proportion of persons with parish experience is thus roughly the reverse of what it was in the 1930s.

There is additional evidence pointing toward a decline in participation of pastors and former pastors in the council's affairs. It is revealing to note the occupational characteristics of delegates to the council's constituent assembly (the "General Assembly"), which now meets once every three years. The assembly, composed of official representatives of the member bodies, elects the council's officers, votes on its budget, and collectively decides broad policy matters. Unfortunately, available records do not permit a year-by-year breakdown of the occupational composition of this body—the council began gathering such data on a systematic basis only in 1957, which is much too recent to use as a base line.[18] A systematic search of existent records of the council turned up only one earlier occupational listing, and this dealt with the founding convention of the Federal Council of Churches in 1908. This permits one to identify some gross changes across a very long span of time (half a century), but rules out charting a more precise trend. It appears that the relative positions of pastors and national church executives in the constituent assembly is now almost exactly the reverse of what it was at the beginning. Whereas in 1908 two out of every five delegates and alternates were identified with local churches, the proportion is now only about one in every six.

To sum up, the persons in policy-relevant posts in the NCC are increasingly without extensive parish experience. While one cannot directly infer from these findings differences in political perspectives between the "parish" and "nonparish" council leaders, it seems likely, in the absence of any clear evidence to the contrary, that the decline in pastors and grass-roots-level laymen is associated with a decline in support for "standpat" political viewpoints. In a broader sense, the data suggest that interdenominational and denominational agencies are increasingly offering professional careers to men just out of seminary. As Protestant church executives come to serve their entire careers in such posts, one may expect that they will less and less take their cues on politics and social issues from an interaction with local church people. It is worthwhile enquiring whether the staff are in a position to influence the council's policies to a significant degree, or whether they largely function as technicians, the broad policy choices being made almost entirely by nonsalaried officials and representatives. As recently as the early 1930s the work of the council was carried on largely through semiautonomous commissions that specialized in such matters as international relations, motion pictures, Jewish-Christian relationships, and so forth. These commissions, composed of representatives of the cooperating denominations serving on a volunteer basis, appear to

---

[18]The 1957 figures, not presented here, were examined, and the occupational breakdowns turned out to be substantially the same as those of 1966.

have been the primary initiators of action in the council. The role of staff was secondary or "supplemental," according to published accounts.[19]

There is reason to think that staff personnel now play a much more active part in policy deliberations, including those in an area of social justice and political representation, which is our main concern here. The trends since the 1930s in the absolute size of the staff are suggestive on this point and suggest that the size of the specialized staff concerned with social and political problems remained fairly constant from the early 1920s until the latter years of the Federal Council of Churches. Beginning about the time of the reorganization and merger of 1950, the number of staff executives working in this area increased somewhat, followed by a very substantial increase ten years later (1963–1966). It may also be noted that the number of persons employed in the Division of Home Missions also increased rapidly in the period 1950–1965. Although this department was not formally concerned with social action and education, this increase in home missions staff was nevertheless significant for the "radicalization" of the council in the 1950s.

Examination of the *Yearbook of American Churches* suggests that during the 1950s the elective staff not only became larger, but became *significantly more specialized*. The council in this period authorized establishment of a Commission on Religious Liberty, with a leading authority on church-state relations (the Rev. Dean Kelley) as its executive secretary; the council was thus in a position to focus attention on this complex and controversial area in a way that had not been possible previously. The staff now clearly possessed the talent and expertise necessary to generate increased involvement in the area of social justice, and interviews suggest that it was more than coincidental that the augmentation in staff immediately preceded major policy changes on the part of the NCC in the 1960s.

CONCLUSION

The "explanation" offered in the present essay for militant liberalism in the National Council of Churches has been necessarily somewhat one-dimensional. Because of limitations of space, it was not possible to introduce several other factors believed to be important causally; for example, the fact that not all the member churches participate actively in the council, the more active churches being the more liberal ones, the more inactive ones being the more conservative. The thesis of this

[19]H. Paul Douglas and Edmund Brunner, *The Protestant Church as a Social Institution* (New York: The Institute of Social and Religious Research, 1935) p. 270.

essay has been simply that changes in the size, career backgrounds, and degree of specialization of staff executives in the NCC has been *one of the more important factors* contributing to a shift (especially in the period since 1940) in the organization's method of confronting social issues from one of "voluntarism" and "education" to one of increasing militancy.

On the basis of having compared the impact of bureaucratization on the council, the hypothesis is suggested that an initial decision to augment the size and specialization of the professional staff has important long-run implications that are seldom apparent at the moment the decision was made. There is, perhaps, a kind of "critical mass" of staff size, at least for the type of groups we have been describing. Except in groups with an extremely narrow focus, a staff smaller than the necessary minimum (the number would vary with circumstances, but ten to fifteen seems to be the critical level for the groups here examined) will be more inclined to narrow its range of concerns to a few problems of compelling urgency for its constituents and attend only rather spasmodically to broader questions. As the organization grows, however, increased specialization becomes possible. The organization is able to hire persons with technical competence in several of the fields once regarded as relatively tangential and lacking in *unique* relevancy to the constituency. These "professionals" forge continuing personal ties with their counterparts in other groups in the interest of attacking problems in a more comprehensive manner. Very informally, at first, and then often more and more officially, the organization begins to view itself as a participant in a series of coalitions (or alliances, depending upon the degree of explicitness of the arrangement) with other groups. Such coalitions help to extend the range of the group's influence, but they also entail new obligations that may threaten its freedom of maneuver. Among the three groups studied here, the leaders apparently strive to maximize the advantages of coalition strategy while preserving as much flexibility as possible. For example, the frequency of establishing *ad hoc* agencies like the Leadership Conference on Civil Rights, to which mass-membership groups lend their prestige but from which a certain distance is maintained, can be interpreted in light of this need.

The present line of reasoning gives some insight into why the NCC responded in one way to the civil rights and civil liberties questions in the late 1940s and in a somewhat different way when roughly analogous issues arose in the early 1960s. In the late forties the council made pronouncements on and did not cooperate closely with the other liberal bodies in confronting major social and economic questions. It was not, for example, among the original participants in the Leadership Conference on Civil Rights in the early 1950s. NCC response to the social and moral problems of the time was largely confined to the issuance of pronouncements, some of them admittedly quite explicit and judgmental, but none squarely committing the organization to much by way of "carry through." The one issue on which the council did go "all out," namely President Truman's announced intention in 1951 to appoint an ambassador to the Vatican (a move the NCC emphatically opposed) in a sense underscores the point. Since this was a matter that touched a sensitive "Protestant" nerve, the NCC could address itself forcefully to the matter in its capacity as a Protestant "status group." The matter was apparently not viewed as part of a larger pattern of social and political concerns, however, and once settled to the NCC's satisfaction, the organization's involvement in politics subsided.

In the 1960s, however, the council's interest in controversial policy questions with important moral dimensions did not subside after the "flash point" of a given problem had passed. While its participation in the March on Washington (1963) and "Freedom Summer" (1964) earned it more publicity for its civil rights activity than for other matters, the council has been less spectacularly involved in a series of other matters of roughly equal significance. In 1964 it joined Jewish, civil liberties, and other Protestant bodies in efforts to block the "Becker Amendment"—a measure which aimed to overturn United States Supreme Court decisions prohibiting prayers in the public schools.[20] In 1967 it spoke out jointly with the ACLU concerning the rights of conscientious objectors and demonstrators against the war in Vietnam; in the same year it formally joined various civil rights groups in a suit pleading that Congressman Adam Clayton Powell be reinstated by the House of Representatives on the grounds that his expulsion from that body in 1967 denied his constitutents "equal representation."[21] It would appear that, whereas in the late 1940s the council simply did not have the specialized staff of sufficient size to achieve sustained involvement in many of the moral and political problems emergent at that time, by the late 1950s and early 1960s an augmentation in staff and a change in staff perspectives helped to facilitate such involvement. The more specialized staff made it possible for the council not only to broaden its range of concern, but to become more self-conscious about how major social issues overlap the boundaries separating one group from another and how they require like-minded voluntary agencies to act in concert.

[20]William M. Beaney and Edward N. Beiser, "Prayer and Politics: The Impact of 'Engel' and 'Schempp' on the Political Process," *Journal of Public Law,* 13 (1964), pp. 496–498.

[21]Interview with the Rev. Dean Kelly, Department of Social Justice, NCC, 1967.